PRINCIPLES OF
DEVELOPMENT
ECONOMICS

Henry J. Bruton
Williams College

PRENTICE-HALL, INC., *Englewood Cliffs, N.J.*

To F.B.B.

PRENTICE-HALL INTERNATIONAL, INC., *London*
PRENTICE-HALL OF AUSTRALIA, PTY., LTD., *Sydney*
PRENTICE-HALL OF CANADA, LTD., *Toronto*
PRENTICE-HALL OF INDIA (PRIVATE) LTD., *New Delhi*
PRENTICE-HALL OF JAPAN, INC., *Tokyo*

Current printing (last digit):
11   10   9   8   7   6   5   4   3

Library of Congress Catalog Card No.: 65-15566
C-70895

Printed in the United States of America

PREFACE

The appearance of another book on economic development calls for some explanation, perhaps even mild apology. The quantity of writing in this field in recent years is unmeasurable, and considerable courage is necessary to submit a general text that makes claims to freshness and originality in its discussion of development problems. Despite the vast literature, the subject matter of development remains ill-defined and unwieldy, and in no sense does there exist a widely accepted set of principles that lend themselves to presentation in the conventional textbook manner. This means that textbook writing in development is not the writing of received doctrine, the details of which have been worked out in the journals and monographs, but rather involves a sifting of the literature in a search for a corpus of ideas that may serve as the basis around which to build a course.

The scope of the present book is much more limited than most other comparable texts in the field. My basic aim has been to establish a broad framework within which economic problems of the low-income countries can be examined and from which appropriate policies can be derived. The emphasis is therefore on the principles governing the process by which a contemporary underdeveloped country can achieve its development objectives, rather than on history or on actual practices. This limited scope springs from a number of considerations.

The most important consideration is simply that I believe the failure to have a coherent set of principles in mind or available on paper is a major source of our many difficulties in the teaching, researching, and practicing of economic development. It is especially essential in teaching to provide the student with a framework in which he can find some order to the great sprawling mass of material with which he must come in contact. The approach worked out in this text has been tried for several years in a variety of teaching environments and has been found reasonably effective in meeting this objective.

This emphasis does not mean that I think that historical evidence and the examination of actual development policies are not part of a course in development economics. They most assuredly are. The bibliographical material at the end of each chapter is intended to lead the student to the more empirical and historical material that I have found helpful in teaching a course built around the framework presented here. These readings are suggestions as to the kind of material that I think can be used to provide the real-world examples and detailed elaborations that give content and substance to the principles covered in this book.

To rely on other books and articles for this part of a course in development is surely appropriate. The inclusion of a few one-chapter surveys of individual countries in a text may help a bit, but they can hardly cast more than fleeting, partial insights into the many sides of the development process. Also, since any real application of a set of principles or of a given principle requires a great deal of very careful discussion, I have found efforts to include in a single volume evidence that is intended to support general principles or to illustrate arguments to be little more than made-up examples. On the other hand, the inclusion in the syllabus of material that does in a more or less complete way explore actual historical cases and present carefully worked-up data is effective. This procedure has the further advantage of acquainting the student with a variety of viewpoints on development which is itself healthy, as well as with empirical and descriptive material presented with a degree of care and completeness that could not be matched even in the fattest textbook.

The fact that no text in development economics can claim to be presenting "received doctrine" also means that results and arguments are more tentative and preliminary and open to debate than is the case with texts in other areas of economics. The language used in the following chapters is meant to keep the student aware of this fact. A further consequence of the youthfulness of development economics is that some of the material is necessarily treated in a loose, unrigorous fashion. Elegance and rigor are important attributes of effective economics, but they must take second place to relevance and applicability. The student or teacher who likes his economics in the form of neat theorems is alerted that few have been found in the field of technology, education, population growth, and a dozen other aspects of development. I have tried, however, to treat the material as formally and systematically as seemed possible without losing touch with the reality which is our basic concern.

Interest in economic development also has lead economists into areas of inquiry that earlier were assumed outside the boundaries of the discipline. Indeed a large literature on the "noneconomics" of economic development exists and is expanding rapidly. It is readily admitted that politics, the military, religion, and other factors are important in understanding the economic performance of a given society. At the same time to try to examine all aspects of social life in one framework is likely to yield merely truistic generalizations. This book is in no sense an interdisciplinary effort, but an attempt has been made to recognize the role played by certain "noneconomic" characteristics of the society in the development process. However, the student or teacher or development practitioner who views economic development as a minor aspect of general social evolution will not find the treatment very satisfactory. Further issues related to this general question are noted in the following chapters.

This is a textbook and not a survey of the literature. I have not concerned myself with tracing the evolution of the ideas and arguments that I have tried to develop, but have drawn freely on the work of many people as well as on my own observations during extended stays in several developing countries. My main objective is to present a unified and understandable body of thought about an urgent world problem. It is not that of writing a treatise.

The organization of the book is quite simple. In Chapter 1 the definition of the problem is given as specifically as possible, and the ground rules of the approach are spelled out. Chapters 2 through 6 of Part One describe in very general terms the process by which an economy—any economy—achieves a rising per capita income. What is presented here is not a theory of growth and certainly not a growth model, but rather a detailed description of the sources of growth and processes of growth. The analysis is built around the activities of the individual producing unit (public or private) and how its growth affects the rest of the system. I have found it desirable to avoid a high degree of aggregation simply because the heart of the growth process seems so easily shrouded by aggregation.

Given this description of how any economy grows, Chapter 7 of Part One contains a detailed account of the nongrowing economy, the underdeveloped economy. This chapter is an attempt to define the characteristics of underdevelopment that seem crucial in explaining that underdevelopment. This chapter must come after the discussion of how growth takes place, because it would not be possible otherwise to identify those characteristics that from the standpoint of achieving growth are most relevant. The aim is to establish a representative underdeveloped country. Although this is a risky undertaking because of the great diversity among the low-income countries of the world, there are a number of factors common to all such countries that are alien to the achievement of growth. The general task of development may then be defined as the transformation of the economy described in Chapter 7 to meet the conditions laid out in Chapters 2 through 6 as essential to growth.

The primary requirement to achieve this transformation is the availability of resources in excess of those necessary to maintain the economy at its existing level. Part Two is therefore a detailed account of the various methods by which an economy of the type described in Chapter 7 can make available investible resources to be used to change that economy in ways suggested by the arguments of Part One. After this, attention must be given to an explicit consideration of how these extra resources can be used to effect the metamorphosis defined as the objective of development. Included in this discussion (Part Three) are chapters on technology, the quality of labor, population change, and social and institutional arrangements.

Because there are many ways that the investible resources can be used, the question of criteria for their allocation calls for considerable attention, and Part Four is concerned with this subject. Finally in Part Five an account of the role of money and finance (including the price system) in the development process is given. In the last chapter of the book, "Strategies of Development," a brief survey of various proposals for an approach to development policy that are extant is undertaken in the context of the framework worked out in the preceding seventeen chapters. The discussion of these strategies—import substitution, the Big Push, Agriculture or Industry, the Take-off notion, and others—constitute the main explicit contact with the literature. The main purpose here, however, is not to review the literature as such, but rather to show how specific hypotheses as to development can be analyzed in the framework developed and to examine some general conclusions that emerge from such an analysis.

The book is designed for students who have had a good elementary course in economics, and an effort has been made to avoid repeating material covered in that course. A junior-level theory course taken prior to or along with a course using this book will help, but it is not essential. The book is designed to be taught by a live teacher, and I have purposely not written everything that I think should be called to the attention of the students. Perhaps in the field of development economics, making students think about problems is more important than providing them with possible solutions to those problems.

William B. Gates and Gordon C. Winston of Williams College, Robinson G. Hollister of the Organization for Economic Cooperation and Development, Gustav Ranis of Yale University, and the Prentice-Hall reviewer read all or significant parts of the various drafts of the manuscript. I am indeed grateful for their many comments and criticisms. I have also at one time or another profited from conversations with my other colleagues in the Department of Economics of Williams College, and am pleased to acknowledge my obligations in this respect.

I would like to acknowledge the persons and publishers who granted their permission to adapt and reprint material. Table III and the surrounding discussion is adapted from Hollis B. Chenery's "Comparative Advantage and Development Policy," *American Economic Review*, LI (March 1961). Diagram IX was redrawn from a diagram in Harvey Leibenstein's *Economic Backwardness and Economic Growth* (1957) published by John Wiley & Sons, Inc. Selected paragraphs from my book *Inflation in a Growing Economy* (1961) published by the University of Bombay appear in Chapters 5 and 17.

H. J. B.

CONTENTS

CHAPTER 1

INTRODUCTION

The purpose of this introductory chapter is to establish the ground rules and foundation for the rest of the book. The ground rules have to do with the general assumptions and their justification that constitute the boundaries of the argument worked out in the following chapters. The *foundation* has to do with the definition of terms, the establishment of the central task of the analysis, and the approach to this task that is employed.

I. The Problem

The initial task is to define *economic development* in a manner that permits measurement, and that meets other criteria such as commonsense appeal and general interest. A useful and frequently employed approach is to identify various characteristics that are generally felt to be desirable—literacy, "good" housing, life expectancy, and so on—and to define economic development in terms of the extent to which an economy is able to provide these services to its people. The notion that economic development is a multidimensional concept is of course an extremely important one to recognize, but it would appear unnecessary to insist on a multidimensional measure. In almost all instances, per capita output is an effective surrogate for any identifying characteristics of development ever mentioned, and in those cases where it is not, that fact is well known and the reasons easy to discover. Thus no one would argue that Kuwait or Qatar is more developed than Italy or France, yet the per capita income in the two former areas greatly exceeds that of the two latter areas. Such exceptions, however, do no more than impose on the analyst some general knowledge of the state of the world. A more significant difficulty has to do with income distribution, and one might wish to add a requirement about income distribution in the definition of development. But such a requirement has normative implications that are outside the context of the present argu-

1

ment. Even if output per capita is a satisfactory index of development in that it provides a measure of the capacity of the economy to supply goods and services to its people, problems still remain.

No one should confuse output of goods and services with happiness or welfare. What it is that makes people happy is even more a mystery than what makes them rich. Neither does the question whether a country "ought" to develop lend itself to the tools at the disposal of the economist.

Other problems are more severe. There are problems associated with the measurement of output: the valuation of nonmarketed products, which nonmarket services to include, definition of intermediate goods, and so on. It is difficult to answer such questions in other than a rather arbitrary fashion, although of course some arbitrary solutions are more appealing than others. These difficulties are compounded when, by use of exchange rates, an effort is made to compare levels of per capita income among different countries. Thus, the rough statement that per capita income in the United States is about 25–30 times as high as that in India is open to all sorts of objections, but there is no doubt at all that the United States economy supplies its citizens with many more goods and services that they (and Indians) want than does the Indian economy. For this reason it appears reasonable to speak of India as poor in relation to the United States.

If a list of all countries were drawn up in the order of their per capita product as conventionally measured, then by an arbitrary decision all countries with a per capita income of less than (say) $300 might be classified as poor or underdeveloped, and those over $300 might be classified as rich or developed. Such a procedure is not quite as arbitrary as it may at first glance seem, since it is possible to define for each country a level of income that would enable the citizens of that country to live in a manner that does not impair health and permits "reasonable" comfort to be attained. And agreement might be reached on what is "reasonable." If the country has a higher income than this level, it is rich; if lower, it is poor. But this approach is unsatisfactory in other ways. Consider the following example.

Country X has a very low level of income per head of population, and in consequence her literacy rate is very low, the life expectancy of her people is very low compared to countries such as the United States, her people are so very poorly housed and clothed that poor health is very common, and so on and on. Suppose, however, that the per capita income in Country X has been growing at the rate of 3 to 4 per cent per annum. Suppose further that a careful analysis of her economy reveals that this rate of growth is built on a firm basis and there is every reason to assume that it will continue. Evidently, Country X is in a very different position from that of a country with an equal level of per capita income but showing no signs of growth.

This latter point suggests a further distinction between rich and poor that helps to identify the problem more clearly. The rich country seems to have an economy that has growth built into it, while the poor country seems to have an economy in which "nongrowth" is built into it. The fact appears a bit more fundamental than mere poverty and richness. Indeed one can say that currently a rich country is rich because in the past decades per capita income has grown more or less consistently, while a poor country is poor because in the past decades it has not grown. This near tautology is helpful because it places the emphasis on growth rather than level, and growth would appear to merit more attention than level. The above distinction leads then to a statement as to the principal objective of economic policy in the poor country, namely the modification of the economy in such fashion that growth becomes a regular feature of the economy. The *Principles of Development Economics* is therefore concerned with the process by which an economy changes in this fashion to achieve the growth objective. Terms such as low income, nongrowing, and underdeveloped may be used interchangeably to refer essentially to an economy the past history of which suggests that there are forces at work that prevent growth from occurring. Of course nongrowth does not mean that no change has ever occurred, but rather that it has not occurred in a fashion that shows it to be indigenous to the system. Indeed one of the strongest pieces of evidence that a country has failed to solve the development problem (as just defined) is one or more short periods of growth sparked by some outside influence—sudden large inflow of capital, discovery of a new natural resource—that does not set the economy off on a sustained and consistent growth experience. This kind of evidence would suggest that the economy was so constituted as to prevent continuous growth from occurring. Similarly, the phrase "routine growth" is not meant to imply that growth of per capita income occurs automatically no matter what economic policies are pursued. It means rather that the economy is so constructed that all the requisites of growth are present, and the objective of growth policy is to maintain the general conditions for these growth-producing sources to function effectively.

Given this definition of the problem of development, the chapter sequence noted in the preface appears reasonable. Chapters 2 through 6 describe the essential nature of a growing economy, Chapter 7 contains a detailed statement of the nature of underdevelopment or nongrowth, and the succeeding chapters discuss the process by which a nongrowing economy becomes a growing economy. The last chapter contains some comments on other approaches to the problem. It is perhaps necessary to note that even if all low income countries were enjoying a 3 to 4 per cent rate of growth in per capita income, it would be many decades before mass poverty was eliminated, and its continued existence creates many problems and heartaches. The only way to eliminate mass poverty is by growth, however, and the very fact that growth is occurring makes the poverty less of a burden and less degrading to the human spirit.

This statement of the problem has further implications that may be mentioned in order to facilitate understanding of later analyses, as well as perhaps to clarify the above definition.

II. Some Implications

A. LONG AND SHORT PERIOD

Emphasis has been placed on the creation of an economy that, as a matter of routine, produces a rising per capita output. Such emphasis suggests a very long-period analysis, but in a slightly different fashion from the usual meanings attached to this term. Long period usually refers to one of two notions: first, to an equilibrium analysis in which all adjustments included in an argument have worked themselves out. This of course is not a calendar time concept, but an analytical concept, employed to isolate the content of the equilibrating forces. It is this long period in which Keynes assumed that we would all be dead. Second, there is the problem of explaining the time path of a variable or set of variables over a relatively long period of calendar time—two, three, or four decades. The task in this problem is to isolate the characteristics of the economy that explain the path these variables follow over the given time span.

Consider a simple example. A supply and demand diagram shows the relationship between price and quantity supplied and demanded of a specific product under certain assumptions. The intersection of these curves then would show the price reached in the long run in a market where the equilibrium process had worked itself out completely. Over a long period of time, however, as income and tastes change, and as technology and the quantity of capital change, the supply and demand curves themselves change. To explain the time path of the long-run equilibrium price requires not an analysis of the working out of the equilibrium process for given curves, but rather an examination of the factors that account for the change in the position and shape of the curves. To find what these factors are, of course, is the purpose of the inquiry.

The relevant "period" in the analysis undertaken here is a bit different from both of these notions. Although no explanation of a time path of per capita income over a relatively long period is given, an effort is made to isolate those characteristics of an economy that are responsible for its growth-generative powers over a long period of time. The problem is "long run" in the sense that the task is not that of tracing the implications of a given set of data that may be assumed given for a short while, but rather that of trying to find those characteristics that do explain the capacity of an economy to generate growth. These characteristics, however, do affect the performance of the economic system in any particular short-run interval. Since the economy is always in a short-run situation, the problem is to explain why and how an economy grows in a given short-run interval. Such a distinction is useful because the sources of growth vary from period to period, and perhaps the key attribute of an economy, insofar as sustained growth is concerned, is its capacity to generate and to exploit a great variety of opportunities for growth. In this fashion, then, the problem of development is both short-run and long-run, and the most useful empirical construct would appear to be a sequence of relatively short periods rather than the equilibrium notion or the calendar time notion mentioned earlier.

B. The Measurement Problem

The empirical evidence needed for this kind of problem is simply the behavior of per capita output over a sequence of short periods. Concentration of attention on growth of output over a relatively short period makes it possible to by-pass some of the difficulties associated with income measurements previously mentioned. No international comparisons of levels of income in various countries are required, and no long-period comparisons within the country are necessary. The problem is the simpler one of determining if growth has occurred over a sequence of short periods, and the task of making meaningful estimates of the rate of change of a variable is, in such a context, manageable. This is true for a variety of reasons. The comparisons of short-period quality changes are much less difficult than for comparisons that are decades apart, new products do not pose major problems, there are few "structural" changes (e.g., the extent to which output enters the market changes only slowly through time), and the basic conditions of the society are much less subject to changes that make questionable per capita income comparisons over long intervals of time.

C. The Boundaries of the Problem

As understanding of development problems grows, it becomes increasingly evident that solutions to the problem cannot be found within the traditional boundaries of economics. This conclusion is painful, not only to the proud economist, but also to the policymaker. The economic phenomena are generally more amenable to formal policies than are those phenomena usually categorized as social, cultural, anthropological, and so on. It will become clear as the argument develops that in many instances the explanation of a given characteristic or "parameter" accounting for the nongrowth of an economy is to be found in the institutional arrangements or social environments that prevail. An effort to understand such an economy then requires some investigation into the nature of these arrangements and of their links with the economy itself. Then, instead of setting the analysis to fit some sort of disciplinary limits, which are extremely vague and ill-defined, it is more useful and interesting to try to make the analysis fit the problem. At the same time, an analysis can become so inclusive that it is virtually barren of verifiable content. Perhaps a satisfactory stopping point may be reached where an analysis leads to rather specific policy proposals. Even with this stopping point, the argument will still go into areas that are usually beyond the sphere of interest of the economist. It is probably unnecessary to add that the formal treatment of some of the problems in this area is in the exploratory stage, and the isolation of specific relationships and links is usually (even) less satisfactory than is the case for variables that the economists' tools have been forged to handle.

D. The Nature of the Results

Economic policy advice is most effective and useful when the economist is able to predict with a fair degree of confidence. It seems safe to say that the ultimate purpose of a theory is prediction, but the longer the time horizon involved, the greater the difficulties in achieving this objective. In a short-run problem it is of course not impossible, even in economics. For example, it is sensible to ask what the *level* of expenditure for a private sector of an economy will be over the next six months, the next year, or two years, and the understanding of economic processes is such that an estimate of this level may be expected to be a reasonable approximation in most instances. This result might be expressed by saying that the freedom permitted the system over a short period of time is sufficiently limited so that it is possible, with the tools available to the economist, to provide a meaningful analytical prediction of the behavior of a given variable for several months or even a year or so into the future. However, to expect a set of principles designed to explain growth to provide techniques for predicting the *level* of expenditure of the private sector for a period of twenty-five, fifty, or one hundred years is surely meaningless. Over such a long period there is so much freedom in the system that it is impossible—except in a sterile, formal sense or as a mere hunch—to eliminate any of a virtually infinite number of possible results. Consequently, it is necessary in a growth analysis to change the aim (as compared to short-run theory) and seek not a theoretical apparatus that will trace the exact path of absolute magnitude of a variable (e.g., per capita income) but one that seeks simply to identify the forces generating economic change and the nature of the response to these change-producing forces, and from this to deduce—if one wishes to go further—what might be called the time shape of the growth process.

III. Which Income Concept?

There are a variety of income concepts used in economics and a brief comment on the concept used in this book is now in order. The concept most frequently measured is gross national product (GNP), although in some sense the most relevant notion in the development context is net national product. The latter requires estimates of depreciation of capital during a given period, and such estimates are virtually impossible to make with any degree of accuracy. Where net national product figures are found, the depreciation figure is almost always an arbitrary percentage of the estimate of gross capital formation with little evidence or argument to justify it. Also, interest is attached to "real" national product, which means that, over a time period, a price level deflator must be used, and deflators are almost as treacherous as estimates of depreciation. These difficulties, however, do not mean that a deflated series of net national product has no meaning: they mean rather that the user of the series must understand the limitations imposed by the method employed in making up the series. Whenever the term national product, income, or income per capita is used in this book, it refers to NNP.

Reference should also be made to a possible terms-of-trade effect on NNP. The simplest definition of the terms of trade is the ratio of the price index of exports (P_x) to the price index of imports (P_m). It is evident that if P_x/P_m falls, a given quantity of exports will purchase fewer imports than it would prior to the deterioration in the terms of trade. The relevance of changes in the terms of trade may be illustrated with the following extreme example. Suppose a country exported everything that it produced and imported all the products used at home. Suppose further that its output of exports rose by 5 per cent, but P_x fell by 5 per cent so that the country realized no increase in foreign exchange earnings. If P_m remains constant, then obviously P_x/P_m falls, and the economy has not experienced any increase in the quantity of product available for domestic use, despite the increase in total production. An improvement in the terms of trade would have the opposite effect. No country fits this extreme example, of course, but it does illustrate how the terms of trade affect the growth of output of an economy.

A terms-of-trade effect plays a very small role in most discussions of growth of rich countries, but it has been given a great deal of attention in analyses of the problems of poor countries, and will be discussed in various places throughout this book. The terms-of-trade effect will, however, always be treated separately, and when terms such as "growth of output" or "increased output," and so on are used, they do not include a terms-of-trade effect.

With this definition of the general problem of the book and the relevant variable also defined, the next task is that of examining how an economy grows.

Bibliography

For details on the quantitative aspects of economic growth, see the various studies by Simon Kuznets appearing in *Economic Development and Cultural Change*. The series began in the October 1956 number and current contributions usually appear in the January number. These are excellent surveys, and contain not only estimates of the value of a large number of economic variables, but a good discussion of the problems associated with their measurement as well. These studies provide a ready source of information on many of the points mentioned in later chapters. A paper by Suphan Andia and Alan T. Peacock, "The International Distribution of Income, 1949 and 1957," *Journal of the Royal Statistical Society,* CXXIV (1961) Pt. 2, contains much that is revealing on recent changes in the international distribution of income. On problems and methods of estimating income see the two United Nations reports, *A System of National Accounts and Supporting Tables,* Series F, No. 2, Rev. 1 and *Methods of National Income Estimation,* Series F, No. 8, both published by the Statistical Office of the United Nations. The United Nations also publishes a *Yearbook of National Accounts Statistics* that is a readily available repository of national income data on the countries of the world.

The most appealing discussion of whether countries should develop that I have seen is Professor W. Arthur Lewis, "Is Economic Growth Desirable," an appendix to his *The Theory of Economic Growth* (London: George Allen & Unwin, 1955). One should, however, also see S. Herbert Frankel, "Concepts of Income and Welfare in Advanced and Underdeveloped Societies with Special Reference to the Intercomparability of National Income Estimates," in *Income and Wealth,* edited for the International Association for Research in Income and Wealth by Milton Gilbert (Cambridge: Bowes & Bowes Publishers, Ltd., 1953). In the same volume the papers by Tibor Barna, "International Comparisons of National Accounts in Economic Analysis," and V. K. R. V. Rao, "Some Reflections on the Comparability of Real National Incomes of Industrialized and Underdeveloped Countries" are also helpful. See also A. J. Youngson, *Possibilities of Economic Progress* (Cambridge: Cambridge University Press, 1959) Chap. 1.

On the problems of time in the development problem I have found Kenneth Boulding's "In Defense of Statics," *Quarterly Journal of Economics* LXIX (November, 1955) and W. C. Hood, "Some Aspects of the Treatment of Time in Economic Theory," *The Canadian Journal of Economics and Political Science,* XIV (November, 1948) useful. See also Redvers Opie, "Marshall's Time Analysis," *Economic Journal,* XLI (March, 1931). On the problem of the scope of development economics, one can read with profit Appendix C to Alfred Marshall's *Principles of Economics* (8th ed.) (London: Macmillan & Co. Ltd., 1920).

The preceding is an example of the kind of bibliographical material suggested by the remarks on this subject in the preface. Evidently one could include many more citations of a quality equal to those that are included. The purpose of the bibliography is not to provide a complete list of relevant supplementary reading, but rather to provide the interested student with reading material that I think will help him to appreciate the quantitative and historical significance of the arguments presented in this book, and will also enable him to begin to probe more deeply or widely into the various theoretical notions developed.

Part One

ON ECONOMIC GROWTH AND UNDERDEVELOPMENT

This part of the book has two objectives. First, a description of the process by which the output of an economy increases is given in Chapters 2 through 6. Although the growth process is worked out in a way believed to be especially helpful in the specific context of the development problem, the analysis is meant to be general enough that no specific assumptions as to *developed, underdeveloped, socialist,* or *capitalist* are necessary. The objective of these chapters is to identify what in Chapter 1 was called the growth-producing forces of an economy. Once identified, an effort is then made to show how these forces act on the economy so that total output rises. Chapter 2 presents a quick survey of all elements in the analysis. Chapter 3 examines how an economy made up of independent sectors grows. Chapter 4 introduces the assumption that growth of one sector has major implications for other sectors in the system, and explores some of the consequences of this fact. To this point, attention will have been devoted to the supply problem, so Chapter 5 considers the various ways that demand enters the growth argument. Finally, Chapter 6 is a summary and restatement of the growth process as it was worked out in Chapters 2 through 5.

The second objective of Part One is to present a detailed statement of the characteristics of the underdeveloped economy. Chapter 7 emphasizes those characteristics of the nongrowing economy that are relevant to explaining its underdeveloped status, and to devising policies that may achieve the development objective.

9

Chapter 2

THE GROWTH PROCESS:
A GENERAL VIEW

Per capita output has been accepted as the chief criterion of economic development. The theory of development, then, may begin with a statement of the determinants of the level of output at a given time, and from this base go on to explain how these determinants change and how their change affects total output. It is also necessary to introduce here population change in order to arrive at a growth-of-output per capita figure. The immediate task is to discuss these matters generally, and then work into more explicitly formulated hypotheses about growth in the three chapters that follow.

I. The Aggregative Production Function

In a given short interval, the productive capacity of an economy is a datum given from the past; it is usually expressed in the form of an aggregative production function. Such a function may be written in the following way:

$$Y_t = f(K_{nj} L_t : T_{tj} R_t S_t) \tag{1}$$

Where Y refers to the capacity output of the economy; K is the stock of capital services available for productive purposes; L is the labor force available for production purposes; T refers to applied technical knowledge; R to natural resources; and S to the social and cultural characteristics of the society that affect the ability of the economy to produce. The subscript t refers simply to a short-time period, and the subscripts nj and tj will be explained later.

Technology, resources, and the environmental factors act on output chiefly via their effect on capital and labor. They may be called *position variables* as they affect the position of the relationship between output and the direct inputs. The productive capacity of the system at time *t*, then, depends on the quantity of capital and labor as they function in a setting provided by natural resources, the state of technology, and a social and cultural environment.

Expression 1 is a great simplification of reality—possibly more harmful than helpful. The following pages seek to explain each component of this production function in a way that clarifies its meaning, and that justifies succeeding discussion. The approach suggested here is very simple, but seems satisfactory for the purposes for which it is used. The references in the bibliography may be consulted for more detailed discussions of these components.

A. CAPITAL

Capital services, K_{nj}, refers to the quantity of capital services available for use in production at time *t*. Therefore, it represents a heterogeneous complex of specific capital items. Such a complex cannot, of course, be added up to give a total, and K_{nj} should be thought of as a list of items—as a vector—rather than as a single number. Such a notion creates major problems for measuring the change in the capital stock from one period to the next, since one list of capital items can be said to represent more capital than a second list only if the former list contains at least as many of each item as does the second list, plus more of some items or plus some items not on the first list. The form of the physical capital does change from period to period, and the evidence that the United States has more capital than India is not that the former country has at least as many of all types of physical capital items as India, and more of some items as well. In commonsense terms, the evidence is that over the past periods the United States has been able to allocate "more" resources to the production of physical capital items than India. At time *t*, the country that had more capital during previous periods has employed more resources available in those periods to produce capital than has a country with less capital. To have capital at time *t* means that some of the labor and capital services available in periods previous to *t* were congealed into a form that allows them to be used for current production in period *t*. The quantity of capital in Expression 1 refers, then, to the quantity of resources of previous periods congealed into the various forms of physical capital that are available in period *t*. The problem now is to measure this quantity of resource.

The historical cost of the vector of capital would represent the values placed on these resources by the economy during the periods in which they were used to produce the physical capital available in period *t*. If expectations were realized, if there were no capitalized rents, and if factor markets had been perfectly competitive, this historical value would equal the then present value of the earning stream generated by the capital and the opportunity costs to the economy that produced the capital. The chief —not the sole—problem in using cost of capital (corrected by a price change index and for depreciation) as the measure for the quantity of capital arises from increased productivity in the capital-goods-producing sector of the economy. Suppose that technical change takes place in the capital goods sector between periods one and two in such a way that the productivity of resources in this sector doubles, but the physical characteristics of the capital items themselves remain unchanged. Thus twice as many capital items are produced in period two as in period one, but in terms of congealed inputs of capital and labor the same quantity of capital was produced in both periods. The difficulty is that along with congealing capital and labor, the capital created in period two also congeals knowledge that was not available in period one.

If the labor and capital costs rise commensurately with their productivity so that the value of the capital produced in period two is double that produced in period one, the quantity of capital is no longer measured by the quantity of resources used in its production but by the value of these resources. However, in period two, if expectations are realized, there are no capitalized rents, and factor markets are perfectly competitive, then this valuation of the capital items created in period two is equal to their discounted income stream and to the opportunity cost for the economy at the time of their production. At the end of period two, the economy has a capital stock made up of items produced at two different time periods. Thus, at time t, there is available a complex of capital goods produced in various periods prior to t. The value attached to this complex is the sum of the costs of their production minus any depreciation. If the assumptions are pursued far enough, this value figure represents the opportunity cost of producing the capital to the society that did in fact produce it, and the then present value of the income streams generated by the items.

The capital stock available at time t refers to a series of vectors—a matrix. Each vector lists the different capital items produced during period j that are still available for productive activities at time t. Hence, the symbol K_{nj}. These entries are numbers of individual machines, buildings, and so on that are included as capital. No total is available. Another matrix would have value entries, computed as described above, that reflect the money value attached to each physical item of capital available; these values may be added. This value figure is relevant for many problems, but it is apparent that if the purpose is to separate technical knowledge accumulation effects on output from capital accumulation effects it will not work, because the "value" of the technological change effects is built into the value of the capital stock.

To enable the separation of technological change effects from the effects due to an increased quantity of capital, capital must be measured exclusive of change in quality. To do this, it is necessary to identify the capital-goods-producing sector, and to value the resources in this sector in terms of base period productivities. The value of the capital that is measured in this way and produced in period zero—the base or initial period— attaches itself as the quantity of capital produced in this period. In period one, if no new resources were added to the capital-goods-producing sector, the quantity of capital produced would remain as in period zero, and (abstracting from any price level changes) a change in the value of capital would be explained in terms of factors that affected the productivity of capital. If new resources (capital and labor) enter the capital goods sector in period one, they must be valued at the same "unit value" as were the resources in this sector in period zero. Thus, the quantity of capital produced in period one is equal to the quantity of capital produced (equal the value of capital) in period zero, plus new resources added to the capital goods sector between periods zero and one valued at the prices prevailing in period zero, i.e., valued at the factor productivity prevailing in period zero. For period t, the summation process would be the same except that it would extend over all the periods between the initial period and period t, and consequently, methods of estimating depreciation become crucial.

The great difficulty with this approach is the problem of identifying a "unit" of capital in periods subsequent to the initial period to which to apply the period zero price. If there were no changes in the physical characteristics of the capital items, the difficulties would be insignificant, but, of course, successive doses of new technical knowledge alter the form of capital goods in a manner that precludes a comparison of units of capital to which a base period price may be applied through successive time periods. Assume that the quantity of labor and the wage rates are known for a given capital goods sector in the initial period. Further, assume that the value of capital and its rate of return for this sector are also known for the initial or base period. Then, the increment in the quantity of capital produced by this sector between the initial period and period one will be $w_1 \Delta L + r_1 I$ where w_1 and r_1 are the base period wage rates and return on capital respectively, and ΔL and I are the increment in labor employed and the amount of investment respectively in this sector. Then, a unit of capital may be any arbitrarily selected quantity, e.g., that which results in $\Delta K = 100$. Total capital available from this sector in period one will be the sum of the capital in period zero plus that just computed as the addition to capital stock. Similar summing may be done over t periods. As a practical approximation, the use of the average product of labor during the initial period in the capital goods sector may be used, and the increment in the quantity of capital in period one would be simply the increase in the labor force for this sector times the average product of labor in the initial period. Another variation would be to estimate the rate of the "normal" return on capital in this particular sector of the initial period in order to correct for possible temporary distortions in this rate that do not reflect productivity considerations. The importance in this approach of being able to identify the capital-goods-producing sectors is to be emphasized. The figure for the quantity of capital—for K_{nj}—in Expression 1 is the sum of the output of the several capital-goods-producing sectors measured as just described. The subscripts $_{nj}$ are included as a reminder that actual existing capital in period t consists of n different items produced over j different time periods. This attribute of K_{nj} is a strategic part of later arguments.

B. LABOR

The labor symbol is only moderately less complex. The supply of labor available to an economy is a group of workers with various endowed and learned skills. (In the latter category is the skill to learn new skills, perhaps the most important of all skills.) The L in Expression 1 may then be thought of as a vector of particular skills embodied in human beings, just as the capital vector consists of physical objects with technical knowledge incorporated in them. The labor vector is, therefore, a categorization of skills with the number of individuals possessing each skill. The extent of the categorization depends on the problem, and in some instances merely a breakdown between educated through elementary school and uneducated is all that is required. In other instances, a breakdown that isolates specific skills such as lathe operating, teaching, managing, supervising, and so on is essential. If all members of the labor force were "educated," and the quality of the education was such that each member could learn any skill in a brief period, then, a categorization would not be necessary.

To use the number of workers available in the economy as a one figure estimate of this labor vector is rarely more than a rough approximation. If between periods zero and one, each category of labor skills in the labor vector increases in the same proportion and no new skills come into existence, the increase in total work force does provide an appropriate index for the change in the labor vector from one period to the next. If, however, skill categories do not increase in the same proportion, a weighting system applied to the skills is necessary to construct an index. The most obvious system of weights would be the marginal product (a term to be examined in detail in the next chapter) of the various categories of skills. The direct measurement of the marginal product of a given type of labor is extremely difficult. A workable alternative would be a weighting system based either on prevailing wage rates, which may but probably do not equal the marginal value product of labor, or on an independent appraisal of the contribution to the national product of the various categories of skills in the initial period. Such an independent estimate might be able to correct for distortion in the labor market that the use of wage rates would not. The value of L_t would represent a weighted index of the number of workers available in period t with the actual wage rates or "corrected" wage rates of the initial period as weights. (The choice of the initial period is arbitrary, and other weighting schemes can be defended.) A mere increase in numbers in a skill category with weight zero would obviously add nothing to the capacity of the economy. The system of weights defined here will also be employed in Chapter 12 when the role of labor in the development process is explained in detail.

C. POSITION VARIABLES

Technology, natural resources, and the social environment lend themselves even less than do capital and labor to exact, quantifiable formulations. Technology is discussed fully in Chapter 11, and all that is required here is to note that improved technology will shift the function of Expression 1 to a higher position. The increased technical knowledge works through capital and/or labor, and is evidenced by an increased output with unchanged quantities of inputs or an increase in output in excess of that that can be explained by the increase in the quantities of inputs. The improved technology may require gross investment in order to build the new technical knowledge into the physical capital, but this is not necessarily the case. Organizational changes or changes in the production routine that result in an increase in output may be accomplished with unchanged physical capital and unchanged labor inputs, and may be effected after the physical capital is already in place. The technology effective during period t is therefore made up of that prevailing during previous periods when the capital existing in t was constructed, and the "organizational technology" that could be imposed after capital is already in place. In Expression 1, the symbol for technology is to be recognized as referring to this range of technical knowledge, and, as a reminder of this fact, the subscript tj is employed where j refers to the j periods over which physical capital usable in period t was constructed.

The inclusion of natural resources in Expression 1 is necessary for several reasons. Evidently, where nature has provided abundant, fertile land, capital and labor in agriculture will yield larger outputs than when no such land is available. Similarly, the deterioration in the quality of the land due to natural causes will reduce the productivity of the direct inputs. At the same time great care is needed to separate the effects of natural resources from those of capital and technology. It is of course recognized that what is a resource depends on the state of technology, and that changes in technology affect the quantity and quality of natural resources available to the system. It does not appear possible to construct an index that would reflect in a meaningful way the contribution of natural resources to total output. At the same time it is clear that in any given period the relative incomes of various nations may be explainable primarily in terms of their nature given resources in the context of prevailing technology. The role of natural resources is discussed later, but for the most part the common practice of treating it as a peripheral matter is followed here.

Finally, consider the social environment component of Expression 1. The content of this factor in the production function depends largely on the ambitiousness of the analyst for in general terms, every aspect of the environment has some relevance. Fortunately, some are more relevant than others, and the practical question has to do with ferreting out those characteristics that appear to be the most important and then tracing through their effects on the productivity of capital and labor. For the most part, the components of S refer to such things as the organization of the market and entrepreneurial activity, the extent and effectiveness of the price system in allocating resources, labor's work habits, and other institutional arrangements of the society that bear on the effectiveness with which the economy operates. As already noted, it is generally recognized that in a long-run development analysis some attention must be given to an examination of the changing social and institutional environment within which the narrowly defined economic sector operates. In any short-run interval it is acceptable to assume that this environment does not change, whereas over a longer period it not only changes but, more importantly, it changes in response to economic policy and to economic decisions generally. It is the purpose of Chapter 13 to explore the *modus operandi* of this mutual interaction between the growth of output and the social environment. All that is required here is to emphasize that in time period t the productivity of capital and labor—and hence the position of the function in Expression 1—depends in part upon the characteristics of the environment within which the function is assumed to be effective. It is also clear that S refers to a set of specific characteristics, and not to some amorphous mass.

II. The Problem of Demand

Actual output depends not only on the capacity of the economy to produce goods and services but also on aggregate demand. The aggregate demand side of the problem poses fewer conceptual problems than does the aggregate supply side, and little need be said at this point. The essential problem is to establish means of effective control over total spending brought to bear on the capacity of the economy. Of equal importance with the analysis of the determinants of total demand is the examination of the composition of demand as to the customary aggregates—consumption, investment, and exports, and the changes in the composition of these components as growth occurs. These issues are discussed fully in their logical place.

III. The Growth of Output

A theory of the growth of output for an economy requires an explanation of the increases in the quantity of capital and labor, and the effect of these increases on productivity, as well as the process of change in the position variables, changes in the quality of labor, and the effects of these changes on the productivity of the direct inputs. Further, since interest is focussed on output per capita, it is necessary to have a theory of population growth to add to the picture. Finally, actual output depends on aggregative demand as well as capacity, so it is necessary to include also an argument relative to the effects of demand. The latter task leads into the monetary and fiscal activities of the government and an examination of private sector response to the operation of the traditional instruments of government policy.

The preceding definition of the economic development problem may be summarized at a very high level of abstraction with the following equations:

$$\Delta K / \Delta T = k \ (Y, K, L, T, R, S : t : a_1 \, a_2 \ldots) \tag{2}$$
$$\Delta L / \Delta T = l \ (Y, K, L, T, R, S : t : b_1 \, b_2 \ldots) \tag{3}$$
$$\Delta T / \Delta T = g \ (Y, K, L, T, R, S : t : c_1 \, c_2 \ldots) \tag{4}$$
$$\Delta R / \Delta T = w \ (Y, K, L, T, R, S : t : d_1 \, d_2 \ldots) \tag{5}$$
$$\Delta S / \Delta T = s \ (Y, K, L, T, R, S : t : e_1 \, e_2 \ldots) \tag{6}$$
$$Y_t = y \ (K_o, L_o, T_o, R_o, S_o : t : \epsilon_1 \, \epsilon_2 \ldots) \tag{7}$$

Under appropriate mathematical restrictions, such a set of equations will define a set of time paths generated by the a's, b's, c's, and so on (parameters) for the several variables. The equation for total output is an expanded version of Expression 1, and states that the level of national product at time t depends upon $K, L, T, R,$ and S in the initial period—period zero—and the lapse of time until period t. The determinants of the level of Y_t change from period zero to period t in the manner described by Expressions 2–7. The parameters in all expressions refer to the coefficients that would appear if the expressions were written out explicitly. The fact that Expressions 2–6 are written in the form that they are does not mean that the explicit explanation of capital accumulation or growth of labor supply, for example, must be written specifically in terms of $Y, K, L, T, R,$ and S. They may (and will) be written in terms of other variables, which are in turn governed by some or all of the variables in Expressions 2–6. If, however, it is claimed that Expressions 2–7 define a complete system, then it is necessary that these subsidiary variables be governed by the actual variables in Expressions 2–7.

This way of writing a theory of growth has very little substantive content, and to a large degree says simply that growth depends on almost everything. The building of a specific growth model consists in making assumptions as to form and content of some or all of the Expressions 2–7, and then tracing their implications. To write the growth problem as in Expressions 2–7 does, however, point up several aspects that are very relevant.

First, the initial conditions are explicitly included in the argument. The role of initial condition is especially relevant in the context of a development effort. It is assumed that at period zero the conditions prevailing are given, i.e., are not to be explained by the theoretical arguments to be established. A new development plan, for example, necessarily begins within the context of a prevailing set of circumstances about which nothing can be done. How the economy moves from this initial starting position depends very much on the characteristics of the initial position. A country may be "overpopulated" at the outset, or it may have a large existing capital stock, or it may have a set of values particularly alien to development, and so on. These characteristics are assumed to have developed over the periods prior to the date of period zero, and therefore cannot be explained by the theory that seeks to explain how the system grows subsequent to period zero. A simple example illustrates the point. A compound rate of interest of 4 per cent per year (a parameter) will double the capital in about 17 years but how much money one has at the end of 17 years depends not only on this fact but also on the amount of the initial investment. In most instances, the initial conditions will enter the process in a more complicated fashion than as a proportional factor. In particular, they may affect the existence and the nature of the stability of an economy as well as facilitate or inhibit the achievement of sustained growth. The *initial conditions* of underdevelopment are set forth in Chapter 7 and constitute the datum from which the development process is assumed to start. From Expressions 2–7 and the discussion here, it is seen that these initial conditions necessarily enter the formal characteristics of any theory of growth.

The parameters of Expressions 2–7 describe those behavioral and technical characteristics that are relevant in the argument. As noted above, they would form the coefficients (e.g., saving rate, propensity to import, and so on) of Expressions 2–7 if the latter were written out explicitly. The structural parameters emerge from the complex of social and economic characteristics that form the society, and they affect, in an obvious fashion, the variables of the system, as well as the extent and source of its stability. To alter the value of some or all of the parameters may be an objective of economic policy, and the very process of growth may cause some of them to alter. Therefore, it seems appropriate to consider a particular set of parameters as effective for a given short-run interval and to diagnose the performance of the system in this period. In the next period, new parameters may be effective and part of the analyst's problem is to explain how and why the new parameters came into existence.

Finally, it is to be noted that Expressions 2–7 have no "exogenous" component, but the actual development of any economic system in the real world is to a great degree shaped by the autonomous events that originate outside the system and impinge on it. The system defined in Expressions 2–7 does state how the economy will respond to these exogenous shocks once they occur. Such shocks are by definition outside the arguments of the explanatory apparatus in use, and cannot be predicted by it. In many instances it is convenient to treat the government's actions as autonomous, to analyze how the system acts with no government action in a given sphere, and then to analyze the effect of the government entering into the picture in a particular fashion.

The very general statement of the growth process contained in Expressions 2–7 places primary emphasis on initial conditions, on structural parameters, and on exogenous shocks as the major sources of the explanation of how an economy grows. This is a very abstract statement, but it does provide the general framework that may lead to more explicit formulations. To seek such formulation is the objective of the next three chapters.

Bibliography

The discussion of the aggregative production function and capital theory is rather complex and this chapter presents only the basic principles. For supplementary reading I suggest that students begin with J. E. Meade's *A Neo-Classical Theory of Economic Growth* (London: George Allen & Unwin, 1959) because it is most easily understood. Robert Solow's "Technical Progress, Capital Formation, and Economic Growth," *American Economic Review*, LII (May, 1962) and his "Technical Change and the Aggregate Production Function," *The Review of Economics and Statistics*, XXXIX (August, 1957) and B. F. Massell's "Capital Formation and Technological Change in United States Manufacturing," *The Review of Economics and Statistics*, XLII (May, 1960) are helpful references. Solow has other important papers, for example, his *Capital Theory and the Rate of Return* (Amsterdam: North-Holland Publishing Company, 1963). See W. E. G. Salter, "The Production Function and the Durability of Capital Goods," *Economic Record*, XXXV (April, 1959) and Hollis B. Chenery, "Process and Production Functions from Engineering Data," in Wassily Leontief (ed.), *Studies in the Structure of the American Economy* (New York: Oxford University Press, 1953) for further discussion of the production function. The International Economic Association volume, *The Theory of Capital* (London: Macmillan & Co., Ltd., 1961), has a readable introduction and Chapter 1 by Friedrich Lutz as well as some interesting empirical papers by Tibor Barna and Walther G. Hoffman. See also J. R. Hicks, "Thoughts on the Theory of Capital," *Oxford Economic Papers*, XII (June, 1960). Mrs. Joan Robinson has written extensively on capital and production functions. Students might look first at Chapter II of her *Essays in the Theory of Economic Growth* (London: Macmillan & Co., Ltd. 1963) before referring to her other works.

For the labor input see bibiliography for Chapter 12, for technology the bibliography of Chapter 11, and for the other position variables the bibliography of Chapter 13.

An excellent monograph by Trygue Haavelmo, *A Study in the Theory of Economic Evolution* (Amsterdam: North-Holland Publishing Company, 1954) and

Irma Adelman, *Theories of Economic Growth and Development* (Stanford: Stanford University Press, 1961) were used to secure material for Part III of this chapter.

Numerous efforts have been made to give empirical content to the aggregative production function. See Gerhard Tintner *Econometrics* (New York: John Wiley & Sons, Inc., 1952), pp. 51–57 for a virtually endless listing of such efforts as well as the Solow and Massell papers previously listed.

The papers in the Income and Wealth Series VIII, *The Measurement of National Wealth,* ed. by Raymond Goldsmith and Christopher Saunders (London: Bowes and Bowes, 1959) present a rewarding study of the great difficulties associated with the measurement of capital. See also Kuznet's series of studies listed in the bibliography to Chapter 1.

CHAPTER 3

THE GROWTH OF AN ECONOMY
WITH INDEPENDENT SECTORS

At the beginning of the growth process—period zero—the economy has a particular endowment of capital items and labor skills. The technical knowledge available to it is reflected in the capital items and in the manner in which production is organized. The other relevant determinants of the productivity of capital and labor are subsumed under the heading of natural resources and social environment, and a level of output is given by Expression 7 of the preceding chapter. The problem now is to provide an analysis, much more explicit than that given at the end of the preceding chapter, of the *modus operandi* of the growth of output through time from period zero. The aim is to be specific enough to isolate the strategic factors and relationships of growth, but not so specific that a given interval of economic history of a particular country could be explained by a simple and direct application of the argument.

In this chapter, attention is given to an economy made up of independent sectors. Independence here means that no sector uses as inputs the products of any other sector. Thus, all sectors produce all their own raw materials, capital, and so on and sell only consumer goods. The analysis is conducted step by step through the elements of the production function worked out in the previous chapter. The simplest case will be that in which more capital and labor of precisely the same quality as that already in use becomes available to the sectors. This case is examined in Section I. Then in Section II, the case is examined in which not only more direct inputs are available, but the new capital items incorporate technical knowledge that was not available earlier. Later in this section, attention will be given to new products, and to increases in productivity that are not embodied in physical capital, i.e., organizational and administrative improvements. In Section III, changes in the quality of the labor input will be considered along with scale and terms-of-trade effects. Finally, the effects of changes in environmental factors will be introduced in Section IV. Throughout the assumption is made that there are no problems on the demand side.

I. Effects of Increasing Direct Inputs

A. The Process of Adjustment to New Factor Supplies

To begin, assume that the position variables of Expression 1, Chapter 2–technology, natural resources, and social environment—remain unchanged in content and effect from period zero to period one, while net- and replacement-capital formation and an increase in the labor force do occur. It is further assumed that the gestation period for the construction of capital and the accounting period are of the same length, so that the investment occurring in period zero is ready for use as capital in period one. This capital will therefore embody the technical knowledge available in period zero. Capital accumulation means the construction of specific physical items for use in further production. The fact that capital accumulation is taking place implies the existence of a capital goods sector with a quantity of resources—labor and other capital—available to it. The extent to which resources can be transferred between the capital goods and consumer goods sectors is a matter of concern later in the argument. As it has been assumed that replacement investment is also occurring, it is convenient to assume at this point that no change in the quantity of technical knowledge available in the economy has occurred since the capital being replaced was constructed. If this assumption were not made here, then technical change would enter the analysis via replacement-capital formation even though no change in technology took place between period zero and the preceding period.

Under these assumptions the only source of growth of output is the increase in the quantities of the direct inputs, capital and labor. Two possible situations may be identified. Net-capital formation may result in the same percentage increment for each item in the capital vector corresponding to period zero. This would mean that the economy had more of each physical capital item in period one than it had in period zero. Similarly, the increase in the labor supply may take the same form, i.e., each item in the labor skill vector grows by the same percentage increment, and this percentage increment is equal to that of the increase in capital. If there are constant returns to capital and labor, then the capacity of the economy will also grow by this percentage rate while the capital-labor ratio remains constant, and growth imposes few adjustments on the system.

A second situation is more interesting and more important practically. Suppose that the percentage increment in the quantity of capital exceeds that of labor. Continued full utilization of capital requires that the new capital vector—the one referring to the list of capital items created during period zero and first available for production uses in period one—be altered sufficiently to make possible a capital-labor ratio different from that obtaining during period zero. If it is assumed that once capital is created no further substitution between capital and labor is possible, then for the capital-labor ratio to rise in this manner it is necessary to have available blueprints that may be followed to produce capital items that effectively substitute capital for labor compared to the technique used in period zero. It is further necessary for the relative prices of capital and labor to move in a way to make the second technique the one chosen. In Expression 1, the T_{tj} means that there are alternative techniques of production available (it does not mean that there are an infinite number of such techniques) the choice of which depends on the relative cost of capital and labor. The result, then, is a rise in the capital-labor ratio induced by a rise in wage rates and a decline in the cost of capital, consequent to the fact that the supply of capital has grown relative to the labor supply.

The economy during period one in relation to period zero is shaped in the following way. A new capital vector has been constructed in which the physical items that have been added are such that the combination of direct inputs is optimal with respect to factor prices prevailing in period one. (Since capital is built in period zero to be operated in period one, some accurate prediction is required if exact optimality is achieved.) This "marginal vector" includes both the net- and replacement-capital formation of period zero, but only the net-capital formation adds to the quantity of capital. The concept of a marginal vector is crucial to the subsequent analysis, and it is convenient to think of it either as a vector of capital items or as a vector of the optimal capital-labor ratios for the factor prices prevailing in the most recent time period. Stretching behind this marginal vector is a series of other vectors of capital items and capital-labor ratios created in periods prior to period zero, and therefore reflecting the influence of different technical knowledge and different factor prices prevailing during the periods that the capital was constructed. These vectors may be designated as inframarginal vectors, and the vector (or vectors) of capital items replaced is the submarginal vector of period zero. Several characteristics of the marginal and inframarginal vectors are noted.

It is asserted here and argued later that equilibrium prices are such as to allow normal profits (or zero profits) on the products flowing from the marginal vector. Costs of production in the inframarginal vectors are higher than in the marginal vector due to a number of reasons. Wage rates in the same sector will tend to equalize, and the inframarginal capital vectors are (by definition) designed to exploit a different capital cost—wage-rate ratio from that currently prevailing. On the present assumptions that capital is increasing at a faster percentage rate than labor, and input proportions are fixed once capital is created, wage rates in later periods will be higher than in earlier periods, so the inframarginal capital-labor vectors are more labor intensive than is currently optimal. When the assumption of no change in technical knowledge is relaxed, then costs in the marginal vector will be lower than in the inframarginal vectors because of changes in the productivity of inputs as well. Since costs are higher in the inframarginal than in the marginal vector and the prices of the product are the same, then profits are evidently lower in the former than in the latter vector. In the submarginal vector, profits have fallen so low that replacement is justified.

The fact that the marginal vector includes replacement as well as net-capital formation has an effect on the quantity of labor available for combining with the newly created capital. There are in effect two sources of new labor to work with the new capital. First, there is simply the net increment in the labor supply. Second, some of the capital, built in previous periods to combine with a given amount of labor, is being replaced with capital designed to combine with a smaller quantity of labor. This replacement will thereby release some of the labor that was previously employed with what has now become submarginal capital. This released labor must be able to adapt to the new types of capital items. If the labor were not able to adapt, then the kind of capital created would have to be identical to that used up, or there would be more capital created than could be used and some labor would be idle. It is also necessary to assume that the new additions to the labor force have the skills to operate the new capital, but that there is not qualitative change in the nature of the labor input. This assumption has the equivalent effect on labor that the no change in technical knowledge assumption has on physical capital and organization.

B. The Productivity of New Factors

To isolate the effect of an increased quantity of capital and labor on output, it is convenient to introduce a diagram, which will also illustrate the adjustment process just described and which can be used in later analyses as well. Diagram I shows the "technology" of one sector, for instance sector r, in an economy in which the only source of increase in capacity is an increased quantity of capital and labor. The quantity (as measured earlier) of K_r (the kind of capital required to produce product r) is shown on the vertical axis, and that of labor (L_r) along the horizontal. The three rays—identified as A, B, and C—show there exists at the time of the construction of K_r blueprints that would enable r to be produced by any of three possible combinations (techniques) of capital and labor. Rates of output are measured by a given interval along a ray. For example, length Oa may represent output of 100 units when Technique A is employed. Length Ob would represent the same output (100) when Technique B was used, and so also for Oc. There is no need for a given length on one ray to represent the same output as it does on other rays. Constant returns to capital and labor would be evidenced by a given length on a ray representing the same output irrespective of the level of output. Unless otherwise stated, the constant returns assumptions will be made. The line connecting points a, b, and c would then connect the points representing an output of 100.

The three rays drawn in this fashion also mean that at the time K_r was constructed, there is a choice as to technique, and substitution between capital and labor is possible. To produce an output of 100 with Technique

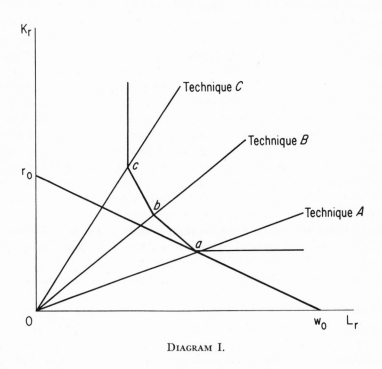

DIAGRAM I.

A requires more labor and less capital than to produce the same output with Technique B. Under present assumptions however, once the technique is chosen and the capital is constructed, no further substitution between capital and labor is possible. This diagram may then represent the technology prevailing at a given time.

To determine which technique (combination of capital and labor) will produce a given rate of output at least cost requires information about the relative costs of labor and capital. If the line $w_o r_o$ is drawn so that any point on it represents the same total outlay and any point northeast of the line a larger outlay, then it is easily seen that production of the given rate of output at minimum cost is achieved by building capital of the kind required to use Technique A. The available technology and relative prices will determine the least cost combination—the least cost technique—required to produce a given rate of output. Since no post-construction substitution between the inputs is allowed by present assumptions, if factor prices change after the capital is constructed, then costs rise and the particular capital-labor ratio built into the capital may no longer be the least cost one.

Consider the effect of the new resources on capacity. This effect depends obviously on the productivity of the new resources, and the problem is to measure this productivity. It is not a simple thing to do.

Suppose that Sector r is producing now with Technique A only, and relative costs of capital and labor are accurately represented by the slope of $w_o r_o$. Sector r is part of the economy described above in which the rate of capital formation is exceeding the rate of growth of the labor force, and therefore it is assumed that the price of capital is declining over time relative to the price of labor. In Diagram II, Sector r decides to expand as well as to replace some of its old capital. It finds that relative costs of capital and labor have changed, and that Technique A is no longer the least cost technique. Suppose then that net-capital formation of type r takes place in the quantity of OF' (Diagram II) and $F'F$ of the existing capital is replaced so that a total of OF of new capital is formed. Since $F'F$ of old capital (Technique A type capital) is scrapped, output from Technique A must fall by an amount equal to $S'S$. The labor released from employment in Technique A as a consequence of scrapping $F'F$ of A–type capital is FS minus $F'S'$ or NS. This entire amount of labor will not be required to combine with the replaced capital $F'F$, as a more capital intensive technique is now to be employed. Consequently, some labor (for example, Og_1) is available for combining with the newly created capital. So with no net increase in the labor force there is OF' of new capital to combine with Og_1 labor that can produce an output of OP as read from Ray C. There is also $F'F$ of replacement capital combining with $g_1 g_2$ of labor that can produce PM output. Since there has been no increase in the labor supply to this point, the increment of output is entirely attributable to the increment in the quantity of capital.

If $PM = SS'$, then OP would represent the net increase in output due to the new capital. But SS' must exceed PM because on the new ray the same quantity of capital ($F'F$) is combined with a smaller quantity of labor than was the case when Technique A was used. If output represented by SS' did not exceed that represented by PM, it would mean that Technique A was "technologically inefficient," i.e., would never be used no matter what relative factor prices were (as long as the least cost combination is the criterion of selection of techniques). This difference between $S'S$ and PM—call it D—must then be subtracted to get the net increase in output due to the increase in the quantity of capital with no increase in the labor supply.

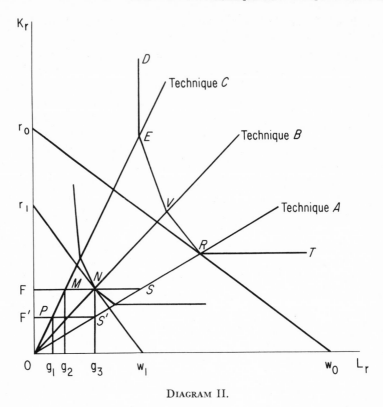

DIAGRAM II.

Let $OP - D = OP'$ and then let $OP' + PM = OM'$. If OF' represented a "unit" of capital (as previously measured), then the increment of output of OP' would be attributable to an increase in one "unit" of capital, i.e., it is the marginal product of capital when capital is of the type to produce commodity r. If there were *no* net increase in the supply of labor then, with present assumptions as to total (net plus replacement) capital formation, capital of type C must be accumulated no matter what factor prices are if all available resources are to be used.

But there has been a net increase in the supply of labor, by an amount equal to $g_2 g_3$. With this increase in the labor supply the maximum increase in output now achievable is on Ray B, and is shown by ON. Therefore ON minus OM' is attributable to the net increase in the labor supply. Suppose that $g_2 g_3$ represents a "unit" of labor, then ON minus OM' is the increment output due to the increase in one "unit" of labor, i.e., it is the marginal product of labor. (The factor limitation lines of F and g_1, g_2, and g_3 have been drawn to intersect on a ray, and the initial output of OR was assumed to be produced by one technique only. This simplifies the exposition, but is not necessary to the argument. For further information on these points see the articles by Dorfman and Eckaus.)

This rather involved method of defining and measuring the marginal products of capital and labor has considerable advantage. In the first place, it emphasizes that reorganization of production is necessary before it is meaningful to use the concepts, and this reorganization may impose heavy adjustment burdens on the economy. If *no* labor were available from any source to work with the new capital, then a net increase in the quantity of capital would yield no increase in capacity. If this description of the reorganization of production is granted, the increment in capital does result in an increase in capacity that may realistically be called the marginal product of capital. A similar argument holds for labor. It is also clear that these marginal products apply only to the newly created capital, and not to all existing capital. It now seems appropriate to write, in the traditional manner, the increase in total capacity in terms of marginal products and increases in factor supplies. Thus

$$\Delta Y_r = MP_k \, \Delta K_r + MP_l \, \Delta L_r \tag{1}$$

where the *MP* refers to marginal product, and the subscripts k and l to capital and labor respectively.

To get the total increase in output in all sectors of the economy due to the availability of new capital and labor, the equivalent of Expression 1 for all sectors would be summed. Total new capital is the sum of OF' and the total increment in the labor force is the sum of $g_2 g_3$. If it is assumed that one type of capital and one type of labor combine to produce one type of product and there are no links at all among the several (n) sectors, then this sum may be written very simply.

$$\sum_{r=1}^{n} \Delta Y_r = \sum_{r=1}^{n} [MP_k \, \Delta K_r + MP_l \, \Delta L_r] \tag{2}$$

In the second place, Diagram II and the accompanying discussion help to clarify the marginal vector notion. The diagram shows that in period one, two vectors of capital are operating in the economy, those illustrated by Techniques *A* and *B*. With the factor prices of period one, shown by $w_1 r_1$, Technique *A*, used to produce output $OR - SS'$, becomes inframarginal, and the costs per unit of output here are necessarily higher than with Technique *B*. As time goes by, more capital is accumulated and its price falls relative to labor's, Technique *B* also becomes inframarginal. Diagram II could be enlarged to show how new techniques, and hence new vectors of capital, become optimal and then eventually some techniques are abandoned completely.

Third, the argument tells something about distribution of the output and the profitability of capital formation. The marginal product of capital at any given output declines from Ray A to B to C in Diagrams I and II. Suppose for the moment that the decline in the marginal product of capital is exactly offset by the rise in the quantity of capital used per unit of output, so that capital's share of the increment of output is the same as its share in the previous level of output. As the marginal vector is created, however, the cost of labor and capital in all of Sector r may be expected to follow those in the marginal vector. As the capital-labor ratio in the "old" capital items is nonoptimal from the standpoint of the "new" factor prices, the distribution of the output from the old capital is altered. If the amount of existing capital exceeds by a wide margin the increment of capital, this income distribution effect may be quite important. As long as the percentage rate of increase of capital exceeds the percentage rate of increase of labor and there are no technical innovations, and factor payments for all vectors are set by the marginal product of the marginal vector, capital's share of output from the inframarginal vectors must decline. This statement holds no matter whether the proportionate change in the marginal product of capital equals, exceeds, or falls short of the proportionate change in the capital-labor ratio as the system moves counterclockwise from Ray A. As discussed in Chapter 5, these points are relevant to the maintenance of price level stability and control in a growing economy.

Finally, the argument gives a role to replacement investment that is important, and will become more important when technical change is introduced into the analysis.

The assumption of post-construction fixed input coefficients is somewhat unrealistic. If some organization and administration changes occur as relative prices change, then some of the deterioration in the position of the inframarginal vectors is countered. In certain instances such changes may be important, but they cannot offset the full effect of a changing factor environment. It is also clear that if unemployment exists, the change in least cost techniques does not take place even if the rate of capital formation does exceed the rate of growth of the labor force. Unemployment is a relatively important characteristic of the nongrowing economy, and is discussed in Chapter 7.

II. Effects of Increasing Technical Knowledge

The continuous flow of new applied technical knowledge has a wide variety of effects on the growth of capacity of an economy, and of the demand brought to bear on this capacity. The task now is to separate these effects, and to devise a method of introducing them into the argument. The most immediate effect of the introduction of new technical knowledge into the production process is that the productivity of the direct inputs is raised so that a larger output with given quantities of inputs becomes possible. The discussion begins with an explanation of the implications of this particular aspect of the technological change.

A. PROPORTIONATE INCREASES IN THE PRODUCTIVITY OF THE DIRECT INPUTS

The simplest assumption to make about the accumulation of technical knowledge is that it has the sole effect of increasing the productivity of capital and labor proportionately. In this case the introduction of the effects of knowledge accumulation is a simple matter. Consider first a situation in which the newly available knowledge is of the type that must be incorporated into physical capital items. Refer again to Diagram I. Under present assumptions, new applied technical knowledge is illustrated by the creation of new rays, superimposed on the existing ones, on which a given length represents a greater output than on the existing rays. In this case the results for period one are obtained as before, except now operation is on a new ray that did not exist earlier. The increment in output between periods zero and one due to the net increase in direct inputs and improved technology may now be written as

$$\Delta Y_r = t_k \, (MP_k \, \Delta K_r) + t_l \, (MP_l \, \Delta L_r) \tag{3}$$

where t_k and t_l are the ratios of the marginal productivities of capital and labor respectively after technical change to those obtaining prior to the introduction of the new techniques. The MP_k (MP_l) is the marginal product of capital (labor) in period one as it would have been in the absence of the technical change that produced the increased productivity. It is assumed here that $t_k = t_l$, and the right-hand side of Expression 3 may be written as $t_r \, (MP_k \, \Delta K_r + MP_l \, \Delta L_r)$.

[There is a complication with respect to introducing technical change into replacement investment. In terms of Diagram II, it was noted that the difference between *PM* and *S'S*—called *D*—had to be subtracted from *OP* to get the net increase in capacity due to new capital. With rising productivity a modification or two is required. If there has been no improvement in technical knowledge between the period of construction of the capital items to be replaced and period zero, then *D* is equal to $t_r(PM) - S'S$ in terms of Diagram II. If, however, technical knowledge has been accumulating at a constant percentage rate (equal to $t - 1$) between the period when it was constructed and period zero and the capital item is more than one period old, things are a little more confused. Now replacement-capital formation results in new capital being created that embodies several periods of new knowledge accumulation relative to that being replaced rather than to only one period. Thus *PM* is corrected not by t_r, but by $(t_r)^x$, where *x* is the number of periods between construction and replacement. But it is unnecessary to become too concerned about this point in the present context.]

It has been assumed that $t_k = t_l$, but this is not the same thing as saying that the t_k's and the t_l's are equal in all sectors. Indeed a major part of the subsequent argument rests on the realistic assumption that the t_k's and the t_l's differ from sector to sector and from time period to time period.

The marginal vector of the economy may now be defined as the vector that employs the most productive technology as well as the least cost combination of inputs. On the assumption that labor and capital costs in all of Sector r are the same and are equal to the respective marginal products in the marginal vector, the costs in the inframarginal vectors are raised relatively more than is the case with no technical change. The submarginal vector—the replaced capital items—become submarginal because of the change in the optimum combination of factor inputs and also the change in technical knowledge.

Finally, the aggregative production function for period one differs from that for period zero in that the quantity of capital and labor has increased, and the level of applied technical knowledge has risen. The change in capital stock for the entire economy (the n independent sectors) would be

$$\sum_{r=1}^{n} \Delta K_r$$

minus depreciation

$$\sum_{r=1}^{n} (F'F)_r$$

the increase in the labor supply would be

$$\sum_{r=1}^{n} \Delta L_r$$

and the technical knowledge position variables would be T_{1j}. They would be an index determined from a weighted average of the t's (weights would be the proportion of output of a sector in total output) of the various sectors. The difference in total output between periods zero and one shown by two production functions equals the ΔY given by Expression 3.

If $t_k = t_l$, the effect of increasing technical knowledge is simply to increase the increment in output that is achievable with the quantity of new direct inputs above the level that would have been attained in the absence of new knowledge. The least cost technique remains the same as in the case with no technical change effect, merely a rise in the capital-labor ratio. Also the percentage increment in the marginal product of each direct input equals the increase in output, i.e., $t_k = t_l = t$, and consequently the distribution of the increment of output is unaffected by the introduction of new technical knowledge into the analysis. Because of these characteristics it seems reasonable to refer to this kind of technical change as neutral. It is evident, of course, that neutral technical progress does not alter the conclusion reached earlier as to the effect of the change in the factor price line on the distribution of the output from the inframarginal vectors.

B. Nonproportionate Increases in the Productivity of Direct Inputs

There is no argument or empirical evidence to suggest that $t_k = t_l$, and indeed there are some reasons to think that there are forces tending to produce a t_k in excess of t_l in a growing economy.

If t_k equals the ratio of the marginal product of capital in period one with no change in technology to that in period zero, the decline in the marginal product of capital due to the rising capital-labor ratio is precisely countered by the new knowledge, and the profit rate (assumed to be the marginal product of capital) remains constant from period zero through period one. If the percentage rate of capital accumulation continues to exceed the percentage rate of increase in labor as further periods evolve, the least cost technique becomes increasingly capital intensive. If the technical change effect continues to be neutral then a constant profit rate equal to that of period zero requires a rising t.

However, if t_k exceeds t_l, then the maintenance of the marginal product of capital may be achieved with a constant t but a rising t_k. With a constant t (t is a weighted average of t_k and t_l where the weights are the shares of the increment of output accruing to capital and labor) and a rising t_k there are further implications as well. In particular it means that the share of capital in output is rising, as the successive increments in the marginal product of capital are exceeding the increments in output. If the process continues, capital's share will approach 100 per cent of the increments of output due to the increase in applied technical knowledge, and the change in the productivity of labor will be limited to that due to the rising capital-labor ratio.

The distinction between neutral and nonneutral innovations may be further clarified with an explanation of Diagram III. The "isoquant" marked I is drawn so that points A, B, and C all represent the same output level, say 100. The isoquant II appears after a neutral innovation has made it possible to produce a rate of output of 100 with a smaller quantity of inputs than was possible before the innovation. Isoquants II and III and the rays that create them are applicable only to the capital to be constructed after the knowledge has reached the blueprint stage. Points A', B', C', on the new isoquant also represent outputs of 100 and are all nearer the origin in the same proportion on their respective rays than are A, B, and C. A price line that dictated the use of Technique A before the innovation would also dictate its use after the neutral innovation. Suppose now another innovation results in isoquant III and here t_k exceeds t_l.

Again C'', B'', and A'' represent points of an output of 100. Now, however, C'' is closer to the origin relative to C than B'' is relative to B, and B'' is closer to the origin relative to B than A'' is relative to A. The greater the capital intensity of the technique, the greater the input saving effect due to an innovation in which t_k exceeds t_l. It is for this reason that it seems appropriate to identify such innovations as "favorable" to capital.

In Diagram III, the factor price line $w_o'r_o'$ is identical to $w_o r_o$ except

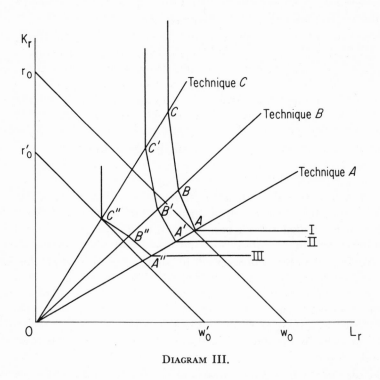

DIAGRAM III.

that it represents a smaller expenditure. The neutral innovation, as just noted, does not produce any change in the least cost technique. The innovation producing isoquant III has the effect of changing the technique that maximizes output (for the price line $r_o w_o$) from Technique A to Technique C. Thus an innovation favorable to capital will lead to a choice of technique that is more capital intensive than that produced by a neutral innovation for a given price line. In the extreme case (the one shown in Diagram III), innovations favorable to capital may in effect substitute for changes in the factor price line to produce changes in the least cost technique. Suppose that the percentage rate of capital formation exceeds the rate of growth of the labor force between period zero and period one so that Ray C becomes optimal, but for reasons of market imperfections, the factor price line does not change to reflect the changed relative scarcities. If innovations occur that are favorable to capital, then with unchanged factor prices, the technique chosen as new capital becomes available is more capital intensive than are the existing techniques. In this case, an innovation favorable to capital will result in a larger increment in output than would a neutral innovation with the same overall t. This is true because the innovation favorable to capital has effects on the choice of technique that enables a more effective exploitation of resources than would be possible with neutral innovations.

Innovations that result in points A, B, and C moving nearer to the origin, the greater the labor intensity of the technique, may for similar reasons be called innovations favorable to labor.

This discussion shows that innovations enter the argument not only by increasing the increment of output achievable from a given quantity of new inputs, but also possibly by altering the optimal combination of inputs. This fact has relevance as a possible source of stability in the economy and for exploiting to greater advantage existing resources. These latter points are explained in detail in the following pages.

C. THE ROLE OF NEW TECHNIQUES

The preceding discussion assumed that three techniques were known in period zero, and that the effect of new knowledge consisted exclusively of increasing the rate of output available from each of these techniques. The assumption that there were only a very limited number of techniques (*i.e.*, of factor combinations) known at any one time was made simply because it seems to conform much more closely to reality than does the assumption of a smooth isoquant that allows an infinite number of combinations of inputs. A further elaboration is necessary. The creation of a technique places demands on resources. Sometime prior to period zero resources were used to design the blueprints and other data necessary to create Ray C of Diagrams I, II, and III, and part of the innovational activity consists of this kind of work. As factor prices change in a manner that favors techniques that are relatively capital intensive, efforts may be expected to be concentrated on producing new rays—Ray D—between C and the ordinate of the diagrams. Also an input saving innovation that is applicable to one ray is not generally applicable without cost to all other existing rays. It, therefore, seems safe to argue that as the rate of capital accumulation continues to exceed the rate of growth of the labor force and as labor becomes increasingly expensive relative to capital, or more readily available, little attention is given either to creating new rays in the area of the diagram where labor intensity is relatively high or to devising input saving innovations applicable to these rays. It therefore seems safe to argue that in an economy where capital growth has long exceeded the growth of labor, innovations may be expected to be largely favorable to capital.

Consider again Diagram III. The argument just stated suggests that as the capital-labor ratio continues to rise, Technique *A* becomes of little interest, and the innovational effort is concentrated on reducing the input requirements for Techniques *B* and *C*. Later, if the capital-labor ratio keeps on rising the technique represented by Ray *B* becomes equally un-interesting and attention is aimed at creating a new ray *D*, and at raising the productivity of inputs combined in the ratio given by Ray *C*. Indeed, it may be that Ray *A* becomes technologically inefficient as a consequence of innovations that affect Ray *B*. If an innovation is applicable only to Rays *B* and *C* and has the result of placing *B″* southwest of *A″*, then Ray *A* is no longer of interest as it now requires more of capital and labor for each output within the range considered here.

This argument has considerable relevance for the problem of trans-ferring technology from a rapidly growing economy to one that has not experienced growth or between economies with differing factor endow-ments. The argument also means that economies seeking rapid growth cannot acquire cost-free technical knowledge but must allocate resources to the task of adaptation of imported knowledge if they wish to exploit all resources. Innovations favorable to capital may now be defined to include the creation of new rays in the relatively capital intensive area, and inno-vations favorable to labor will include the creation of new rays in the part of the diagram that represents relatively labor intensive techniques.

D. The Role of New Products

The preceding arguments have been built on the assumption that in-creases in technical knowledge were reflected simply in a reduced quantity of inputs per unit of output of an unchanged product. Changes in the na-ture and quality of the product, however, are an essential part of the im-pact of knowledge accumulation. The introduction of changes in the characteristics of the product into the analysis is at best exceedingly crude, but is necessary for reasons connected both with supply and demand.

It was pointed out above that if the percentage rate of growth of capital exceeds that of labor and innovations were neutral in effect, a rising *t* was required to keep the marginal product of capital constant at the period zero level. And if the assumption were made that *t* is constant, then a con-stant marginal product of capital requires a continuously rising t_k/t_l ratio. Neither assumption has much to recommend it as applicable over a long period of time. Empirical evidence is slight and is open to many doubts, but what there is does not support either condition, and the a priori argu-ment leads to the conclusion to reject both assumptions. The inclusion of the creation of new techniques as part of the innovation process slightly relieves the pressure, but does not alter the conclusion just stated. At the same time the evidence available for countries that have experienced long periods of growth does not suggest any long-run tendency toward a sys-tematic decline in the profit rate for the economy as a whole, although for short periods it may decline drastically and for specific sectors it may decline permanently. It would appear then that it is necessary to introduce further effects of innovations into the arguments.

Part of the answer at least is to be found in new products that open the way for further technological progress. The argument may be stated in the following terms: the design of a new product is completed and the details of its production put to blueprint. In the language of the diagrams used earlier, this means that a new diagram comes into existence with at least one technique of production. It is possible to construct hypotheses that these "initial" rays are likely to be relatively labor intensive and relatively inefficient and thereby to leave "room" for both technological progress in general and technological progress favorable to capital in particular. Detailed examination of this hypothesis is made in Chapter 11, but it has appeal with respect to available empirical data and to material describing the innovative process.

The major difficulty with the argument is the conceptual one of defining a new product. In a very broad sense there have never been any new products as almost everything can be classified as food, clothing, shelter, or machines, and all of these have been available in one form or another from any date of interest to the modern economist. On the other hand, the slightest modification in a product in some sense changes "the nature and quality of the product." Despite these difficulties about which legitimate debate may take place, the argument not only seems reasonable but indeed essential not only because products have very obviously changed but also because the alternative assumptions of a rising t or a rising t_k/t_l are, for reasons already discussed, less acceptable.

Therefore, part of the knowledge accumulation process includes the creation of new products, and the production of these new products is generally at the outset relatively labor intensive and costly. (Defense of this hypothesis is given in Chapter 11.) After the conception of the product, the technical knowledge effect consists of reducing input requirements in a manner favorable to capital. New products have a role on the demand side of the problem as well, but this matter is best treated in the general discussion of demand.

E. ORGANIZATIONAL CHANGES

The discussion has assumed that all new technical knowledge was necessarily incorporated into physical capital, and therefore could not be introduced without some replacement- or net-capital formation. There are other types of new knowledge that when made available can be introduced directly into existing plant and equipment. Such knowledge may be referred to as organizational and administrative, since for the most part it will be of the kind that will affect the manner in which production is organized, and controlled, as contrasted with the means by which it is carried out. The chief difference between this type of innovation and that previously considered is that the existing resources are affected as well as those newly created. Thus the assumption is made that the organizational changes are applicable to a plant already in operation as well as to one just beginning to be built. Examples would be a new manner of handling inventories that reduced the quantity required to be maintained, or a new way of arranging the production routine so that a larger throughput of raw materials would be possible with existing supplies and form of capital and labor. One might also include in this type of new knowledge that which is actually incorporated or embodied into physical capital, but which can be effected by a modification in the existing capital. For example, modifications of existing machines may permit a more rapid operation or may enable a reduction in wastage of raw material.

In terms of the diagrams already introduced, this type of innovation differs from that requiring incorporation into physical capital simply by virtue of its applicability to the existing capacity. The previous innovations applied only to the marginal vector of physical capital, while these will apply to the existing capacity as well. In terms of Diagram III if innovations are all of the organizational variety, isoquants II and III will change in a way that the whole capacity has been increased by the amount of the innovation. It is immediately evident that organizational innovations of a given magnitude will have a greater output effect than those of a similar magnitude that require embodiment in physical capital, because the former applies to all existing capital, while the latter applies only to the marginal vector of capacity. If organizational innovations are measured as the percentage increment in the capacity of Sector r, then the effect of such innovations on output may be introduced into Expression 3 simply by addition. Thus if $t_k = t_l$ for Sector r,

$$\Delta Y_r = t_r \left(MP_k \, \Delta K_r + MP_l \, \Delta L_r \right) + p \, Y_r \tag{4}$$

where p is the percentage increase in output due to organizational progress between period zero and period one.

Organizational innovations affect the whole of existing capacity, and thereby do not add to the discrepancy between the marginal and inframarginal vectors as to costs and profits. If all innovations were organizational and there were no changes in relative scarcities of capital and labor, then the distinction between marginal and inframarginal vectors would disappear. It seems clear, however, that all innovations are not of the organizational variety, and attention must therefore be given to both types of technical change. It is evident that organizational innovations may also be neutral, favorable to capital, or favorable to labor with the same consequences as those already outlined for the embodied innovations.

F. CONCLUSION

A quick summary of the role of the accumulation of applied knowledge may be helpful. Most simply it results in an increase in the productivity of the direct inputs in the various sectors of the system in a manner that may affect each input in exactly the same way or may favor one or the other of the inputs. The innovation may be applicable only to the capital yet to be created—embodied innovations—or it may be of the kind that is applicable to all of the existing capacity—organizational innovations. If the long-run constancy of the marginal product of capital and (at some point) a rising capital-labor ratio are assumed to be requirements of growth, then it may be concluded that one or more of the following must occur: innovations must be favorable to capital, or new products must appear that open new potential for input-reducing innovations, or innovations must be great enough to offset the change in the capital-labor ratio. A "theory of technical progress" must address itself to each of these issues, and it is with these issues in the context of an underdeveloped country that the subject matter of Chapter 11 is concerned.

III. The Role of the Quality of Labor, Economies of Scale, and the Terms of Trade

The sources of growth considered to this point were increases in the quantity of capital and labor and increases in technical knowledge. Increases in technical knowledge were assumed to affect the forms of the capital or the manner in which the production process is organized. Throughout the discussion the quality of the labor input has been assumed to be such that the skills required to operate the capital equipment were present, but no independent source of growth due to the changing quality of labor was introduced. However growth from this source is not only possible, it is probable, and it must have a place in the growth story. So too must economies of scale and the terms-of-trade effect be introduced. It is the purpose of this section to discuss the *modus operandi* of these three sources of growth.

A. THE QUALITY OF LABOR

In the previous argument the marginal product of labor increased either because labor had a larger quantity of capital or more productive capital with which to work or because it was organized in a more productive manner. The marginal product of labor may increase also because labor skills change, and consequently with the same quantity of inputs and technical knowledge output rises because the quality of the labor input changes. The productivity of labor does not rise merely because of the passage of time. It improves because other resources become embodied in it or because of a learning process. The capital formation previously discussed took the form of machines or buildings, but capital may also take a form that is embodied in a human being. The obvious example is specialized training. The training process is a form of capital formation as its achievement requires saving, and it is not destroyed by use, and may become obsolete. Presumably after the training period, the labor is more productive than it would have been in the absence of training, and this extra output constitutes the return to the capital invested in the form of the training. A discussion of the process by which the quality of the labor input is improved is the subject matter of Chapter 12, and the task now is to show how this type of increase in labor's productivity affects output.

In Diagram II the marginal product of labor was worked out in the situation in which the capital-labor ratio was rising. Now suppose that the new entrants to the labor force (g_2g_3 in Diagram II) have had more or better specialized training than the workers already in the labor force (Og_1) who will also be employed with the new form of capital. The OM' represents the same rate of output as in Diagram II, but ON will be larger now than previously and so of course will $ON-OM'$. Therefore, with the same increment in the quantity of direct inputs a larger increment in output is now secured than in Diagram II. For the better trained workers to be effective requires that the capital stock be of a kind that permits variable skills to be applied or it may mean a different kind of capital must be created to be combined with the different quality of labor. If the capital stock were not adaptable in this way, the extra training given to the workers would yield no output and so no return would be realized on the cost of training the g_2g_3 quantity of labor.

In this case it has been assumed that only the new entrants to the labor force possessed the new training, and therefore only this marginal vector of labor could contribute the higher rate of output. This assumption would mean another source of a marginal-inframarginal category of inputs. In general, however, this is an extreme assumption, for just as physical capital may be altered to reflect new knowledge, so existing labor may be retrained. For many professional workers retraining is doubtless impossible and, as will be argued later, a major policy question for the development planner is what training programs to establish. Nevertheless, it seems appropriate at this point to assume that a greater proportion of the labor force than that constituted by the new entrants can be affected by a training program.

Of equal importance to formal specialized training programs is on-the-job training. This source of increase in the marginal product of labor may be especially important in the new developing countries where the labor force is unfamiliar with the more demanding tasks of modern production methods. In this case it is the product of the existing labor force that is rising, and the new entrants to the labor force would be less productive than those who had gained considerable experience in operating new types of equipment. In terms of Diagram II, this kind of learning process would mean that $ON-OM'$ gradually increased as labor learned to perform its role in the production process more effectively.

In all these cases the increased productivity of labor may be considered simply as an innovation favorable to labor, and would be reflected in the value of t_l. It is important, however, to keep the various sources of the value of t_l distinct for they imply very different policy actions. Finally, from the arguments in the previous section, a t_l in excess of t_k means that, with a given cost line, a more labor intensive technique will become optimal for the sector.

B. ECONOMIES OF SCALE

Economies of scale are only mentioned at this point. They would be reflected in the diagrams by an increase in the quantity of output represented by a given length along a particular ray as output increases. There are no reasons to suppose that if one ray in a diagram is subject to increasing returns to scale all rays will be equally blest. Indeed there is some evidence to suggest that the more capital intensive rays are more likely to enjoy increasing returns than are the more labor intensive techniques. The existence of economies of scale means that the least cost technique is not independent of the size of output. Also in explaining divergent rates of growth between several time periods, the availability or unavailability of economies of scale may be a strategic part of the explanation.

The possibility of increasing returns to scale is most relevant in the context of a country just beginning to grow. There it may have—as shown later—considerable implications for investment decisions as well as for problems associated with marketing and foreign trade.

C. TERMS OF TRADE EFFECT

In Chapter 1 the way the terms of trade enter the income picture was briefly noted. Their effect arises out of the fact that changes in the terms on which a country sells its product to the rest of the world obviously affects the quantity of imports it can acquire with a specific quantity of exports. As noted earlier, a rise in the price of exports relative to imports results in a larger quantity of goods and services becoming available for domestic use without any increase in the domestic output. The opposite occurs if the terms of trade deteriorate, i.e., if the price of imports rises relative to the price of exports.

The diagrams that have been used show rates of physical output and imply nothing about the terms of trade. They may be introduced easily enough by assuming that the output of the export sector is import capacity. Suppose Sector x is the export sector, and new capital and labor are allocated to this sector. Then the physical output of export commodities will rise in accordance with Expression 4 above. What happens to import capacity (ΔM) is then given by

$$\Delta M = \frac{P_x}{P_m} [(t_k \, MP_k \, \Delta K_x) + (t_l \, MP_l \, \Delta L_x) + p \, Y_x] \tag{5}$$

where P_x/P_m is the ratio of the price index of exports to that of imports. Expression 5 shows that the increase in import capacity depends not only on the determinants of physical output, but also on the terms of trade. It also shows that P_x/P_m may be introduced in the argument very much in the manner of innovations. If there were no changes in the terms of trade, then all the other sources of growth identified as affecting physical output of exports would affect import capacity in the same way that they affect the output of exports.

The terms of trade however are not completely equivalent to technical innovations because of the fact that their behavior depends in part on a variable over which the country itself has no control, namely foreign demand. This means that along with the adjustment problems already discussed—and to be discussed—one must add another, similar in kind but different in the degree of susceptibility to domestic policy. The terms of trade are considered later in the book.

IV. Environmental Factors

The other position variables included in the aggregative production function—natural resources and the social environment—are necessarily treated differently from the sources of growth already discussed because they change much more slowly than do the other variables, and because they lend themselves much less satisfactorily to the tools of the economist. Except in rare instances do natural resources and environmental factors change at a speed comparable to changes in the quantities of direct inputs available or in their productivities. It therefore seems misleading to talk of changes in these variables between period zero and period one. For example, the apparent slowdown in the rate of growth of output in the United States in the few years following 1955 can hardly be explained in terms of changes in natural resources or environmental factors. This does not mean, however, that such changes are not as important as changes in factor inputs and in technology over a longer period of time. There is no doubt that the environmental factors relevant to the operating of the United States economy were different in the mid-1950's from what they were in the mid-1920's, and that these differences should enter into an analysis of why the economy seemed to perform so differently in these two periods thirty years apart. Thus sometime and for some reason between 1925 and 1955 the environment changed, and its change introduced elements into the 1955 situation which constitute part (probably a minor part) of the explanation of the differing performances of the economy in these two periods.

Of equal importance is the fact that the relevant environmental factors can be affected by the operation of the economy and by government policies. If the components of the environment changed haphazardly or changed in response to factors over which no control could be exercised, then they would be of less interest in the kind of analysis undertaken here. There seems little doubt that market organization, extent of the "urge to maximize," extent of labor mobility, and so forth can be influenced by particular policies. Finally—and this is the source of many analytical and practical difficulties—the environmental effects have long gestation periods and policies that are taken in period zero may have no effects in period one, but may appear very important indeed in period 25 when the rest of the economy is quite different from what it was in period zero. The identification of some specific environmental features that seem especially relevant, and the further exploration of their impact is discussed in Chapter 13. Now it is necessary only to show how changes in the content of the S of the aggregative production function affect the capacity of the economy to produce.

The environmental factors act in two different ways: they act on the rate of capital and technical knowledge accumulation, and on the effectiveness with which existing inputs are used. The latter effect would be shown by an increase in the rate of output from already available resources. For example, if an improvement in the allocation of production between domestic and foreign sources were achieved, then under a variety of circumstances output from resources already in place would increase. Similarly, if attitudes toward maximizing changed, a reorganization of production may be such as to bring about a larger output. In these two examples the changes would be applicable to all resources, not just those in the marginal vectors.

It is with respect to the effect on the rates of increase in inputs and knowledge and of changes in the attitudes of the economic agents that the S factors seem most important. For example, attitudes toward saving and toward forms of assets that are acceptable are subject to change and may obviously affect the rate at which the economy is able to accumulate capital. Equally evident is the fact that changes in attitudes and ideas about risk taking and venturesomeness of entrepreneurs affect the rate at which new techniques are sought and employed.

Both conceptually and practically there are major difficulties in measuring the effect of changes in the environment on output and particularly in separating this effect from the innovation effect. In a larger measure a set of policies conducive to rapid technical change is also conducive to creating an environment that encourages further growth. Still there is real merit in separating the "environmental" effect from the technical change effect for all types of economies, but especially for the underdeveloped ones. As will be argued in Chapter 7, the social milieu in which the nongrowing economy functions is a major factor interpreting this nongrowth. The analysis explaining the existence of this sort of environment, and the process by which it may be changed, involve a different approach from that seeming to be most helpful in understanding the *modus operandi* of technical change.

The little consideration that is given to natural resources is in the context of technical change and capital accumulation.

V. Conclusion

This chapter has considered the sources of growth of capacity of an economy made up of individual, independent sectors, and tried to establish the manner—the *modus operandi*—of their growth-producing influence. Since each sector was assumed to be independent of other sectors, there were no objections to summing up the increment in output of the several sectors to get the total increase in output. The sources of growth of capacity that have been isolated follow from the aggregative production function introduced in Chapter 2, and in general terms are the changes in the quantity of direct inputs and changes in the position variables that affect the productivity of the direct inputs. More specifically, growth of total output has been assumed to result most directly from increases in the quantities of capital and labor. The increase in capital is embodied in new physical plant and equipment or in human beings. A second source of increase in output capacity is the increase in technical knowledge that, by altering the form of the physical capital and organization of the production process, increases the productivity of the direct inputs. The social and environmental characteristics that determine or help to determine attitudes toward risk, toward work, toward innovations, toward profit maximizing, and the like also affect the extent to which the immediate origins of growth function in a manner that produces growth. Finally, note was taken of the fact that the productivity of resources producing for exports depends in part on the terms of trade, and that the scale of output may affect productivity or changes in productivity of the direct inputs.

The precise form in which these several growth generative forces enter the growth equation vary considerably, and for their clarification chief reliance was placed on a simple diagram. The diagrams illustrated how growth occurs as these forces become effective, and the adjustments on the economy that growth imposes. Also the growth process was found to create what were identified as marginal, inframarginal, and submarginal vectors of capacity. The chief difference among these vectors had to do with costs of production and hence profits realized from output and growth. The chief problem created by their existence had to do with pricing policy, and the extent to which the economy can exploit existing opportunities.

Bibliography

For a more formal explanation of the approach employed in this chapter see W. E. G. Salter, *Productivity and Technical Change* (Cambridge: Cambridge University Press, 1960). This is an excellent book, and merits detailed study. See also Robert Dorfman, "Mathematical or 'Linear' Programming," *American Economic Review*, XLII (December, 1953) for a lucid exposition of the various aspects of the kind of diagram used in this chapter. Material similar to that in the Dorfman article is found in Chapter 6 of Robert Dorfman, Paul A. Samuelson, and Robert M. Solow, *Linear Programming and Economic Analysis* (New York: McGraw-Hill Book Company, 1958). See also the excellent paper by Richard S. Eckaus, "The Factor Proportions Problem in Underdeveloped Areas," *American Economic Review* XLIV (September, 1955). For material on the marginal-inframarginal notion see Anne P. Grosse, "The Technological Structure of the Cotton Textile Industry" in *Studies in the Structure of the American Economy,* edited by Wassily Leontief (New York: Oxford University Press, 1953). Robert Solow, "Investment and Technical Progress" in *Mathematical Methods in the Social Sciences,* ed. by Kenneth Arrow, Samuel Karlin, and Patrick Suppes (Stanford: Stanford University Press, 1960) and Benton F. Massell, "Is Investment Really Unimportant" *Metroeconomica,* XIV (April-August, 1962) have helpful suggestions on the material covered in Parts I and II of this chapter.

The assumption of alternative factor combinations to produce a given rate of output was not defended in the text. It is surely a reasonable assumption. There are some interesting empirical studies of alternative techniques of production done by the Netherlands Economic Institute, Division of Balanced International Growth, Rotterdam. This series provides some very detailed data on a variety of production processes in a variety of economies, and also data on capital-labor ratios for the same industry in different countries. Another interesting book on this subject is the United Nations, Department of Economic Affairs, *Labor Productivity of the Cotton Textile Industry in Five Latin American Countries* (New York: United Nations, 1951).

There are many papers on the classification of innovations. The best place to begin is perhaps J. E. Meade's *A Neo-Classical Theory of Economic Growth* (London, George Allen & Unwin, 1961), Chapters 4 and 5. See also William Fellner, *Trends and Cycles in Economic Activity* (New York, Holt, Rinehart & Winston, Inc., 1956) especially Chapter 8, and J. C. H. Fei and Gustav Ranis, "Capital Accumulation and Economic Development," *The American Economic Review,* LIII (June, 1963).

For a general treatment of the contribution of labor training to capacity begin with Theodore W. Schultz, *The Economic Value of Education* (New York: Columbia University Press, 1963) and John Vaizey, *The Economics of Education* (London: Faber & Faber, Ltd., 1961). Schultz's book has a long bibliography. More specific supplementary reading is given in the bibliography to Chapter 12.

The United Nations, especially the Economic Commission for Latin America, has a number of publications that discuss the terms-of-trade effect in an enlightening way. See, for example, United Nations, Department of Economic Affairs, *Relative Prices of Exports and Imports of Underdeveloped Countries* (New York: United Nations, 1949).

CHAPTER 4

SOME IMPLICATIONS
OF INTERDEPENDENT SECTORS

The analysis just completed rested on the assumption that each sector of the economy could be examined in isolation. The assumption in effect was that capital and labor were the only inputs employed in each sector to produce a given commodity or service. Consequently the whole analysis could be conducted by examining the growth process of one sector, and then summing over all the sectors of the economy to get the results for the whole economy. The argument must now be expanded in order to recognize the fact that one sector may use as inputs not only capital and labor, but also the products of other sectors as well. To do this some kind of interindustry model is necessary, and in Section I a very simple model is presented. The objective of this section is to identify the way in which sectors of an economy are linked together, and what these links mean for the choice of least cost techniques. Also it is shown in this section how international trade enters into the computation of least cost techniques. In Section I the economy is assumed to use all of its resources for the production of consumer goods or for the replacement of capital goods, and further that there are no other sources of growth present.

In Section II of this chapter a growth sector is introduced into the interindustry model. Here capital formation takes place that will add to the quantity of building and equipment, or to technical knowledge, or to the quality of labor, etc., i.e., adds to the capacity of the economy to produce goods and services. Then some brief attention is given to how these sources of increases in capacity affect the growth process of an economy in which the sectors—or some of the sectors—are linked together, in contrast to one in which there is no linkage among the sectors.

Finally in the concluding section, an effort is made to identify the particular characteristics of the interindustry models that seem most directly relevant to the development problem.

Information about interindustry economics can be found in the references listed in the bibliography, and this chapter is in no sense a complete survey of this area of economics. The objective here is limited to showing how the sectors of an economy are linked together, and how this fact affects the growth of an economy. In particular, no attempt is made to discuss the mathematical properties of an interindustry model.

I. The Interindustry Model

A. THE ROLE OF INTERMEDIATE GOODS

Table I provides the raw material for the discussion. The term "intermediate good" is applied to a product produced by one sector and used in another for production purposes. In Table I the intermediate goods are designated as the X_{ij}'s. For example, X_{12} shows the amount of the commodity produced in Sector 1 that is used in the production of the products of Sector 2 when output of the latter sector is at a particular level. Then W_1 measures the total amount of the output of Sector 1 that is used as an intermediate good in the production of all other products in the economy. Thus $\sum_j X_{ij} = W_1$. Total production of Sector 1 is then X_1. The factor in-

SECTORS	INTERMEDIATE GOODS							FINAL USE	TOTAL USE	SUPPLY	
	1	2	$\cdot\cdot$	j	$\cdot\cdot$	n	TOTAL INPUT			M	X
1	X_{11}	X_{12}	$\cdot\cdot$	X_{1j}	$\cdot\cdot$	X_{1n}	W_1	Y_1	Z_1	M_1	X_1
2	X_{21}	X_{22}	$\cdot\cdot$	X_{2j}	$\cdot\cdot$	X_{2n}	W_2	Y_2	Z_2	M_2	X_2
$\vdots$	$\vdots$	$\vdots$	$\cdot\cdot$	$\vdots$	$\cdot\cdot$	$\vdots$	$\vdots$	$\vdots$	$\vdots$	$\vdots$	$\vdots$
i	X_{i1}	X_{i2}	$\cdot\cdot$	X_{ij}	$\cdot\cdot$	X_{in}	W_i	Y_i	Z_i	M_i	X_i
$\vdots$	$\vdots$	$\vdots$	$\cdot\cdot$	$\vdots$	$\cdot\cdot$	$\vdots$	$\vdots$				
n	X_{in}	X_{n2}	$\cdot\cdot$	X_{nj}	$\cdot\cdot$	X_{nn}	W_n	Y_n	Z_n	M_n	X_n
FACTORS											
CAPITAL	K_1	K_2	$\cdot\cdot$	K_j	$\cdot\cdot$	K_n					
LABOR	L_1	L_2	$\cdot\cdot$	L_j	$\cdot\cdot$	L_n					
OUTPUT											
X	X_1	X_2	$\cdot\cdot$	X_j	$\cdot\cdot$	X_n					

TABLE I.

puts, capital and labor, refer to the nonproduced inputs required for the production of a particular level of output in a sector. For example, K_2 and L_2 refer to the payments to capital and labor in Sector 2 for producing whatever output is being produced in that sector. The payments to K_2 and L_2 would measure the value added by Sector 2 to the inputs from other sectors that it processed. The K_j's and L_j's constitute the capital and labor vector defined in the preceding chapter. It is recognized, of course, that during any short time interval the capital stock and labor skills available are primary inputs, i.e., not produced in the current period, but in a longer period their variations are subject to explanation. At the moment attention is centered on a short period during which these primary inputs are fixed.

The Final Use column shows the amount of each commodity that is used by an ultimate consumer. The exact content of final use depends upon how complete one wishes to make the analysis. At the present time it is assumed that no capital accumulation is occurring, so that Y_i refers to consumption and exports. Thus Y_1 is the mount of the output of Sector 1 that is consumed at home plus the amount exported. In the previous chapter the assumptions were that all X_{ij}'s were zero, and the only inputs were capital and labor, and the total output of Sector i was shown by Y_i. Evidently, the total supply of a commodity available to the community is net domestic output plus imports, and this total is designated by Z_i in Table I.

With these definitions and symbols, the following "balance" expressions are essentially self-evident.

$$Z_i = M_i + X_i = \Sigma X_{ij} + Y_i \tag{1}$$

This expression states that the total supply of commodity i is equal to domestic production plus imports, and that total supply must equal total demand composed of intermediate and final use. And then

$$X_j = \underset{i}{\Sigma} X_{ij} + K_j + L_j \tag{2}$$

which states that the total production of commodity j is equal to the sum of the value of produced and primary inputs. If joint production is ruled out, Equation 2 implies a production function of the form

$$X_j = F_j (X_{ij} K_j L_j : T R S) \tag{3}$$

The difference between this production function and the one used in the previous chapter is simply the inclusion of the intermediate products. It is, of course, evident that including X_{ij} precludes writing F_j as an aggregate economy-wide function.

In conventional national income accounting, imports are subtracted from final demand, so

$$\underset{i}{\Sigma} X_i = \underset{i}{\Sigma} \underset{j}{\Sigma} X_{ij} + \Sigma Y_i - M_i \tag{4}$$

and

$$\sum_j X_j = \sum_j \sum_i X_{ij} + \sum_j K_j + \sum_j L_j \tag{5}$$

Since $\sum X_i$ and $\sum X_j$ are equal, Expressions 4 and 5 are equal to each other, (one is a row addition, the other a column addition) and the intermediate goods, $\sum \sum X_{ij}$, may be cancelled out leaving

$$\sum_i Y_i - \sum_i M_i = \sum_j K_j + \sum_j L_j \tag{6}$$

which is the usual form of the basic national income identity: total factor payments on the right-hand side and total demands on the left-hand side. It is Expression 6 that is implied in the summations performed in the previous chapter to get the increases in total output.

The preceding expressions are, of course, simply definitional or book-keeping relationships to show the relationship between the interindustry model and an aggregate model, and more is needed. At the outset of Chapter 3, the assumption was made that there were three different techniques of production available that represented three different combinations of capital and labor. The choice of technique was based on the relative prices of capital and labor and once the technique was selected and the capital constructed there was no substitution possible between these inputs. This argument may now be expanded to include the produced inputs. It is now assumed that a limited number, for instance three, techniques are available for the production of X_i. Each technique involves not only a particular capital-labor ratio, but also particular input coefficients for the several produced inputs. Which technique is chosen depends here on the prices of all the inputs, produced and primary, and evidently there may be, in a given sector, substitution between a produced and primary input. Again for the moment, once a process is established and in operation no further substitution in that process is assumed possible. For each process, i.e., for given prices of primary inputs and intermediate goods, a technological co-efficient may be defined that shows the extent to which the output of one sector uses as inputs the output of another sector.

$$X_{ij} = a_{ij} X_j \tag{7}$$

where the a_{ij} is a technological coefficient showing the requirements of the ith input per unit of output of the jth sector when a particular technique is employed. And if a particular technique is employed in each sector, Expression 1 may be written in a slightly modified form,

$$M_i + X_i = \sum_j a_{ij} X_j + Y_i \tag{8}$$

or

$$X_i - \sum_j a_{ij} X_j = Y_i - M_i \tag{9}$$

The latter expression states that the quantity of the ith product not used for inputs into other sectors will equal the part of final demand not covered by imports. Under present assumptions there are n unknown production levels to be determined from the n expressions, the parameters (for given prices) a_{ij}'s, and the autonomous variables Y_i and M_i whose values are determined outside the system as it is now constructed.

The primary inputs have no effect on the solution, but when the expressions for the use of capital and labor are added it is possible to compute the magnitude of outputs achievable with existing quantities of primary inputs. The expressions for the use of primary inputs are of the same form as Expressions 8 and 9. For capital, the relevant expression would be $K_i = k_i X_i$, and for labor it would be $L_i = l_i X_i$. The k_i and l_i are interpreted in a fashion similar to the a_{ij} as given above.

To answer the question as to the amount of each commodity producible with a given quantity of primary inputs, it is necessary to solve the system of n expressions in the n unknowns. This solution has the following form:

$$X_i = A_{i1} Y_1 + A_{i2} Y_2 + \ldots + A_{ij} Y_j + \ldots . \qquad (10)$$

where now the total demand for X_i is explained in terms of the final demands only, the Y_i's, and the new coefficients, the A_{ij}'s are derived from the a_{ij}'s. The method of solution is not considered here, but it is important to recognize that the A_{ij}'s measure the total (i.e., direct and indirect) requirements for a given level of production for final use. If Y_2 is produced at a level of 100, A_{12} indicates the quantity of the ith product used directly in the production of Y_2 plus the amount of the ith product used in the production of other commodities that are also required in the production of this quantity of Y_2.

Once the level of production in each sector corresponding to the preassigned Y_i is determined from Expression 10, the requirements for primary inputs is obtained simply from the capital and labor coefficients and the computed levels of output. In any given period, the quantity of capital of various categories and of labor of various skills are fixed as are the a_{ij}'s (hence the A_{ij}'s) and thus the supply of primary inputs impose a limit on the Y_i. This result is shown in the aggregative production function of the previous chapter.

There is one more side of the argument, that having to do with prices. In a stationary, competitive economy the price of a commodity will equal its cost of production, and in terms of the present argument the costs of producing a given commodity equals the cost of the primary inputs used directly and indirectly in its production. More specifically, the cost of producing commodity j is equal to the cost of the primary inputs used directly in its production plus the cost of the produced inputs used. Thus,

$$P_j = l_j P_l + k_j P_k + \sum_i a_{ij} P_i \qquad (11)$$

If the price of each primary input is equal to its marginal product (as computed in Chapter 3), the P_j computed in this fashion is defined as the marginal cost of producing the products of the jth sector. Prices of products and inputs defined in this way are referred to as shadow prices, and are important in later analysis. The shadow price of a particular product, e.g., the jth, therefore measures the value of the resources required for its production when a particular set of techniques is employed throughout the system. To assume that Expression 11 holds requires either a perfectly competitive economy or a very powerful set of taxes and subsidies. In this chapter the assumption is made that it does hold; in Chapter 5 and those that follow, attention is given to the difficulties involved in making such an assumption realistic.

B. IMPLICATIONS FOR ALLOCATION

At a given time interval, the economy has at its disposal a given quantity of types of physical capital and of labor skills and given "position variables" with which it may produce a variety of goods for final use. The static allocation problem is to maximize the value of the output achievable with this quantity and composition of capital, and this quantity and composition of labor skills. Suppose that for several periods there has been no net increase in the quantity of capital or of labor, and no change in the quality of the labor input or in technical knowledge available. As a result of these assumptions, no change in the relative price of capital and labor or in the least cost technique of production in any sector has occurred. Suppose further that the pricing system is such that Expression 11 holds exactly for all commodities. Then over these periods, it is expected that each sector will move to the least cost technique as replacement-capital formation takes place, and further that capital and labor will move into those sectors where returns are higher. In this fashion, then, the economy will move toward a situation in which total output is a maximum. Under present assumptions, the rate at which the economy approaches maximum output is determined by the rate of replacement-capital formation, and the rate of "replacement-labor formation."

The profitability of a sector is defined as the value of output of that activity less the cost of its inputs when the latter are computed using the shadow prices of the primary inputs. Under the conditions hypothesized —no change in the supply of capital and labor, no technical change, and no change in factor prices—the process by which the system moves toward the maximum output achievable with the available quantities of primary inputs is simply the elimination of those activities whose profitability is negative, and the expansion of those whose profitability is positive. So then it is assumed that by the period from which the present analysis is to begin—period zero—the system has reached the point where output is a maximum.

C. An Example

A very simple example may help to make the argument clear. Consider Table II. The section identified as Sector I shows three columns within it, designated as *A, B,* and *C.* Each of these columns shows a technique by which the product of Sector I can be produced. In all cases, output is taken to be at the unit level, and inputs are therefore inputs per unit of output. Output is indicated by the absence of a sign, and inputs by a minus sign. See Column B under Sector I as an example. It shows that one unit of output—the 1.0 in Row I—is produced with (reading down the column) .10 units of the output of Sector III, .6 units of capital, and 1.1 unit of labor. These are the input coefficients of the produced inputs and the primary inputs. To produce the output of Sector I with Technique *C* requires less inputs of Sector III's output (.05 units), less capital, and more labor. The columns *A, B,* and *C* then are the equivalent of the rays of the diagrams in the previous chapter, but with produced and primary inputs rather than only the latter. The other sectors of Table II are interpreted in a similar fashion.

The import section shows that each commodity can be imported as well as produced domestically. For example, the .80 states that one unit of

SECTOR	SECTOR I			SECTOR II			SECTOR III			EX-PORTS	IMPORTS		
	A	B	C	A	B	C	A	B	C		I	II	III
I	1.0	1.0	1.0	−.10	−.06	−.06					1.0		
II				1.0	1.0	1.0	−.15	−.18	−.18			1.0	
III	−.04	−.10	−.05				1.0	1.0	1.0				1.0
EXPORTS										1.0	−.80	−1.25	−1.05
CAPITAL	−1.2	−.6	−.4	−1.5	−1.1	−1.0	−2.1	−2.0	−1.6	−.4			
LABOR	−1.0	−1.1	−1.2	−2.0	−2.2	−2.5	−2.4	−2.6	−3.0	−1.5			

Table II.

Sector I output can be obtained for .80 units of exports. The export sector itself is also shown in Row 4.

Table II then corresponds to Diagram I, except now the assumption of the interdependence of sectors is explicitly considered. Table II may then describe the technology of the economy (more accurately, the technology of this very simple example). As in Diagram I, which technique is the least cost technique cannot be told without reference to factor prices (unless all techniques except one are inefficient).

To work out an example with prices, it is necessary to make even further assumptions in order to keep the purely mathematical manipulations in bounds. (This discussion is principally based on Professor Hollis B. Chenery's article in *The American Economic Review*.) Consider Table III where only one technique for each of the sectors is assumed, and a third primary input, natural resources, is added. Thus, it is assumed that by some clever, unspecified way it is known that if a given commodity is produced domestically, a certain technique will be the least cost one.

The first prices needed are those for the primary inputs. Consider the price of capital arbitrarily to be 1.00, and then suppose that it is known that the shadow price of labor (equals the opportunity cost of labor) is .5 of capital and that for "natural resources" is 2.20 the price of capital. With these prices given, the price of producing a unit of each commodity domestically, or the cost of importing it, is determined by direct application of Expression 11. The cost to the community of producing a unit of exports is $2.20(1.00) + 1.00(.50) + .10(2.20) = 2.92$. This figure is shown in the price column for Row 4. With this figure for the cost of earning a unit of foreign exchange, the cost of importing a unit of commodities I, II, and III is obtained by applying the import coefficients given in Row 4. To import item I imposes a cost of $.85(2.92) = 2.48$, for II the cost is $1.20(2.92) = 3.50$, and for III it is $1.10(2.92) = 3.21$. All these cost figures are shown in Row 9 in the respective import columns. The cost of producing the same commodities domestically is computed by applying Expression 11 again. For example, to produce II at home costs $.08(2.19) + 1.0(2.70) + .20(.50) + .25(2.20) = 3.52$. Domestic costs of production for other commodities are computed the same way, and all are shown in Row 9 in the respective production columns.

The price (shown in the price column) is then set by the cost of production or import, whichever is lower. To get the profitability of either producing or importing, simply subtract cost from prices. Thus to import a unit of the products of Sector I requires the export of resources valued at 2.48, while to produce a unit domestically requires resources valued at 2.26. The profitability of importing then is $-.22$, and that of domestic production is zero. The same procedure may be applied to work out the profitability of the other activities. The price data applied to the technology data therefore will yield prices and costs—when both are based on shadow prices—of the various activities included in the table, and will determine thereby which products are produced domestically and which are imported to find the least cost of supplying the society with particular list of commodities.

SECTORS	PRODUCTION				IMPORTS			PRICES
	I	II	III	EXPORTS	I	II	III	
I	1.00				1.00			2.26
II	−.22	1.00				1.00		3.50
III		−.08	1.00				1.00	2.19
EXPORTS				1.00	−.85	−1.20	−1.10	2.92
CAPITAL	−.70	−2.70	−.50	−2.20				1.00
LABOR	−.70	−.20	−.30	−1.00				.50
NATURAL RESOURCES	−.20	−.25	−.70	−.10				2.20
COSTS	2.26	3.52	2.19	2.92	2.48	3.50	3.21	
PROFIT-ABILITY	0	−.02	0	0	−.22	0	−1.02	
LEVELS	1000	0	0	1464	0	1220	0	

TABLE III.

One can easily trace the implications of a higher exchange rate or a higher price for labor relative to capital. Also one can compute, for example, the cost to the society of having an overvalued exchange rate or of having labor receiving a wage in excess of its opportunity cost.

Consider the specific example in the Chenery paper previously mentioned. Suppose the community demands 1,000 units of Sector I and 1,000 of II for final consumption, what is the least cost method of supplying this bill of goods? From the coefficients of Table III, the given final demands, and the assumption of no build-up or draw-down of foreign exchange reserves or capital inflows, it is evident that the following must be satisfied (write X_1 for the output of the product of Sector I and M for imports):

$$X_1 + M_1 = 1,000$$
$$-.22\,X_1 + X_2 + M_2 = 1,000$$
$$-.08\,X_2 + X_3 + M_3 = 0$$
$$X_4 - .85\,M_1 - 1.20\,M_2 - 1.10\,M_3 = 0 \qquad (12)$$

Also from Table III, it is evident from Row 9 that X_1 and X_3 would be produced domestically more cheaply than they can be imported, and that

X_2 can be imported more cheaply. So Expression 12 can be filled as follows:

$$1000 + 0 = 1,000$$
$$-.22(1000) + 0 + 1220 = 1,000$$
$$-.08(0) + 0 + 0 = 0$$
$$1,464 - .85(0) - 1.20(1,220) - 1.10(0) = 0 \qquad (13)$$

These production and import figures have been entered in Row 11 of Table III. Whether these levels of production and import are possible depends on the quantity of available primary inputs. To produce the 1,000 units of I and 1,464 units of exports requires

Natural Resources	$.20(1,000) + .10(1,464) =$	346
Labor	$.70(1,000) + 1.00(1,464) =$	2,164
Capital	$.70(1,000) + 2.20(1,464) =$	3,921

If these quantities of primary inputs are not available, then evidently the demands for 1,000 units of X_1 and X_2 cannot be met because there is no lower cost method of producing this bill of goods.

Finally, it may be noted that the value (in terms of capital) attached to the primary inputs is $2.20(346) + .5(2,164) + 1.0(3,921) = 5,764$. Now if shadow pricing holds throughout, the value of total output must also equal this figure. The value of total output is given by $2.26(1,000) + 2.92(1,200) = 5,764$. The 1,200 is 1.2(1,000), i.e., the number of export units exported in order to import 1,000 units of X_2. Why isn't it 1.2(1,220)? Because the 220 imports used in the production of X_1 have already been included in arriving at a value figure for X_1, namely 2.26(1,000). Thus, the competitive equilibrium condition that the value of the flow of final goods equals the value of the primary inputs used directly and indirectly in its production is illustrated. In an arithmetic sense, this equality always holds because profits are computed as a residual and are added in, but that is not the same thing as a static equilibrium.

The role of intermediate goods is also clarified by this discussion. For example, the fact that some of X_2 is used in the production of X_1 means that to produce X_1 the economy must also have access to X_2. Also in this example, no X_3 was produced or imported, but if X_2 had been produced domestically, some X_3 would have to be made available. Other implications of these tables are to be explained, but now it is important to introduce growth into them.

II. The Effects of Capital Accumulation

The preceding discussion assumed that all available resources were used to produce goods and services that were consumed during the period in which they were produced. The quantity and quality of primary inputs remain the same from period to period with the only investment taking place being replacement. The very object of development policy, however, is to increase the quantity and improve the quality of the "primary" inputs. To introduce these effects into an interindustry framework, the tables must be expanded in a rather obvious, but cumbersome, way.

A. CAPITAL FORMATION

The simplest way to enter growth into a system is to introduce net capital formation. Assume now that capital formation is taking place. How do the tables, and the accompanying equations change? Net capital formation means that some of the resources available in period zero are employed in producing commodities that add to the capacity of the system in later periods.

In Table IV, Columns 1–4 repeat Table I. The final demand here is consumption only, and this part of the table may be designated as the stationary part, or the consumption goods sector. The factor inputs are also defined as in Table I, but now all available factors are not required to produce the final bill of consumption goods, and so some are available for capital formation. Columns 5–7 show this capital formation, and these columns may be called the dynamic part or capital goods sector of the Table. The K_{23}, for example, shows the amount of commodity 2 used by Sector 3, for purposes of capital formation. The primary inputs, K'_3 and L'_3, show the amount of capital and labor used in the production of capital goods by Sector 3. The summation of Column 7 shows ΔK_3, the increase in the quantity of capital of that particular type. In the next period, therefore, more of this type of capital will be available either to produce consumer goods or more capital goods.

Expression 1 must now be rewritten to include the resources used in capital formation.

$$M_i + X_i = \sum_j X_{ij} + \sum_j \Delta K_{ij} + Y_i \tag{14}$$

which states that total supply (imports plus domestic production) of commodity 1 is equal to its intermediate demand plus investment demand, plus consumption. The quantity of investment, i.e., the ΔK_i, is assumed to be given exogenously here, but will be considered later. It is evident, however, that the increase in K_j is related to an anticipated increase in the output of the jth sector, which in turn is related to an anticipated increase in the final demand for Sector j's output or to an increased use of j for an intermediate good or both combined.

Just as a flow coefficient, a_{ij}, was defined for a given technology and given factor prices, so too may a technical relationship between increases in the quantity of physical capital of a particular type, and inputs from a given sector be defined under the same assumptions. Conventionally, this

SECTORS	CONSUMPTION				INVESTMENT			TOTAL AVAILABILITY	
	1	2	3	4	5	6	7	8	9
1	X_{11}	X_{12}	X_{13}	Y_1	K_{11}	K_{12}	K_{13}	M_1	X_1
2	X_{21}	X_{22}	X_{23}	Y_2	K_{21}	K_{22}	K_{23}	M_2	X_2
3	X_{31}	X_{32}	X_{33}	Y_3	K_{31}	K_{32}	K_{33}	M_3	X_3
CAPITAL	K_1	K_2	K_3		K_1'	K_2'	K_3'		
LABOR	L_1	L_2	L_3		L_1'	L_2'	L_3'		
PRODUCTION	X_1	X_2	X_3		ΔK_1	ΔK_2	ΔK_3		

TABLE IV.

coefficient is designated as b and then $\Delta K_{ij} = b_{ij} \Delta K_j$. Expression 14 may be written in terms of the two sets of coefficients a and b.

$$M_i + X_i = \sum_j a_{ij} X_j + \sum_j b_{ij} \Delta K_j + Y_i \qquad (15)$$

The primary input coefficients for the capital-goods-producing sectors are defined as for the consumption goods sectors.

Suppose now that the economy, as just described, is operating in such a fashion that, in period zero, output is a maximum and that the amount of resources allocated to capital formation is determined by government policy. What will be the picture of the economy in period one?

The simplest possible development would be that in which the proportionate increase in capital and the proportionate increase in labor were equal, and in the absence of technical innovation, the least cost techniques will be the same in period one as they were in period zero. Then each K_1 may be increased in the same proportion so that if labor is allocated in a similar way, the capacity of each sector will be larger by the same proportion in period one, relative to period zero. If the capacity of each sector rises proportionately, then the ability of the economy to supply intermediate and final goods rises in the same proportion. In this case, the only difference in the economy between periods one and zero is that every sector is proportionately larger in the former than the latter period. This situation implies that the autonomously given final demand functions are of an exponential type. Indeed, if it is hypothesized that the the Y_i's are all growing at the same percentage rate between periods zero and one, and the rate of capital formation and labor growth are equal, and there is no

technical change, then productive capacity in each sector must also grow
at this same percentage rate. This statement holds, of course, even though
some goods are used only as intermediate goods. If this were the only way
that growth of total output took place, then the introduction of the interdependence characteristics of the economy would hardly be worth the
effort.

The adjustment process when the rate of capital formation exceeds the
rate of growth of the labor force and there is no unemployment is more
complicated. In this event, the k_j and l_j of the newly created capacity will
differ from those obtaining for the existing capacity. The reason for this
difference is the same as that discussed in the previous chapter, simply that
capital costs are assumed to decline relative to labor costs, and the least
cost combination of inputs would dictate a greater use of capital relative
to labor. These changes in k_j and l_j will—except under extremely forbid-
ding assumptions—result in changes in the relative prices of the products
the community produces, and will thereby alter the matrix of a_{ij}'s, the
A_{ij}'s, and the b_{ij}'s. In this case, the counterpart of the marginal vector of
Chapter 3 is a marginal matrix of input coefficients. In period one, therefore, a new set of technical coefficients (a_{ij} and b_{ij}) comes into existence
alongside the one prevailing in period zero. If it is further assumed that
Y_i is larger in the same proportion in period one relative to period zero,
then the capacity of each sector must also expand proportionately, and
each sector will have a larger capital stock and labor force in period one
than it had in period zero.

The assumption is made that the equation for the pricing of products
and factors is determined in the marginal matrix. Optimal allocation now
means that Expression 11 holds exactly only for the new matrix and consequently the combination of capital and labor and the flow of inputs imposed on the inframarginal matrix by the existing stock of capital is, in
period one, less than optimal. It is evident then that the profitability of a
sector operating in the inframarginal matrix is less than that of the same
sector in the marginal matrix. It may again be noted that when the assumption of no post-construction substitution is relaxed and some adaptation is achieved, the distinction between marginal and inframarginal
matrices is reduced.

At this point, further demands on the growing economy are revealed as
to the role of prices and the adjustment process. In particular it is seen
that the maximum increment in output accompanying the increase in the
capital stock of each sector requires the use of activities different from
those employed in period zero, and consequently different techniques and
production routines must come into being alongside existing ones, if the
new capacity is to be fully exploited. And then, of course, there must be
changes in prices to reflect accurately the changes in relative supplies of
the primary inputs. A new weight is thus placed on the entrepreneurial

and management talent in the society, and on the price setting forces of the economy due to the rising capital-labor ratio.

B. THE IMPACT OF TECHNOLOGICAL CHANGE AND IMPROVED LABOR

Capital formation is not the only source of increased output, and both increases in technical knowledge and improvements in the quality of labor must also be introduced into the dynamic sections of the interindustry framework. Later chapters will develop in detail the argument that research for and development of technical knowledge and the training of labor constitute an economic activity in the same sense that the production of bicycles or machine tools does. Consequently, some of the resources available for capital formation must be used for these purposes as well as for the building of more physical capital items. The dynamic sector of Table IV includes the activities devoted to accumulating new technical knowledge and to the training of new labor. A brief comment on both types of activities is useful at this point.

1. Technical Change. The introduction of technical innovation into the interindustry framework can be done in a fashion very similar to that followed in the previous chapter. If technical innovation occurs along with a rising capital-labor ratio, then the marginal matrix differs from the inframarginal one both because of different combinations of inputs and because of the different knowledge incorporated into the capital stock. The scheme of classification and the several effects of technical change discussed earlier are equally applicable to the interindustry framework.

The major new effect emerging from the introduction of technical change into an interindustry model has to do with the effect of such change in one sector on other sectors. To examine this effect, the assumption is made that the income elasticity of demand for goods for final use is the same in all sectors, but that there is no policy that all the Y_i's must necessarily grow at the same percentage rate. Suppose now that technological change in the simple form of increasing productivity of capital and labor occurs in only one sector, for example Sector j, and suppose further that the output of Sector j happens to be used only in final demand and does not require any produced inputs. Here the impact of the increased productivity of K_j and L_j is limited to Sector j as it was in Chapter 3. The consequences of this innovation would be that the price of the jth product (equal to $l_j P_l + k_j P_k$) would decline relative to the price of other products. Then, unless the price elasticity of demand for Y_j was less than unity, Sector j would grow more rapidly than other sectors, and the system must change in such a way that this difference in relative rates of growth of the various sectors is reflected in the allocation of resources. Whether newly available resources must move into or out of Sector j depends on the magnitude of the productivity increasing innovation and the price elasticity of demand for the jth product. At any rate, there is now the increased problem of allocation created by the recognition that innovations in one sector affect the extent to which new resources flow into that sector as well as into others.

On the other hand, suppose that Sector j was used as an input in a large number of sectors. Now as a cost-reducing innovation in Sector j becomes effective and its price falls (by assumption), the cost of production of the sectors using j as an input also falls. So the prices in these sectors decline, and this in turn reduces costs in sectors where they are used as inputs, and so on and on. Many sectors will have an incentive to expand in addition to that provided by the assumed rising incomes, namely falling costs of production due to an innovation in a single sector. The impact now of a productivity increasing innovation is much more far reaching than was the case when Sector j was not linked with the rest of the economy.

Since there is no reason to assume that the magnitude of cost-reducing innovations will be the same in all sectors, the present argument isolates a source of dynamism for the entire economy, namely the appearance of cost-reducing innovations in a sector that has extensive links throughout the system. Such an innovation will have the effect of reducing (indirect) inputs of primary factors in many sectors, and thereby allows a greater expansion of output with the available new resources than would otherwise be possible.

One can also see that an innovation in Sector j that reduces the requirement for a particular produced input also saves primary inputs of another sector in the same way, and the flowing of the effects through the system is the same as when there are innovations that reduce the primary input requirements in Sector i.

2. *The Role of Skilled Labor.* The labor input L_i refers to a specific type of labor skill, and to increase the magnitude of an activity requires an increase in the number of workers possessing the necessary skill. Also even if labor possesses the minimum skill to allow some increase in the rate of output, further training may so increase skills and hence output that the additional training is profitable to the system. An "educational" activity is therefore part of the dynamic section of the tables and the expressions, and hence of the economy.

The improvement in the quality of labor, as noted earlier, can be treated in the same way as a technical innovation that is favorable to labor. Thus the tracing of the implications of labor with new and advanced skills is similar to that just described for new technical knowledge. There are, of course, many other problems associated with education and training in the developing country, and these are discussed in Chapter 12.

III. Conclusion

There are several major implications of an interindustry model for the development problem.

(*a*) The process of adjustment to changing factor supplies, changing technology and labor quality is a great deal more complex now than it was with the assumptions of Chapter 3. Now adjustment includes not only primary inputs, but also produced inputs as well. Also pointed up in this adjustment process is the role of pricing. Expression 11, defining the shadow price of a product, and the attachment of the opportunity cost (equals marginal product) as the price of primary inputs are both of great importance in a wide variety of ways. In the discussion in this and the preceding chapter, it has been assumed that the pricing mechanism in the economy is such that Expression 11 holds. This is a very strong assumption, and difficulties in the way of making it realistic are severe indeed. In the following chapter some of the problems of achieving "correct" pricing are discussed, while in still later chapters policies are explained that are aimed at trying to assure the applicability of shadow prices as those governing the decisions of economic agents. As will be emphasized in Chapter 7, one of the ways in which the nongrowing economy fails is in the pricing and adjustment process.

(*b*) Under the assumptions of this chapter, growth is characterized not only by the creating of marginal and inframarginal matrices, but also by a jagged edge with respect to the expansion paths that the various sectors of the economy follow. This jagged edge is the outcome of the assumptions of a variety of rates of increase in labor and capital productivity in the various sectors, the appearance of new products, differing price elasticities of final demand, and the possibility of substitution among inputs and final demand. This jagged edge of growth plus the interdependence of the sectors will have important implications when attention is given to the problem of allocating the newly available resources among the several sectors of the system.

(*c*) The interindustry model also points up the implications of intermediate goods. The fact that a $10 million chemical factory may lie idle half the time because of the failure of other sectors of the system to supply enough power or raw material, or a particular labor skill, cannot be seen in the absence of an interindustry framework. Also the production of a given product may use only modest amounts of a particular input directly, but require a produced input whose production uses the primary input in very immodest proportions. A look simply at the direct inputs may therefore leave a misleading impression as to the cost of production of particular commodities.

(*d*) International trade was introduced as merely another sector of the economy. To get imports, exports had to be produced, and whether production took place at home or abroad depended simply on relative costs of production. There are many aspects of foreign trade of relevance to development (some of which are discussed in the following chapters), but it is especially important to appreciate the implications of trade for the cost of producing a given bill of goods in the current period. As noted, the cost of an overvalued exchange rate may be quite high. Also the interindustry model enables one to define the shadow price of foreign exchange in a clear way (at least conceptually) as well as to trace the implications of changing terms of trade on the distribution of production between domestically used products and exports.

(e) The interindustry framework also suggests a rather specific growth mechanism that is of interest. As already noted, all sectors of an economy do not grow equally rapidly, rather some sectors move ahead quite fast while others tend to lag, or even decline absolutely. Those that lead are the ones favored with either supply or demand advantages. Then, when one or a few sectors move ahead for these reasons, they tend thereby to provide incentives for other sectors to expand by virtue of the technological links with the other sectors. The term "leading sectors" is sometimes applied to this kind of argument. A leading sector is a sector that grows at a rate above the average for reasons not connected with the growth of other sectors, and because of its links with other sectors provides an incentive for them to grow. There are difficulties with the leading sector notion (see Chapter 18), but it is helpful in suggesting that the growth of an economy does not proceed in an even, across-the-board manner. It also helps to emphasize that when one sector does expand it thereby provides incentives for other sectors to expand.

(f) Finally, a comment on the question of the empirical content of an interindustry table is necessary. It can easily be seen that even a table with a very small number of sectors is extremely demanding of data if all slots are to be filled. There are several such tables in existence for a number of very different countries (see bibliography at end of this chapter), and a study of them is rewarding. However, it is important to recognize that the source of enlightenment shed by the interindustry approach does not depend on the availability of numbers to fill in all the cells. No country will have, in the next decade or more (much more), enough data for more than an enlarged example of such a model, and such data are almost sure to be out of date by the time they are compiled. The real advantage of the interindustry framework—of interindustry thinking—is to call attention to the importance of flexibility and adaptability in the economy as part of the growth process. A major part of the achievement of this flexibility and adaptability depends on how well the economy solves the pricing problems, i.e., how well the economy achieves the lowest possible costs and transmits them in terms of low prices. It will be argued later that one of the chief tasks of the government—no matter how much central planning is done—in the development process is to try to devise ways and means of making the price system produce the signals that help induce economic agents to exploit all opportunities that the economy offers. If this can be done, then using resources to get numbers to put in Tables I–IV is probably not very rewarding. But such a statement does not mean that interindustry thinking is not essential for one seeking to understand growth or one seeking to devise policies to promote growth.

Bibliography

A complete and very lucid discussion of input-output and linear programming is contained in Hollis B. Chenery and Paul G. Clark, *Interindustry Economics* (New York: John Wiley & Sons, Inc., 1959). After Chenery and Clark one can go on to the Dorfman, Samuelson, and Solow volume mentioned in the bibliography to Chapter 3. More empirical studies are in a collection edited by Tibor Barna, *Structural Interdependence and Economic Development* (New York: St. Martin's Press, Inc., 1963). Chapters 1, 11, 12, and 13 are especially helpful. Another view of interindustry models for the development problem is presented in the paper by A. T. Peacock and Douglas Dosser, "Input-Output Analysis in an Underdeveloped Country, A Case Study," *Review of Economic Studies,* XXV (October, 1957). For two major efforts to use interindustry models in an analysis of a developing country see *Analyses and Projections of Economic Development* (III) *The Economic Development of Colombia* (Geneva: United Nations, Department of Economic and Social Affairs, 1957), especially Part 2, Chap. III, and Michael Bruno, *Interdependence, Resource Use and Structural Change in Israel* (Jerusalem: Bank of Israel Research Department, 1962). See also Hollis B. Chenery, "Comparative Advantage and Development Policy," *American Economic Review,* LI (March, 1961).

For information on the "leading sector" issue use W. W. Rostow, "Some General Reflections on Capital Formation and Economic Growth" in *Capital Formation and Economic Growth* edited by Moses Abramovitz (Princeton: Princeton University Press, 1955) and William Fellner's "Comment" in the same volume. A more elaborate statement by Rostow in his "Trends in the Allocation of Resources in Secular Growth," in *Economic Progress,* ed. by Leon H. Dupriez (Lourain: Institut de Recherches Economiques et Sociales, 1955). See also Hollis B. Chenery, "Pattern of Industrial Growth," *American Economic Review,* L (September, 1960) for an excellent empirical and theoretical discussion of some of the issues raised in the text. A short, but very convincing, statement questioning the usefulness of the leading sector notion and pointing up the empirical difficulties associated with its use is Hans W. Singer's comment in *The Economics of Take-Off into Sustained Growth,* ed. by W. W. Rostow (New York: St. Martin's Press, Inc., 1963), pp. 302-303.

CHAPTER 5

DEMAND AND PRICING PROBLEMS

In the preceding chapters the discussion has, to the extent possible, been limited to the problem of growth in the capacity of the economy, and where some nod to demand considerations was essential it took the form of an arbitrary assumption, e.g., income elasticity of demand for all consumer goods equal, and so on. Evidently, however, capacity will not grow whimsically with respect to demand, and something more than arbitrary assumptions about the nature of demand is required. Also to this point, strong assumptions as to the pricing of products and factors have been made. These assumptions were not only strong, but were also strategic to the preceding arguments, and some attention must be given to the conditions necessary for their applicability. The purpose of this chapter is to discuss these demand and pricing issues in some detail. Section I explains the ways in which the composition of demand enters into the growth picture. First, an effect of the composition of demand on the degree of utilization is noted, followed by a discussion of how demand affects the pattern of growth. In Section II, considerations that affect the control over aggregate demand are discussed in Part A, and in Part B attention is given to the problem of individual product and factor pricing both as they affect the control over aggregate demand, and as they affect the achievement of the pricing objectives that were assumed in previous chapters.

I. The Composition of Demand

The assumption is made that no aggregate demand problem exists, and now the question is what implications for growth can be found in an analysis of the composition of demand. Two particular points will be examined. As has been repeatedly emphasized, the capacity of an economy to produce goods and services is not an amorphous mass that may be used to produce any product at all, rather it is a complex of specific capital items and labor skills designed to produce a fairly specific set of products. Thus capacity may become inframarginal or submarginal because of changes in the composition of demand. This fact creates both problems and opportunities for the growing economy. The second reason why the composition of demand is important has to do with the almost certain existence of divergent income elasticities of demand, and the fact that these elasticities are sure to change from period to period as the economy grows. Therefore, the question arises relative to the implications of demand for the products of a few sectors growing much more rapidly than is the case for the products of other sectors. This section is concerned with an examination of these considerations.

A. EFFECT OF CHANGING COMPOSITION OF DEMAND ON UTILIZATION OF CAPACITY

Consider first the extreme assumption that new capacity created in a particular sector can be used only to produce a single product, and that the capacity once in place cannot be modified to produce any other commodity. The building of capacity during period zero therefore requires that a prediction be made and acted on as to what the composition of demand will be in period one when the capacity is ready for utilization. Note that the prediction is really a prediction of a demand schedule, and applies to both consumption and investment goods. A one-period prediction in most instances will pose no major problem if data on investment plans are widely available and known, and the newly created capacity may generally be assumed to match the composition of demand brought to bear on it. The problem is different for the existing, older capacity. As periods go by and income grows and tastes change and new products appear, the composition of demand will change and, given the extreme assumption as to no adaptability, some capacity cannot be used. Just as a portion of capacity may become inframarginal (or submarginal) because of changes in technology and relative scarcities of input, so may it become because of changes in demand.

The problem arises chiefly because of technical changes that create new products. Merely changing income elasticities as income grows would rarely result in an absolute decline in the quantity of a product demanded. In this case, the only adjustment called for would be to assure that newly created capacity was designed to meet the demand of the rapidly growing sectors. When technical change is introduced, the possibility of shifts in demand away from a sector becomes much greater. It is especially clear that with respect to investment goods and intermediate goods, a technical innovation in one sector may mean that the output of one or more other sectors is no longer used in the productive process. The same general argument is applicable to consumer goods also, as the appearance of a new product on the market frequently attracts consumer expenditure away from traditional products. Also of course demand for some consumer products seems to change rather whimsically, leaving a sector with no market for the product it is able to produce.

This sort of structural change, therefore, results in a form of excess capacity in the system. It is evident at once that a mere increase in total demand will not make use of this capacity. However, changes in relative prices will have at least some effect on the utilization of this physically effective capacity. The fall in demand for the output of a given sector means that the earning power of the capital in that sector is greatly reduced. To the extent that the capital value is reduced to reflect the changed structure, and prices are also reduced to reflect the writing down of capital values, the nonutilization of the existing capacity will be to some extent lessened. It is evident that if this type of price adjustment occurs, the level of output in any one period, and its rate of growth over several periods, will be greater than in the case where the valuation of capital and price adjustments did not occur.

A further source of adjustment is international trade. Since the world market is much larger and probably more diversified than the domestic, having access to foreign markets adds a major source of flexibility to the economy in meeting changes in the composition of demand. As already noted, foreign demand is an element in the growth picture over which a country has little or no control, but this does not mean that trade cannot provide a significant source of flexibility for an economy. Again, however, some price changes are necessary.

Adjustments internally or through foreign trade, by way of price changes, are facilitated if the assumption of no flexibility or adaptability at all in existing capital equipment is relaxed. Some modifications can usually be made that allow existing capital to be converted to a form that enables it to be used to produce a product more consistent with the new structure of demand. Such modifications may be expected to require net investment, and perhaps the creation of new technical knowledge. Some flexibility in the capital stock may indeed be built in initially in the sense that the original design of the equipment be such that it lends itself to alterations in later periods.

In general, however, it is likely that most of the burden of adjustment will be via price changes and substitution. At the same time, it is to be emphasized that complete adjustment is extremely difficult if not impossible, and continuous *full* utilization of *all* existing capital equipment is an extremely severe definition of equilibrium growth. On the other hand, it may also be recognized that an economy that has the wherewithal to force the writing down of capital values to a point consistent with demand, that has a pricing system that forces the prices of the affected products down accordingly, and that has production managers who recognize the advantages of substitution and adaptation will enjoy an advantage in maintaining growth over that economy where these things are absent. In a rapidly growing economy, the size of the advantage may well be substantial.

A corollary aspect of the role of the composition of demand is conveniently noted at this point. Attention has already been directed toward the adjustments that are required if all resources are to be utilized in an economy where the rate of capital formation exceeds the rate of growth of the labor force. Suppose that there is only one technique available for the production of each product, and so no adjustment in technique is possible despite the fact that the price of capital is declining relative to the price of labor. If the price of capital falls compared to labor, then the price of commodities produced by the more capital intensive methods will decline compared to products produced by less capital intensive methods. Then, assuming some price elasticity for most consumer goods, demand for the capital intensive produced goods will rise more rapidly than that for labor intensive produced goods. New resources would then go into the sectors of the economy requiring relatively more capital in their production process, and adjustment to changing factor supplies is thereby aided. Indeed under extreme enough assumptions, it is possible to devise a system in which no change in the techniques of production is required as the economywide capital-labor ratio rises, and full adjustment is made through changes in the composition of output. Such extreme assumptions are not likely to be realized, however, and the argument here is that changes in the composition of demand facilitates adjusting to a rising capital-labor ratio, but that changes in the techniques of production are also necessary for full adaptation.

B. Effect of Composition of Demand on the Pattern of Growth

The composition of demand is relevant to the growth story in another way. Consider the following illustration. Suppose that the economy is experiencing an expanding circular flow of the type already described, i.e., all sectors of the economy are expanding at the same percentage rate, and the economy is becoming larger and larger while all sectors maintain the same proportionate size relative to each other and relative to total output. Suppose now that a new product is introduced into the system. As this product becomes known and finds its place in the economy, demand for it will grow more rapidly than demand for the products of other sectors. This higher than average rate of growth of demand will also have repercussions, via the input coefficients throughout the economy. In this case then, a new sector imposing itself on the existing system would pull the economy away from the routine expanding circular flow that it was previously experiencing. The new product by virtue of its rapid growth and links with the rest of the economy creates a net investment allocation that causes the economy to move forward, not as an expanding circular flow, but in an uneven, jagged way.

More generally, it may be argued that in one period or sequence of periods the income elasticity of demand for some products is very high and for others it is very low, and for others it is about average. It is the first category of sectors that provides the major opportunities for new capacity creation, and as these sectors expand, certain other sectors will also expand because of the existence of the interdependent matrix. In the same manner that innovations were described earlier as favoring one or more sectors relative to others and thereby causing them to move forward rapidly, so income elasticities may also favor specific sectors and cause them to grow at a rate of greater than average rapidity. In both instances a source of growth is isolated: in the one case a technical innovation and in the other case a high income elasticity of demand. The manner by which the rest of the economy is affected is the same in both cases, and can be traced through the input coefficients, and the ability of the economy to respond to the incentives and demands created by the leading sectors.

Finally, in discussing the composition of demand, it is safe to assert that unless a very broad categorization of goods is employed, demand for any single product will have an upper limit, and no matter what happens to per capita income after this point, demand for the product will not grow more rapidly than population growth. If there are no new products forthcoming and no new entrepreneurs to bring about their production and introduction into the market, then an aggregate demand problem will emerge at some point. Although this particular difficulty is of little concern to low income countries, a variation of it may be of great relevance. The achievement and maintenance of export markets may depend to a very great degree upon the ability of the developing country to provide the world with new products.

The point is made here because the source of the problem is to be found in the composition of output rather than the level of output. The upshot of the argument is that the pattern of income elasticities, and their change through time, impose on the economy the requirement that it have the capacity to produce a more or less continuous stream of "new" products.

II. Aggregate Demand

The preceding discussion has been built around the assumption that aggregate demand in the economy was always brought into equality with aggregate supply without changing the price level. It is now necessary to examine exactly what such an assumption means, and the precise nature of the problems associated with its implementations. First, it is convenient to make the assumption somewhat more general. Thus rather than imposing the assumption of a continuous equality between planned aggregate spending and actual supply, it is more advantageous to seek to maintain a situation in which the monetary and fiscal authorities always have control over total spending. This more general objective is necessary simply because a range of situations may present themselves in which price level stability with full utilization of all resources is not the policy objective of the society. For example, the policy objectives of the community may dictate that a changing price level be used to achieve a specific aim such as income redistribution or a change in the rate of capital formation. There is indeed some evidence (to be examined) to suggest that the deliberate creation of a temporary state of excess demand may be effective under certain conditions as an instrument of development policy. There is, on the other hand, abundant and convincing evidence that a spiralling inflation is most likely to raise major havoc with any development effort. The central objective on the aggregate demand side would therefore seem to be the firm establishment of an arsenal of tools within the economy that permits constant control over the demand brought to bear on that economy.

To see the nature of the problem of this control consider the simplest kind of aggregate demand model. Let

C = consumption	S = savings
I = investment	R = government tax receipts
G = government expenditure	$D = G - R$
X = exports	$F = X - M$
M = imports	Y' = total demand

then by definition

$$Y' = C + I + G + X - M$$

and in an *ex post* sense also by definition

$$S + R + M = I + G + X$$
$$S = I + D + F \tag{1}$$

In an *ex post* sense these expressions are simply definitional identities, but if the expenditures are thought of as planned expenditures in real terms, then an inequality in Expression 1 would mean that output would have to be different from that planned. Suppose that $S < I + D + F$ in the planning stage, and that planned output is the capacity of the system. It is at once evident that all plans cannot be realized, and some adjustments have to be made. In an economy with no price controls and certain other characteristics to be discussed, the adjustment process will be through rising prices. The rising price level will force a reduction in actual expenditures below the level planned when the former are measured in constant prices. Which component of aggregate demand will be reduced below planned levels cannot be told without further specification of the origin and nature of the price rise. To determine how much the price level must rise to eliminate the excess demand also requires greater detail as to the exact nature of the inflation process.

A further detail of great interest in a growing economy has to do with the behavior of individual prices. Excess aggregate demand is reflected in an excess demand for individual goods and services. Write P_i for the price of the ith product in period zero, and x_i for the difference between the quantity supplied and demanded at P_i in period one, then at the beginning of the period

$$I + D + F - S = \Sigma \, P_i \, x_i \tag{2}$$

and if there is excess demand in the economy $\Sigma \, P_i \, x_i > 0$. The sum of the individual excess demands in period one, measured in period zero prices, is thus equal to aggregative excess demand.

To write the excess demand expression as it is in Expression 2 indicates the obvious point that the effect on the price level of aggregate excess demand depends upon the reaction of the prices of individual products to the excess demand for them. Evidently price behavior varies widely from market to market. It depends not only on the competitiveness of the market, but also on the quality of entrepreneurship, on ease of entry, on public relations position, and so on. Similarly, monetary and fiscal policies react differently on different markets. It may also be noted that some of the x_i's may be negative even when there is no total excess demand. Since prices rarely react symmetrically to upward and downward pressure, some examination of the downward rigidity or flexibility of prices therefore constitutes part of the demand problem. Finally, it may be noted that for a number of reasons chiefly having to do with costs, prices of individual commodities may be raised in a manner that affects the price level as a whole, as well as the extent to which Expression 11 of Chapter 4 holds. In general then, part of the problem of maintaining full control over the level of demand involves an understanding of factors affecting the prices of individual products, as well as the factors affecting the level of expenditures on the particular components of total demand just defined. There is thus both a macro and micro side to the problem defined in the first paragraph of this section. These will be examined separately, although the two sides are very closely related.

A. The Macro Problem

The usual weapons at the disposal of a government to control the level of aggregate demand—aside from direct controls and foreign loans—include changes in the ease with which credit is made available to investors, changes in the level of government spending or in the magnitude of the government budget deficit, changes in the exchange rate, and changes in the supply of money. Changes in these aspects of the system are assumed to have effects on one or more of the components of demand listed above.

The simplest argument to make, and the one which has the greatest appeal for the low income country, has to do with the ease of acquiring funds and the level of investment. (Ease here includes, but is not limited to, changes in the rate of interest.) If in the present period demand is less than that currently thought appropriate, then funds for investment are made easier for the private entrepreneur to acquire, and thereby the rate of investment in the current period is increased. As the rate of investment is increased, then by a conventional multiplier analysis, consumption will rise so that both the investment and consumption components of total demand will increase. Since there are inevitable lags in bringing about such effects on a system, monetary authorities must—if demand is to be at the desired level in each period—initiate the change in credit policy enough in advance to allow time for the working out of the new policy.

The lag or forecasting problem is only one of several difficulties associated with this approach. Investment opportunities may be such that a mere change in the ease with which credit is made available will not produce the desired change in the outlay on investment. If the problem is to increase demand, then a whole series of factors—economic and noneconomic—may militate against investment increasing despite an easing of credit. If the problem is to curtail demand, then in most economies it is easily possible to continue investment projects despite reduced availability of credit. In some cases then, complete reliance on changes in the interest rate or in the availability of credit generally will be inadequate, or if pushed to extremes may create more problems than are solved. For example, if credit is eased greatly in order to encourage private investment, then the economy may become so liquid that the monetary and fiscal authorities lose control over the level of demand. Complete reliance on this method does not therefore provide a very safe approach to the control of demand problem.

A more reliable weapon is changes in the level of government spending or in the magnitude of the government deficit of surplus. Variations in the level of the government deficit of surplus may be analyzed in the same fashion as variations in private investment. The greater reliability of this method over that described in the previous paragraph is simply that the spending decision is made directly, rather than an attempt to influence the spending decision of many economic enterprises by altering the terms on which finance is available. As the other methods mentioned above—changes in money supply and in the rate of exchange—are also of questionable merit in affecting the level of spending in the economy, a manageable government deficit appears as a strategic condition for maintaining full control over aggregative demand. Difficulties of course must be recognized. Not the least of these is the possibility of major objections to a deficit from strong social and political elements in the community. There are, however, more fundamental difficulties. Chief of these is the problem of controlling the size of the deficit. Rarely can a government limit its expenditures from period to period strictly in response to the needs of affecting total demand. Programs once begun can hardly be interrupted without major losses, and the very nature of development planning requires that long-range commitments be made. Control of the deficit requires, therefore, that the tax system be such that it can be used to achieve the necessary variation in the government deficit. Furthermore, reliance on variations in tax receipts to affect the deficit modifies the impact of the deficit on the economy, for the impact depends in part on the reaction of the private sector to the changed tax schedules. This is surely a minor difficulty, but what is not a minor difficulty is the establishment of a taxing bureaucracy that can devise and implement a tax program that meets the necessary standards. Since such a program will almost always require a heavy reliance on direct taxes, the point can be made in terms of direct taxes.

The conclusion may then be stated that, as an initial attack on the demand objective, reliance is placed on changes in the terms on which finance is made available to potential investors. This initial attack must, however, be supportable with a set of tools that enable the government to affect its deficit without major disrupting effects on its own or the private sector's investment programs. Included in this tool kit is a practical set of direct taxes.

The notion of controlling aggregate demand can be deceptively simple, but the practical problems and complications that arise often are of a most severe kind. It is useful to mention some of these problems at this point as they are not only relevant to understanding the growth principles outlined here, but also enter the discussion later in other ways. The following are of particular interest to the development analyst.

(*a*) The most important complication has to do with the creation of financial assets that will, in most circumstances, accompany the creation of new capital. Financial assets may be defined simply as claims against the real assets of the economy. They range from highly liquid assets that the owner assumes to be fixed in price and redeemable into the most liquid of assets—money—on demand or at short notice, to claims that are subject to a high risk of capital loss. The existence of such assets (other than money) and the existence of financial institutions that issue them complicates the control of demand by the monetary authorities in a variety of ways. In general terms, their existence means a source of finance exists for expenditure, or more accurately control over a source of finance exists that is quite independent of the customary monetary controls. And if this independence is curtailed, there remains the fact that a great variety of means and sources of financing greatly complicates the problem of predicting what total expenditure will be in the next period. To understand the impact of a projected change in interest rates or tax rates or government spending requires also an analysis of how these sources of finance will respond, as well as how the direct spenders will respond. It is evident, then, that financial assets and the institutions that create them are of great importance in the growth story, and full attention will be given to both in Chapter 17.

There are also less far-reaching complications that may be mentioned at this point.

(*b*) A given level of $I + D + F$ may or may not exceed S depending on the mobility of labor and the adaptability of capital stock. Attention has already been given to the problem of adaptability of existing capital stock. The extent to which labor moves in response to changes in demand is equally difficult to ascertain. Thus a situation could result where an improvement in labor mobility or capital equipment adaptability would greatly increase the capacity of the economy, and so affect the relationship between capacity and aggregative spending.

(*c*) Similarly, a specific input shortage may obtain that, because of the linkages in the system, affects the level of output that the system can achieve. In this event, the appearance of unused capacity in a number of sectors of the economy may represent a bottleneck on the supply side rather than an aggregate demand problem. Here the question of the "right" level of total demand requires not only an appraisal of the bottleneck problem, but also the extent to which the bottleneck may yield to demand pressure. As detailed in the previous chapters, the allocation problem of growth is at once complicated and important, and supply bottlenecks are certain to appear. Even with the most complete information, such bottlenecks will greatly complicate the question of how much spending the economy can safely absorb.

(*d*) Expectations as to interest rates, prices, tariffs, taxes, and the like may also be relevant. Expectations as to future events of course affect current spending decisions, and in appraising a current demand situation, some attention must be given to the extent to which expectations are responsible for the existing and predicted future situation.

(*e*) The existence of unemployed labor complicates the analysis in several ways. Maximum capacity is itself a difficult notion to define, and even more difficult to measure, but the presence of unused resources adds further to these difficulties for they, too, must be measured. More importantly, some decision has to be reached as to the incentives and conditions that will attract the unemployed into productive enterprise. These tasks may be relatively easy in an urban area where data on the labor force and capital stock are available. The task is much less easy in a rural, agricultural region where unemployment, idle labor, and membership in the labor force are extremely vague concepts. In appraising the capacity of the system to accommodate spending, it is, however, necessary to consider a wide range of questions having to do with the size of unemployment and the extent and manner to which such resources respond to incentives.

(*f*) A final source of difficulty and complexity has to do with import and export prices. These prices are worth separating from other prices because their movements are dependent to a large degree on forces outside the economy. In particular there are two points that bear on the question of total demand. In the first place, fluctuating export and import prices may obscure inflation. Temporary, or apparently temporary, price movements arising out of events abroad may make it exceedingly difficult for the analyst to define the underlying price level situation. In the second place, stabilization schemes, if operative, may tend to interfere with an efficient allocation of resources and thereby affect the capacity of the system. These remarks mean simply that in an economy where foreign trade is important, and especially where export trade is concentrated on a few commodities, the already complex problem of defining capacity and aggregate demand is made more complicated.

These various considerations are mentioned to emphasize the importance of understanding the "structural" characteristics of the economy in appraising the capacity of the system. In some economies—developed and otherwise—the structural characteristics of the kind just described are so marked that making absolutely sure that there will be no increase in the price level may mean that the economy suffers costly under-utilization of capacity. In the event that this is the case, measures that weaken these "structural" obstacles become part of the battle against inflation. This argument is not meant to imply that excess aggregate demand or excess aggregate supply has no meaning, but rather to stress the fact that the task of appraising the size of the economy, and understanding the implications of a particular level of spending is a great deal more complicated than the mechanical manipulation of the equations stated in the beginning of this section would seem to imply.

B. THE MICRO PROBLEM

The analysis of the aggregate demand problem cannot be completely divorced from an analysis of the mechanism by which payments to factors are determined and prices of products set. Earlier, the point was made that excess aggregate demand is reflected in an excess demand for individual goods and services and could be written as $\Sigma P_i x_i$, where P_i is the price of the ith good in period zero and x_i the excess demand at that price of the ith good in period one. The problem now is to inquire into the mechanics by which price setting of products and factors enter into the aggregate demand problem. This inquiry will also lead into contact with some of the problems associated with maintaining a pricing mechanism of the kind required to make Expression 11 of Chapter 4 something more than an abstract assumption. It is convenient to separate the argument into two different areas of problems, one flowing from the simultaneous existence of the marginal and inframarginal vectors and matrices described in the preceding chapters, and the other flowing from the possibility that labor or capital may seek to increase their rates of return without reference to increases in their productivity.

1. Implications of the Marginal and Inframarginal Vectors. The principal source of complications arises from the adjustments of factor returns due to the emergence of new techniques. It has been argued that the returns to the factors in a given sector are determined by the marginal productivity of the factors in the marginal vector, i.e., in the most recently created capacity. In period one, as the capital-labor ratio rises and technical innovations are affected in a given sector, the wage rates that lead to the adoption of the new and different techniques also apply to all the labor in that sector. Because of the limited extent to which existing capacity can be modified, the factor combination in the inframarginal vectors is no longer optimal for the new prices of inputs. In most cases, this means that wage rates have risen above the level that they were when the inframarginal vectors of capital in this particular sector were constructed. If there is no change in the price of the product then the quasi-rent on inframarginal capital equipment must fall, and a shift in the distribution of income in favor of labor must occur as described earlier. On the other hand, if the price of the product of this sector is raised in order to protect the return on invested capital, complications are created for the monetary authorities. In this event, the increase in price is made without reference either to demand or to the productivity of capital in this particular activity, and the system moves away from the stabilizing comfort of the marginal productivity conditions. The result must be either an accumulation of inventories (for at the higher price and prevailing level of money income the total stock cannot be moved) or the monetary authorities must allow an increase in money income and hence a rise in the price level that justifies the price increase. In the latter case, the monetary authorities have lost control over the level of demand, and in the former case full utilization of resources is prevented.

The achievement of price level stability and full utilization of resources requires that the owners of inframarginal capital equipment be willing to accept reduced quasi-rents on their investment, which is in effect the writing down of the capital values of these inframarginal capital items. If this does occur, then a shift in income distribution will take place in favor of labor, and this shift may have some effect on aggregate demand. More important than the possibility of a shift in income distribution, however, is the simple fact that the very process of growth creates a situation in which there is a decline in the quasi-rents of invested capital, and capital owners will have a strong incentive to protect their quasi-rents, and thereby create the kind of difficulty outlined here. Another possible way of protecting quasi-rents, which will be examined later, is that technique changes are not made with the speed that they are available, and thereby the growth of the economy is penalized.

The extent to which technical change is foreseen will modify the seriousness of the problem somewhat. If perfect foresight is assumed, then the foreseen new techniques available several periods in the future would be included in the profit calculations on current investment. Perfect foresight is neither a realistic assumption nor a very meaningful one, and it must not be confused with a purposeful refusal to introduce cost-reducing innovations merely to protect the capital values of what should become the inframarginal vector.

2. *Wage and Relative Price Considerations.* Independent of the difficulties arising from the existence of the inframarginal vectors, additional problems relating to the control of demand may emerge as the economy grows. One of the major characteristics of growth as it has been described to this point has been the diversity of growth rates among the several sectors of the economy. The consequence of this diversity for the present analysis is the adjustments that it imposes in the allocation of resources among the sectors, and the fact that, except in a rigidly centrally directed economy, these adjustments require changes in relative prices of both products and primary inputs. The discussion has already noted the nature of these changes in relative prices and the mechanism to bring them about, and the problem now is to examine how such changes may affect the price level and the power the monetary authorities have over aggregate demand.

Price flexibility can be defined in such a way that there is no problem at all. Suppose the monetary authorities seek to maintain a stable price level with full utilization of resources. This they do by seeking to bring about, in an *ex ante* sense, $I + D + F = S$ at full capacity output. Except under extreme assumptions it is quite unlikely that excess demand for each product is zero, rather it will be the case that some are positive and others negative. If there is positive excess demand in some markets and prices rise there until it is eliminated, while in other markets there is negative excess demand and prices fall until it is eliminated, then if $I + D + F = S$ *ex ante,* there will be no change in the price level. If price adjustments are rapid enough and if the speed of adjustment up and down is the same in all sectors, then downward price movements will offset upward price movements, and the price level will remain the same. But this is a very idealized kind of price flexibility, and can hardly be expected to obtain as a matter of routine. In particular, it appears likely that in a newly growing economy the monetary authorities must be prepared to face a situation where such flexibility is lacking.

The major area of the inflexibility is on the downward side. It may be taken as an unusual market situation in which downward price flexibility equals upward price flexibility, and a safe generalization is that prices respond much more quickly to excess demand than to excess supply. This result stems from a variety of factors chiefly associated with cost and competitive position that make firms reluctant to reduce prices except in the face of long continuing under-utilization of capacity. In a situation where the various sectors of the economy are growing at divergent rates and price signals are necessary—in the absence of "perfect" foresight—to direct new resources into the faster growing sectors, upward price movements are unlikely to be matched by downward price movements.

There may be similar developments with respect to factor payments. It has already been assumed that factor payments are set in the marginal vector of a sector and that these payments prevail throughout that sector. In some instances, an even greater spillover effect may take place. Suppose, for example, that while a stable price level monetary policy is being successfully pursued, an innovation occurs in Sector i that raises the marginal product of labor in that sector and wages go up to reflect this increase in productivity. Now then suppose that for reasons associated with union pressure, political and social pressure, and various other pressures, wages in other sectors where no technical change has occurred also rise. In the latter sectors (as well as in the inframarginal vectors of Sector i) money wage rates go above the marginal product of labor and costs of production rise, and again the decision-making unit is faced with the problem of accepting reduced returns on capital or to try to raise prices of the products. At this point the argument joins that in the previous section, but where the sources of the problem earlier emerged from the very nature of the growth process, the problem now comes from the possibility—not necessity—of all wage rates following the leading wage rates upward. In this latter event, prices must rise or labor will have priced itself out of the market at some point.

The same general argument applies to the price-setting mechanism in the system. If producers, for whatever reason, raise the prices of their products above that given by Equation 11 of Chapter 4 ($P_j = l_j P_l + k_j P_k + \Sigma\, a_{ij} P_i$), then the quantity of products demanded must decline unless money income is allowed to rise. If money income does not rise, then eventually the system will necessarily fall below maximum utilization of resources.

The type of wage and price developments just outlined means that the monetary authorities lose control of the situation in that they have been pushed into action independent of a policy decision on changes in the level of prices, or they must allow the maximum utilization of resources to be sacrificed. Full control of aggregate demand by the monetary authorities requires an effective wage and profit policy or it requires an economy in which all factor and product markets are perfectly competitive. The exact content of a "wage and profit policy" is difficult to define, and once defined, imposes major implementation problems on those responsible for carrying it out. The problem at this point, however, is the simpler one of isolating a necessary condition for assuring control over aggregate demand without violating other conditions such as full employment, rate of capital formation, and so on that are also strategic to the growth process. Also these various considerations impinge directly on the extent to which ruling prices are those that satisfy the "shadow price" conditions of the previous chapters. They therefore affect the way in which resources are allocated, and hence the contributions that available resources can make to output. To solve these problems by the assumption of perfect competition in all markets, without at least some discussion of the difficulties and procedures by which the competitive result is achieved, seems to be solving an important problem by assumption rather than by understanding the nature of the problem. This further examination is made in succeeding chapters.

III. Conclusion

The arguments of this chapter have been concerned with issues associated with demand and prices. Several points emerged. First, changes in the composition of demand may affect the ability of the economy to utilize all its capacity if adjustments and adaptations are difficult and slow in appearing. Second, changing income elasticities of demand contribute to the divergent rates of growth among the several sectors. As to the problem of aggregate demand, the objective of maintaining control over total spending was seen to be complicated by structural characteristics that not only make difficult the measurement of the total capacity of the system, but also complicate the task of predicting how various spending units will respond to monetary and fiscal policy. The conclusion that much depends on the capacity of the government to manipulate its own spending is perhaps the most important issue with respect to aggregate demand. Finally, attention was directed toward how the price-setting machinery for individual products and factors affects the ability of the monetary authorities to maintain control over total spending and the achievement of the allocation objectives.

In all these cases, assumptions could be introduced that would relieve the problems. For example, it might be assumed that private investment could be effectively controlled by manipulating the rate of interest, or that competition solved the factor and product-pricing problems. However, any such assumptions or any set of relationships on the demand side seem much more precarious than corresponding supply relationships. Therefore, rather than developing a demand model, the purpose of the chapter has been to isolate those problems on the demand side that appear relevant to the making of development policy. As policy issues are discussed in later chapters, these problems and methods of meeting them will be given attention.

Bibliography

On the composition of demand I suggest Herman Wold and L. Jurien, *Demand Analysis* (New York; John Wiley & Sons, Inc., 1953) passim but especially Chap. 1; Richard Stone, *The Measurement of Consumers' Expenditure and Behavior in the United Kingdom, 1920-38* (Cambridge: Cambridge University Press, 1954), Vol. I, Pt. 11; and Hendrik S. Houthakker, "An International Comparison of Household Expenditure Patterns, Commemorating the Centenary of Engel's Law," *Econometrica*, XXV (October, 1957). Somewhat less formal treatment of similar issues is found in Arthur F. Burns, *Production Trends in the United States Since 1870* (New York: National Bureau of Economic Research, 1934) and Walther G. Hoffman, *British Industry 1700-1950* (Oxford: Oxford University Press, 1955).

On the issues raised in Part II of this chapter, further elaboration can be found in Charles L. Schultze, *Recent Inflation in the United States*, Study Paper No. 1 of materials prepared for the Study of Employment, Growth, and Price Levels of the Joint Economic Committee, United States Congress (Washington: United States Government Printing Office, 1959); Fritz Machlup, "Another View of Cost-Push and Demand-Pull Inflation," *Review of Economics and Statistics*, XLII (May, 1960); Dudley Seers, "A Theory of Inflation and Growth in Underdeveloped Countries Based on the Experience of Latin America," *Oxford Economic Papers*, XIV (June, 1962); and Geoffrey Maynard, *Economic Development and the Price Level* (London: Macmillan & Co., Ltd., 1962), especially Chap. III. See also references at end of Chap. 10 and 17.

CHAPTER 6

ECONOMIC GROWTH:
A SUMMING UP

The next task is to summarize and put into focus the kind of growth process that has been described in the preceding chapters. This can be done quickly, and to do it will help to isolate the characteristics of the underdeveloped or nongrowing economy that appear to be strategic in explaining its nongrowth. This latter explanation is the task of Chapter 7.

The growth of per capita income is the major problem of interest, and by definition this means that the rate of growth of output from period to period must exceed the rate of growth of population. The question to this point has been the growth of total output as population is to be treated separately. It is convenient to discuss separately three aspects of the growth of output: (1) the sources of growth, (2) the conditions for these sources to be effective, and (3) the *modus operandi* of growth.

The sources of growth refer to the processes that function in a manner that results directly in an increase in the capacity of the system. As summarized at the conclusion of Chapter 3, they consisted of increasing quantities of capital and labor, increasing technical knowledge, improved quality of labor, and changes in those environmental characteristics that affect the productivity of capital and labor. Capital formation means the creation of specific output yielding assets that may take the form of plant and equipment or a qualitative change in the labor input. An increase in technical knowledge is reflected in the changed form of physical capital that enables a given quantity to yield a larger rate of output or in a change in the organization of the productive process that results in a larger flow of output from a given quantity of inputs. The distinction between quantity and quality of capital and of labor is essential to the argument. The change in the quality of labor is due to the embodying of skill in labor, while the change in the quality of capital is due to the embodying of new technical knowledge in the physical capital, in the plant and equipment. The changes in the environmental factors refer to such things as entrepreneurial activity, allocative mechanism, work habits, and the like that affect the productivity of capital and labor or the extent to which they are increased in quantity and quality. Changes in these characteristics occur much more slowly than do changes in the other sources of growth, and are probably less amenable to specific policies than the other growth-producing sources as well.

To define these several processes as the sources of growth means that some or all must be present if the rate of growth of output is to exceed zero. But their presence also requires that the economy meet certain conditions that allow these growth-producing agents to be effective. These conditions refer to several things. With respect to the pricing of factors and changes in those prices to reflect relative scarcities, a response on the part of entrepreneurial talent and managers is required. Otherwise, full advantage will not be taken of the changing supply of inputs. This condition is made more important and more difficult to meet because of the existence of the marginal and inframarginal vectors of capacity. The existence of produced inputs places greater emphasis on the pricing mechanism (or on planners) to signal potential supply bottlenecks, and to transmit the growth-producing effects of investment and innovation from the originating sectors to the other sectors. Conditions for growth also include control of aggregate demand. One of the firmest conclusions about growth that can be established is that a condition for growth is that demand be pressing against capacity. At the same time, mere excess demand does not produce growth, and runaway inflation is surely harmful on all counts, so the existence of the means to control aggregate demand is a major condition of the growth story. Finally, the institutional arrangements that provide the framework in which the economy functions must be such that the adaptations and adjustments required by growth can be effected easily and quickly.

The *modus operandi* of growth refers to the mechanism by which growth occurs, to the question of stability and equilibrium growth, and finally to the relative importance of the various sources of growth in accounting for growth of total output.

This general argument developed about the mechanism of growth is one that is commonly referred to as leading sectors. For reasons associated with increases in technical knowledge in a specific sector or to increases in the final demand for specific goods, one sector or a few sectors will experience a major incentive to expand capacity. Because of the linkages among sectors—because of the role of produced inputs—expansion of a few sectors results in increased demand for the output of other sectors in order to supply the necessary produced inputs. Thus, the system made up of many sectors linked together by the technological coefficients presents what was called a jagged edge of growth with some sectors leading the way and others being pulled along perhaps equally rapidly, and still others dropping by the wayside. An investment opportunity is presented to a sector or two by virtue of demand changes or by virtue of new knowledge. The exploitation of these opportunities creates further opportunities through the rest of the system via the existing linkages, and the economy as such grows in the jagged edge manner just mentioned. Only in rare instances and for short periods does an economy grow evenly in all sectors, and for most of the time it is expected that some sectors are growing rapidly while the rest of the economy simply responds to the incentives created by these leading sectors. The fact that growth is expected to take place in this fashion adds further to the adaptation and adjustment burden that an economy must carry if it is to continue to grow with regularity and stability.

The definition of full employment equilibrium growth appears rather complicated because capital is to some degree fixed, and only the marginal vectors of the system can be expected to be ideally suited from the standpoint of technology, factor supplies, and the composition of demand. An extremely idealized growth pattern is one in which all available capacity in each period is fully utilized and there is optimal allocation of resources in the sense defined earlier. This ideal is, however, regarded as extremely difficult to attain, since changes in the composition of demand, in technology, and in factor prices tend to make some capacity that is physically usable of no economic value. The fact that much of the existing capital equipment is less than ideally suited to technology and demand conditions means that an economy that can adapt its equipment, and then can achieve the necessary price changes to make the adjustment work has another source of growth compared to that economy that is unable to exploit so completely its existing capital equipment.

A less idealized pattern of equilibrium growth is one in which all capital equipment is thrown on the market and the quasi-rents allowed to seek their own level, even by falling to zero. It is clear, of course, that the simultaneous existence of marginal and inframarginal vectors means that equilibrium growth is not such that all activities are conducted with the least cost techniques. Indeed it means precisely that they are not, and that, consequently, there are pressures created that change the income distribution and the profitability of certain techniques. Also growth may create incentives to adjust prices in a manner that is not consistent with a stable price level and full utilization of resources. Because of these adjustments the monetary authorities must, in order to keep control over aggregate demand, have an effective wage and profit policy as well as weapons to affect total spending in the economy.

The notion of an equilibrium growth requires some sort of adjustment mechanism unless the equilibrium is to be strictly fortuitous. A stable equilibrium growth means that as the system experiences change—an in-

crease in the capital-labor ratio, new technical knowledge, new social arrangements,—it adapts in a way that makes the new situation consistent
with the technological and behavioristic expressions describing the economy. In the growth process as it has been described here, there is no equilibrium path on which the economy must tread or go off into an undefined
unknown, but rather there is a sequence of equilibrium positions that are
defined with respect to the conditions prevailing in that period. The adjustment mechanism assures that the equilibrium positions are such that
the factor combinations in the marginal vectors are optimal with respect
to factor prices. In order to obtain such a sequence of equilibrium position, considerable adjustment is required within the economy, and it is
useful to list specific adjustment mechanisms on which the preceding argument is based.

(*a*) The argument includes the assumption that there exists more than
one technique of production available during any single period, and
changes in prices of inputs result in changes in the technique employed.
Since a growth of per capita output usually means that the rate of capital
formation exceeds the rate of growth of the labor force, full utilization of
all resources requires changes in the techniques employed in the marginal
vectors relative to those employed in the inframarginal vectors. In the new
vector, the capital-labor ratio is higher than in the old ones and the rate
of return is lower—unless this latter result is qualified by innovations. Unemployed labor with suitable qualifications will relieve the necessity for a
changing capital-labor ratio as long as it lasts. Unemployment is discussed
in Chapter 7.

(*b*) Technical innovations may also provide a source of stability in several ways. In the first place, if the relative prices of inputs do not change,
no matter what happens to relative scarcities, innovations may provide the
source of adjustment to the rising capital-labor ratio. This innovation effect may be in the form of the creation of new techniques of production,
or a new product, or it may be in a form that is favorable to the factor
(capital) whose supply has increased relatively more. This last effect would
then result in the choice of technique being the one that utilized the most
capital intensive method. In this case, the innovation effect is a substitute
for changes in the relative prices of inputs. This discussion has included
no argument that suggests that this innovation effect is induced by factor
price behavior or any other development in the system. Before innovations
can be secured as a reliable source of stability such an argument must be
introduced. Two things are noted here and examined in detail in Chapter
11. In the first place, the economic history of growing countries suggests
that innovations have, with great regularity, been favorable to capital.
Second, even if there is no inducement mechanism available in the routine
operation of the economy, a careful government can determine that such
an innovation would have a stabilizing effect on the system and so direct

its research resources toward producing technical change effects favorable to capital. The chief point is that the innovation effect is not considered to be completely exogenous to the needs of this particular aspect of the economy.

(c) A further source of adjustment to changing factor supplies has to do with the composition of final demand. A decline in the price of capital relative to the price of labor means that the price of the products that are produced by the more capital intensive techniques will decline in relation to the price of the less capital intensive techniques. Therefore, rather than adjustment to changing factor supplies taking place via changing techniques or changing technology, it may take place via changing demand. As the price of products, whose production process makes greater use of capital, declines, the quantity of these products demanded will increase more rapidly than the products whose production calls for relatively more labor. Consequently, even with only one technique of production, adjustment to changing factor supplies is possible via changes in the composition of demand. It is recognized that adjustment in this manner is also limited, and cannot be relied on as a solution to the whole problem.

(d) As to the question of control of aggregate demand, the argument places initial reliance on variations in the ease with which credit is made available to investors. It is also assumed, however, that supportng this weapon are direct changes in the government deficit or level of government spending. Part of the aggregate demand problem includes consideration of the determination of wage rates and product prices, and an effective policy to maintain control over total demand requires the existence of a mechanism or policy that prevents factor payments from rising without reference to the productivity of the factors.

(e) Another possible source of stability at the aggregate level has to do with monetary factors. Thus, the desire to save may be satisfied by adding to claims on physical capital or by adding to the real value of the stock of money, and this fact may impose another source of stability to the system. This argument has not been developed yet and is considered in detail in Chapter 17.

These several sources of stability, and the assumptions as to the speed with which they may be expected to work, suggest that the growing economy described here is neither perfectly stable nor uselessly unstable. It is neither always and necessarily in equilibrium nor is it running off into an unknown unstable area. It is therefore believed to be quite realistic in the sense that it describes a phenomenon that can be observed in the real world. This kind of situation also means that the various decision-making and policy-making units must always be on guard for disequilibrating developments. Equilibration is not something that occurs automatically and can be forgotten about.

As to what source of growth is most important in accounting for the growth of capacity, the answer is not the same from period to period. The empirical and a priori evidence cannot be used to conclude that it is innovations, or investment in human beings, or investment in buildings and equipment that are always and invariably the dominant source of growth. If this were the case, the theory could be greatly simplified. Two things can be concluded however. First and most importantly, at any given time it may be possible to isolate a particular source that at that time will yield the greatest growth. If this is possible, it has obvious policy implications. Second, and somewhat contradictory to the first, it is dangerous to ignore any of the aspects of growth just mentioned. The policy maker, therefore, is faced with the task of deciding where to concentrate the major attack on growth, but this decision must emerge from an examination of the economy as it is characterized at a given time, and not from an assumption as to the universality of the importance of a given source or condition of growth.

More specific theories or models of growth may be devised from the tools and framework outlined here. Thus one can assume only one production technique available or one can assume some substitution among the factors, and assume that empirically the capital coefficients have been constant, and design a theory to account for this alleged stability. Similarly, one may ignore the complications created by the fixity of capital equipment, and assume that all capital is always ideally designed from the standpoint of technology, factor prices, and the composition of demand. Many other varieties of assumptions may be made and their implications explored. This argument has been made as general as possible without losing touch with reality. It seems quite clear, for example, that the assumptions of a few techniques of production is a much more revealing one than is that of an infinite number of such techniques, at least in the present context. Similarly, the assumption that the growth process generates inframarginal vectors is surely directly applicable to a growing economy. It also seems clear that capital equipment created five years ago is less suited to current opportunities than is capital equipment created yesterday, and this fact is general enough that ignoring its implications is to miss one of the key parts of the growth process. It is of course recognized that the more specific the assumptions are that can be made, the more directly applicable is the theory. At the same time, carrying specificity too far not only endangers the generality of the argument, but also may lead to far-reaching conclusions that rest on a specific assumption, the validity of which is yet to be established or is strictly limited in time and place.

The present argument appears to be realistic in that it provides an apparatus of sufficient generality to enable all sources of growth to be examined, and it provides the maximum degree of specificity consistent with the objectives of this book. In Chapter 2, it was shown that growth depends not only on the growth parameters, but also on the initial conditions from which the analysis is assumed to begin. The initial conditions of interest here are the general characteristics of the underdeveloped country that is seeking to alter its economic structure so that it may achieve, as a matter of more or less routine, a rising per capita income. These general characteristics of underdevelopment are described in the next chapter.

Bibliography

Formal growth models abound, and some attention should be given to such models in any study of a developing economy. Benjamin Higgins, *Economic Development* (New York: W. W. Norton & Company, Inc., 1959) and Gerald M. Meier and Robert E. Baldwin, *Economic Development* (New York: John Wiley & Sons, Inc., 1957) both contain surveys of a number of theories of growth and long lists of references. See also Bert F. Hoselitz, ed. *Theories of Economic Growth* (New York: The Free Press of Glencoe, 1960). William J. Baumol, *Economic Dynamics* (2nd Ed.) (New York: The Macmillan Company, 1959) is also a good general treatment of growth model building, especially in the early chapters. The most famous growth model is the so-called Harrod-Domar model: R. F. Harrod, "An Essay in Dynamic Theory," *Economic Journal,* XLIX (March, 1939) and E. D. Domar, "Capital Expansion, Rate of Growth, and Employment," *Econometrica,* XIV (April, 1946). Two models of great elegance are J. E. Meade, *A Neo-Classical Theory of Economic Growth* (London: George Allen & Unwin, 1961) and Robert M. Solow, "A Contribution to the Theory of Economic Growth," *Quarterly Journal of Economics,* LXX (February, 1956).

There are hundreds more possible references, but a sample from the above list will give the student a good notion of the variety of approaches and degrees of rigor. A reading of a few of them would also provide further material for examining and expanding the approach employed in this book.

CHAPTER 7

THE NONGROWING ECONOMY

In Chapter 2, the argument was made that the full story of the growth of an economy depended not only on the *modus operandi* of the growth process itself, but also on the initial conditions from which growth is assumed to begin. The preceding four chapters have outlined a process of growth, and have identified the conditions that have to be met in order for an economy to achieve sustained growth of *per capita* income. The purpose of the present chapter is to establish the initial conditions from which this growth process is assumed to begin. Therefore, it is now necessary to specify the characteristics of the nongrowing economy that appear to be strategic in accounting for the inability of such a system to experience growth, and that are relevant characteristics in getting growth under way. This chapter must come after those on the process of growth because without an understanding of the mechanism of growth, it is not possible to isolate the barriers to growth.

Even the most cursory look at the world's nongrowing economies shows a tremendous diversity. The basic characteristic—absence of growth—itself is not true to the same degree in all poor countries. Some countries have achieved some growth, others none, still others have probably suffered a reduced *per capita* income in the last fifty or one hundred years. Indeed, it would be difficult to find a single characteristic that was equally applicable to all the countries that are usually classified as underdeveloped. The general conditions as to natural endowments, basic capital equipment, and population pressure vary from country to country. Similarly the state of technology, of research, and of education evidence sharp and important contrasts. The mores and conventions of the societies differ substantially, especially as to attitudes toward accumulation, toward economizing, and toward social change. Also social arrangements and economic organizations, e.g., land tenure, family life, and so on will be found to differ widely among underdeveloped countries.

Nevertheless there is enough similarity that it is meaningful to seek a general analysis, as opposed to studies of individual countries. When this general analysis is applied to an individual area, it is necessary to introduce specific assumptions into the argument that make it applicable to a given area at a given time. The approach here is to establish a "representative" nongrowing or sporadically growing economy, and explore in some detail the explanation of this condition. Some of the problems and analyses may not be at all applicable to a specific low income country, but for the most part a simple modification of qualification will be all that is necessary to localize the argument to the extent to make it applicable.

This chapter is divided into seven sections that more or less reflect the characteristics of the growth process just discussed. The sections are: I. Production and Consumption, II. Supply of Resources, III. Technology, IV. Employment, V. The Productive Process, VI. Population, and VII. Social and Institutional Setting.

I. Production and Consumption

The most identifiable characteristic of the low income, nongrowing economy is that it is predominantly a primary producing and consuming area. In most instances, production is food grains and fibers, although in several countries mining is an activity of importance. Along with primary production, a whole series of service activities are indigenous to the kind of economy that is of concern here. Manufacturing activity is of course not completely absent, but in most instances it is newly established and is yet to become an integrated part of the economy. One characteristic of an economy making substantial progress is the development of an industrial sector that is indigenous to the society. More accurately, it is the development not of an industrial sector as such, but rather the development of the capacity to exploit opportunities presented, and the capacity to do this requires an industrial sector or at least the capacity to create one. The lack of this capacity is perhaps the key explanation of the primary production characteristic of these economies.

If there were no international trade, then a country could use only what it produces, and the explanation of the concentration on food production is simple. If income is around the subsistence level, then by definition most resources must be devoted to producing those things required for keeping people alive—food, clothing, and shelter. Thus, about 50 per cent of total expenditure on consumption goods in Australia goes for food, clothing, and shelter, while in Ghana, Nigeria and Peru the same percentage usually is over 70 per cent. If food alone were taken, the differences would be even greater. Undoubtedly, any small increase in *per capita* income is used for food, and so the expenditure elasticity of demand for food is generally quite high. In terms of proportion of output, the agriculture sector accounts for at least one third of total output and possibly up to and over one half in some instances. There are of course major exceptions. For example, the figures for Venezuela, which most people would classify as an underdeveloped country, show that only 8 per cent of Gross Domestic Product originates in agriculture. Even allowing for some underestimation, it is clear that this sector in this country is relatively small. Imports into Venezuela are much more heavily consumer goods than is the case for any other major South American country, and domestic production and exports are dominated by oil. In the representative low income country, productivity of agriculture is usually below that of industry, and the proportion of the labor force in agriculture therefore usually exceeds the proportion of total output produced in that sector.

If international trade is introduced, it is not so easy to explain the continuation of the concentration on primary production. Obviously, a low income country could produce a nonfood product for export, and then import food. Further, it is useful to note that rich countries that are usually thought of as agricultural—e.g., New Zealand and Denmark where about 20 per cent of total product originates in agriculture compared to about 5 per cent in the United States—are countries that have long engaged in international trade in significant amounts. This statement, of course, does not mean that were present-day low income countries to engage in more international trade, their difficulties would end, but it does suggest that failure to trade and failure to grow have a common root. The story is further complicated because many low income countries have a high ratio of foreign trade to national income ratio. Thus Ceylon, Iraq, Ghana, and Venezuela are heavy traders, but unlike the rich countries that are very dependent on foreign trade these low income countries depend principally on a single commodity for export that is either a mineral or an agricultural product. There seems to be no example where a poor country has concentrated its own production on non-primary commodities, and has also imported all or most of its food. The question asked at the beginning of the paragraph is why.

There is no exact set of explanations that is as applicable if no trade were possible, and consideration must be given to institutional and organizational factors. The most important of these have to do with the extent to which the economy is market oriented and market directed. In many of the poor countries, subsistence farming means simply that very little output enters the market, or if it does, it is a local market with minor connections or links with the rest of the system. Partly as a contributing factor and partly as a consequence of this, the market organization is not geared to effective and extensive trading. Market organization here refers chiefly to financial arrangements for conducting internal or international trade as well as to transportation facilities available for such trade. In that single sector in which foreign trade is important, the market organization is directed only toward the handling of this specific product and little else. Generally, it is possible to say that the primary production designed for foreign trade is usually conducted in a more efficient manner than is subsistence agriculture.

The concentration on agriculture is also due, to a significant degree, to matters of history and it is dangerous to overload the analytical arguments. In many instances, the single export crop (or mineral) had its origin as an industry in a foreign company or by foreign entrepreneurs entering the country and establishing the industry. The organization was designed merely to take advantage of this particular asset rather than contributing to the general development of the entire economy. Whether the latter was possible at the time of the establishment of the industry is an issue well beyond the present objective, but it does seem clear that the explanation of the simultaneous existence of a sector in which international trade is extremely important and methods of production of recent origin, and a sector in which no trade takes place and production is of a primitive subsistence kind must go beyond analytical matters and consider the historical evolution of the economy. However, it is unnecessary to account for a situation presented to the initial conditions by history.

The other category of production that is surely indigenous to the nongrowing, low income country is that usually identified as the service industry. A widely accepted body of thought relates the development of a service industry to the achievement of high incomes on the assumption that only then can people devote any sizeable part of their income to purchasing services. This is an acceptable argument in certain contexts, but there is a great variety of services and a great variety of reasons for buying them, and those prevalent in low income countries are not to be explained in terms of income. These services consist chiefly of retail selling and a great many types of personal services.

The great number of personal servants results from a variety of circumstances. The most narrowly economic reason is simply that personal servants are considerably cheaper than the same services performed by consumer durables, and of course there are some services that consumer durables cannot perform, e.g., marketing. Families who are able, therefore, to avoid doing tasks that are tedious and uninteresting do so by hiring personal servants, not by buying a washing machine, refrigerator, and so on. This behavior is completely rational from the most exacting economic interpretation. However, it is important not to overload the economic argument in explaining an observed situation that the social mores of the community dictate, i.e., the use of personal servants by all who can afford them. To a very large extent employing servants approaches a form of transfer payment—a means of redistributing income—since extra leisure time to the person buying the service is not the primary objective of the purchase (and it certainly is not—except here and there—to free the purchaser so that he or she can do more important things), but rather the objective is to live within the security of the conventions of the society. It is not so much leisure that is sacrificed if a servant were dismissed, as it is prestige or position in the community that is sacrificed. At the same time it is evident that rising wage rates produced by a rapid rate of capital formation would make it necessary to change this prestige element.

Household servants do not, of course, exhaust the categories of services. In terms of manpower involved, what is loosely called retail trade is of great importance. This category includes many services such as buying one package of cigarettes and "retailing" them individually, selling iced water by the glass on the streets, selling "air" pumped into a bicycle tire, as well as services of the more orthodox shop clerk. Furthermore, many of those people whose major task is in agriculture have free time to do the little selling there is to do or to maintain a small retail establishment as a sideline. Though both types of such service categories are an essential part of the economic routine, they do not constitute a very large proportion of total output simply because of the very low productivity of the resources employed in this manner. The resources are grossly underutilized and to a very large degree are engaged in such activities merely as an alternative to starving. Entry and exit from such activity is easy since virtually no commitment is necessary. There seems little doubt that if suitable alternative employment opportunities were presented, a large proportion of labor now engaged in service activities would readily accept it. The condition of suitability is no small one and, as is argued later, complicates the problem significantly.

Also in the service category are the civil servants, bank clerks, teachers, religious leaders, landlords, and others who constitute a small proportion of the labor force. Though small in number, they are important, usually because they possess some education and other characteristics that set them apart from the vast majority of the population, including others in the service category.

Although there is some manufacturing activity, this is relatively minor as a proportion of total output, and employs a relatively small proportion of the labor force. In particular, it is appropriate to say that there is no widespread industrial activity and no existing basic industrial equipment in terms either of a capital plant or supply of appropriately trained labor. There is, therefore, an absence of that essential groundwork—environment, physical plant, and technical knowledge—that constitutes the heart of a thoroughgoing industrial sector, or even one that is just beginning a sustained growth toward development of a major industrial sector. The industrial sector that does exist is superimposed on an economy and society that is not equipped to handle it. This is the case not only with respect to industries owned and operated by outsiders and designed to supply a foreign market, but also true of industry that has its origin in domestic entrepreneurship. The result is likely to be difficulties in production, idle capacity, and the like. Even so, labor productivity in the industrial sector is higher than in the other sectors. This is due in part to a higher capital-labor ratio and more modern technology in the industrial sector, but also in no small measure to the extremely low productivity and underutilization in agriculture and services. So for these reasons, the industrial sector is somewhat alien to the rest of the community, and unlike agriculture and services that are really indigenous to the economic community.

The production side of the nongrowing, low income economy shapes up as follows: a large proportion—from 35 to 50 per cent—of the total output originates in primary production activities and an even larger proportion of the labor force is engaged in this sector full or part time, and a still larger proportion of the population depends on agriculture for a livelihood. A large proportion of the agricultural output does not enter the market, but is produced and consumed on the farm and part of the output that does enter the market does so only at a very local, village level. Here, there are essentially barter arrangements between farm workers and retail stores or small producers of low income consumption products. At the other extreme, there is production on a larger scale primarily for the market, large domestic urban markets, and foreign markets. There will be some commercial and financial organizations to support foreign trade, and much less to carry on internal trade. Although manufacturing activity is minimal and limited to small scale undertakings, it is designed chiefly to process locally available primary products such as fibers, food grains, and perhaps minerals, or to supply such minor manufactured goods that the economy finds essential. The production economy is unconnected and markets tend to be separate and distinct with little linkage among them. The subsistence sector lives a more or less isolated existence as does the export sector—both agriculture and mineral. The tertiary industries exist largely as a means of occupying the otherwise unemployed.

This kind of productive system has some rather far-reaching implications. In particular, as noted above, a large segment of it is more or less isolated from price effects, and therefore will have no incentive to change in consequence of price changes. The method of response and incentive to expand outlined in the preceding chapters is not applicable. At least one product may be tied very closely to foreign markets, and the profitability of its production is therefore heavily dependent on events over which the economy itself has no control. It also means that the range of output is sorely limited, and the productive system is ill-equipped to respond to changes in world demand, and thereby to adjust to the changing composition of demand as it occurs throughout the world. This is especially true in a given short run, but for this kind of system it is also true for the long run.

The consumption pattern is explained simply in terms of the level of income. A large proportion of expenditure goes for food and most of the remainder for other necessities. Housing in particular shows the effect of low levels of income not so much by the proportion of expenditure paid for this service but by the extremely low quality. A similar statement is true for clothing, but the implications of poor clothing are probably not as significant as those of poor housing.

II. Supply of Resources

Here, too, it is convenient to begin with an extremely obvious point, the relatively large supply of labor compared to other inputs used in the production process. The labor is in general unskilled, but in some instances there is a body of people with high school diplomas who are available for work. It is accurate to say that whatever skills are possessed are generally not those that are suitable for the initiation of development. It is not then a matter of a relatively large well-trained labor force at hand, but rather a labor force that only potentially may be a source of development. The question of employment is important, and is discussed in Section IV.

The explanation of the low capital supply relative to labor (a low capital-labor ratio relative to that in richer countries) is usually made in terms of the saving capacity of the economy. If income has never risen very much above subsistence the saving ability of the society is, by definition, extremely limited, and since capital formation requires saving then the rate of capital formation is extremely limited. However, both population and the labor force have grown continuously through the years, and although in some countries the aggregate capital-labor ratio has probably declined, there is little evidence to suggest that it has changed very much over the first half of the twentieth century in most of the low income countries. It is also probably true to say the same thing about *per capita* income. Now, if population has risen consistently while *per capita* income has remained about constant, then it is evident that this society has chosen children over saving or possibly higher consumption, has in a sense chosen —to use rather harsh language—to accumulate children rather than physical assets or claims on physical assets and eventually to have a higher level of consumption. The result has then been the growth of population occurring at the expense of capital formation.

This way of stating the undersaving problem emphasizes the role of demand for capital goods. The role of population growth is examined in Chapter 14. There are two arguments of merit. On the one hand, the demand for children is so great that it outpulls the existing demand for resources for capital formation. On the other hand, there is evidence to suggest that the general quality and quantity of entrepreneurship and organizing ability is such that there is really very little demand for capital, and children win by default. Even more extreme is the view that resources available for capital formation are being underutilized because of the inability of the system to supply the necessary entrepreneurial ability to see and exploit investment opportunities. These various arguments have different policy implications, and it is important to appreciate the differences. The first hypothesis implies that the economy fails to generate other investment opportunities of sufficient attractiveness to bid resources away from families wishing to have children. This may mean that even though investment opportunities are strong, the institutional and cultural milieu surrounding the family is such that a high rate of return is attached to children. The second hypothesis suggests rather that the economy fails to provide investment opportunities that the entrepreneurial talent available can recognize and exploit, and even further that the problem is not really one of competing claims of resources at all. Part II is concerned with capital formation and the key thing here is to recognize that the total explanation of the relatively low capital-labor ratio is not simply a subsistence income that permits no saving. Population growth belies this, and then there are many reasons to look into the demand side of the problem.

The latter two hypotheses also stress the role of that nebulous and undefinable "factor" entrepreneurship. Although the definition and measurement of this factor cannot be done very revealingly, it is an essential ingredient of the problem, and it seems clear that whatever definition is employed and however measurement is attempted, the entrepreneurial function is less well performed in the underdeveloped world than in West Germany, Japan, or other rich, growing countries. The source of this particular supply characteristic is of course a major problem. Since this "factor" cannot be simply equated to labor—although entrepreneurs are men —population growth alone is not a sufficient explanation as it is in the case of labor. Rather appeal must be made to a general social atmosphere that places particular prestige value on the organizing, the securing of finance, and the carrying through of an economic undertaking. The general features of this "social atmosphere" are to be discussed later, but it is useful to emphasize the fact that this particular supply phenomenon has an impact on a wide variety of aspects of the system. The one aspect of interest now is that having to do with the relative supply of capital and labor. With respect to the subject matter of Section I, the entrepreneurial talent problem is part of the explanation of continuing concentration on agriculture. For with a weak entrepreneurial supply, the "objective" conditions for economic change must be greater and last longer than is the case with an alert and strong source of supply of entrepreneurship.

The situation that involves land and other natural resources varies to an extent that defies generalization. There are countries where land is so crowded that it constitutes the single most important constraint on economic development. East Pakistan is probably an example of such an area. At the other extreme, there are countries with equally low incomes where cultivatable land is no constraint at all. The same is true of other natural resources. One has only to mention oil to see that a natural resource advantage is not a sure way to achieve development. The result then is simply that the land-natural resource base is a conditioning, not a determining factor in the development process. For the representative underdeveloped country described here the assumption may be made that its natural resources are average, which means that they impose no major barrier and give no major boost.

III. Technology

Over most of the system the technology prevalent in the economy is "primitive." Primitive means two things: first, that it is the same technology that has been in use for decades or centuries past; and second, that it is less productive than the technology in other, richer countries. Less productive means that with the same quantity of inputs, output would be less than in other countries. It is technological considerations that account for results contrary to what the variable proportions argument suggests. For example, with larger quantities of labor employed per unit of land in Country A than in Country B, output per *acre* may be expected to be higher in the former country than in the latter. The fact that it usually is not if Country A is a low income area and B a high income area is explained partly in terms of capital that is used, but largely in terms of quality of seeds, methods of cultivation, fertilizers used, control of insects, control and use of water, and so on. The qualifying phrase "over most of the economy" is important because one observes many instances where the most modern of technology is in effect. More accurately, it should be said that one observes examples of the most modern technology available from abroad. There are then three general questions: (1) Why has not technology in general advanced in these economies? (2) Why is there an advanced, imported technology in use in isolated instances? (3) How can the two—advanced, imported and primitive, indigenuous—coexist?

The technical progress argument presented in Chapter 3 implies that in any one period of time a growing economy will be characterized by a variety of technologies due to the fact that some technology is built into physical capital, and that capital lasts for several periods. The observed difference in the technology in the underdeveloped country just mentioned is not, however, in this category, and the explanation outlined earlier is not applicable here. The use of new, imported techniques can be explained by several factors. The most obvious is that these advanced techniques are employed only by firms controlled and operated by foreigners. It is generally accepted that outside firms bring the technology of their home country with them and install it, independent of the relative factor prices in the underdeveloped country and with only the minimum adjustments. It is not, however, correct to say that only foreign firms use modern, imported techniques. In many new plants, the equipment is imported from abroad or, if built at home, is constructed from blueprints obtained from abroad. It is indeed a cliché of development that at the same time that an atomic energy power plant is being built in a given locality, five miles away a barefoot farmer is struggling with a pair of bullocks and a wooden plow. This is a cliché, but it is not devoid of content.

There are several reasons that may be offered for domestically instigated new firms using modern, imported technology. The most cogent of these is the argument developed in Chapter 3 having to do with the evolution of technology. Consider Diagram IV drawn on the same basis as the similar diagrams used earlier. Line VRT connects points of equal output, and the

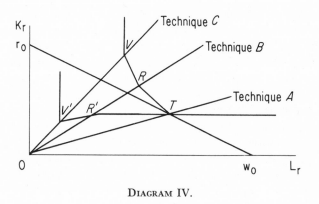

DIAGRAM IV.

presumption is that given the factor supply situation described in Section II of this chapter the technique described by Ray A will yield the largest output for a given cost in the underdeveloped country. In a rich, growing country, however, Ray C is probably chosen and for reasons already discussed, innovational activity in the rich country will be concentrated on improving the productivity of resources combined according to Technique C, or on the creation of a new ray between C and the ordinate of the diagram. Innovations then are likely to be of the favorable to capital variety. Suppose as a consequence of an innovation, a new isoquant is created as $V'R'T$ that shows the same output as VRT produced with a greatly reduced quantity of resources for Technique B or C, but since the capital rich country is no longer interested in the technique shown by Ray A, no effort is made to adapt the new knowledge to fit a labor intensive technique such as A. In this case then the labor rich, capital poor country that borrows technology chooses that represented by Ray C no matter what the factor prices are in the borrowing country and for completely rational reasons: the most modern is also the most economic. The new technique C

would not be the most economic had innovations been developed that were applicable to Ray *A*, and resulted in pushing point *T* back southeast of *R'*. A similar kind of argument may be made in terms of scale of output. Often because of indivisibilities, a new technical advance increases the most economic size of a plant or equipment, and consequently the importing country brings in a technology that does not "match" its market size to capitalize on the innovations. The argument then is based on the absence of a routinized innovational procedure in the low income country that permits the adaptation of newly available knowledge to the relative factor supply situation prevailing in the country, and hence the necessary reliance on imported, unadapted technique. Whether this reliance is unwise from an economic standpoint is, of course, another matter, and its consideration requires inquiry into the cost of adaptation, and the difference in rates of output between the adapted and unadapted techniques.

A second set of reasons is less easily spelled out, but is probably no less important. Skilled labor, foremen, managers, and the like may be a major bottleneck, and an automated or highly routinized plant may require a smaller number of these scarce inputs than a plant or machine complex that is, in terms of Diagram IV more labor intensive. A few highly trained individuals—possibly imported—may be easier to find than a larger number of semi-skilled workers requiring a great deal of supervision and organization. Thus, what at first may appear to be a noneconomic capital using technology may in fact be skill-saving or manager-saving technology.

Finally, economic considerations do not always rule, and the borrowing of technology is sometimes based on misconceived notions of national prestige or pride. National pride is essential to development, but it would be beneficial if it could be expressed in less expensive ways. However, the point now is simply that while the use of the most modern imported technology in newly constructed plants and equipment does not necessarily represent a violation of the economic calculus within the constraints of existing knowledge, it does most surely mean that there is little, if any, innovational activity in the underdeveloped country even of the simple kind of adapting new knowledge available from abroad in the manner necessary to exploit its factor supply situation.

That there is no or very little domestic innovational activity explains in part why most of the productive processes are characterized by primitive technology, but there is still a necessity for explaining why the new technology that is imported—if it is economic—is not copied throughout the economy. The chief explanation seems to lie in the factor supply situation, and in the nature of the imported technology.

On the factor supply side, the capital and entrepreneurial "shortages" described above are both relevant. The entrepreneurial aspect is obvious and needs little elaboration. The introduction of new techniques and new processes requires new routines and new modes of activity, and these changes impose demands on worker and manager alike that usually cannot be met. This is true even if the task is merely copying what is being done in the next field or in the next factory. Indeed, knowledge of new techniques is frequently not available, and where available is not shown in a manner that convinces anyone of its superiority. Of equal importance with these factors, however, is the fact that an innovation is sure to cost something, or to risk something. Consider a simple, but not untypical example. New seeds that will result in an increased output, if used, are available at a somewhat higher price than those seeds that have customarily been used. To buy the new seeds requires, therefore, a larger amount of working capital committed, and if floods or droughts frequently ruin the crop, the extra outlay may mean not extra yields, but rather higher losses. The farmer may be unwilling to take the risk. Also the application of new knowledge will frequently require fixed capital investment in excess of the capital that is merely being replaced. Since labor is relatively abundant and wages low, there is, in many instances, little incentive to assume the risks involved in introducing new techniques and new processes. These two considerations then—available entrepreneurial talent and credit—handicap the emulation of foreign technology by the economy as a whole.

The type of technology imported is also relevant as it is frequently difficult, if not impossible, to use or reproduce in all sectors of the economy. Thus, there is not much technology embodied in large earthmoving machinery that can be used in making shovels, wheelbarrows, or donkeys more efficient. The absence of a large industrial sector means that facilities for copying and adapting are in general absent. The same is true for many other capital items, and consequently much of imported technology embodied in physical capital items has no imitation value.

Finally, then, why is there no domestic innovational activity? Part of the answer to the question is very simple. The building up of a sector of the economy devoted to innovational activity requires resources. It is in effect a form of capital formation and the risk of getting any return on this outlay is quite high—the gestation period is long, and the kind of resources used have a very high opportunity cost. Specifically, the cost of innovation activity is high and the returns most unpredictable, therefore it may appear more profitable to allocate such resources to other activities, the outcome of which is more predictable. Here it is necessary to be cautious about overloading the narrowly economic argument, and probably a large part of the explanation of the lack of innovational activity in the underdeveloped country is due to social and cultural matters to be discussed in Section VII.

IV. Employment

The growth process, as described in previous chapters, was consistent with the full utilization of all resources, though the actual achievement through time of full employment of capital and labor was considered most unlikely because of changes in the composition of demand, the partial fixity of existing physical capital, and the slow adaptation of labor. The more likely condition then for a growing economy is some excess capacity (in the sense that there are physically usable goods that have not been made obsolete by new technology) that cannot be pulled into use by increasing total demand or by changes in relative prices. With this important qualification in mind, it may be said that part of the growth process as described involves continuous full or nearly full utilization of capacity. This is achieved by virtue of the existence of alternative techniques of production in all sectors, changing factor prices, changing composition of demand, possibly changing technology, and, of course, a mechanism by which aggregate demand and supply are brought into equality. Although the topic is controversial, there is considerable evidence to suggest that there is underutilization of labor particularly and even of capital in the underdeveloped country. The purpose of this section is to examine the issues involved concerning the extent to which resources are fully employed in the kind of economy being described.

First, consider the unemployment of labor. The proposition that the quantity of labor is so excessive relative to other inputs that its marginal product is zero is both widely held and widely denied. If the marginal product of labor is zero, then the conditions stated above for full employment are not sufficient as labor would not be employed if its product were zero (even if the wage were zero). Indeed, the only solution is further accumulation of other inputs. It is easy to see that if there is only one technique of production for each product, continual full employment when rates of increase in the factors are not the same can only be achieved by very rigorous assumptions as to changing composition of demand or the behavior of technology. As has been argued, neither required assumption about demand or technology is remotely applicable to the low income areas.

It is correct to assume, however, that there are several techniques available and therefore substitution possible. If the factor combination falls between Ray *A* and the abscissa of Diagram IV, all of the labor cannot be employed due to an inadequate supply of capital. Therefore, even with several techniques available, there is no assurance that full employment of labor is technologically possible. Of equal importance with the question of alternative techniques is the question of the adjustment of relative prices of capital and labor to reflect their true opportunity costs, i.e., their marginal productivities. The discussion of growth in Chapters 3 and 4 placed great emphasis on both factor prices and product prices equalling opportunity costs. Such equality is not a common characteristic of those economies with more developed market mechanisms than the underdeveloped country, and there are several reasons to doubt the efficacy of the market mechanism in this regard in the latter countries.

In the first place, wage rates in a large part of the economy approach subsistence levels, and to drive them below this level is difficult indeed. The organization of much of subsistence farming is such that the product available to the workers is divided among all the people involved, more or less irrespective of individual contributions to output. If a person receives an income of a given magnitude from his family or village in the form of food, a place to live, and clothes to wear, then he has no concern for nor is he capable of exercising much influence on the wage rate. In this sector, at any rate, there is no automatic mechanism to drive the wage rate down below something approximating an average subsistence wage, and there is no reason to assume this wage to be the marginal product of labor. In most instances, all the available labor is thrown into service, and if the supply of land and capital is "enough," then this labor is fully employed. But there is no necessity for this to be the case. There does not seem to be conscious substituting of capital for labor, but rather the simple question of whether there is enough work to go around.

In commercial farming and in industry, the picture is somewhat different, and here the price of capital is also relevant. There is little of share-the-work arrangement here, and the unemployed or less than fully employed are cared for either by direct charity or via the service industries previously described. There is not much evidence of a bidding down of wages and thereby increasing the labor intensity of production. The chief question about capital has to do with the rate of interest, and in most countries there are arrangements and policies that tend to keep the rates of interest below their "equilibrium" level, i.e., below the level that equates supply and demand for loanable funds at maximum output. These rates are chiefly those charged by government lending agencies, and such a policy is advanced as a device to encourage certain types of investment. In this part of the capital market, the price of capital is below its market clearing price. This means that an additional rationing device is necessary, but more importantly it means that the entrepreneurs find it profitable to use "too much capital" relative to its opportunity cost to the economy as a whole. The consequence of this second result is of course that resources are not allocated in the manner that will maximize output, or that makes full use of available resources. By definition, if "too much" capital is used in the input mix, then some labor must be idle or engaged in tasks where its productivity is less than it would be in other sectors.

Reference may also be made to the service activities described earlier. The discussion in Section I outlined the nature of these activities and suggested that not only was productivity very low among such workers, but also that they were so employed because of lack of alternative employment opportunities. Somewhat in the same vein is a situation in which idle labor is not used even though there are things that it might do. This is especially the case in rural, agricultural areas. The most casual (and the most careful) observation suggests many ways that life in the rural areas of underdeveloped countries could be made vastly more satisfying with existing factor supplies if some form of leadership and initiative were present to help get things under way, and help people to appreciate how things may be done with what is now available. This is a particularly relevant point in areas where seasonal demand for labor exhausts the supply, but there is much idle time through most of the year. A further reason, then, for expecting idle labor resources is simply the lack of a capacity to see how a resource may be used to improve living conditions, or how to mobilize it for such use. Also in many instances some work is possible—e.g., on very poor land—but the returns are so low that workers do not deem the reward worth the effort.

The upshot seems to be that in both subsistence farming and manufacturing there are technological constraints on achieving full employment, and reasons for doubting the efficacy of the market mechanism in bringing about the equality between factor prices and economy-wide opportunity costs. With respect to the latter, the market tends to keep wages "too" high and capital costs "too" low. With respect to technology, in some instances at least, substitution between labor and land is not adequate to make full use of all labor even if wage rates fell to zero. Further, there are reasons to believe that labor is idle not only because of these factors, but also because there is lacking in the system insight and understanding of what can be done with available resources to make life somewhat better. Does all this mean that there is excess labor—disguised and undisguised unemployment—in the sense that some labor could be reallocated without reducing the present level of output? The answer is yes. It is to be emphasized, however, that this labor force is not lined up, ready to be pulled into action at a moment's notice. What it does mean is that the system has evolved in such a manner that it makes less than maximum use of what it has. It also means that there *are* labor resources available that can be used for capital formation or other things without reducing current output *if* production is reorganized, *if* most people work more than they work now, and *if* resources—especially entrepreneurship—are found to call them into being. These *if's* are large ones. For example, organizational changes may include changes in the size of land holdings, and to effect this requires far-reaching changes in the social organization of the community. It will be argued later that the most effective way of doing this is to strengthen strongly the demand for labor, but this is *not* to say the explanation of unemployed labor is oversaving.

Consider now capital. Despite the factor supply situation in the underdeveloped country there is abundant evidence that the capital stock is not being fully utilized. The reasons are different from those given in previous chapters as to why such may be the case in a growing economy, although one does frequently find underutilized capital in the export sector because of changing demand abroad. One very simple set of reasons has to do merely with extra work shifts. Physical capital is generally—there are notable exceptions—not used as intensively as complementary inputs would permit. This is due chiefly to barriers against night work, and the like that seem to be more imagined than real.

More important, from an analytical point of view, is unused capacity due to bottleneck supply problems, i.e., specific input shortages. Thus a mill may be ready for production, and not be able to go at full speed because transportation facilities are inadequate to bring in an adequate flow of raw materials, power is insufficient, or imported spare parts are not available and so on. To pinpoint the exact cause of this difficulty is not easy because the causes vary from time to time and place to place, but there is no doubt that it is an important source of underutilization of expensive capital equipment. In general, the cause may be that the economy has failed to solve the interdependence problem as it was discussed in Chapter 4. To some extent, of course, lags cannot be avoided, and discontinuities may dictate building ahead of the market. Some losses due to these causes are inevitable, but the situation in many countries suggests that the difficulty is more fundamental than this. Where planning is widespread, the blame may be placed (to a large degree) on poor planning, and on the failure of the price system to work effectively. The exploitation of this source of supply again requires an attack on the organization of the economy rather than simply on aggregate spending.

Capital like labor (but to a much less extent) is not fully utilized due to organizational matters, and matters connected with the allocation mechanism in the economy. Here is a source of strength and evidence of a major problem.

V. The Productive Process

Given this description of the kind of economic activity that characterizes the nongrowing economy, the relative supplies of the inputs, the state of technology, and the underutilization of resources, what can be said about the productive process in general as it takes place in an economy of this type? There are several things that are worth a specific comment, and although they are all interrelated it will again facilitate discussion to treat them separately.

A. DIVISION OF LABOR

Consider first the division of labor. A "high" degree of division of labor means a high degree of specialization within a given enterprise and within the economy as a whole. Within the single enterprise this means that the individual worker performs a limited number of activities, and consequently the product must pass through many hands before it is completed.

At the opposite end, a low degree of division of labor means that each worker performs many varieties of activities at all stages in the productive process. The rewards of a high degree of division of labor are well known: development of skill, no time or energy lost shifting from one job to another, and a greater likelihood of technological discovery. Where the division of labor is small these advantages are absent. Thus, a country with a "high" degree of specialization would tend to have lower costs and possibly a higher rate of innovation than would a country with a "low" degree of specialization.

The usual statement is to relate the extent of the division of labor to the size of the market; the size of the market is small in the low income country so the division of labor is strictly limited. The size of the market is considered later, but first, some other factors bearing on the division of labor are discussed.

The division of labor is not costless to bring about or to maintain, no matter what the size of the market may be. In particular, the establishment of the facilities necessary for a division of labor in the economy as a whole—such things as transportation and communication facilities, financial arrangements, trained labor, and so on—may be very costly in terms of the use of scarce resources. Once this basic set of capital goods is in place, then costs associated with the division of labor are likely to be much reduced. Also an effective division of labor requires considerable coordination of production in separate areas, and imposes a more difficult task of organization and management than is the case when most workers perform a variety of tasks. Attention has already been called to the existence of unused capacity in the system because of failure to solve the interdependence problem, and now it may be added that a widespread division of labor adds to the interdependence problems.

Now consider the size of the market as it relates to the division of labor. If the market is "small" the demand for any one product is "small," and output cannot be absorbed on a large scale. The result is that demand for single products is so fragmented, and is so limited that resources cannot be allocated exclusively to the production of single products or parts of single products. For if this were to occur, output would be so great relative to the level of demand that prices would fall below costs. As income increases, however, demand for individual products will rise, and this in turn will permit, to an increasing extent, the limiting of activity of a given amount of labor to narrowly defined jobs, i.e., will permit an increasing amount of division of labor. In more general terms, then, it may be said that the low income economy is unable to exploit certain production advantages that are inherent in the production process simply because total demand for output is too low. Immediately, however, it is evident that international trade has to be mentioned. Obviously the world market is large enough for many products, and in some sectors of the economy, division of labor is made possible by reliance on foreign trade. Why is not the same true for the entire economy? The answer to this question is essentially the same as that given to the similar question asked in Section I, namely, institutional and organizational difficulties that impede full exploitation of opportunities provided by foreign trade.

There can be little doubt that the division of labor in the productive process is limited compared to that in the richer countries. On the other hand, an important qualification is necessary. In some parts of the system, division of labor is carried to an extreme that is not approached in the richer countries. Particularly in service activities does one find a very sharp and very fine division of labor. The explanation of this is implied in what was said earlier about the rationale of the existence of these sectors. Individuals seeking to find a niche for themselves in the production activity of the community are able only to do this in a small and insignificant way. The result is a large number of activities that are meant to mesh in some way or another with the rest of the economy. It is doubtful that any of the advantages that Adam Smith and his successors have attributed to the division of labor flow from this particular type. Indeed the exact opposite is the case, as there results considerable underutilization of capacity.

B. The Size of the Market

Since the size of the market is determined by the size of income, and the latter is, by definition, low, then the size of the market is small. The problem here is to examine some of the implications of this statement other than that associated with the division of labor. In some of the larger countries, per capita income is very low but the size of the population is great enough that the total market for some products is very large. The most obvious example is India with a per capita income of perhaps $70 but a total national income of around 30–35 billion dollars. Her total market, then, is larger than that of a number of Western European countries or of Australia or New Zealand where one does not think of the market as being small. Similar comparisons would show that other low income nations with large populations have a total income larger than smaller rich countries. It is no problem to explain why the market for *some* products, e.g., television is much greater in Australia. The problem here is limited to those products for which there is a mass consumption market. Why, then, does market size seem to be a problem in India but not in the Netherlands or Australia or even Italy?

The question suggests that size of market is dependent upon things other than total national income. The answer seems to be found in the fact there are few national markets in the typical low income country, and few instances in which a single firm or small group of firms supply the total output of a particular product to the entire economy. The reason for this is partly due to the nature of the products that are produced and the extent of household self-sufficiency, but more importantly it is found in the fact that the conditions for a nationwide market do not exist. This latter has to do with transportation, communications, and this sort of thing, but it also has to do with the heavy dependence on subsistence farming, limited contact among groups in different parts of the country, and frequently divergent consumption habits. The conclusion seems to be then that not only is the market small because of a low level of income, it is also a divided or chopped-up market that does not lend itself to full exploitation by any one producer. Thus, the market is generally limited geographically as well as in terms of the level of income.

There are numerous implications of this characteristic that will emerge as the discussion proceeds. The most important of these has to do with the productivity of the resources already available, and with the rate of capital formation and the introduction of new technology.

C. The Price System

In the growth process discussed earlier, considerable importance was placed on the pricing mechanism as both an allocation mechanism and as the determinant of the distribution of the product. Emphasis was placed on achievement of the equality between the marginal product of each factor and its price and the applicability of Expression 11 in Chapter 4 $(P_j = l_j P_l + k_j P_k + \Sigma\, a_{ij} P_i)$. In Chapter 5, some of the problems of achieving this pricing objective in a growing economy were examined. The problems in this area are even more complex for the underdeveloped country, and it is well to consider the issue explicitly.

The fact that a significant part of the rural economy makes minimum use of money and monetary transactions inhibits any sort of pricing system from working at all. But the difficulties are more far reaching than this, and if the price system is ineffective over much of the economy how then are the problems solved that a price system is meant to solve. In a large part of many underdeveloped countries, there is little reliance on achievement as the procedure for acquiring economic goods, and goods are allocated to the various agents of the society more nearly on the basis of their position in the society rather than on the basis of what the various agents contribute. In a similar fashion, the allocation of jobs is done chiefly on the basis of social heirarchy (or at least must be consistent with the social hierarchy) rather than primarily on the basis of efficiency in performing tasks. To the extent that this characteristic is applicable to an economy, the allocation of available resources—especially labor—in a way that will maximize output will be purely accidental. If certain jobs in the system are available only to a given social category, then interjob mobility is limited to movement within the eligible group, and workers in other social groups are automatically excluded from consideration. The result is a general inability of the market mechanism to allocate existing resources in such a way as to achieve the maximum output from these resources, and both the allocation of resources and the distribution of the product rest to a significant degree on noneconomic considerations. One may summarize by stating that the institutional arrangements operating on the allocation and distribution mechanism are strong enough to modify to a relevant extent a price mechanism effect, and are generally inconsistent with the results of the effective operation of a price mechanism.

There is, however, danger of making too strong a statement. In most instances the recipient of a share of output performs some function. Thus, the landlord receives a large share of output by virtue of his position in the heirarchy, but also he is the owner of what are often the chief scarce resources—land and credit—and labor's product in agriculture, as previously discussed, is distressingly low. The same sort of reasoning applies elsewhere in the economy. The conclusion seems to be that although the allocation and distribution difficulties imposed by the dominating position of the institutional factors are severe, the more fundamental difficulty arises from the obstacles these same institutional arrangements create for change. Where the kind of price system envisaged for the growing economy not only facilitates the adaptation of the economy to changing opportunities for continuing growth, but indeed encourages it, the kind of arrangement just described inhibits this adaptation process. Therefore, the chief characteristic that will be relevant for later analysis is not so much the deviation from optimal allocation that the institutional arrangements dictate (although this is important), but rather the fact that these arrangements tend to prevent the adjustments necessary to capitalize on newly emerging opportunities.

In parts of the system this description is hardly applicable. In urban centered industrial activity, prices do function in a manner that approximates that in most western countries. The major qualification to this is the employment of individuals to perform services, the importance of which may surely be questioned: door openers, tea bearers, messengers, and so on. Wage rates do perhaps approximate the product of the laborer employed directly in production activity. Profit rates are frequently higher than one suspects the marginal product of capital warrants, a result emerging from the existence of imperfect capital markets. This too must be qualified because of the frequent inclusion in the profit category of payments for entrepreneurial and managerial services, the "marginal product" of which is surely quite high. A more important source of problems is probably a misuse of foreign exchange, but this can hardly be attributed to the market mechanism because foreign exchange policy almost always encourages the use of "too many imports," i.e., the price of foreign exchange tends to understate the value of resources going into earning it. This, however, is the consequence of a particular policy rather than an inherent characteristic of the economy.

The general picture, then, is one in which a very large sector of the economy is more or less insulated from the pricing system by the institutional structure that has grown up as an essential part of the nongrowing, low income society. At the same time there exists a relatively small industrial sector which, with some exceptions, is generally consistent with a pricing system. Superimposed on this picture is a set of government controls and policies that interfere, or seek to interfere, with the outcome of the process in a variety of ways. The net effect of such controls is difficult to state in a general way except possibly for one point: the government probably overestimates its capacity to implement any particular policy or set of controls. The discussion of what the government can do will be part of the story as the later argument develops.

Finally, financial institutions are given consideration. The banking system though not highly developed is usually not a major growth bottleneck. For example, the description just given of the largely non-monetized, rural sector is not so much the result of an inadequate banking system as it is the cause of it. Here emphasis is placed on the activities of the banks. To a very large degree, the private banks are oriented toward financing trade rather than production, and loans are chiefly short-term loans designed to carry a merchant while he conducts his trading operations. In particular, long-term, industrial loans by a private bank are unusual, and problems connected with "finance" often emerge to thwart the entrepreneur who may have a legitimate project of this type. These latter difficulties apply not only to new men seeking entry, but also to established firms seeking expansion. The source of this characteristic of the banking institutions is to be found largely in the nature of the community that it serves. The demand for commercial loans greatly exceeds the demand for production loans, the former loans are much safer than the latter, and rates of interest are probably higher than could be charged on production loans and secure any applicants at all. The task of providing the finance for investment undertakings is one in which the government's action may be crucial.

Banks are not the only source of financing however, and the moneylender in rural areas—not infrequently a landlord—is a major part of the financial system. The small farmer usually relies on such a source for the financing of his crop and for a range of consumption loans to which a poverty stricken community must have access. That the moneylender fills a need cannot be denied, and that he does it in a manner that penalizes the farmer also cannot be denied. The result is an institutional arrangement that is a significant part of the system at the same time that it is an obstacle to the system realizing its full potential. The mere replacement of the moneylender by a strictly supervised commercial bank is not a sufficient condition to change much of anything.

Attention has already been called to the tendency of government lending offices to charge interest rates that are below any sort of equilibrium rate. Commercial bank rates are much higher, and in general one rarely finds a commercial bank whose ability to grant loans is exhausted or even nearly so. One may conclude that their rates—or other criteria for lending —rule out potential borrowers beyond that called for by an effort to equate demand for their loanable funds with their supply. Perhaps a simple explanation in terms of security, safety, and costs of loans is all that is required of this phenomenon. The interest rates on consumption and "crop" loans by the rural moneylenders vary widely, and the evidence suggests that they run extremely high. To the extent that this is not a form of the monopolistic exploitation of a high time preference, it is a payment for the high risk involved in such loans.

As to monetary policy, the chief weapon is probably simply control over the money supply and direct control over lending decisions. There is little evidence of manipulation of interest rates or open market operations as an effective tool, and rarely do changes in reserve requirements—even where ostensibly a part of the repertory of policy weapons—have much effect. The most serious result of this is the uneconomic rate of interest on the use of capital. There can be little doubt that the prevalance of a rate of interest below that justified by the productivity of capital on productive loans (plus an undervaluation of imports) and wage rates above the productivity of labor result in a less than optimal combination of inputs in newly created production enterprises. It will be argued later that the best attack on this problem is—for a variety of reasons—an attack on wage rates.

VI. Population

The "population problem" in the nongrowing economy is one of great importance, and arises out of the particular population structure that exists in this kind of economy. The key feature of this population structure is the high growth potential of the population. This growth potential arises from the existence of a birth rate of about 40 or 45 per thousand compared to a figure of below 20 for most European countries. If the death rate is only slightly less, the increase in population is low, perhaps even below 1 per cent. However, the death rate can be reduced very rapidly and, in many instances, quite inexpensively by control of epidemics, elimination of widespread disease (e.g., malaria), control of famine, and so on. Also as water supplies, sanitation facilities, clothing, and the like improve, the death rate can be reduced even more. The birth rate, however, is susceptible to no such easy and quick reduction, and obviously a sharp reduction in the death rate while the birth rate remains high will result in a sharp increase in the rate of growth of population. It is evident, then, that the solution to this "population problem" is to be found in understanding the determinants of the birth rate.

Another important characteristic of the population structure is its age distribution. A much larger proportion of the population of an underdeveloped country is under 15 years of age than is the case in the richer countries. Thus, the pool of the under 15 age group is large, but a relatively small part of this pool flows into the older age groups. There are two important consequences of this situation insofar as the analysis here is concerned. In the first place, it means that the labor force-population ratio is smaller than in the growing economy. This, in turn, means that the working population must support a larger number relative to its size than is the case in the economy with a low death rate and an older age structure.

In the second place, more importantly, the age composition affects the composition of expenditure with respect to its capacity creating effects. It can easily be seen that expenditures made to care for a child from birth to age ten or older may be thought of as an investment with a long gestation period. If the child dies at the age of ten, then this investment never bears fruit, and the resources used to maintain the child these years are lost. If the child lives and enters the producing age group, then his maintenance "investment" yields a return. The high infant and child mortality rate then results in a significant proportion of total expenditures being used in a manner that, from the limited standpoint of increasing the productive capacity of the society, yields no return.

The population characteristic of the low income country may be summarized as follows: it is a high-growth potential population because the high death rate responds so readily to a variety of easily available methods of control of disease and famine, and reduction in the high birth rate does not occur equally rapidly. Also the age structure of the population places a heavier burden on the economy than is the case in a country with a lower birth rate. These various aspects of the population structure, and some policy implications are fully examined in Chapter 14.

VII. Social and Institutional Setting

Throughout the preceding six sections of this chapter frequent references have been made to particular characteristics of the social environment within which the economy functions. The nature of this environment is to be considered explicitly for, as argued in Chapter 1 and as is clear from the discussion in this chapter, much of the explanation of underdevelopment is to be found in these "noneconomic" characteristics. To do this is a major task because there is no obvious stopping point, and one could consider virtually an unlimited number of facets of the community. The guideline to be followed is to concentrate on those attributes that appear to be most relevant to the growth process as already oulined, and to explain some of the other characteristics of the economy that have been identified in the other sections of this chapter. It is convenient to divide the discussion into subheadings for Social Organization, Economizing Attitudes, and Entrepreneurial Talent.

A. Social Organization

Under this general heading there are several things to note. In the first place the society is predominantly rural. In particular the society may be thought of as made up chiefly of small agricultural villages that are more or less isolated from each other. In these circumstances there is little contact among peoples of diverse origin, habits, ways of thought, or ways of earning a living. Therefore the isolation is more than a physical one; it is primarily and most importantly an isolation from new and/or different ideas about how to approach the problems of living. Since the villages are small and isolated, it is not surprising that a routine has been established in almost all areas of activity. This routine repeats itself with no source of interruption, and no reason for change. Consequently, a traditionalistic approach to all social activity in general and to economic activity in particular is established, and little effort is made or understood as appropriate to alter the existing tradition. Included in this tradition are a number of aspects pertinent to the general question of growth.

Family ties are very strong, and family is interpreted in a manner that is generally very inclusive. This has several consequences of importance to the development question. It creates a barrier of immense proportions against the mobility of workers. Workers are most reluctant to leave the areas in which they were born and raised, and if they do leave they find it very easy to return and very difficult to become attached to new surroundings. The strong and extended family ties also mean that each member of the family has responsibility toward the other members. This is true to the extent that unemployed workers (and lazy ones) are taken care of by other members of the family. This kind of family pension system acts as a barrier to mobility, and to a lesser extent to effort. Especially negatively affected are the incentives to undertake *new* activities. The high priority on family solidarity also reflects itself in large expenditures on weddings, funerals, and other family occasions. This evidently means that some expenditure not directly required for consumption is not used in a way that increases the capacity of the economy.

Furthermore, the loyalty to the extended family often results in widespread nepotism. If a relative has to be supported whether or not he works, it is simpler to give him a job regardless of his productivity. Under these conditions, it is more or less accidental if the best equipped person available is employed in a given job. Indeed it may be that not even the best equipped relative is given the job, but merely the closest. Finally, the family system is one—there are others—reason why in these societies, reward is unrelated to effort. This separation of income from effort is surely one of the most strategic social factors accounting for the adverse behavior of many economic agents, and a careful interpretation of this point is given in the following discussion.

The extended family system is not, however, an anachronism serving no useful function. It is not only a form of insurance against catastrophe, it supplies other needs as well, especially those connected with security, entertainment, discipline, and continuity that in a low income, risk-filled economy are so essential. The extended family system is a typical example of a characteristic of the underdeveloped economy that will often be met: it is at one and the same time a major obstacle to growth, and it serves as a built-in social security system for which no alternative institution exists.

In addition to a strong, extended family system, the society may be characterized by a more general caste system. Such a caste system does not have to be of the iron-clad variety that is associated with earlier days in India, but one that constitutes a bottleneck to movement of individuals up the social and economic ladder. This is further expression of the traditionalistic approach to all problems. Given an existing stratification according to income, land holdings, occupation, and so on, problems are in effect solved by simply carrying on in the same routine that was observed as the generation was growing up. Movement among social and economic levels is effectively discouraged or more accurately not recognized as a possibility.

In terms of income distribution there is one distinct characteristic of considerable importance. There is only a very small middle income group: there are the very rich, a very small minority of the population, and the very poor, a huge majority of the population. This situation, explainable principally in terms of land ownership, tends to discourage effort in two ways. First of all, it is almost impossible to move from the poor to the rich class. With a more or less continuous graduation from poor to rich, it is not so discouragingly hopeless that no effort is made to move up a notch or so. Where there are no in-between notches, however, the challenge is virtually nonexistent. For here as the worker is not confronted with opportunities that are within his capacity to exploit, often no effort at all is made. This is especially true in areas where land ownership is the key to wealth.

The second point in this connection has to do once more with the relationship between reward and effort. To the extent that workers feel that they (or someone that they recognize as a legitimate claimant) do not receive their "just" share of the product, effort is discouraged. The great wealth of a few seems to suggest this to many, consequently increased productive activity carries little attraction. The example often cited is that increases in agricultural productivity is discouraged because so much goes to the landlord, that the peasant cultivator finds little left over to reward him for his efforts.

Most traditionalistic societies give evidence of stratification in some form or another. The one based on income distribution lends itself most satisfactorily to the tools of the economist, and will be examined in some detail, but it may not be the most important barrier to mobility and the exploitation of economic opportunities. The stratification and rigidity created by religious attitudes, racial feelings, education, and so on may be of equal importance and more intractable to economic policy.

Although the preceding discussion emphasizes that the society is predominantly rural, this does not mean that there are *no* cities in such areas. Rather what is meant is that the economic life of the society is only slightly oriented around urban industrial centers. Urban areas that do exist serve more as cultural, religious, and government centers than as the hub of the economic machine. This is less true for those coastal cities that serve as main routes for international trade, but this segment of most of the cities is small relative to the city as a whole, and has no great impact on urban life in general. Even where urban population may be increasing in relation to that in rural areas, it is due chiefly to a push out of the latter regions rather than a pull into the former. There is little evidence that the urban areas in the contemporary underdeveloped country serve as the same kind of center of dynamic economic activity as they did (and continue to do) in countries that began their growth much earlier and under different circumstances. Merely pushing people out of the isolated rural villages into cities by means of hunger or unemployment does not mean that they move into an environment that encourages growth.

Still the urban centers are important in the initial conditions. The industrial activity is for the most part located in them, and generally a more aggressive and alert-minded people inhabit them compared to the rural populace. Similarly, the city provides, almost by definition, much wider contacts among diverse groups and has more frequent contact with foreign ideas and material things. For example, newspapers and radio are found in cities and are uncommon in the rural areas.

B. Economizing Attitudes

Perhaps the clearest notion of an "economizing attitude" has to do with the consciousness and rationality with which decisions are made as to economic behavior. It implies that economic agents appraise a situation, and then choose the action that is most nearly consistent with their particular objectives. Thus economizing means choice, conscious choice, and implies that individuals, firms, and households are free enough from custom, routine, and tradition to make a choice. Probably in no society is there complete freedom (from the bonds of social custom) to choose and economic rationality is usually tempered by considerations having to do with one's environment. But there are greater and lesser degrees, and it is helpful to distinguish between an economy that is largely traditionalistic and one that is largely choice making. Except for a noteworthy qualification to be emphasized in this explanation, the kind of social order that is being described may be classified as traditionalistic rather than choice making. This particular characteristic is reflected in many ways throughout the system.

In a general way, it is reflected most importantly in the prevailing attitude that it is impossible to overcome the difficulties confronting the people, i.e., in the attitude that it is impossible to exercise control over nature so that growth can be achieved: the idea of progress is lacking. If it is hopeless then it is useless to try, and effort is wasted. This attitude may be explained by an appeal to religious convictions or a fatalistic philosophy, but perhaps the most satisfactory explanation is simply the mere lack of precedent. Growth has not occurred over such a long interval of time that prevailing opinion has accepted the view that it is impossible. To overcome this pessimistic point of view, obviously the precedent must be broken. To create an attitude that growth is possible, growth must occur. It would appear as simple—and as difficult—as that.

The absence of the idea of progress as well as low incomes also has an effect on the time horizon of the individual and the investor, and so on their accumulation habits. Apart from the profit rate behavior and from the capacity to save, some disincentive to save or to accumulate exists simply because there seems little purpose for saving. Many motives for saving and investing are present, but all of them involve some expectations about the future. If incomes are near subsistence level, it is easy to understand why a person is not very concerned about the situation a few years hence; he is more concerned with his day-to-day existence. It must be noted that experiences of frequent difficulties—crop failures, floods, illness, and the like —encourage saving to survive these difficulties. Thus one may expect that if an income unexpectedly increases for some reason or other, the peasant will tend to save a large proportion. But this is rainy day saving, and usually is matched by dissaving somewhere in the economy.

Even where income is sufficient so that saving and accumulation as a routine are physically possible, such activity requires some expectation and concern about the future, and an attitude that something can be done to affect the outcome of the future. In particular, it requires that the accumulator believes that his economic status can be improved by a planned investment program. Consequently, resources available for investment are frequently put into highly speculative, quick maturing schemes that contribute little to the productive capacity of the economy. Once again, it seems that concrete evidence must show that investment in productive capital will be a remunerative undertaking over an extended period of time before any savings will be forthcoming on a substantial scale, even from those who have resources available.

Traditionalism also expresses itself in the prevailing attitudes toward technological innovations. Any new technological process involves in some very real sense a process of acculturation. Modern techniques are rarely, if ever, introduced piecemeal, but almost always there are required many corollary changes in the habits and routines of the affected areas. To incorporate into the economy a new way of conducting the production of an old product or the introduction of a new product requires some adjustment, some modification in traditional activity. Where traditions are strong and firmly entrenched, the introduction of a new technology is likely to face a very high barrier indeed. Not only then is technology of an ancient and unproductive kind, but there are also effective obstacles to the development or the borrowing of an improved technology. In a society with an unchanging technology, a worker does as his father and grandfather did; in a society where technology is constantly changing, a worker cannot even do as he himself did a few years earlier. Evidently then, in a society that is bound by tradition, technological change as a continuing, established part of the economic routine is not possible, and at best can occur only sporadically, and in particular places at particular times.

Further, if the tradition oriented economy acts as an obstacle to the introduction of new technology, then it is also to be expected that it will create an atmosphere that is alien to the development of an indigenous source of technological change.

The work habits of the labor force are to some degree affected by this traditionalism. The workers' limited horizon both as to time and as to geography means that their understanding of what extra income can do for them is also thereby limited. Workers may therefore tend to work to the extent necessary to meet the needs that they are aware of, and then quit without regard to wage rates and employment opportunities. The backward-bending supply of labor due to this kind of attitude is perhaps more important for what it represents than for what it is, as there are numerous ways of straightening it. It seems due neither to laziness nor to a high premium on leisure, but rather to a narrow and tradition-determined attitude toward the nature of work and the rewards it can bring.

Along with the possibility of a backward-bending supply curve, another key characteristic of the labor force is its more or less haphazard work habits. The emphasis on subsistence farming and the lack of interdependence in the economy mean that many individual workers are able to choose their own pattern of work. The kind of worker discipline that is associated with work, such as factory work that requires the meshing with other work, is generally lacking. The labor force is not only unskilled in the sense that the workers do not know how to operate particular kinds of machines, but is untrained in the much more fundamental sense of being unacquainted with and alien to the routine required of labor if a steady flow of labor services are to be forthcoming. These considerations impose further constraints on the "disguised unemployment" issue. Even in those instances where labor can be removed from agriculture without significantly reducing output, the attitudes and work habits of this labor may be such as to make it extremely difficult to use effectively in other activities requiring more discipline and more concentration than does the kind of agriculture to which it is currently attached. This does not mean that these laborers are unskilled and unable to learn because, in most instances, the technical problem of learning to operate a machine is not the fundamental difficulty.

On the other hand, most economic agents in the kind of society being discussed here are extremely cost, price, and money conscious and do respond in one way or another to economic incentives. The evidence to support this assertion reflects itself in a variety of ways. The extent to which prices vary, depending on the buyer, is a simple example. The common practice of bargaining over any and all prices is an effort by the seller to scoop out the total area under the demand curve confronting him. There are also numerous examples of wage bargainings and full economic exploitation where possible. More important than this type of example is recognizing that the more one observes such an economy, the more one sees an inherent rationale in it. Refusals to adopt new processes, to employ new techniques, or to try new diets can frequently—indeed usually—be traced to a perfectly satisfactory economic rationale. It does seem clear that when the peasant farmer or the small scale industrialist is convinced that he will profit from a change that is possible for him to make, he is not only willing, but eager to make the change. What frequently meets the outsider's eye and dominates his thinking are major differences between the customs of rich and poor countries—e.g., the role of women—and from such observations it is easy to conclude that the individual economic agent of the poor country is not really interested in profit maximizing, in maximum wages, or in material well being. This is surely not the case.

There is little to convince one that the citizen of the poor country is very much different from the citizen of the rich, except that he is much poorer and lives among people who are and always have been much poorer. What is different are the social institutions that have evolved in the low income, nongrowing society. Because they have evolved to help alleviate the distresses of extreme, mass poverty, it is not surprising that they are frequently alien to growth. That the distinction is in the organization of society and not in the personal, innate characteristics of the individual is an important distinction, for if the economic agents were otherwise, the whole notion of economic development would necessarily rest on principles other than those that the economist is equipped to clarify.

C. ENTREPRENEURSHIP

It is useful to give a more specific interpretation of entrepreneurship. In the chapters describing the growth process, the tasks of the entrepreneur had not only to do with innovations, but also with understanding and implementing the adjustments that are required of the producing units as the capital-labor ratio rises, technology improves, and the composition of demand changes. The entrepreneur must do more than merely adjust, he must appreciate the opportunities that are inherent in a given situation, and he must be able to make opportunities out of a given situation. In this chapter, the assertion was made that the supply of entrepreneurial talent relative to the labor force was less than in the richer countries. This fact was introduced to explain several things, low rate of capital formation and primitive technology among others. The problem now is to examine briefly the factors that account for this situation with respect to the entrepreneur.

One can assume that entrepreneurship must be limited or otherwise the preceding description of the underdeveloped country could not hold, and therefore the entrepreneur supply situation emerges from the nature of the overall social and economic situation. It has been noted that the social organization and the factor endowment of the country militate against change, and that the resources are hardly adequate for risk taking. Similarly, the strong hold that the traditional organization of society imposes on the individual limits his freedom to try new methods, or limits the likelihood of success if new methods are tried. The qualities that entrepreneurs should possess include: open mindedness, unwillingness to rely on socially given doctrines; capacity to see or imagine configurations other than those inherited; mental and emotional detachment from immediate surroundings; self confidence, an optimism that things can be made better. It is evident that these attributes are unlikely to appear often in the personality and attitudes of individuals of the population of the representative underdeveloped, nongrowing economy, and indeed that individuals with these attributes are likely to be alienated from the society.

It would be unusual if such a society never produced any individuals who met the requirements just listed. If these attributes are possessed, they may be channeled into areas that are consistent with the existing order. The most obvious of the latter has to do with acquiring and holding land. One of the most important characteristics of low income areas is that the landlord class is in a strong position, but that it also is at the heart of the traditionalism of the system. Landlords are, however, usually alert and informed, but their knowledge and position are not used to introduce newness into the system, but rather to maintain their strong position in the system. In a similar way merchants—especially merchants dealing in imports and exports—are in possession of talents approaching those of the entrepreneur, but such talents are used rather for trading than for production. Importing in most countries is a highly lucrative business, and the talent attracted into it frequently is comparable to those of the entrepreneurs. Although less important quantitatively, a great variety of illicit businesses (money changing, smuggling, and the like) that operate rather openly here and there take some toll of talented manpower.

One might argue that entrepreneurial capacity as a personality characteristic is distributed in the underdeveloped country in about the same manner that it is in rich countries. The difference is that the organization of the society in the former country is uncongenial to potential entrepreneurs' becoming actual entrepreneurs, while in the latter countries the opposite is the case. This is important because it may be that the best approach to overcoming the difficulty is by exploiting the talent that is there, rather than undertaking the creation (or importation) of new talent, but consideration is given these matters in Chapter 13.

An answer to the entrepreneurship problem in terms of government ownership and operation is not an answer at all. Government bureaucrats are part of the society, just as are private bureaucrats, and are subject to the same limitations, handicaps, pressures, and inhibitions as are individuals in the private sector. Some things (e.g., access to finance) may be easier, but the entrepreneurial problem is much more fundamental than simply the division of labor between the public and private sectors.

VIII. Conclusion

The purpose of this chapter has been to examine the characteristics of the low income, nongrowing economy, and to provide an argument accounting for these characteristics. Not all characteristics could be considered, and only those relating to economic growth as that process has been described in Chapters 2 through 6 were introduced. Evidently a different analysis of growth would have included a different set of characteristics of underdevelopment. The picture that emerges is extremely complex. No single "cause" of underdevelopment has been isolated, and no single clue to its elimination found. Some of the features of underdevelopment do contribute to its existence, and some are the results of its existence, and still others contribute to preventing its elimination. The major emphasis is on the existence of a general consistency with nongrowth at the same time that sources of deviationism, sources of potential inconsistency with this underdevelopment, can be found. For example, it was argued that the general social environment was for the most part inconsistent with the emergence of a large, strong entrepreneurial class, while at the same time there was evidence that some such talent did exist, but was usually shunted into unproductive activity. Both notions are important for policy purposes.

The fact that most of the characteristics of the system were consistent with the general state of low and nongrowing *per capita* income is important in a variety of ways. Principally it means that attacks on specific problems may not work well because to eliminate one problem without eliminating a whole range may not be possible. The role of landlords provides a typical example. To parcel out titles to plots of land to individual peasants who have no access to credit, seeds, fertilizer, or water except from their landlord will surely create nothing but chaos. This consistency notion also has a favorable side in the sense that eliminating one problem may eliminate the need for a particular growth-inhibiting institution, technique, or action. For example, an effective subsidy and tax measure that tends to bring about an equalization of actual wage rates paid by the firm with labor's productivity not only would contribute to a more effective utilization of resources, but also would increase employment that in turn would tend to discourage the productivity depressing practice of make work service activity.

The consistency of the characteristics also means that the chief problems of the economy are solved in such a manner that the functioning of the system produces little or no growth or change of any kind. Whether this would continue to be true indefinitely is another matter. If, for example, population increased sufficiently, the pressure generated might create such misery that it would bring the kind of changes that it is the objective of development to produce in less painful ways. At the present time, however, it seems correct to argue that the consistency of the characteristics of the underdeveloped economy is such that the economy, from its own internal operation, will produce little improvement in existing conditions. This means that the force initiating the change must come from outside the system, or at least from elements sufficiently detached, to view the working of the system externally and is not made helpless by the internal workings of the system.

The term dualistic is often used to describe the underdeveloped country. In general the term is meant to convey the notion that there exists two parts of the society, a large, traditionalistic, rural sector dotted by islands of urban areas where industry and commercial activity are carried on in a manner that more nearly approaches the rational choice-making, textbook type of economy. This is a helpful and generally accurate notion and dualistic is a convenient term. But the dualism is also more subtle than that just defined. It is not merely that there are geographic islands of modern economizing activity within a sea of traditionalism, it is also that within both these sectors there is dualism in the attitudes, motives, and performances of the economic agents. The preceding discussion has shown that although the peasant is limited in his freedom by traditions, so too is the merchant and commercial worker, and similarly the peasant seeks economic rationality as his urban brother does. The differences are largely in the freedom permitted by social and economic arrangements, and the ability of the individuals to help themselves. In this sense the "dualism" is also within the individual economic agent as well as within the geography of the land. It is both these dualisms that provide the leverages for the development effort to use, and where they are completely absent, the problem is such that the economist may have little to contribute.

The foremost problem to be considered is finding resources not currently employed to maintain the system. No matter what activities are anticipated—technical change, social change, reduced population growth, and so on—resources above those needed to maintain the economy are required. Thus it is appropriate to examine the question of how the underdeveloped economy can find resources to devote to the task of altering its essential nature. More precisely, how can it find resources to devote to the task of converting the kind of economy described in this chapter to the kind described in Chapters 2 through 6? In still other words, given the initial conditions as described in this chapter and the process of growth as described in Chapters 3 through 6, how can the nongrowing economy be made into a growing one?

Bibliography

One of the characteristics of underdevelopment is lack of data, but it is a lack not an absence, and one should refer to those that are available. The Kuznets studies mentioned in the bibliography to Chapter 1 is a good place to begin. The United Nations, *Monthly Bulletin of Statistics* is also a readily available source of data. More detailed data can be found in the bulletins issued by the several Economic Commissions (Latin America, Asia and Far East, Africa) of the United Nations and the numerous special reports issued by the various specialized agencies of the United Nations. The International Bank for Reconstruction and Development has had published by the Johns Hopkins Press a number of surveys that always contain a deal of descriptive material on individual developing countries—Ceylon, Guatemala, Mexico, Malaya, Syria, and so on. Almost all data are subject to wide margins of error, but there is no substitute for studying the numbers to become familiar with the characteristics of the low income countries, and to gain insight into the working of the underdeveloped economy.

For other general descriptions see Harvey Leibenstein, *Economic Backwardness and Economic Growth* (New York: John Wiley & Sons, Inc., 1957), Chaps. 1–5, and the collection of papers edited by Lyle W. Shannon, *Underdeveloped Areas* (New York: Harper & Row, Publishers, 1957). Chapters 1–6 are a very good beginning.

Of course, any book or article having to do with development has some material on the characteristics of the developing countries. I have found the writings of Hla Myint especially rewarding. See particularly his "An Interpretation of Economic Backwardness," *Oxford Economic Papers,* VI (June, 1954) and "The Gains from International Trade and the Backward Countries," *Review of Economic Studies,* XXII, 1954–55, No. 58. Everett E. Hagen has a good description of "traditional society" in Chap. 4 of his *On the Theory of Social Change* (Homewood, Ill.: The Dorsey Press, 1962). See also Hans W. Singer, "Obstacles to Economic Development," Chap. 6 in his *International Development: Growth and Change* (New York: McGraw-Hill Book Company, 1964) and the same author's "Economic Progress in Underdeveloped Countries," *Social Research,* XVI (March, 1949).

Of the specific points raised in this chapter perhaps the most controversy has centered on the existence of "disguised unemployment." Theodore W. Schultz has presented the strongest evidence that it is rare or nonexistent. See his *Transforming Traditional Agriculture* (New Haven: Yale University Press, 1964), Chap. 4. A more positive attitude about the existence of disguised unemployed (and efforts to measure it) is expressed in United Nations, Department of Economic Affairs, *Measures for the Economic Development of Underdeveloped Countries* (New York, United Nations, Department of Economic Affairs, 1951) Chap. 2 and Ragnar Nurkse, *Problems of Capital Formation in Underdeveloped Countries* (Oxford: Basil Blackwell, 1958), Chap. 2. See also C. H. C. Kao, K. R. Anschel, and C. K. Eicher "Disguised Unemployment in Agriculture: A Survey," in *Agriculture in Economic Development,* ed. by Eicher and Lawrence Witt (New York: McGraw-Hill Book Company, 1964), which has an extensive bibliography on the subject.

On the technology question see the Netherlands Economic Institute series mentioned in the bibliography to Chap. 3 and the journal *Productivity Measurement Review* published by the Organization for Economic Co-operation and Development, Paris. See also OECD's *Technological Digests* for further evidence on this subject. A very helpful paper on the size of the market and the division of labor is George Stigler, "The Division of Labor is Limited by the Size of the Market," *Journal of Political Economy,* LIX (June, 1951). On institutions see W. Arthur Lewis, *The Theory of Economic Growth* (London: George Allen & Unwin, 1955), Chap. 3. The notion of "dualism" was apparently originated by J. H. Boeke, *Economics and Economic Policy of Dual Societies* (New York: International Secretariat, Institute of Pacific Relations, 1953) and is discussed at some length in B. Higgins, *Economic Development* (New York: W. W. Norton & Company, Inc., 1959), Chap. 12. For references on population, see bibliography to Chap. 14. For an interesting account of the working of the price system in one underdeveloped area, see Edwin R. Dean, "Social Determinants of Price in Several African Markets," *Economic Development and Cultural Change,* XI (April, 1963).

Part Two

ON CAPITAL FORMATION

The arguments of Part One described the process of growth, and outlined those characteristics of a typical underdeveloped country that seem most relevant in understanding such an economy and in devising policies that would permit a successful solution to the development problem. The next step is to find ways to make resources available that can be used to produce changes in those characteristics of underdevelopment that impede growth. In general terms, this means finding resources in excess of those required to maintain the economy at some level, i.e., finding resources that may be used to increase the capacity of the economy. The central purpose of Part Two is to examine the various methods that enable the achievement of this objective.

However, before this discussion can be undertaken, this question must be reconsidered: How much saving is it appropriate for a community to do? This is an especially pertinent question in the developing country where pressures for both consumption and investment are very strong. The discussion in Chapter 8 seeks to clarify the issues involved in trying to reach some practical working rule on this question.

In Chapter 9, methods of making resources available for capacity creating activities that do not require a reduction in consumption are examined. The methods examined include the use of "disguised" unemployed labor and a more effective use of existing capital as well as capital imports.

In Chapter 10, methods of raising the rate of investment that do call for a reduction in current consumption are examined. Here measures for increasing voluntary saving are reviewed, and then attention is given to inflation as a means of forcing people to save.

Finally, the last section of Chapter 10 contains a discussion of the variety of ways in which resources freed from use in maintaining the economy can be used to increase the capacity of the economy. This section introduces Part Three.

CHAPTER 8

THE OPTIMAL SAVING PROBLEM

The issues to be considered in this chapter have to do with the proportion of available resources that should be devoted to activities that add to the capacity of the system as opposed to activities that produce consumption goods. The question is especially important in the low income country, because of the great urgency for both an increase in consumption and an increase in expenditures that will raise the capacity of the system. The heart of the problem then is the conflict between present and future rates of consumption. A formal resolution of this conflict can be accomplished only at a level of abstraction quite removed from reality, and the practical resolution is necessarily of the order "devote as many resources to capacity increasing uses as is possible." Despite this conclusion, the theoretical issues involved should be appreciated by the practical policymaker and the student of development as well. The purpose of this chapter is to emphasize a few of the issues involved in this question—usually called the optimal saving problem—that seem of special importance in the development context.

Assume first that resources can be used either to produce consumption goods or to increase the capacity of the economy, i.e., there is no difficulty at all in substitution between producing one type of goods and another. How much should be allocated to each category of activity?

The usual procedure is to relate "utility" to *per capita* consumption and then seek to maximize this utility. More formally, let C be *per capita* consumption, and then $U_t = f(C_t)$. The policymaker must then find the set of C_t's that maximizes the sum of the U's over the time periods. The U's are utility and are defined in a way that makes them equivalent to "welfare" or other equally vague terms that imply something desirable. *Per capita* consumption is constrained in any one time period by the overall capacity of the economy to produce (and to borrow abroad), and by the central conflict between consumption and investment. The assumption is generally accepted that there is diminishing marginal utility from increasing *per capita* consumption. The further assumption is also usually made that diminishing marginal utility holds over the entire range of the function, but it is doubtful that such is the case when consumption slightly increases from exceedingly low levels.

A whole range of problems immediately presents itself. Assume that some satisfactory definition of utility can be given that makes it the thing to be maximized, there is still the task of specifying the nature of the function. The requirement of diminishing marginal utility for increasing consumption would still permit an infinite variety of functions to be applicable. The problem of the function is further complicated by the possibility of "time preference." The legitimacy of the notion of discounting the utility attached to future consumption merely because it is in the future is frequently disputed, but there are other reasons for such discounting. If the utility of consumption is declining as consumption rises, and if it is believed that income and consumption are rising through time, a "unit" of consumption in the future is valued less than a unit now simply because it is assumed that there will be more units in the future. A more important point has to do with the uncertainty attached to the rewards from saving. This uncertainty is especially great in the kind of economy described in Chapter 7, where the current generation has neither seen nor heard of progress in their society, and it is not surprising that questions are raised about the likelihood of future progress. This uncertainty is not the same as that associated with the life of an individual (or a society) that is of course real enough. If the choice is between consuming now or saving now in order that higher consumption may be enjoyed by someone in the future, and if current income recipients are doubtful as to the capacity of the economy to raise consumption levels, then they are also doubtful about this reason (it is not the only reason) for saving. Part of this difficulty—but only part—arises from doubt that others in the society will save. Perhaps taxation provides a good piece of evidence on this point, as there is evidence that many persons do not pay taxes because they are convinced that many other people do not pay taxes.

The problem is made more complicated by the fact that "present" and "future" are usually not specific enough alternatives, as the problem involves (or may involve) choice between current consumption and later consumption for the present generation or between the present and future generations, or between different future generations. If foreign loans are introduced, it becomes possible for the current generation to increase its consumption, and impose a burden on a future generation. In this event the usual relationship among generations is reversed, and it is the future generation that is sacrificing consumption in order for the present generation to enjoy higher consumption than it could without the loans. Whether such a sacrifice is "good" or "bad" depends on a number of factors con-

nected with the level of consumption in the periods, and the utility attached to that consumption. These remarks suggest the obvious point that
decisions to save must be made by the current generation, and future generations who are also affected by the decision to save can have no "voice"
in that decision. This means that any effort to use a utility function involves some sort of prediction as to what consumers yet to be born will
like.

Then finally, one may question whether or not *per capita* consumption
is the sole pertinent source of utility. One may define utility so that it
originates only from consumption, but if this is done then the question
arises as to why seek to maximize it. Again this point seems to be especially
relevant for the underdeveloped country where certain forms of new capital formation give satisfaction to all members of the community. Although
in some instances such satisfaction may spring from a misunderstanding
of the notion of national pride, it may also rest on a deeply felt desire for
one's country to acquire the respect of other members of the world community, and such respect is not a unique function of the level of *per capita*
consumption attained.

Under assumptions usually identified as perfect competition and neo-
classical, the amount of saving is determined by consumers reacting to the
rate of interest, the level of income, and whatever else determines saving
habits. The decision to spend on consumption or to save then is treated in
the same fashion as the decision to spend on white shirts or blue shirts,
and the conditions for and meaning of optimality in the latter case are
equally applicable in the former case—with one exception: the choice between blue and white shirts affects only the person who makes it (and possibly the people who have to look at the shirt) while the saving decision
can affect the level of consumption of persons (future generations) who
have no voice in the decision. When the decision is taken from the consumer and given to a central authority that, by means of fiscal and taxing
policy, largely determines the rate of saving, the assumption is sometimes
made that such authorities are better able to appreciate the needs of
future generations than are individual decision-making units, i.e., governments do not have "pure" time preference. It may be argued that individuals may prefer governmental action in this regard because it is
believed that only by such action will it be possible to achieve the rate of
saving that is in fact the rate that society prefers. For here it is frequently
noticed that the great majority of the population prefer development, recognize that it imposes a cost (in more ways than merely foregoing consumption), but are unwilling—or unable—or believe others to be unwilling
—to acknowledge this cost without some acceptable compulsion from an
authority that is recognized as legitimate. Again a particular tax structure
provides a common example.

Suppose then that dependence on an unfettered consumer sovereignty is ruled out insofar as the "how much to save" issue is concerned, and the government, via the conventional monetary and fiscal weapons at its disposal, acts to affect the level of present saving. The justification for this is twofold: in the first place, it may be assumed that population recognizes that government decisions in this sphere are necessary if development is to take place, and it is assumed that the population "wants" development to take place. Second, the government decision on the saving level is assumed necessary because in many instances saving can be accomplished only if the government takes specific action. In this category are taxes, inflation, and foreign borrowing. If the government then assumes the responsibility of deciding on the "optimal" level of saving for the community, can something more than simply "save as much as possible" be said?

If the assumption that there is perfect substitutability between the capital goods and consumer goods sectors is modified, then for technological reasons there may not be a great deal of freedom for changing the average rate of saving in a given short period. Suppose there were no substitution between these sectors, then the capacity of the economy to accumulate capital would be limited by the size of the existing capital goods sectors and the ability of the economy to export consumer goods and import capital goods. Clearly to save in excess of this level—more accurately, to try to save in excess of this level—results in underutilization of resources. There is, of course, some substitution between the capital goods sector and the consumer goods sector (the most obvious would be the accumulation of inventories of consumer goods), and exactly how much can be exported in in any one period without depressing foreign prices so much that no increase in foreign exchange earnings is possible cannot be stated with exactness. Despite the ambiguity as to the exact upper limit of the capacity of the economy to transform resources into capital goods, it is reasonable to think in terms of the upper limit of saving being that determined by these constraints. There is, however, no reason why the saving level that results in the full exploitation of the economy's capacity to accumulate capital goods is the "optimal" level of saving.

On the other hand, it may be that it is impossible to increase consumption goods output without first increasing the quantity of capital in the economy. In this case, too, the policymaker has no choice; if output is to increase, then resources from somewhere must be found to go into capital formation. This may be the situation when there is unemployment due to the kind of structural difficulties that were discussed under the employment heading in the preceding chapter.

There are other constraints as well. Except under rather specific conditions, it is virtually impossible to reduce *per capita* consumption below that level that has come to be accepted as an historical minimum. If attempts were made to push down consumption below this level, the community would be expected to offer significant resistance. This fact is especially important in a society where population is growing rapidly, and the community seeks to maintain a constant level of average consumption. A bind may be created by such an effort, for in trying to maintain *per capita* consumption for a growing population by reducing saving now, a society is reducing its capacity to provide this same level of consumption to a still larger population in the future. The specific conditions referred to as possible exceptions are two in number. Reduced consumption can be imposed on elements of the society who are rich or whose income is not generally recognized as "legitimate" by the major part of society. Landlords are the obvious example. In general, however, these groups are usually able to avoid those measures that are designed to force reduction in their consumption. There is also the danger of designing a policy that is aimed at reducing consumption, and has the effect of reducing both consumption and investment.

The other way in which the real consumption rate may be affected has to do with the form of the asset that is available for the saver to accumulate. As will be explained, there is some evidence that the motivation of some forms of consumption is essentially that of saving, of accumulating an asset that is believed to be reasonably liquid in case of emergency. Because, however, this demand for assets constitutes a claim on resources, no resources are released for production of capital goods. The approach to this problem is in terms of providing other assets—e.g., bonds, bank deposits—that do not require resources for their creation as a means of releasing resources from producing a commodity that is held as an asset. The best example of this procedure is the use of gold and other precious metals, but other commodities also serve in this capacity in certain countries, e.g., carpets in Iran.

Another possible source of reduction in consumption is one that probably cannot be exploited in the early stages of development. This pertains to expenditures on ceremonial occasions, which could be reduced without impairing health, but it probably would impair something more important than mere physical health to do away with them or try to do away with them.

These specific constraints are less applicable in the long run than in the short run. If the size of the capital goods sector (or the capacity to export) is a constraint in the current period, then to allocate resources to these sectors in the current period means that future levels of saving are expected to be higher than current levels. Similarly, capacity to tax, borrow abroad, and the like may not be very amenable to change in a given short period but are subject to change over the long run.

Conclusion

If consumer sovereignty is allowed to determine the rate of saving, it seems logical to conclude that that rate will probably be so low that the economy will continue to stagnate not so much because the society is unable or unwilling to save, but because of a variety of factors, individual decision units will not save unless there is some form of extra pressure on them and ways for them to do so. Thus it is assumed that the government must, through monetary and fiscal policy, effect to a very significant degree the rate of saving. There is, however, not complete freedom. There is the limitation imposed by the specificity of the existing productive capacity, the virtual necessity to maintain consumption at "conventional" levels, and other things. Given this kind of situation it is not very helpful to speak in terms of an "optimal" rate of saving. The solution is rather of the rule of thumb variety. Allow *per capita* consumption to rise to the minimum extent—possibly zero—and hence concentrate on making the marginal increments in output largely investment if the technological constraints permit. A common procedure is to define a rate of growth of *per capita* income that is believed to be acceptable, and then seek to estimate the rate of saving required to achieve this rate of growth. Such rules of thumb are the most nearly consistent policy with the general objective of the transformation of the economy from the underdeveloped to the growing category.

To obtain this rate, however, is no small task, and attention must be given to the means available for achieving such an objective.

Bibliography

An excellent, nonmathematical treatment of the optimal saving question is A. K. Sen's "On Optimising the Rate of Saving," *The Economic Journal*, LXXI (September, 1961) on which the discussion in this chapter is based. The subject was first systematically treated in Frank P. Ramsey, "A Mathematical Theory of Saving," *Economic Journal*, XXXVIII (December, 1928), and since that time many other economists have examined the problem. See Sir Dennis Robertson, *Utility and All That*, (London: George Allen & Unwin, 1952), Chap. 1. References given to Chapter 16 are also relevant to this problem.

CHAPTER 9

CAPITAL FORMATION WITH
NO REDUCTION IN CONSUMPTION

In the description of the underdeveloped country in Chapter 7, the point was made that there are idle resources in the system that could be exploited *if* some rather far-reaching reorganizations of production and social arrangements were made. It is immediately evident that the least painful way of effecting an increase in the rate of capital formation without outside help would be through an exploitation of those resources not now required to maintain the system at its existing levels. In this case, the "disutility" involved would be the inconvenience attached to the reorganizations required, and this inconvenience is probably less than that associated with a reduction in consumption in an effort to increase the rate of capital formation. The first part of this chapter is concerned with the mechanics by which the rate of capital formation may be increased by the use of those resources currently unproductive. At the outset attention is devoted to the use of labor—the "disguised" unemployed—and later the problem of making more effective use of physical capital is to be discussed. In the latter part of the chapter, the other "painless" way of accelerating the rate of accumulating capital, via international loans and grants, is to be considered.

I. The Mobilization of Currently Underutilized Resources

A. On the Use of Unemployed Labor

It has been argued that the typical underdeveloped country is characterized by a significant number of workers whose productivity is very low, possibly even zero, or whose duties could be easily performed by other laborers working somewhat harder or more hours. This potentially available labor is not now fully exploited largely because of lack of alternative employment opportunities, due to the inadequacy of complementary inputs, chiefly capital and entrepreneurial talent, and to a "too high" wage rate. The wage rate is determined not by productivity considerations but by the institutional arrangements already discussed, especially those arrangements having to do with the sharing of total output among all hands in rural areas and the nature of the labor market in urban areas. The implications of a wage rate reduction are considered in Section B, and now the question is simply—can anything else be done with this "excess" labor? With these assumptions the exploitation of the idle resource—of the resource not required for the maintenance of the economy—requires the creation of complementary inputs. The idle resources (labor) must indeed be used to create the complementary inputs. In other, more optimistic language, the potentially available labor provides a resource from which capital may be created, and the problem is how to use it to this end.

1. The technological and entrepreneurial problems. If there is literally nothing that can be produced with the available labor because of technological reasons, then there is nothing more to say except advise the population to emigrate or to obtain foreign help. This strong statement is not appropriate either for rural or urban areas. There is little doubt that in rural areas the technological problem of how to use the labor can be surmounted. Especially is it evident that capital in the form of canals, roads, field terracing, improved housing can be created with virtually no other inputs. It is less evident, but no less true, that labor may create crude tools out of "nothing"—shovels, weeding devices, earth-moving devices, and so on. A less strong assertion is applicable to the urban labor force. Here, it seems clear that labor working virtually alone can improve housing conditions and sanitation arrangements, and can build simpler forms of capital goods such as spinning and weaving machines, minor transporting devices, and (especially) construction tools.

If this is the case, then the question arises as to why advantage has not already been taken of this potential source of capital formation. The answer (other than that associated with wage rates that are discussed later) is found in the organizational and entrepreneurial attributes described earlier. So, now there must be a recognition by some elements in the community of the possibility of doing something with resources that are available. To expect that this may be possible now—and was not possible thirty-five years ago—is reasonable on several grounds. Technical advice is available from a wide variety of sources, and even "bad" advice sometimes stirs up thought and effort in a manner that over several periods may inspire some action. Also, contact with the rest of the world is much greater now than was the case in pre-World War II years. The latter statement is true even in former colonial territories. In these countries, although colonial supervisors were present, there is little evidence of the kind of contact that results in the spread of ideas and understandings about the workings of an economy. It, therefore, seems appropriate to assume that there is a creeping awareness that something can be done although, in most instances, there remains little clear understanding as to what this something is. Consequently, efforts are often directed chiefly to getting or trying to get foreign aid, but even this suggests that some further awareness of possible improvement is materializing.

If knowledge or awareness is present, then the question of implementation comes next. At the outset, outside pressure must be exerted. The system will not generate its own implementing action, and unless an exogenous force is imposed, nothing happens. Consequently, formal government action is assumed necessary. This action will take the form either of direct operation or of efforts to help organize local communities to get something started. An assumption may be made that entrepreneurial ability is available to a limited extent in this fashion, but it is also to be emphasized that such organizing and implementing ability—such entrepreneurship—is likely to be relatively unproductive, not only because it is itself new and inexperienced, but also because the task confronting it is so severe. It is not appropriate to assume that the latent entrepreneurship referred to in Chapter 7 can be exploited on the type of activity that can be accomplished under present assumptions.

The preceding discussion argued that there did exist technologically possible ways of using the available labor, and that there could be assumed to exist a modest source of organizing talent. The problem now is to examine the process by which capital may be accumulated by use of these resources. If inflation is ruled out (temporarily), and consumption is assumed not to decline, then the specific question is how to bring about the increment in outputs that has been argued to be technologically and organizationally possible.

Begin with the simplest case. Labor in rural areas is used in the area in which it lives to build physical capital in the form of canals and other water control devices, roads, and possibly to make some tools and implements. No wage is paid as the workers continue to live where they have been living, and to eat what they have been eating. The major new input called for is the organizational and leadership skills assumed to be supplied from outside sources. Part of the leadership task is to persuade the community that doing work in this fashion is not only acceptable, but is indeed most laudatory. No increase in money income has occurred so there is no problem of inflation. The incentive to work more for no immediate increase in income is in part some sort of nationalistic—or localistic—spirit, in addition to the fact that at some time in the future the real consumption of the community may be increased or workers may be taxed and thereby forced to work for a money wage to pay the tax.

Another change in routine is simply that those persons performing traditional tasks must do more work than they have previously done. This is a point worth emphasizing because it may not be easy to accomplish. In some instances, for example, it may mean that a modification in job hierarchy is necessary or that women may be asked to perform tasks that they have not previously performed. If these obstacles can be surmounted, real income will rise due to the increased output made possible by the new physical capital.

That this is not a completely idealistic argument is clear. Village self-help programs of this sort are not only possible but have been observed in several places and are being tried in one form or another in a wide variety of places. There are two major difficulties, one having to do with convincing labor to work more for no immediate gain, and the other having to do with the limited range of output that can be produced in this fashion.

2. *The Inflation Problem.* To persuade workers to apply themselves more diligently may require incentives in addition to those provided by moral suasion and hopes for the future. To persuade them may in fact require payment of money wages; and if money wages are paid, the complexity of the process is greatly increased. Since, under present assumptions, no increment in saving is assumed to supply the loanable funds out of which new wage payments may be financed, an increase in money wages must be paid from an increased money supply. Technically the operation could proceed in the following way: New money is made available to pay wages to labor to build the new capital, but there is no immediate increase in output (except partially completed capital projects) resulting from this increased wage payment. Since it must be assumed that the workers will spend a large part of their new money income more or less immediately, there will be an increment in demand for consumer goods with no increment in output. To prevent the price level from rising, expenditure somewhere else in the system must be curtailed. There are several spots where this might be accomplished.

Suppose that the workers buy food from those persons remaining on the farm. In order to prevent this latter group from increasing their consumption, they must be taxed. In the neatest of all worlds, the new workers receive a money wage with which they buy the food that they had been consuming when they lived and worked on the farm. The people remaining on the farm maintain a constant rate of consumption, and by "selling" (previously they were "sharing") the part that they do not now consume, receive a money income that they did not previously receive. They are taxed the exact amount of this income; and consequently, there is no increment in total expenditure, no reduction in anybody's real consumption, and physical capital is accumulated. At the end of the gestation period for the capital constructed, the capacity of the economy is increased—in the example here, agricultural output is increased. When real output rises, taxes may be reduced and consumption allowed to increase; or the rate of capital formation may be stepped up.

Now the simple logic of the preceding argument is acceptable, but the practicable difficulties involved in its implementation and the narrow scope within which it is applicable must be recognized. Not only is there the burden on the new entrepreneurial talent previously identified, but also now there is an even larger burden placed on the taxing bureaucracy. The implementation of the kind of tax required to prevent inflation would challenge the most sophisticated of taxing bureaucracies, and the tax levying and collecting skills in most underdeveloped countries are far from sophisticated. Furthermore, if the capital formation requires the physical movement of labor, then not only is there the likelihood of greater wage incentives being required but also a transporting of food burden is placed on the economy that it did not have to meet before the project began. Both add pressure to the inflation threat, and the latter subtracts from the net gain attributable to the investments.

There is not much that can be said about the composition of the increments of output as it is so dominated by what is technically possible. It does seem that the increment in output flowing from the new capital will be almost entirely consumer goods, as the quality of the labor available and the absence of complementary inputs does not permit the building up of a capital goods sector, at least not within the interval of time of interest to the policy-maker of a country pursuing a development program. As a damper on inflation, this fact has advantages, but it also imposes obvious limitations on what can be accomplished by this method. It is possible that agricultural output may be increased by the capital created in this form. This method of capital formation is also important in that it emphasizes the use of the most plentiful factor available—labor—and at the same time it imposes (relatively) minor demands on the social organization of the system.

The discussion has been applied to agriculture, but it is also applicable to urban unemployed workers as well. If used in the urban areas, the incidence of the tax will need to be on those people who were supporting the unemployed workers. If the tax does not reach these persons, then they may increase (or try to increase) their consumption by consuming that which they previously shared with their friends and relatives. It may be that taxes are easier to collect in urban areas than in rural areas, and that workers are more easily organized into work groups in town than in the countryside. However, this is not something that seems very amenable to generalization.

One may conclude that the use of the "disguised unemployed labor" to build capital is limited in quantity, especially so long as the no inflation assumption is imposed. Yet, there may be successive rounds of capital formation using the methods discussed here. Capital formation by these means is also limited in scope in that it can contribute little to the building up of the more complicated activities. It may, however, be a method of increasing exports that in turn make possible an increase in imports of any type product, complicated or otherwise. At the same time, it is important in that it can contribute to the output of consumer goods, and may help to impose on the community—especially an isolated community —at least one important new notion; namely, that living standards can be raised.

B. On a More Effective Use of Capital

The assumption that there is no capital available with which the "disguised" unemployed can work is an extreme one; and, as explained in Chapter 7, the existing physical capital stock is rarely used to full capacity. Although the amount of unused capital capacity is decidedly less than that of unused labor capacity, it may have important implications, and how it may be used is to be analyzed.

1. Sources of Unused Capital Capacity. Some of the idleness results from rather obvious and mundane causes such as the failure to employ multiple shifts of labor where possible. This form of idleness is evident in a wide variety of cases, including (especially) educational facilities and the capital that is in the form of a trained teacher. To devise remedies for this requires no great analysis, although any particular remedy may run into institutional and social obstacles when implementation is undertaken. Perhaps it should be noted that some capital is used in multiple shifts, and the preceding sentences are not meant to apply across the entire capital vectors. Also, the necessity (because of lumpiness) for building ahead of the market may result in the appearance of capacity in given sections that cannot for a time be utilized. If there is unused capacity due to these reasons, then—as already noted—an increase in aggregate demand would produce price level rises rather than solve the problem. In other instances, an increase in total demand would tend to call forth a more intensive use of existing capital. In Chapter 10, the effects of inflation as related to use of existing capital are discussed; but it is important to recognize that capital of a specific form may be underutilized for this reason. A final reason why capital is underutilized (noted in Chapter 7) is simply the lack of complementary capital. Labor is not the only complementary input with capital, and idle capital capacity in one sector may be due to a lack of capacity in another sector. The discussion of interdependence in Chapter 4 emphasized this possibility, and the obvious fact that further capital formation in the relevant sectors is required before full utilization can be achieved.

These are all important reasons why the existing capital stock is not fully utilized. There is, however, another much more important reason why the quantity of existing capital does not yield full return. This pertains to the prevailing factor price combination in the underdeveloped country and the resulting form of the capital that is created. This point merits further attention.

To set the argument, use may be made of the diagram introduced in Chapter 3. Suppose Diagram V describes the production possibilities of a typical industry or firm in an underdeveloped country. Three techniques of production are known as shown by the rays marked A, B, and C. Reasons have already been given why wage rates are higher relative to capital costs than relative scarcities would indicate, (i.e., the ratio of actual capital and labor costs does not also measure the ratio of the opportunity costs of these factors). In light of this argument, suppose that the actual price line is $w_0 r_0$ and output is OB with OK of capital and OL of labor. The opportunity cost line of the inputs is, however, $r_1 w_1$. It is immediately evident that were the ratio of the prices to change to reflect the ratio of opportunity costs, output with the same quantity of capital would rise once the new technique (Technique A) became effective, i.e., $OA' > OB$ (unless Technique A is inefficient). If this change in relative costs occurred, the quantity of capital now available in this sector could be redistributed over a larger quantity of labor, and a larger output would result. But R-type capital cannot simply be squeezed in order to alter it in a fashion to make it suitable for Technique A rather than B. The position then is this. As a consequence of the institutional factors affecting input prices, capital representing Technique B has been constructed and currently exists. Such prices, however, overprice labor and probably underprice capital services

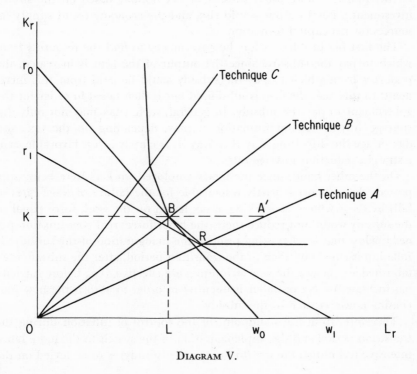

DIAGRAM V.

compared to their economy-wide opportunity costs. If policies can be effected that will result in the effective cost line shifting from $w_o r_o$ to $r_1 w_1$ as replacement capital formation occurs, output will rise not because a larger quantity of capital is available or because new technology becomes available, but because of a more efficient use of the resources that are already available. The increment in capacity may then be utilized for capital formation without reducing the output available for maintaining the economy. Two specific issues require additional comment: At least some replacement investment must occur; otherwise the sector is technologically bound, and second, the institutional barrier to changing $w_o r_o$ must be surmounted. Consider the second problem first.

To say simply that the economy must be made more competitive is no answer at all. The most likely approach is in terms of a system of taxes and subsidies or possibly a cost of living dole. It is evident that the government could design a subsidy system to compensate firms for wage-rate payments in excess of the economy-wide opportunity costs of labor. Suppose this latter figure were estimated to be about 1 and the current wage rate was 2. The government then would give each firm in that sector 1 for each employee, and the effective wage rate to the firms is then 1. Presumably through time, Technique B would be replaced by Technique A in order to exploit reduced labor costs as replacement investment and reorganization of production takes place. (Incidentally, such a subsidy is quite different from the more usual subsidy or tax holiday based on the size of investment.) Total output would rise, and the economy could supply resources for net capital formation.

The first big problem is for the government to find the resources from which to pay the subsidy. Since the output of the firm is increased, the resources from which to pay the subsidy could be paid from this increment. In this case, the firm is subsidized but is then taxed in order for the government to pay the subsidy. In general, such a tax may not only discourage further capital formation it may, depending on the tax, also discourage the shift from Ray B to Ray A. It clearly is less favorable than a straight reduction in wage rates.

On the other hand, since the newly employed workers were being supported (this support is partly responsible for the failure of wage rates to fall) by those who were working, a tax levied on the work force equal to the subsidy would not reduce their (the labor force) real consumption per head below that level existing prior to the inauguration of the subsidy. If inflation is ruled out, then in the transition period, after the subsidy is established and before the new techniques are effective, (i.e., before capacity has increased) a tax on labor is essential in order to absorb the new purchasing power created by the subsidy.

Therefore, from the standpoint of the control of inflation during the transition period and the implementation of the switch to the more labor intensive technique, the tax (to finance the subsidy) is to be levied on the labor force—more accurately, on a specific part of the labor force. The argument is similar to that outlined in the discussion of disguised unemployed labor. Suppose that employed workers are now supporting the idle workers who will become employed after the change in technique is effected. The tax on the currently employed worker reduces his after-tax earnings, but the increased employment also reduces the number of people he must support, and his consumption, therefore, need not fall. Once the new technique is in operation, the output is higher than it was when Technique *B* was used, and the whole operation can then be thought of as a method to increase employment and output without any prior reduction in consumption and with no net capital formation.

With this technique, there are major practical difficulties that can easily be seen. The tax to be levied is again a difficult one to implement in precisely the manner that assures its incidence on the "right" people. The same taxing constraint appears here, therefore, that appeared in connection with the direct employment of the "disguised unemployed." Similarly, the recipients of the subsidies, the firms, can easily find ways of abusing the arrangement by manipulating the number of their employees. Thus, much depends on the ability to diagnose the actual production opportunities available. These practical difficulties, especially the latter one, suggest that the approach probably cannot be applied on an economy-wide scale but is best limited to the more highly organized sectors where its implementation appears feasible.

There still is the necessity for some replacement investment. The existing capital has to be replaced or modified in a way that makes it technically possible to exploit Technique *A*, and this in an underdeveloped country may be a bottleneck. First of all, there is not much capital to depreciate; and, more importantly, the depreciation accounts and methods do not lend themselves to a very accurate appraisal of the profitability of gross capital formation. Finally, replacement does not always occur in the area and manner implied here, and in an economy where there are major gaps in the linkages among the sectors, this source of capital formation may be further handicapped. These facts add further to the previous conclusion; namely, that the policy is sure to be more effective when applied to firms that are organized in a fairly sophisticated manner. It may even be more directly applicable to new products and new firms, but even this would help. It should also be noted that to the extent that existing capital is flexible enough to permit a shift from Technique *B* to *A* without significant investment of any kind, the difficulties here considered are reduced.

In view of these limitations, what can be said about the importance of this kind of policy? The answer is very simple: It is of very great importance. The earlier chapters on growth explained the importance of choosing the least cost techniques and the role of shadow prices in this allocation procedure. The actual increase in output made possible by the change in factor prices can be read from Diagram V. It is equal to RA', and its quantitative importance depends very much on the productivity of labor, known to be small. More importantly, the original output OR is now possible with less capital, and the new capacity may be allocated to other things. But, the immediate net increase in output due simply to the change from Technique B to A is perhaps the least important advantage accruing from the shift. The increment in capacity here can be of widely varied forms and is not so limited as the use of disguised unemployed labor was. The most important consequence, however, is that the private sector entrepreneur is benefited in that the rate of return (the marginal product of capital) has risen as Technique A replaces Technique B. There are few institutional barriers—except implementing the right tax—and the process once implemented should also help develop a greater consciousness about the importance of using all resources economically. These advantages are further emphasized if the possibility of technical progress that is favorable to labor are introduced, and the taxing to finance the subsidy problem is greatly reduced if a net import surplus is possible.

The role of interest rates is more complicated than that of wage rates because of their effect on the rate of investment. It seems quite clear that, for reasons noted in Chapter 7, interest rates do not accurately reflect the scarcity and productivity of capital. It is not so clear, however, that given the uncertainty and risk inherent in undertaking productive capital formation in the underdeveloped country, it is a satisfactory approach to the factor combination problem to raise interest rates above the conventional levels prevailing at the outset of the development effort. In a later chapter an argument is introduced to suggest "high" interest payments to lenders and "low rates" to borrowers seeking to finance productive capital formation. Here, it is merely asserted that wage rate policies probably must bear most of the burden of achieving a more economic use of available resources.

A further area in which there is surely a misallocation of resources has to do with imports. The world is filled with overvalued currencies (import controls are the most ubiquitous of all controls). But controls and red tape do not seem to have the economizing effect that simply a high price has. Also, controls and red tape are frequently best tolerated by persons least concerned with productive investment. The advocacy of a completely free exchange market is probably not the right solution, and is nonsense for practical reasons anyway. It is, however, an important part of the factor combination problem to find and make effective the shadow price of foreign exchange. In the absence of a free market, to determine the shadow price is no simple matter (except conceptually, see Chapter 4), and some contact with the market is essential. But, these matters are beyond the scope of the issue at hand.

2. *Capital Accumulation Implications.* Suppose now that a policy has

been effected to bring down the effective wage rate (i.e., the wage the firm pays to its workers) to a number of firms in the organized sectors of the economy. As already noted, the marginal product of capital rises as the move from *B* to *A* occurs, and the firms may thus have an incentive to increase their capital stock. To examine this point, assume the movement to Technique *A* has occurred. Both profit rate and the total amount of profits are now higher than they were when Technique *B* was used. Now suppose that all or almost all the profits are saved, a not unreasonable assumption for most societies: then it may also be assumed that saving will increase because profits have risen. As these profit earners invest their new saving, they will find that the new higher rate of return does not decline, i.e., that labor is forthcoming at the effective (reduced) wage rate in sufficient quantities that the capital-labor ratio represented by Technique *A* can be maintained. The entrepreneurs simply crawl out Ray *A* as they continue to reinvest their earnings, and the profit rate remains constant. Furthermore, since it is likely—though not certain—that these sectors are growing more rapidly than the rest of the economy, the saving income ratio for the economy as a whole is rising; and, of equal importance, the sector dominated by the "industrial mentality" is expanding as a proportion of the total economy.

The impact of innovations may also be introduced into the argument. If innovations are neutral, the only effect is a more rapid increase in total profits, in total saving, and in total investment. On the other hand, if innovations are favorable to capital, there will be pressure to move back toward Technique *B* at the existing effective wage rate (i.e., market wage rate minus subsidy). Thus if the capital formation process is accompanied by innovations favorable to capital, then the wage subsidy to firms must rise. By similar argument, it is evident that innovations favorable to labor may be accompanied by a decline in the subsidy without pulling the entrepreneur away from the technique that, from the standpoint of the economy, is optimal.

This whole argument as to capital formation obviously rests very heavily on the assumption that labor is forthcoming simply if employment opportunities open up at the "existing" wage rate. *Existing* means a wage rate somewhat above the amount being received by members of the labor force from their current activity. Pulling this labor away from its current activities imposes some reorganization within the activity; but generally, this imposition should not be extreme enough to constitute a bottleneck to the operation. Also, even if there is a reduction in output due to the withdrawal of labor from certain sectors, the increment in output in the sectors receiving the labor is sure to be greater than that reduction. Note further that there is no inflation problem once the transition to the new technique is completed as the profit earners are by assumption saving. In general, this sort of process would appear most directly applicable to urban manufacturing activity and the labor drawn on is likely to be the low (or zero) productivity urban workers, although as the process proceeds, an increasing number of workers will be pulled into the urban area from the agricultural sectors. And, of course, there is no reason why the whole process is not applicable to the more highly organized agricultural sectors.

Through how many periods can such a process continue? The answer is obvious: As long as labor is forthcoming at an unchanged wage rate. The wage rate may begin to rise for a variety of reasons, the most evident of which is that capital formation outruns the growth of the labor force and eventually the pool of "disguised" unemployed labor is used up. This end to matters may happen soon or late depending on the size of the backlog of the labor supply. There are other possibilities of pushing up (down) the wage (profit) rate.

As the labor is pulled in from rural areas, the average output of those remaining in agriculture rises (by assumption that output has not fallen or has done so only slightly, and the number of workers has declined so average product rises), and even though additional workers could be spared without reducing output, they may be no longer willing to leave their traditional stations at the existing wage rate. As their real output rises, the push out of the routine is reduced and the attractiveness of new employment must be increased to maintain a constant inflow of workers. If the tax system can be made to work, then average consumption of those remaining on the farms will not rise; and this particular problem is not present.

Also, if the expanding sectors trade with those sectors that are not expanding, the price of the purchases of the former sector from the latter may rise relative to the price of the product they sell. This result is not at all unlikely because demand and output are increasing much more rapidly in the expanding sector. This deterioration in the terms of trade between the sectors will cut into the profit margins directly and will also contribute to the entrepreneur having to pay higher wages to attract his workers. If the expanding sectors do not trade with the labor-supplying sectors, this problem does not arise; but such a no-trade assumption is rather unrealistic over any significant time span. The more important conclusion would seem to be rather that productivity must increase in the labor-supplying sectors also. The problem falls into a traditional pattern if the labor-demanding sectors are designated "manufacturing," and the labor-supplying sectors "agricultural." The argument would be that productivity in the agricultural sector must rise rapidly enough to prevent the price of the products sold to the manufacturing sector from rising. At the same time, however, the rising productivity in this sector must not be permitted to result in rising wage rates, for if that happened, then the profit margins in the manufacturing sectors would be reduced. Thus, the real wage rate in the agricultural sectors must be prevented from rising even though productivity there is rising, and this can probably be accomplished only through taxation or possibly through increases in rent. And again, the strategic role of taxation is emphasized. But the terms "manufacturing" and "agricultural" are misleading as the argument applied to any labor demanding, labor-supplying sector arrangements.

All of these difficulties may be met by adjusting the wage subsidy paid to the firm and some prolongation of the process may be accomplished in this fashion, but a general assumption to the effect that the subsidy be manipulated to offset developments elsewhere is probably too much to expect.

What conditions are necessary for the process to work in the manner described? The process was set off by a government policy that brought about a higher profit rate and larger total profits by virtue of a subsidized shift in production techniques. Is this a sufficient incentive? The answer is that it depends on the supply of entrepreneurial talent available. Indeed, the whole process implies that somewhere in the economy there exists an organized, monetized sector that has economic agents that will respond to the kind of incentives provided by the subsidies. The discussion in Chapter 7 suggested that for the typical underdeveloped economy the assumption of an organized, commercial sector was reasonably realistic as was the assumption of the existence of latent entrepreneurship. Despite these assumptions, it is probably correct to assume that, even if neatly implemented, the process will produce a rather low rate of capital formation at the beginning; but perhaps one that rises rapidly as the effects become known to the entrepreneurs and as innovations enter the picture.

The process may also run into trouble because of natural resource limitations, but this possibility though relevant does not seem important.

Finally, the capital accumulation process does result in some modification of the social and institutional environment right from the beginning. The most important dimension of this is the gradual growth in the relative size of the profit oriented, entrepreneurially dominated sector of the economy. This fact, although an essential ingredient of the development process, is also another reason to expect a rather slow start, for the breakdown of the environmental factors is necessarily a slow process as there are major obstacles to violating traditional arrangements. Part of this environment changing process may involve attracting entrepreneurial talent away from traditional occupations—trading, banking, landholding, and so on. To do this may require simply time and demonstration of the effectiveness of the policy, but it may also require more direct action than the subsidy. These are important difficulties and not to be taken lightly, but they do not appear severe enough to warrant discarding the whole approach.

II. Capital Imports

Capital imports enter the analysis of capital formation in a wide variety of ways. Most obviously they permit the rate of expenditure to exceed the rate of output. In the expression used earlier $S = I + D + F$, capital imports mean that F is negative, and hence investment plus the government deficit may exceed saving by the amount of the import surplus. It is then evident that a positive import surplus permits a higher rate of capital formation than does a zero import surplus. Perhaps more revealingly, it may be said than an import surplus permits a rate of capital formation in excess of domestic saving. The import surplus enters the story in other ways as well. For example, it permits access to products that may not be available from domestic sources, it may serve to catalyze domestic savings, it may facilitate the achievement of a particular domestic policy such as the subsidy system discussed in the previous section, and it may provide the source of new technology. It may, however, permit the economy to avoid painful structural change. Section B examines some of these more specific aspects of capital formation in detail. In Section A, an analysis is developed to show the general process of capital importing under a variety of assumptions.

A. The Process of Importing Capital

To see the process clearly it is helpful to work through a simple model that, though it rests on specific assumptions, does enable the isolating of the strategic factors that appear relevant to the general argument.

Suppose that a nation has access to foreign loans for a specified period of time only, and then within an additional period of specified length it must also be free of foreign debt. This means that during the period when it is importing capital, the rate of investment may exceed the rate of domestic saving, but during the interval in which the loan is repaid, the domestic saving rate must exceed the rate of domestic capital formation by the rate of the loan repayment. It is evident that the efficacy to the economy of this arrangement depends very much on the extent to which capacity is raised during the period of the capital inflow. In the ideal case, the capital inflow plus other sources of capital formation results in income rising to the extent that, when the repayment period begins, voluntary savings are sufficient not only to repay the debt but also to permit a rate of capital formation sufficient to maintain that rate of growth achieved during the period of the import surplus. In the least advantageous case, the capital inflow would add nothing to the productive capacity of the economy (would all be used to raise consumption temporarily), and to repay the loan would mean that consumption must fall below the level that was obtained before the capital inflow began. These general remarks suggest that a country's capacity to profit from capital imports depends upon several things: (1) the increase in productive capacity that can be achieved with the capital from abroad, (2) the increase in the saving rate consequent to the increase in output, (3) the "size" of the investment rate needed to maintain growth after the capital inflows cease, (4) the terms on which the foreign capital is obtained—terms include interest charges and the time periods involved, and (5) the terms of trade that prevail over the two periods. (The two periods refer to the period when capital imports occur and to the period during which the loans are to be repaid.) Consider now a specific example suggested by Gerald M. Alter in his paper, "The Servicing of Foreign Capital Inflows by Underdeveloped Countries."

1. The Limited Payoff Period. Suppose that a planning authority makes the following diagnosis of the economy. A percentage rate of growth of 3 per cent per annum is an acceptable target rate. A careful study of the resource and technological situation in the country suggests that to accomplish this, at least through the next few decades, requires a rate of investment of about 12 per cent of income. Data are available to show that the current average saving rate is about 5 per cent, but given a hoped-for improvement tax policy plus a growth of income, the assumption could be made that the marginal saving rate for the next 15 years would be about 20 per cent, and after that about 30 per cent. Investigation indicated that foreign loans were available at a 5 per cent interest rate. These were loans, however, and had to be repaid. To make the story complete, it is assumed that income in the country in period zero is 1000. What kind of foreign loan arrangement should be made?

Table V and Graph I summarize a particularly simple approach to the problem. In the early years, the country must borrow not only to add to the rate of capital formation, but also to pay interest costs, and these capital imports must continue until the marginal saving rates have resulted in a volume of domestic saving sufficient to meet the demands for capital formation (i.e., until average saving equals 12 per cent of national product). However, as the loan must be repaid, and the 3 per cent rate of growth is to be maintained, the saving rate must rise above the 12 per cent by a sufficient amount to release resources to produce products with which to repay the loan. On present assumptions, as the table and graph show, arrangements must be made for a net capital inflow for the first nineteen periods, and it is only after that date that the saving capacity of the economy is great enough that domestic capital formation can be supported and loan repayment begin. The country would be free of external debt before the end of the 33rd period, and at that time the economy may either expand its growth rate quite markedly or it may reduce its rate of saving. In this example then, loans must be available for nineteen periods, and the repayment period be at least fourteen periods.

2. Some Implications. Several things may be said about this argument.

TABLE V

	Income	Investment	Saving	Imports	Interest	Foreign Exchange	Exports	Increase in Debt	Total Debt
0	1000.00	120.00	50.00	70.00	0.00	70.00	0.00	70.00	70.00
1	1030.00	123.60	56.00	67.60	3.50	71.10	0.00	71.10	141.10
2	1060.90	127.31	62.18	65.13	7.05	72.18	0.00	72.18	213.36
3	1092.73	131.13	68.55	62.58	10.67	73.25	0.00	73.25	286.61
4	1125.51	135.06	75.10	59.96	14.33	74.29	0.00	74.29	360.09
5	1159.27	139.11	81.85	57.26	18.00	75.26	0.00	75.26	435.35
6	1194.05	143.28	88.81	54.47	21.75	76.22	0.00	76.22	511.57
7	1229.87	147.58	95.97	51.61	25.58	77.19	0.00	77.19	588.76
8	1266.77	152.01	103.35	48.66	29.44	78.10	0.00	78.10	666.86
9	1304.77	156.57	110.95	45.62	33.34	78.96	0.00	78.96	745.82
10	1343.91	161.26	118.78	42.48	37.29	79.77	0.00	79.77	825.59
11	1384.23	166.09	126.85	39.24	41.28	80.52	0.00	80.52	906.11
12	1425.75	171.08	135.15	35.93	45.30	81.23	0.00	81.23	987.34
13	1468.53	176.21	143.71	32.50	49.37	81.87	0.00	81.87	1069.21
14	1512.58	181.50	152.51	28.99	53.46	82.45	0.00	82.45	1151.66
15	1557.96	186.94	161.59	25.35	57.58	82.93	0.00	82.93	1234.59
16	1604.70	192.55	231.41	0.00	61.73	61.73	38.86	22.87	1257.46
17	1652.84	198.32	245.85	0.00	62.87	62.87	47.53	15.34	1272.80
18	1702.42	204.27	260.73	0.00	63.64	63.64	56.46	7.18	1279.98
19	1753.49	210.40	276.05	0.00	64.00	64.00	65.65	−1.65	1278.33
20	1806.10	216.71	291.83	0.00	63.91	63.91	75.12	−11.21	1267.12
21	1860.28	223.21	308.08	0.00	63.35	63.35	84.87	−21.52	1245.60
22	1916.09	229.91	324.82	0.00	62.28	62.28	94.91	−32.63	1212.97
23	1973.57	236.80	342.07	0.00	60.65	60.65	105.27	−44.62	1168.35
24	2032.77	243.91	359.83	0.00	58.42	58.42	115.91	−57.49	1110.86
25	2093.75	251.23	378.12	0.00	55.54	55.54	126.89	−71.35	1039.51
26	2156.57	258.76	396.97	0.00	51.97	51.97	138.21	−86.24	953.27
27	2221.26	266.53	416.38	0.00	47.66	47.66	149.60	−101.94	851.33
28	2287.90	274.52	436.37	0.00	42.57	42.57	161.85	−119.38	731.95
29	2356.54	282.76	456.96	0.00	36.60	36.60	174.20	−137.60	594.35
30	2427.23	291.24	478.17	0.00	29.72	29.72	186.93	−157.21	437.14
31	2500.05	299.97	500.01	0.00	21.86	21.86	200.04	−178.18	258.96
32	2575.05	308.97	522.51	0.00	12.95	12.95	213.54	−200.59	58.37
33	2652.30	318.24	545.69	0.00	2.91	2.91	227.45		

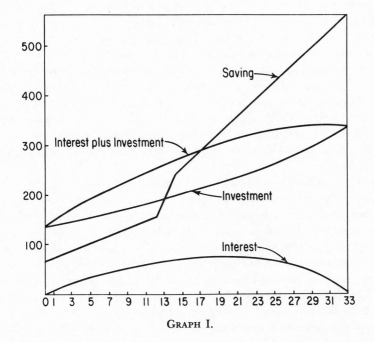

GRAPH I.

(*a*) The graph suggests the particular impact of all the variables. It is evident, for example, that if the marginal saving rate were .30 from the outset, independence of foreign debt could be achieved before the 33rd period or a larger rate of borrowing could be supported and possibly a higher rate of growth achieved. Or, if the jump in the saving rate from .20 to .30 did not occur, the payoff period would be lengthened or the rate of borrowing reduced. Similar statements may be made about the rate of interest that is assumed and the investment rate that is assumed to be required. Indeed, it is intuitively clear that the rate of interest paid must bear a certain relationship to the growth of income made possible by the capital inflow, or independence from foreign debt is not possible without increases in the saving rate or future reductions in the growth rate.

(*b*) It is further evident that to achieve the continuous 3 per cent rate of growth requires a continuous inflow of capital for nineteen periods. The argument is completely altered if capital imports are available for a shorter period or on a one-shot arrangement. Suppose, for example, the flow of imports shown in column 4 of Table V were available only through period seven and that repayment had to begin in period eight and be completed over ten years. In this case, from period eight through period seventeen, domestic saving must exceed domestic investment by about 76. If this were done, on present assumptions, it would leave less than 20 to meet domestic investment requirements in period eight, when over 150 is required to maintain the rate of growth of the economy. This is below the quantity of saving available for domestic investment in period zero before the loan was inaugurated, *if* the change in the marginal saving rate could be effected even though no foreign capital flowed into the country, then by the 18th period there would be little difference between the level of income with capital inflows and without capital inflows. Generalization from specific arithmetic examples is, of course, unwarranted, but the point does seem well established by the model that merely more foreign loans is not a sufficient condition for achieving a permanently higher rate of capital formation. Much depends on the other variables isolated in these examples.

(*c*) These difficulties are added to when note is taken of the transfer problem inherent in the above argument. It is evident that not only must domestic saving exceed domestic investment by the amount of the loan repayment, but this excess must be transferred, i.e., exports must exceed imports by this same amount. Even under ideal conditions of world trade, such a transfer may not be easy to effect, and the modern underdeveloped country is not beginning its development effort in a world trading network that facilitates such a transfer. If, for example, the transfer can be effected only by a deterioration in the terms of trade, the argument that capital imports may not add to the long-run rate of capital formation is enforced. The introduction of the transfer problem serves to indicate the role of the countries with whom the developing country trades. If the lending country is the chief trading partner of the borrowing country, then repayment of the loan requires that the former country recognize its obligations toward permitting an import surplus from the latter country to materialize.

The conventional mechanisms to effect the transfer have to do with price and income changes. Thus, prices and incomes fall in the paying country and rise in the receiving country, and due to the consequent changes in the quantities of goods demanded in the respective countries, trade occurs in sufficient amount to bring about the export surplus in the paying country. In a world where, to the maximum extent possible, the internal economy of a country is isolated from the effects of international trade there is little reason to believe this mechanism to work smoothly. The difficulties associated with the transfer have lead to some efforts on the part both of public and private investors to invest in specific projects that earned the required foreign exchange. It is implicit in the argument developed in Chapter 4 with respect to the multi-sectored growth model that such an approach may lead to a reduced growth rate.

(*d*) The saving rates assumed in the examples were abstractly drawn. The abrupt change in the marginal rate (from .20 to .30) was made to suggest the fact that a higher income may permit a higher marginal rate of saving, and that possible improvements in the taxing machinery may facilitate the achievement of a higher saving rate. Though the abrupt change between the 15th and 16th periods is of course quite unrealistic, a general rise in the marginal saving rate as income grows does seem a reasonable assumption. Further, the assumption that an investment rate of 12 per cent was required throughout the thirty-three periods has been made, and again there are many reasons why such a rate may yield higher or lower rates of growth than the 3 per cent assumed. For example, economies of scale may be realized as income expands or a particularly productive innovation may become accessible as the economy acquires more capital. On the opposite side, the available labor force may begin to become exhausted and force the use of more capital intensive techniques with the result—evident from previous analysis—that 12 per cent investment rate will not produce a 3 per cent rate or growth of capacity. This latter result, coupled with deteriorating terms of trade, could produce a major reduction in consumption rates as loan repayments are made.

(e) All of these difficulties emerge because of the assumption that capital inflows would end and repayment becomes necessary. The difficulties would be removed if repayment were not required, or if a given supply of foreign exchange of an adequate size were available for an indefinite number of periods. Although there have been a large number of grants in recent years, it does not appear feasible for an underdeveloped country to rely on grants, and ignore the problems of repayments completely. A conclusion that is even more far-reaching is that foreign loans can create difficulties for the developing country of a more intractable nature than those that it solves. Whether or not problems are created depends very much on how the loans are used. Merely having more resources is not enough, but if the additional resources are used in a way that some of the growth-defeating characteristics discussed in Chapter 7 are changed, then the difficulties are greatly overshadowed by the return. Part of the capital import analysis then includes attention to the specific impact that they might have.

B. SOME SPECIFIC USES OF CAPITAL IMPORTS

In Section A, the role of capital imports as a means of accelerating the rate of capital formation was examined, and as the analysis developed, obvious pitfalls emerged. The task now is to look more specifically into precisely how foreign capital may be used to increase its effectiveness, and possibly to permit the avoidance of some or all of the difficulties referred to in the previous sections. The discussion is primarily concerned with the effects on capital formation—on releasing resources from necessarily contributing to maintaining the economy—but it also considers a few other aspects of the international transactions as well.

1. Capital Imports as a Means of Implementing Domestic Policies. In Section I of this chapter, several processes of capital formation were identified, the success of which depended very strongly on the capacity of the country to levy and implement a rather specifically defined tax program. At the same time, it was noted in Chapter 7 and elsewhere that the tax-implementing skills available to the system were extremely limited. An import surplus is frequently an effective substitute for taxation as a means of controlling inflation. Particularly is this true during the various transition and gestation periods involved in the capital formation processes already described. For example, in the policy to bring about the use of generally more labor intensive productive techniques, a major problem area was the maintenance of control over aggregate demand during the period between the initiation of the subsidy and the realization of the increased output arising from the improved allocation. To pay the subsidy without taxing produces inflation, and to tax prior to the increased output limits the effectiveness of the subsidy. An import surplus aimed at supplementing the resources available to the community during this transition interval may, therefore, be especially strategic in the successful carrying through of such a general policy. The same kind of argument applies to the redirection of the "disguised unemployed" labor.

This is a very simple, but very important point. The shift in resource allocation from a rather institutionally determined system to a system that approaches economic rationality is of far-reaching importance to the development problem. The chief aim of an import surplus in the present argument is not simply to permit a higher rate of capital formation *per se* as in Section A, but it is rather to provide part of the resources necessary to carry through a much more fundamental policy. The argument further implies that unless the complementary activities within the economy are undertaken, the import surplus may contribute less to the capital formation process than is technically possible. Perhaps this can be stated in more general terms: Where a long gestation period is necessary before the fruits of a domestic policy are available, capital imports may provide an essential ingredient to the success of the implementation of the domestic policy.

2. *The Catalyzing of Domestic Entrepreneurship and Domestic Saving.* Capital imports also may serve as a device to set off domestic investment and saving simply by supplying a product that is or is thought to be a bottleneck to action. There are many examples that show the use of capital imports in this way. Many individuals with resources and some drive are genuinely thwarted, or are so circumscribed by their environment that they believe themselves to be thwarted, unless some access to imports is possible. Thus, a particular product—machine, vehicle, and the like—may be an essential ingredient to an investment project, and its availability from abroad may, therefore, encourage domestic entrepreneurs to commit their energies and their domestic resources when otherwise they would not. How important such an effect is varies widely from country to country and time to time. In many instances, the effect is probably very small or

absent entirely, but in other cases it is surely of great relevance. The need for outside light, i.e., for a source of pressure or encouragement from without the system to enable the economic agents within the system to appreciate the possibilities at their disposal, is most relevant. In many situations, this can be done by making exact use of capital imports to provide an immediate solution to a shortage of a specific produced input that may, because of the interdependence of sectors, be preventing full utilization.

Again, the precise nature of this role of the import surplus should be clear. Its primary achievement is not simply supplying more resources that thereby permit a higher rate of capital formation, but rather it is the extent to which specific imports of physical items induce a commitment of domestic resources to capital formation that would otherwise not have occurred. The chief difficulty is to appreciate the imports that have this kind of catalyzing effect, but there is little evidence to suggest that such information is impossible to come by. If no other way is available, a simple learning by experimentation may be profitable.

3. Technological Considerations. Chapter 11 is concerned with the general problem of the sources of new technical knowledge to the underdeveloped country. Here, however, an examination of the way in which an import surplus may contribute to the knowledge accumulation process is made. Capital imports may take the form of training personnel brought into the country or of trainees sent abroad for technical training. Although the evidence is far from conclusive on the impact of these activities, there is little doubt that some increase in technical knowledge is spread through the system in this way. Perhaps more important than direct formal training is a sort of on-the-job training. Specifically, imported products that provide or require new routines and new applied knowledge if they are to function at all may induce a training effect of considerable magnitude. In this case financing through capital imports may be necessary in order to prevent output from falling, because there is little doubt that a long and risky gestation period is involved. Great care and a great deal of information are required to make much of this argument. It is much easier to find evidence where a machine or tool of some sort was imported under terms of a grant or loan to serve precisely as a training device, and nothing happens: no training, no increase in the number of skilled workers, and no ultimate effect on output occurs. The source of the difficulty is partly that the necessary homework has not been done. Because it has not worked very well in the past does not mean that it cannot be made to work in the future, and one of the key sources of technical improvements emphasized in Chapter 11 is this kind of on-the-job training.

4. Capital Imports to Finance Specific Projects. Capital imports may also help provide the resources for the construction of a specific capital item. In general, such capital formation takes one or two forms: first, private imports may be used to build a branch factory or supply source; and second, public loans may be obtained specifically to help build a particular large project, e.g., dam, railroads, highways, and so on. The effectiveness of such capital import depends on a variety of things. If the opportunity cost of the capital is zero, i.e., if capital will come in only for that project and nothing else, then everything hinges on the repayment arrangements relative to the growth of the economy. On the other hand, the opportunity cost is rarely zero because some domestic resources are necessarily committed, and they may have more productive alternative uses if capital were available for other purposes. Where a special project foreign loan has the greatest advantage is a situation in which it is used to fill a niche in an overall investment program. In this case, one may say that the import is being used as it would be used even if it were not tied to a specific project. Where it is most likely to be harmful—in the sense that the repayments plus interest amount to more than the increment in income due to the capital import—are those occasions where such imports have little impact on the rest of the economy, and where they are not part of a general development effort.

5. *Capital Imports to Solve the Transformation Problem.* A situation may arise (it is discussed in Chapter 18) in which a country is able to save, but cannot accumulate capital. This would be the case if the domestic capital goods sector were not large enough to exploit fully the saving propensity, and if it were not possible to find additional export markets for current output (at least in the short run) without depressing the price to the extent that no increase in foreign exchange earnings were achieved. In this case, a development effort is thwarted, not because the country cannot supply "enough" resources for capital formation, but because it is not able to use the resources it has to acquire any form of capital. In the language to be used in Chapter 18, the economy lacks the transformation capacity necessary to exploit its saving propensity. Capital imports may then help to solve this kind of problem. This transformation difficulty is a short-run problem, but may be especially crucial in the middle of a major development program.

In this discussion of foreign loans and grants, a distinction has been between capital imports simply as the importation of foreign saving, simply as a means of raising the rate of capital formation, and foreign loans and grants as a means of implementing essentially domestic policies. It is the import surplus of course, that provides these means. At the same time, however, the distinction seems to be helpful because it leads to the isolation of what appear to be the more strategic aspects of capital imports. The most important suggestion that emerges is that such imports are more important as a method of facilitating the implementation of domestic policies than they are as mere additions to the supply of investible resources. This suggestion gains considerable weight in the next chapter where further domestic sources of saving are discussed.

III. Conclusion

This chapter has reviewed some methods of capital formation that the description of the underdeveloped country in Chapter 7 suggested were feasible without reducing consumption. Because they do not require reduced consumption, they might be identified as "painless" methods of capital formation, more accurately, painless methods of making resources available for development purposes. The most important of such methods had to do with changing techniques of production and using foreign loans and grants in an effective way. "Painless," however, does not mean easy or simple. Throughout the discussion emphasis was placed on the organizational and institutional changes that were demanded if full advantage were to be taken of these methods, and the fact that a heavy burden was placed on the entrepreneurial talent available.

The review of foreign borrowing was concentrated on the difficulties involved in making sure that such borrowing yields full returns. It is important to realize these difficulties, but at the same time it is important to appreciate that foreign loans—and grants—are essential to almost all developing countries making any headway in their development efforts. The question is how to make sure that such borrowings are used effectively, not whether they are necessary or desirable. There are other problems associated with international capital movements, e.g., tied loans—that have not been discussed in this chapter.

Bibliography

On the use of "disguised unemployed" labor to increase the rate of capital formation see the famous article by W. Arthur Lewis, "Economic Development with Unlimited Supplies of Labor," *The Manchester School of Economic and Social Studies,* XXII (May, 1954). It is reprinted in several "Readings." Also, James S. Duesenberry, "Some Aspects of the Theory of Economic Development," *Explorations in Entrepreneurial History,* II (December, 1950); Gustav Ranis and J. C. H. Fei, "A Theory of Economic Development," *American Economic Review,* LI (September, 1961); H. J. Bruton, "The Short Run Problem of Growth in Underdeveloped Countries," *Kyklos,* Fasc. 3, 1957; and Ragnar Nurkse, *Problems of Capital Formation in Underdeveloped Countries* (Oxford: Basil Blackwell, 1958), Chap. 2; and J. R. Hicks, "World Recovery after War: A Theoretical Analysis," *Economic Journal,* LVII (June, 1947) provide further elaboration of this issue.

On the effect of choice of technique on capital formation see especially Professor James E. Meade, "Mauritius: A Case Study in Malthusian Economics," *Economic Journal,* LXXI (September, 1961), which was very helpful in the writing of this section. See also Hollis B. Chenery, "Development Policies and Programmes," *Economic Bulletin for Latin America,* III (March, 1958).

On capital imports the approach in the text draws heavily on Gerald M. Alter, "The Servicing of Foreign Capital Inflows by Underdeveloped Countries," in *Economic Development for Latin America,* Howard S. Ellis (ed.) (New York: St.

Martin's Press, Inc., 1961). Mr. Alter develops much of the argument very rigorously in a mathematical appendix to his paper. See Gerald M. Meier, *International Trade and Development,* (New York: Harper & Row, Publishers), Chap. 5 and Sir Donald MacDougall, "The Benefits and Costs of Private Investment Abroad: A Theoretical Approach," *Economic Record,* XXXVI (March, 1960) for a slightly different approach to the capital import question. On the broader question dealing with measures to facilitate the flow of international private capital see the United Nations study, *The Promotion of the International Flow of Private Capital* (New York: United Nations, 1961) and on the quantitative side the UN's *International Flow of Long-term Capital and Official Donations,* 1951–1959 (New York: United Nations, 1962).

Chapter 10

CAPITAL FORMATION INVOLVING
A REDUCTION IN CONSUMPTION

The discussion in the previous chapter considered methods of making resources available for capital formation without reducing consumption at all. Because these methods did not require that the population sacrifice present consumption, they were referred to as "painless" (but not simple) methods. But current consumption rates, though very low, can only be regarded as sacrosanct at great cost to the development effort, and examination of methods of reducing consumption is clearly part of the problem of this book. The available methods are neither painless nor simple. Two general categories of approaches are considered. In Section I, those methods that involve a voluntary reduction in consumption or forced reduction via increased taxation are examined. In Section II, inflation as a means of reducing real consumption, and raising the rate of capital formation is discussed. First, however, some comment on the very idea of reduced consumption is necessary.

Among large segments of the population, average consumption is currently so low that health standards are seriously deficient. In terms of the language used in the discussion of the optimal saving problem, the utility of present consumption relative to future consumption is extremely high. If it were possible that consumption could be higher in the future than now (or possibly even the same as now) without saving, then real questions would arise as to the appropriateness of a policy that calls for a current reduction in consumption. The difficulty, of course, is that available evidence suggests strongly that some reduction in domestic consumption is required if the demands of development are to be met. Painless methods are important, indeed essential, but they are inadequate to do the complete job. They are inadequate in terms of the magnitude of the rate-of-capital formation, and in terms of producing the kind of reorganization and adjustments that are necessary to achieve the development objective.

Besides this consideration there is evidence that there is at least some saving room even in the lowest income society that may be exploited. For example, there are many instances where countries have increased the size of their armed forces by a sizeable margin, and there is no doubt at all that were a war to break out, any modern underdeveloped country would make available for the war effort a good deal more (at least for a short time) than the 15-18 per cent of its output usually thought necessary for development. There is also evidence that many, if not most, households accumulate assets of one kind or another that represent saving at some point in their history. The main motive for this sort of nonconsumption expenditure is for emergency, rainy day use, and as rainy days are quite ubiquitous in a poverty-ridden community there is a great deal of dissaving. The evidence does suggest that if the economy is so managed that rainy days are reduced, net saving will increase. Finally, there is evidence that decisions are made that clearly do reduce average consumption below what it would be if other choices had been made, for example, employing servants, supporting relatives, and the like. And, of course, there is a part of the community where conspicuous consumption is rampant, but this part is so small that it cannot contribute very much to the saving effort even if taxation reduced the consumption in this sector to only just above subsistence. That this is true is no reason why the extremely wealthy should not be made to curtail their consumption by a large margin.

The conclusion then may be accepted that there is a saving potential in the underdeveloped country not exploited in the initial conditions. Now the question is how to take advantage of this potential in a manner that has minimal ill effects on the other aspects of the development effort.

I. Noninflationary Methods of Increasing Saving

A great many schemes and proposals are extant for persuading people in underdeveloped countries to save a larger percentage of their low income. It would be a useful undertaking to examine these proposals in detail, to try to ascertain how effective they were or are, and the conditions under which they would be generally applicable. In the present context, all that is appropriate is to consider some of the more general propositions relating to increasing saving in terms of their applicability to the underdeveloped country, and in terms of the extent to which they lead to specific policies.

In an economy where one half of total output originates in agriculture a sizeable increase in domestic saving must necessarily come in part from this sector. This follows simply because of the dominant size of this sector in the economy. Also the evidence is strong that the sector of the society where saving is most likely to take place voluntarily is out of profits, as opposed to rents and wages. The basis for this assertion is that the profit earner's social position is such that he gains prestige as well as personal satisfaction through saving and accumulating productive capital. In most instances the landlord, the militarist, the politically ambitious find their prestige and satisfaction dependent on spending rather than on accumulating. The other sectors—service, professional, salaries—have saving potential but do not offer quite the target that the first two sectors mentioned offer.

The most important single thing that can be done to exploit the saving potential that does exist in the economy is to improve the tax system. (Indeed one may go further and assert that improving the tax system is the single most important task confronting the government of the underdeveloped country.) A well-designed tax program may exploit saving potential where it exists, and may effect its incidence in a manner to cause the least discouragement to capital formation. If the tax program is really well designed, the landlord could be taxed and the entrepreneur subsidized without reducing the real income of the peasant worker. But such an improvement in the tax machinery is a long, slow process, and until it is effected, resort must be had to second best schemes. However, the general point must not be lost sight of: the highest priority is attached to the development of effective tax instruments.

A. Specific Methods of Increasing Saving

Granting that tax improvement is the heart of the matter what else can be said, i.e., the question now is what to do until the good tax system arrives.

1. Moral suasion. Perhaps the most strategic thing that may be done is to convince the society that development is really taking place, and that its saving is really bearing fruit. As already noted, to save in order to secure a higher income later is not a common characteristic among the nationals of underdeveloped countries, and, especially in those new countries where growth pains are just beginning, to convince the population that saving matters and that development depends on it is no small task. The comparison of a development effort with a war effort is revealing in this respect. There are many examples of major sacrifices being made during a war, e.g., people standing in line to contribute gold hoardings or precious gems to help acquire resources to fight an enemy, but it is difficult to find examples of the same actions for the purpose of achieving economic development. Perhaps the only way to stir up the necessary enthusiasm is to demonstrate that development is actually taking place, and that saving today really means that income a few years—or few decades—hence will be higher because of the saving. It is evident that if there is a general enthusiasm for the development effort, the more mechanical approaches to the saving problem are much more likely to be successful than if they are im-

posed on a population that has a desultory attitude toward the very idea
of saving.

2. Direct incentives to save. Inducements to save through payment of
high interest rates and the making available of particular financial assets
will have some effect. Both interest rates and financial assets play a complex role in the development story and they are discussed in Chapter 17.

3. Increasing investment opportunities. A major means of increasing saving in some sectors of some economies is to increase investment opportunities. In particular activities, investment will generate its own saving,
and in these areas the task confronting the government policy maker is
simply to make sure that such investment opportunities are readily ob-
servable. There are several ways that economic policy can contribute to
this end. The more obvious include a tariff—an infant industry tariff—or
other forms of subsidy. The government may also invest in limited areas
of its own, and thereby generate obvious investment opportunities elsewhere in the system through the interdependence effects described in
Chapter 4. To argue that in all or most cases investment demand creates
its own saving in the underdeveloped country is to argue that there is no
saving problem as such, only a demand problem. This is surely an inaccurate and dangerous generalization, and a policy that acted on the assumption that it was generally true would result in inflation or bottlenecks
that produce investment opportunities but no investment, and no growth.
What does seem to be the case is that there are recurring instances where
the appearance of an investment opportunity will generate saving that
otherwise would not be made, and the availability of a method that will
permit full advantage to be taken of this saving potential may, at particular times, be of great importance. The difficulties involved in isolating
those sectors where this effect will be operative are severe, but perhaps not
insurmountable. Especially would it seem likely that going concerns would
react favorably in terms of saving if further investment opportunities become available.

A similar point has to do with the location of the physical capital that
is accumulated. There seems little doubt that most persons are more willing to sacrifice in order to contribute to the building of something that
they can see and benefit from directly than they are if they are merely
told of the usefulness of the investment activity. Thus a community may
be willing to reduce consumption in order to help build a feeder road or
school in their own area, but would be unwilling if the road or school
were to be built 200 miles distant.

4. Saving in particular sectors. Note has already been taken of the probability that profit earners save a larger portion of their income than do
wage earners and landlords. This assumption may be generalized to the
effect that certain sectors of the system will save more than other sectors or
are more easily taxed than other sectors. Expansion of output in such sec-

tors may, therefore, result in saving in the economy as a whole being higher than it would be if output had expanded in other sectors. To the extent that this point is empirically valid, it is important and useful. Because of the practical difficulties of discovering which sector or sectors will produce more saving and how much more they will produce, a more immediately relevant argument involves a slight modification of that just stated. The point is that rather than seek to allocate investment in a manner that maximizes the saving rate in the economy, the study of ways and means to increase saving should be done with those sectors in mind that growth of output considerations dictate should expand. This approach seems more appropriate than allocating or seeking to allocate investible resources where it is believed that saving rates will be highest or taxing rates will be more effective. It is easier to ascertain which sectors are going to move ahead rapidly in the near future than it is to discover which sectors have the highest saving rates, and also no sacrifice of immediate output is involved with this approach. That different techniques or incentives are required to induce a farmer to save from those that are required to induce the white collar worker or the factory worker to save seems quite clear.

5. *Substitution effects.* Finally, consideration is given to decisions that are made by the population, and the fact that policies to alter these decisions may be found. The chief examples have already been noted, spending for ceremonial affairs, hoarding gold or other precious metals, buying physical items as a hedge against rainy days, and so forth. A change in some relationship or tax or prestige factor may then induce changes in patterns of expenditure that result in a lower demand on resources. The point here is simply that certain forms of consumption outlays may be primarily a form of asset accumulation, and where this fact can be ascertained, alternative forms of assets may be supplied that are less demanding on resources. The data problem again is quite severe and demanding, but its solution does not impose insurmountable difficulties and once the analyst is aware of the relationship to look for, appropriate data may be made more readily available. Another form of substitution has to do with imports. Some evidence is available to suggest that, at least over a short period, the curtailing of consumer imports may induce saving. If direct taxation of the rich is not effective, indirect taxation through import curtailment may be an effective substitute because the type of consumption goods imported are usually not obtainable at home, and hence some increase in saving will take place if imports are stopped. This effect is probably only short run, as adjustment in consumption patterns will surely be made in a longer run if the affected individuals do not want to save the new higher proportion of their income. Again, however, as a spot policy, this source of saving may be extremely helpful.

Conclusion. No single proposal—except taxation—emerges from the list as a sure fire method of inducing or forcing the population to save more of its income, and a great deal of information and implementing skill is called for in all cases. In some instances, the method would clearly work only in very special circumstances, and only for a given interval of time. Despite these conclusions the arguments are rather convincing that given the existence of the saving potential, approaches to its exploitation along the lines discussed above will be profitable. It also seems clear that with respect both to the size of the profit and the certainty of its appearance, that these methods or others like them cannot bear the full burden of the saving problem. But, of course, a small increment in the saving rate may mean the difference between success and failure of the development effort, and at any one time having access to the kind of approaches described here is very important. Further, any activity that trains the taxing bureaucracy and contributes to its emergence as an effective organization may be expected to yield significant returns.

B. On the Marginal Saving Rate

The previously mentioned generalizations apply equally well to saving from increments in income, and the implementation problem in this case is probably easier than in the case where consumption must be reduced. To persuade people that not increasing consumption despite a rise in income is surely easier than convincing them that reducing their consumption is essential to the development effort. The same assertion would appear to hold for the other forms of inducements to save discussed in the preceding section.

On the other hand, there are two complications to which reference should be made that may affect the extent to which consumption is held down as income rises. In the first place, there is the possibility of a backward-bending supply curve of effort. Such a phenomenon may arise if there appears no reward for increased labor that is acceptable to a large majority of the population. If such were the case, then an effective policy to prevent consumption from rising may create bottlenecks on the supply side. Thus rather than workers straining to spend their newly acquired income and thereby creating inflation problems or slowing down the rate of capital formation, they may simply refuse to supply the additional effort that the concentrated development effort requires. Presumably the argument could be applicable to all levels of labor, from the least skilled to the highest skilled, but the argument is usually applied to the relatively unskilled. Empirical evidence does not reveal very clear conclusions as to the general applicability of this hypothesis, although there are examples of laborers working until they have accumulated enough to buy a particular and unusual consumer good (e.g., watch, bicycle, and the like) and then quitting. Granting these examples and the general validity of the logic of the argument, there are several reasons for doubting that it should affect policy considerations in any significant manner. A labor bottleneck of this type is not likely to appear in most developing societies for some time after development is underway, certain types of capital formation have equal incentive effects on labor that consumption goods have, and inducements in the form of income earning assets may also be an effective substitute for consumption in some instances. This last consideration is particularly relevant in light of the rainy day saving argument introduced in Section A, and the conclusion following from it that the voluntary marginal saving rate may well be "quite" high, say .25 or .30. Such a high marginal rate—high relative to the average rate—may be a short-run affair if dissaving is reduced through an effective development policy, and savers find their assets growing more or less regularly. By the time these happy circumstances arrive, the tax system should be in a position to control consumer spending in a fairly effective way. Finally, for reasons associated with welfare considerations and with higher consumption that will enable many workers to supply more effort because of the resulting health effects, the argument would not dictate a zero rate of increase in consumption as income rises. There seems no evidence to suggest that the rate of increase in consumption called for by these considerations is below that called for by the necessity to straighten out any potentially backward-bending supply curve of labor.

The other point to be made in connection with the marginal-saving rate is more important and easily stated, but more difficult to put into quantifiable terms. A high marginal-saving rate may be wasted if the capital goods sector is small and incapable of expansion in the short run and if export markets are weak. In such conditions, the high-saving rate simply means lower income or less rapidly growing income than a lower saving rate would mean. In an economy with a 5 per cent average saving rate and little past growth, the capital-goods-producing sector is necessarily small, and most of the resources and organizational arrangements are geared to consumption-goods-producing activities rather than capital-goods-producing activities. Consequently, a quick upsurge in saving may catch the economy unprepared to exploit it. This, then, is simply a reminder of the argument referred to in the discussion of the optimal saving rate, namely that saving rates are necessarily limited by the capacity of the economy to supply capital goods. In a given short period, especially early in the development effort, the incremental saving rate may release resources from consumption goods production at a higher rate than they can be absorbed into the capital goods-producing or exporting sectors. Evidently, then, in appraising policies for affecting the marginal saving rate, some attention must be given to the ability of the economy to use the resources released to produce capital goods of one kind or another.

Here again, however, the major problem is in almost all cases one of a marginal-saving rate that is too low, rather than too high for the economy to exploit effectively. The capital goods sector is generally expansible.

Especially if effective wage rates to firms reflect true relative scarcities, then it will be unusual for the marginal-saving rate to outstrip the capacity of the economy to use the released resources effectively.

The preceding discussion considered some general arguments about ways to convince people to reduce their consumption or at least not increase it very rapidly. The methods assumed zero inflation, but it is commonly recognized that inflation may facilitate the capital formation process. An inquiry is made to reveal how inflation is used for capital accumulation.

II. Inflation as a Means of Inducing Saving

There are few economic ills that have not been explained in terms of inflation, and it is easy to argue that simply pumping too much money into the system can and has produced a great variety of economic problems. At the same time, it is necessary to recognize that just as saving is not all good so inflation is not all bad, and that under some circumstances inflation may be used as an instrument of policy rather than defined in a manner that makes its suppression necessarily an objective of policy. The principal objective here is to work out the details of the process by which a rising price level forces a reduction in consumption and thereby makes available additional resources for capital formation. The primary purpose of this section is to consider the conditions necessary for this process to resolve itself without producing a runaway inflationary situation. These are given attention in Section B, but some recognition of specific problems created by inflation is necessary as a prologue—so Section A is concerned with a brief review of long recognized, traditional ills that may be created by inflation. The inflation process considered here is that usually identified as produced by excess aggregate demand. In Chapter 17, other sources of inflating pressure are discussed, and uses of inflation other than as a capital formation instrument are examined.

A. The Problems of Inflation

Inflation means a rising price level, and of course is not to be confused with rising and falling relative prices. How high must prices rise before inflation exists? In some sense, any rise in the price level means, by definition, that inflation is occurring. But price level changes must be measured by a price index and price indices are tricky things. A modest rise (e.g., less than 2 per cent per year) probably does not mean much of anything, but once the price index shows an increase in excess of this, then perhaps even the strongest index number critic would agree that the price level really is rising. Also for reasons connected with the difficulties inherent in index number construction, long range comparisons do not make much sense. For example, the statement that the price level is five times (or two times or twelves times) as high now in Country X as it was in 1900 does not have a great deal of content. The reasons are obvious. Changing weight, changing quality of products, changing institutional arrangements, and the like mean simply that it is not possible to construct a single value index of changes in the general purchasing power of money for such a long period of time. "Inflation" then means a relatively short-run situation in which prices are rising by a rate say in excess of 2–3 per cent per annum. The specific question is simply what problems does such a situation create.

On the one hand, there are what may be called income distributional problems. Such problems refer to the fact that fixed (money) income groups are penalized, and these groups often include persons who most members of the community agree should not be penalized. This kind of attitude is, of course, a welfare judgment about which no firm assertions can be made. Thus there is no machinery that will enable the demonstration that the income distribution before inflation was "better" than the one produced by the inflation. Therefore, whether the income distributional effects of inflation are of great relevance depends on the precise welfare function that one employs. Less strongly, one may say that unless certain groups—e.g., widows—are penalized to the point of impairing their members' physical health, then no firm conclusions can be drawn about the welfare implications of the income distributional effects of inflation. In the underdeveloped country, the group most harshly affected by inflation are the urban workers who buy most of their consumption goods in the market, and, as noted earlier, this group may be the most difficult of all groups (except the landlords) to tax. The peasant farmer with little or no contact with the market will be only moderately hurt by rising prices. It is tempting then to argue that inflation may be the tax in the urban sector, and the taxing bureaucracy then concentrate its energy on the rural areas. And of course, as shown in the next section, capital formation via inflation requires an effect on the distribution of income.

On the other hand, there are also effects that may be considered in a more objective manner. These are familiar and need be only briefly discussed.

Inflation discourages voluntary saving. Inflation means that the value of money is declining, and people who become aware of the inflation seek to rid themselves of money and acquire goods. But whether or not inflation not only results in a flight from money but also away from saving depends upon the nonmoney assets that are available to the community. If assets are available that have built-in inflation insurance, then there is no important reason why voluntary saving should be discouraged by a rising price level.

Similarly, arguments are frequently presented that inflation results in an allocation of investment that is less than optimal. Thus even if the rate of capital formation is increased by inflation, the larger quantities of investible resources are used in a fashion designed to exploit rising prices rather than designed to take advantage of long-run productivity considerations. Luxury housing is frequently mentioned as an example of the kind of investment induced by inflation. Supporting empirical evidence for this argument is difficult to discover, but there is probably some such effect present in prolonged inflations. However, it should also be kept in mind that until growth begins and until factor prices are adjusted to match the relative scarcities of the factors, much of private investment—whether occurring in a stable price level environment or in an inflation environment —will aim at the higher income groups and seek areas where capital gain is likeliest. Inflation accentuates this tendency. There are some controls however. The origin of inflation of the kind discussed now is either an increase in credit to private entrepreneurs or a government deficit. In both instances, the investment projects at the outset can be controlled simply by limiting the access to the finance to those who invest in areas that satisfy acceptable criteria. Investment following the originating projects may be less easily controlled, but attention has already been called to the fact that investment finance will not be rationed solely by the rate of interest. Hence some control system on investment allocation is assumed to exist, and this control may affect the allocation subsequent to the initial inflationary burst. The longer the inflation continues the more difficult it will be to maintain full control, and hence the more likely an undesirable allocation is to emerge. The accumulation of inventories especially is encouraged by rising prices. Again emphasis should be placed on the argument that the misallocation of investment caused by inflation is probably small compared to that induced by a malfunctioning factor price system and a generally static economy. If inflation contributes or can be made to contribute to solving either or both of these problems it may earn a return on its costs.

Finally, inflation can play havoc with the balance of payments, and attempts to correct the balance of payments may add still further to the inflationary pressure. The balance of payments effect is perhaps the most difficult of all the problems created by inflation. The balance of payments of a developing country is a fragile thing in the best of situations, and an inflation adds greatly to the difficulties confronting the policy maker in this area. To assume trade and exchange controls as a solution is not enough, because the kind of controls that may become necessary if inflation continues unchecked will impose severe limitations on the effective functioning of the price system. The practical difficulties of implementing a program of subsidies to exports and taxes on imports to counteract the effect of inflation, though not insuperable, are severe enough to warrant little confidence in their efficacy. Especially is this the case if inflation continues indefinitely with no effects on output.

There are other problems created by inflation, but they are of lesser magnitude and more easily manageable than the ones just mentioned. Several general points about inflation dangers emerge from the preceding discussion. The most significant point is that the great evils of inflation occur only after it has continued so long that the monetary authorities have lost control of aggregate demand. Indeed, almost all sweeping condemnations of inflation rest on the assumption that a spiraling phase is an inevitable consequence of any inflation. Once the price rise has begun to feed on itself and is no longer subject to control, then there is no question as to harmfulness. In this event, a major danger of an inflation is that it impedes the establishment of an economy-wide pricing system. These consequences of spiraling inflation, however, cannot be applied to an inflation that does not reach spiraling proportions, and to one that is accompanied by changes in other parts of the economy. Consequently, an essential ingredient of the use of inflation as an instrument of policy depends very much on the sophistication of the monetary authorities, and on their ability to implement the policies necessary to keep inflation under control.

The effects of inflation also vary depending on what else is happening in the system along with the inflation. The important question to be answered is whether or not aggregate capacity is actually being increased. For if it is, then the control of the potential spiral is simplified. Capacity may be increased not only by raising the rate of capital formation, but also by adjusting factor prices, by breaking bottlenecks, by strengthening the mobility of factors, and by spreading the use of the price system. As shall be argued in the next section, controlled inflation tends to contribute to accomplishing all of these objectives.

The position now is this: uncontrolled, spiraling inflation is recognized as an unqualified impediment to development. Under certain conditions inflations will not degenerate into spirals, and if these conditions are met, inflation may be used as an effective instrument to achieve certain key objectives of development. The most important of these "certain conditions" are a monetary and fiscal authority that can devise and implement controls of several types, and an economic system that responds to the incentives and opportunities opened up by inflation.

The task now is to examine more specifically how inflation may serve as an instrument of development policy, particularly as an instrument to raise the rate of capital formation.

B. CAPITAL FORMATION THROUGH INFLATION

To begin the discussion of the *modus operandi* of capital formation by means of inflation, an interpretation of the meaning of inflation and the process by which it occurs or can be induced to occur is given. A more complete treatment of this question is presented in Chapter 17.

One way of defining monetary equilibrium in an economy with no international transactions is in terms of the *ex ante* equality at full capacity of saving (S) plus changes in the money supply (ΔM_s) and investment (I) plus changes in the demand for money (ΔM_d). In conventional terminology $S + \Delta M_s$ is referred to as the supply of loanable funds and $I + \Delta M_d$ as the demand for loanable funds. If the *ex ante* equality does not prevail, then changes in the rates of interest are assumed to occur, and given the customarily assumed shapes of the several schedules, changing interest rates induce changes in the magnitude of the other variables until the necessary *ex post* equality is achieved. For example, if $S + \Delta M_s$ exceeds $I + M_d$, then the rate of interest is assumed to decline and $I + \Delta M_d$ increase until equality is achieved. There are many difficulties with this argument, i.e., the several schedules may be completely unresponsive to changes in the rate of interest, or the rate of interest may not respond to changes in the supply of loanable funds. These difficulties are compounded (as will be discussed) in the underdeveloped economy, and their existence is the reason that manipulation of the government budget deficit must be included in any argument of the determination of the level of aggregate demand. Despite these shortcomings the simple equation is a convenient starting point for a discussion of the excess demand inflation that is of concern here. How then does this type of inflation begin?

Suppose that in period zero, the economy is in full capacity equilibrium, and that for the next period, when a higher output obtains, $S = I$ at full capacity but $\Delta M_s > \Delta M_d$. This situation could occur for any number of reasons: the monetary authorities simply overestimate the demand for money to hold as an asset, an improvement in banking facilities reduces the transactions demand for money unexpectedly, unexplained changes in expectations occur, and so on. So the rate of interest falls, investment plans are changed, and the rate of consumption is increased. By assumption, the system was operating at full capacity before the increment in spending, and consequently these increments cannot be realized in real terms, so prices are pushed up until some of the demand is choked off. This brief argument stresses two things of importance to the capital formation effects of inflation. In the first place, the argument calls attention to the role of finance and, as noted in Chapter 5, finance can be supplied in many ways. The argument further calls attention to the fact that price rises do choke off demand. If, then, finance is supplied to those who will engage in productive capital formation and is not available to those who wish merely to consume, it is the demand of the latter that is choked off and the demand of the former that is implemented. The consequence is, therefore, a higher rate of capital formation and a lower rate of consumption. The details of this process in an underdeveloped country are now examined.

1. Inflation, Capital Formation, and Stability. The simplest way to initiate a capital formation inflation effort is for the government through the central bank or treasury to make available to itself funds in excess of tax revenues. This process may consist merely of printing money, but usually a less incriminating term will apply to whatever process is employed. An almost equally simple way is for the banking system, through any of a variety of techniques available to it, to make available to the private investor credit at a rate that is acknowledged to be in excess of that rate consistent with price level stability. In terms of the general argument, there is no difference between these two sources of inflationary finance. In either event, elements of the community that will invest in productive capital formation are given access to finance with which to gain control over the real resources necessary to effect the capital formation.

The investors (government or private) armed with their new finance are now in a position to bid for available resources. Since the present assumption is that full utilization of all resources was enjoyed before the inflationary finance was made available (otherwise the new finance may not be inflationary), these investors must bid resources away from other uses, and this they do by offering a higher wage or quasi-rent than the resource is now receiving. Suppose the resources are bid away from consumer goods industries, and consequently the output of consumer goods falls absolutely. Prices of consumer goods rise because of the increase in money income accruing to the community, and because of the reduced flow of output from the consumer goods sectors. The sequence of events is then as follows: Investors receive finance and bid resources (chiefly labor) from the consumer goods industries. Output in the latter industries declines, and prices of their products necessarily rise. Money wage rates have risen, but prices of consumer goods have risen more so the quantity of consumer goods demanded declines. There is now an increase in the quantity of resources available for investment, and a reduced quantity available for the production of consumer goods. A shift in the composition of output has occurred in favor of the production of capital goods, and profits have risen relative to wage rates.

The shift in income distribution from consumer to investor must continue until the overall saving rate equals the new higher rate of investment. If no further rises in wage rates after the initial one occurs, then this price increase may be relatively modest. This is particularly true if the investors—or profit earners generally—have an average and marginal-saving rate much higher than that for the community as a whole, and if the wage earner has a money illusion. In the event that there is no effort to restore the level of consumption, the new higher rate of investment continues without additional pressure on the price level. After the new investment is completed, an increase in output is possible. If this increased output is in the form of consumer goods, a rise in real wages can then be allowed. The fact that real wages have been reduced initially and that holding them down is essential to achieving the increase in the rate of capital formation suggests that if the new capacity is in the consumer goods sectors, the control of further inflationary pressure will be simplified. Thus, if the reduction in real consumption is followed by an early increase in consumption, the pressure for further increases in money wage rates may be thwarted and the higher rate of investment may then continue. In this case, a one shot injection of new money into the system used to create productive capital has permanently shifted the allocation of resources in such a way that the proportion of total output invested has increased.

2. *Continuous Inflation, Continuous Capital Formation.* A second possibility is the delicate situation in which new money is made available to the investors more or less regularly, and money wage rates rise steadily, but lag behind the price level in such fashion that real consumption cannot catch up. In this case, the continuously rising price level is an essential part of the mechanism to maintain the shifted distribution brought about by the original injection of new money. As long as the lag of wage rates behind the price level continues, the higher rate of capital formation will also continue, and output will rise at a higher rate than in the absence of the inflation.

There is no a priori reason why this kind of situation must turn into a harmful spiraling inflation. The increased flow of output, especially consumer goods, is continually dampening the inflation pressure. Furthermore, if the possibility of a more rapid rate of technical innovations or of increasing returns to scale are introduced, as investment continues, the dampening pressure is increased.

In both these examples of capital formation, success hinges heavily on the ability of the system to direct the inflationary finance into the hands of the investors, the ability to control or at least impede labor from preventing any reduction in its share of output, the ability to protect the balance of payments by noninflationary means, and the ability to prevent the burden of the inflation from falling on other investment rather than on consumption.

3. *Spiraling Inflation, No Capital Formation.* The most damaging of all situations is a wage-price spiral that has no effect on the rate of growth of capital or output. In this case, the price level increase is immediately matched by a wage rate increase and hence no decline in real consumption takes place and no resources are released for use in capital formation. As such a process continues, the wage earners may even be able to anticipate future price rises, and gain wage rate increases that lead the price level increases. In this event, the rate of investment will fall, and the economy is in the midst of a situation in which nothing can be done but stopping the process through the control of finance, reestablishing full control of demand, and trying again. This particular type of wage-price spiral may not be especially important in the underdeveloped country with "disguised unemployed" labor, but when the labor supply runs out then the argument is more nearly applicable. In some countries, inflation pressure is reflected most immediately in a balance of payments problem,

and the direct source of the spiral may be in import controls or the effects of a devaluation, if the latter should occur, in response to a deteriorating payments position. Further the tax rates—or more accurately, the taxes collected—are frequently such that when money incomes rise, additional deficit financing is forced on the government to meet current outlays. If the marginal ratio of government receipts to national income is less than the average ratio, the costs of government rise more rapidly than its revenue as money income increases. The resulting deficit is unlikely to be met by reducing noncapital expenditures, and the inflation pressure is thus fed by further deficit financing. All of these factors suggest ample reason why an inflation produced to raise the rate-of-capital formation can quickly turn into the kind of spiraling affair that does nothing but damage to any development effort.

4. Problems of Implementation. These remarks suggest several things. First of all, the argument is quite convincing that the longer the rise in price level continues the more dangerous it becomes, i.e., the less likely it is to produce a higher rate of growth of output than would obtain with no inflation. This conclusion is based on the simple assumption that as inflation continues, all of the factors contributing to turning it into a spiraling process—wage rate behavior, balance of payments deficits, the government deficit, and the allocation problem—increase in strength and become much less subject to control via the conventional monetary and fiscal policy weapons.

If this conclusion is accepted, then an essential part of the inflation model is to bring about its end in a manner that does not create either panic or depression. Obviously, the safest way to do this is simply through increased output as described in the first inflation model. That the end may not always come in this neat fashion hardly needs to be said, and that the monetary and fiscal authorities must have a mopping up program ready is essential. The greatest difficulty here will arise in economies with a network of financial intermediaries that can supply finance to investors more or less irrespective of the monetary and fiscal authorities' wishes. More to the point, however, is the conclusion that the use of inflationary finance be limited, and that such inflation episodes be followed by a period in which no such finance is made available. Perhaps the simplest rule of thumb is that the employment of inflationary finance be limited to specific schemes, the output effect of which is fairly predictable as well as quickly realizable. The emphasis on the usefulness of consumer goods output mentioned earlier may again be noted.

These arguments do not imply that the inflation is a "mild" one. In fact for reasons to be discussed in Chapter 17, a mild one (of the order of 2–4 per cent per annum) is surely a necessary continuing part of development. An inflationary burst that has any effect at all may then mean a 10–15 per cent per year price rise for 5 to 7 years with 10 years an outside limit. (These numbers may be misleadingly exact as they can hardly be defended by any sort of theoretical argument, but rest rather on a general appraisal of the institutional arrangements that prevail in the underdeveloped countries. Some countries have such primitive weapons to control the inflation process that they should not consider inflation at all.) Less pressure than this as well as less time will surely be less than that required to effect the necessary transfer of resources from the consumption goods sectors to the capital goods sectors.

To try to raise the rate of capital formation through inflation is without a doubt a risky undertaking, and complete success depends very much on a degree of fiscal and tax sophistication that is rarely present in the kind of economy described in Chapter 7. Indeed a major question that has to be answered is this: Inflation is a form of taxation and any capital that can be accumulated through inflation can be accumulated through taxation, and since the latter is much safer than the former why include inflation at all as an acceptable means of raising the rate of investment? The answer cannot be simply because the taxing bureaucracy is too ill-equipped to do the job, because the successful implementation of the inflation method requires that taxation policy also meet high standards. There are several aspects to the answer.

The demands on the taxing bureaucracy are in both instances quite severe, but they are not the same. To collect higher taxes at a time when no prospect of economic growth is apparent requires a much stronger political position and taxing machinery than does imposing taxes to end an inflation after output has already begun to rise. Indeed the ability of the government to impose taxes to reduce consumption may be completely lacking, and temporary inflation the only way to do so, or it may be the only way to reduce the consumption levels of certain elements of the society who are usually gifted at avoiding taxation. Especially in a country where efforts are being made to exploit "disguised unemployed" labor or to bring about a change in the choice of technique, inflation may be a much more ready tool than taxation.

Finally, and perhaps most important, to effect a shift in resources of the magnitude required to move toward the development goal at a pace that is politically acceptable may not be possible without a strong dose or two of inflation. The defective price system, the weak tax system, the entrepreneurial bottlenecks, and the immobility of labor due to social rigidities of all sorts result in a situation where price pressure to induce modifications into the system must be much more powerful than is the case in any economy long accustomed to reacting to price incentives. This result from inflation may be met alternatively by larger or longer periods of capital imports, unless they tend to inhibit this adjusting process by lightening the pressure on the resources to transfer. The comparison of the transfer of resources in the development effort with a shift from a peace to a war economy is revealing. The wartime problem is (at least was) that of achieving rapid and large scale transfer of resources from the production of one category of product to another. Evidence available suggests strongly that such a transfer cannot be effected without inflation (or direct controls), and the problem is more intense in the low income country than in the developed country converting to war. To pull part of the labor force away from traditionalistic, agricultural jobs imposes a much more demanding task on the allocative function of prices than does shifting from automobile to tank production. However—always the however—the fact that inflation of the magnitude mentioned is part of the development problem does not mean that the policy-making authorities can lose control of the demand side. It means rather maintaining control during episodes of induced inflation, and this is difficult indeed to do even in systems where conventional monetary tools are assumed to work smoothly. All of these conclusions apply to a particular kind of inflation, not just any inflation. No doubt price level stability is a simpler goal to achieve than the ideal inflation episodes, but this observation is of little relevance: non-development is an easier goal to achieve than is development. Also, the method may not be applicable to all countries. Note has already been taken of the fact that the monetary system of some economies may be too primitive to risk the process at all. And finally it is again emphasized that if inflation is undertaken in the manner just described, it is assumed that other things are happening as well, particularly a more rational pricing of labor, an increasing concentration of resources on productive capital formation, a concentrated effort to use the "disguised unemployed" in the uninflationary manner already described, and hopefully an import surplus as well.

III. Conclusions on Capital Formation

A. A Summary View

The arguments in this and the preceding chapter have shown that there is a saving potential in the underdeveloped country and that there are policies available that, if successfully implemented, will enable the exploitation of this potential. From the discussion of the several methods of increasing the saving rate, four points emerged that are general enough and important enough to be given further emphasis. In the first place, the ability to devise and implement a specific tax program has been a strategic factor in almost every method discussed. The failure to recognize and accept the implications and limitations inherent in it may mean that any and all methods not only fail to achieve the announced objectives, but that their initiation creates more difficulties than are solved. In particular, it should be clear that taxation is important not merely as a device for reducing consumption, but also as a device for directing resources into various sectors, for preventing increases in consumption, for effecting pricing policies, and for effecting the combination of inputs. All of these aspects are highly relevant for the success of the effort to release resources from maintenance uses.

Second, the full exploitation of the saving potential requires that the community be able to take advantage of a variety of types of opportunities. Opportunities to affect the saving rate appear here and there, now and then and full exploitation requires that a number of policies be always ready for application. To know when, where, and how much to tax, to inflate, to borrow abroad, to subsidize employers places heavy demands not only on the implementing machinery as such, but also on knowledge and understanding of the economy. To a great extent, the kind of empirical knowledge and understanding required can only be acquired by learning from observing a changing economy. To delay action until all "necessary" knowledge is available is to delay the beginnings of development indefinitely and, of course, would not be advocated. There does seem reason to believe that as the economy experiences change, more will be learned that will permit a more effective exploitation of the saving potential than is possible at the outset of the development effort when knowledge is in such short supply.

A third point has to do with the role of capital obtained from abroad. Such capital—unless outright grants—imposes repayment demands that can possibly nullify the advantages to be gained from the initial import surplus. Especially is it important to recognize that capital imports are most effective when they are used as means of implementing development policies of a sort more fundamental than merely a higher rate of capital formation. For most developing countries, capital imports obtained merely to achieve a higher rate of capital formation can be harmful, as capital formation obtained in *this* painless way may serve solely to relieve the pressure to make the environmental and other changes that are part of the development objective.

Finally, attention is again directed toward the constraints imposed by institutional factors, including the administrative machinery of the government and private sector. Tax-levying capacity has been repeatedly referred to, but there are other constraints as well. The existence of an extended family system, of social customs alien to entrepreneur activity, of widespread technical and economic ignorance, of noneconomic practices toward employment, and so on, severely limit the extent to which the necessary policies can be put into effect. A fairly safe general conclusion is that the maximum upper limit on the saving rate is not to be found in the simple necessity of allowing resources to be used for the production of consumer goods, but rather it is to be found in the category of constraints that fall under the heading of "institutional constraints" on the implementation of policies. This conclusion is of great importance to the development story in a wide variety of ways especially those having to do with the speed at which the development objective can be achieved.

B. Is Capital Formation Enough?

The exact consequences of capital formation taking place "while everything else is constant" is contained in the production function introduced in Chapter 2 and the arguments worked out in Section A of Chapter 3. Suppose that the factor price subsidy scheme has been put into effect and the production technique of the typical firm of the system is described by point *A* on Diagram II in Chapter 3. This point is optimal for the firm and from the standpoint of economywide opportunity costs of the two inputs. As capital formation proceeds, the firm will move along Ray *A* as long as the cost line remains intact, i.e., as long as the effective wage rates do not rise in consequence of the capital formation. When capital formation does occur, to the extent that wage rates begin to rise relative to capital costs, the firm begins to shift to Techniques *B*, then to *C*. If no new techniques are introduced, then maximum capital intensity is defined by Ray *C*, and when all production is carried on with this process, increases in capital must be matched by increases in labor if all the capital is to be used.

For the underdeveloped country the movement from Ray *A* to Ray *C* may require a long period of calendar time. During this time, *per capita* income is growing and the economy as a whole is expanding. It is tempting to conclude, therefore, that until Ray *C* describes the production process for the whole economy, the only requirement for the development program is simply net capital formation in excess of the rate of growth of the labor force. The important consequence of this conclusion would be that at the outset of the development effort and for a long time thereafter, the only problem to solve is that of finding ways to increase the rate of capital formation. This conclusion, however, cannot be accepted for several reasons. The rate of growth of *per capita* income will, obviously, be lower than would be the case if the resources were becoming more productive as the capital-labor ratio rises. This statement may hold even if resources are required to devise the new technical knowledge. Thus, *per capita* income may grow more rapidly if some resources available for building more capital and increasing the capital intensity of production are in fact used to find new techniques of production, and thereby raise the productivity of the existing resources. The same argument applies to the other components of the production function. Thus, the use of resources to alter the social and institutional environment in some way, or to improve the quality of the labor input, or to create a new product out of a natural resource available in great supply may result in a higher rate of growth of income than would be the case if all resources released from maintaining the economy were devoted to the building of physical capital defined in K_{nj} of the aggregate production function.

Also the population growth rate must not merely be less than the rate of growth of output, it must also be under control. Resources used to discover an applicable population policy, and to put it into effect may therefore be the "best" use of the available investible resources.

The conclusion that emerges then is not simply for the economy to move as rapidly as possible from Technique A to Technique C. Rather it is to use the resources released from maintaining the economy at some agreed upon level to make the maximum contribution possible to increasing the capacity of the economy to produce. This may involve capital formation *pur et simple,* but it may not. How investible resources may be utilized to change characteristics of the system other than the quantity of physical capital, and the measurement of the relative size of the effect of alternative uses of these resources on the development objective are considered in Part III.

Bibliography

On the general question of taxation in developing countries begin with A. R. Prest, *Public Finance in Underdeveloped Countries* (New York: Frederick A. Praeger, Inc., 1963), especially Chaps. 1–6; Jack Heller and Kenneth M. Kauffman, *Tax Incentives for Industry in Less Developed Countries* (Cambridge: The Law School of Harvard University, 1963); and U Tan Wai, "Taxation Problems and Policies of Underdeveloped Countries," *International Monetary Fund Staff Papers,* IX (November, 1962). On taxation in agriculture, see Haskell P. Wald (ed.), *Papers and Proceedings of the Conference on Agricultural Taxation and Economic Development* (Cambridge: Harvard University Printing Office, 1954). Studies of the consequences of policies to effect saving are as difficult to make as are estimates of saving and (especially) saving propensities. See, however, I. M. D. Little, "Tax Policy and the Third Plan" in *Pricing and Fiscal Policies* ed. by P. N. Rosenstein-Rodan (Cambridge: The M.I.T. Press, 1964); Richard W. Hooley, *Saving in the Philippines: 1951–60* (Quezon City: Institute of Economic Development and Research, University of the Philippines, 1963); United Nations, "Saving of the Federation of Malaya," *Economic Bulletin for Asia and the Far East,* XII (June, 1962); Stephen R. Lewis, Jr. and Mohammad Irshad Khan, "Estimates of Non-corporate Private Saving in Pakistan: 1949–1962," *The Pakistan Development Review,* IV (Spring, 1964); William I. Abraham, "Saving Patterns in Latin America," *Economic Development and Cultural Change,* XII (July, 1964); and three articles on saving in the *Economic Bulletin for Asia and the Far East,* XII (December, 1962).

On the process by which inflation may be used as a means of raising the rate of capital formation see the excellent paper by E. M. Bernstein and I. G. Patel, "Inflation in Relation to Economic Development," *International Monetary Fund Staff Papers,* II (November, 1952). Also, W. Arthur Lewis has much to say on inflation in this respect that is helpful: see especially the reprint of his speech, "Observations on the Relationship between Development and Inflation," in *Development Research Digest,* I (April, 1963) and his *The Theory of Economic Growth* (London: George Allen & Unwin, 1955), pp. 216–25.

The *International Monetary Fund Staff Papers* frequently have articles that analyze the various effects and dangers of inflation. See, for example, Graeme S. Dorrance, "The Effect of Inflation on Economic Development" (March, 1963) and Gertrude Lovasy, "Inflation and Exports in Primary Producing Countries," (March, 1962).

Part Three

ON THE USES OF
INVESTIBLE RESOURCES

In Part One, an account of the process by which total output of an economy grows along with a detailed description of the underdeveloped country has been given. Then in Part Two, a variety of methods of releasing resources from use in maintaining the economy at some level was examined. Now the question is this: how may these resources—these investible resources—be used in order that they will make the maximum contribution to development, i.e., make that maximum contribution to altering the economy described in Chapter 7 so that growth of output occurs, more or less, as a routine matter. The aim of Part Three is to explore the process by which the strategic characteristics (strategic from the standpoint of growth) of an underdeveloped country may be changed.

In Chapter 11, the process by which technical knowledge suitable for application in the underdeveloped country is accumulated and applied is considered. In Chapter 12 the process by which an appropriately trained labor force is created occupies attention. In Chapter 13, consideration is given to certain aspects of the social environment that seem amenable to economic policy, and population growth is explicitly introduced into the development problem in Chapter 14.

In these chapters, a description is made of the process—e.g., accumulation and application of technical knowledge, labor training, and so on—and, on the basis of this description, plans for a policy by which such a process may be implemented are outlined. With discussions of these various processes behind us, the problem will then be to choose the methods of determining in which of the areas will expenditures be most useful. The examination of this problem leads to Part Four.

CHAPTER 11

THE ACCUMULATION
AND APPLICATION
OF TECHNICAL KNOWLEDGE

In Chapters 3 and 4, the manner by which the availability of new technical knowledge affected the rate of growth of output was described. Three effects were identified: in the first and simplest case, the new knowledge simply increased the productivity of the direct inputs, capital and labor. In the diagrams used in Chapter 3, this effect was represented by a new production ray, superimposed on the existing one, in which the same interval on the new ray represented t times the output on the old ray. The symbols t_k and t_l were used to designate the percentage increase in the marginal product of capital and labor, respectively, with the new technique relative to the old. In the interdependent system of Chapter 4, an increase in the productivity of inputs would be represented by a reduction in primary or produced inputs.

A second part of the effects of the knowledge-accumulating process had to do with the fact that the consequence for the productivity of capital might differ from that for labor. If t_k exceeded t_l, the effect was referred to as favorable to capital and vice versa. The biasness of new knowledge had consequences for the rate of return on capital and for the combination of direct inputs employed.

Finally, new technical knowledge results in the creation of new products not previously known.

It was further argued that a technical innovation that was applicable to one production process—to one ray in the diagrams of Chapter 3—is rarely adaptable without cost to the other existing processes, and that in an economy where the rate of growth of capital had long exceeded the rate of growth of labor, innovational activity would be concentrated on the relatively capital intensive processes and little interest directed toward the relatively more labor intensive techniques. From these arguments, the conclusion was reached that an essential part of the growth machinery in a given country was a flow of new technical knowledge in a form that could be directly applied to productive techniques. It was further argued that the transfer of blueprints from one economy to another economy with different factor endowments and different economic organization may not be appropriate. Therefore, a growing economy must have its own indigenous source of knowledge accumulation.

The underdeveloped country described in Chapter 7 has no such source. The task now is to explore the various ways that a society can proceed from the state of virtual absence of knowledge-accumulating activities to one in which there is a more or less steady flow of new technical data that can be used in the production process.

Section I will be concerned with some general principles of knowledge accumulation, and the specification of the exact problem confronting the underdeveloped economy. In Section II, the discussion is concerned with the process by which the nongrowing economy can perform the task defined for it in Section I of this chapter. The final section of the chapter discusses the problem of the demand for the new technical knowledge produced by the methods described in Parts I and II.

I. The Knowledge-Accumulating Process

The term knowledge has been used with only the adjective "technical" applied to indicate that the kind of knowledge of concern was that which, when put into effect, would produce a change in the production process in one of the three ways just reviewed. It is necessary to be more specific, and to try to isolate exactly what kind of knowledge is of interest to the developing country in the present context. That concern is with knowledge as an intermediate good and not a final good is clear, of course, as is the fact that currently, attention is directed toward technical knowledge as opposed to knowledge about society, institutions, or environment.

A. THE SPECTRUM OF ACTIVITIES

When new technical knowledge has reached the stage that it can, if applied, alter the production process, it is in the form of a blueprint. Technical knowledge, however, is not born in this form. It is convenient to think of a spectrum of knowledge-accumulating activity extending from "basic research" on the left to the drawing of a blueprint of a practical invention on the right. A practical invention may be defined as one that, when used, will reduce costs of production of a good or will make possible the production of a new good, the demand for which will cover its costs of production. After the blueprint is available, the decision has still to be made by the entrepreneur to put the new knowledge into effect, but this final act is not part of the knowledge-accumulating process, and is discussed in a separate context. These activities constitute a continuous spectrum, but for discussion, an acceptable approximation is to isolate three separate categories of knowledge-accumulating activities: basic research, applied research, and "blueprinting." That the process is not simply a one way left to right movement will become clear as the argument proceeds.

The general notion behind "basic research" is that it results in the accumulation of general knowledge—in "basic" knowledge—that serves as the raw material for applied research. The output of basic research consists of propositions and generalizations about real world phenomena that themselves have no practical (as defined above) value because of their very generality. It would seem then that the primary characteristic that distinguishes "basic" from "applied" is both in the motivation of the researcher and in the nature of the output. The principal aim of the former is to achieve a more complete understanding of the problem researched, and the final good is a report, memorandum, and so on that presents the findings in a way that reveals this new knowledge about the subject. Knowledge at this stage is in the pure form of a mental construct and, as such, has no physical or actual counterpart, and hence no immediate application. Thus, one may think of an accumulation or stock of propositions that represents an inventory of current scientific knowledge, and the purpose of basic research is to add to this inventory. The notion of a "stock of propositions" and increments thereto implies measurement, i.e., implies that it is meaningful to speak in terms of a larger or smaller inventory, and a more or less rapid rate of accumulation. A unit of measurement does not seem available, but despite this lacuna, reliance on intuition and common sense may be appealed to in order to speak in terms of more or less "basic knowledge."

Applied research, the second section of the spectrum, is much more motivated by practical considerations than is basic research. Its outputs are patented or patentable inventions, or are technical papers describing processes that may have practical implications. Again the definition of the activity depends as much on the motivation of the researcher as on the particular nature of the output that emerges from the activity. The language "basic" and "applied" imply that the output of the basic research provides the "basis"—the groundings—that the applied researcher uses. More generally, the applied researcher draws from the inventory of propositions and generalizations about the real world the basic knowledge that he requires for his efforts to develop practical knowledge. Two qualifications to this notion are: first, all of the outputs in the applied stage do not rest on basic propositions, and second, and more important, problems and bottlenecks that arise in the applied stage may induce further basic research.

Finally, even after the applied researcher has done his part, further work is required before a directly applicable technique or product is available. The blueprinting or development stage is also a nonroutine activity concerned with adapting technical knowledge into processes or products. The emphasis is on "nonroutine" and "adapting" as well as on the constructing of the blueprint or design. This notion is that the adaptation process will not only reflect the kind of applied knowledge that has become available, but also the characteristics of the economy where the new process or product is designed to serve. For the first time, explicit considerations may be given to such things as factor prices and market size as well as to purely technological matters. The output here is a set of blueprints that defines precisely a technique for the production of a good or service. Also at this stage bottlenecks or problems may arise that have to be referred back to one of the research stages, or in the very process of working out the blueprints a problem that is essentially a research problem is solved.

Throughout the length of the spectrum, there are two common characteristics having to do with the nature of some of the inputs and the nature of the activity itself. In all three stages, a category of labor called scientists is necessary, and to produce the outputs it was necessary to draw upon scientific knowledge. To the extent that hunch or revelation were relied upon, then the formal argument—the reason for the argument—breaks down. Scientists are—as noted earlier—themselves incorporators of capital, and their production therefore requires saving and time. Thus capital in the form of highly trained labor is an input into the knowledge-accumulating process, and if machines and laboratories are employed, additional capital is required. One may conclude then that the knowledge-accumulating activity is an extremely capital intensive undertaking. Except for the usual office workers, clerks, helpers, and the like, the input is largely capital embodied in the scientist as training or in laboratories and equipment.

Of equal importance with the nature of the input is the nature of the activity. The above description of the knowledge-accumulating process was in terms of inputs and outputs as in the case of the production of a product. There is a difference, however. In the production of a product, e.g., a pair of shoes, the entrepreneur knows that if he combines so much of a particular kind of capital with so much of a particular kind of labor along with a flow of raw leather inputs, a fixed rate of output of a given quality of shoe will emerge. In this case, the production process and product are set, and there is no (or very little) uncertainty on the technical side. The same cannot be said for the production of knowledge. The very definition of the process by which knowledge at any point on the spectrum is brought into being implies that the fixity and certainty that resides in the conventional production function is not applicable. This uncertainty might be expressed by attaching an error term to the function describing the relationships between inputs and outputs. This inherent uncertainty in the activity arises out of the fact that the search for new knowledge is a search for that which is currently unknown, and consequently no assurance can be given as to what will emerge from a particular set of inputs.

It also seems likely, although there is no necessary condition involved, that the uncertainty is greatest in the basic research end of the spectrum. The scientist searching for new general knowledge about the world has less to guide him and less to limit him in his pursuit. The result is not only uncertainty as to whether any new knowledge at all will emerge from the inputs, but also there is doubt as to what precisely will emerge. The evidence is fairly clear that one of the conditions necessary for output of basic knowledge is a high degree of freedom for the investigator to go where his researches lead him, not where profit considerations, specific problem considerations, or immediate needs of the community dictate that he should go. As movement to the right along the spectrum takes place, the second source of uncertainty diminishes as constraints on the actions of the investigator increase. Since the applied researcher is not free to wander (or wonder) where his intellectual curiosity leads him, the chance that he will be pulled away from the imposed objective is small. Also, the nature of the unknown being sought at the applied stage is more identifiable, more specific than in the case further leftward on the spectrum, and it is therefore to be expected that the investigator in the applied stage may proceed more systematically and assuredly in his operations than can the basic researcher. For similar reasons, the uncertainty attached to activity in the blueprinting stage is expected to be still less than in the applied research stage. The maker of the blueprint has a fairly well-defined task, and the kind of labor skills and other inputs required to accomplish the task is much more specific and identifiable than is the case for inputs into basic and applied research. One might express this result by saying that the outcome of the engineer's work is more nearly predictable than that of the purer scientists, and this is due to the reduction in the necessary degree of empiricism inherent in the work of development relatively to that of basic and applied research. Nevertheless, the differences as to the technical uncertainty inherent in the production function for knowledge along the spectrum are differences in degree, while the difference between the knowledge-production function and one that is set for producing shoes is a difference in kind.

Several results are to be emphasized. Knowledge of all sorts is looked upon as produced, and consequently the notion of inputs and outputs is applicable. This production function is sure to be very capital intensive (with little substitution possible, no matter what factor prices are) and the production of the capital—mainly embodied in the scientists and engineers—has an extremely long gestation period. Also, the production results are uncertain in the sense that the function is not set, and there is necessarily an error term attached to the function at all positions on the spectrum. The variance of the distribution of the error term is assumed to decrease as the activity being undertaken approaches the right side of the spectrum of activities.

B. RETURNS TO INVESTMENT IN TECHNICAL KNOWLEDGE ACCUMULATION

The final output of the knowledge-accumulating process is a blueprint that permits the production of an established product at reduced costs or of a new product. Consider first a blueprint that if used will result in the saving of inputs in the production of a given, established commodity. Suppose further that these blueprints have resulted from identifiable research activity at the basic and applied stages conducted by a firm. A reasonable estimate of the cost of the new blueprints may then be made. The return on this investment in knowledge accumulation is the increased total profit accruing to the firm due to its decreased average costs. Thus, with the same quantity of direct inputs, the firm would be able to produce a larger flow of output with the newly created technique than with the one already in use. The profitability to the firm supporting the research, then, will result from a comparison of the costs of producing the basic research, the applied research, and the blueprints with the present value of the increments in output achievable with the new knowledge and the existing quantity of resources. If the resources used in the research activities are valued at their economy-wide opportunity costs, then the profitability to the firm of its actions is also the social profitability *if* there are no further uses to which any of the new knowledge can be put. In this case, the basis of the decision to allocate resources to knowledge accumulation is no different from the basis of the decision to invest in new capacity. Specifically, it should be noted that the costs of the research include the costs of the failures that may have preceded successes as the knowledge evolved into more and more concrete forms. A firm or industry may thus have a research department that requires an annual outlay of a definite amount. From this department, there is a constant flow of blueprints incorporating new knowledge. These new blueprints, when applied, yield a return measured as just indicated. The profitability criteria would then be determined by comparing this annual return with the cost of maintaining the research department.

The same kind of argument would apply to new knowledge that lead to the creation of a new product.

The basis of the decision to invest in knowledge-accumulating activity is the same, therefore, as that to invest in anything else, but the relevant variables are much more difficult to identify. The uncertainty and long gestation period on the cost side have already been discussed. On the returns side, the strong likelihood of economies external to the firm, the returns on which the firm producing the knowledge may have difficulty in capturing, are sure to be important. External economies are particularly likely in the basic research stage where the general knowledge that emerges may be of great interest to a wide range of workers in the applied and engineering fields. Conceptually, the value of these external economies may be estimated in the same way that the value of the internal economies were, but practically, the task is much more difficult.

The argument as to the profitability of undertaking knowledge accumulation is not modified if a government or nonprofit organization undertakes it. As long as concern is with the creation of technical knowledge as an input into the production process, the criterion of the profitability of use of resources for finding new knowledge, rather than using old, remains the same.

The question now is reasonably specific: Given the account of the knowledge-accumulating process just described and given the characteristics of the underdeveloped country in Chapter 7, what can be said about the use of the resources freed from maintenance duties in the underdeveloped country for purposes of the accumulations of technical knowledge?

C. Research Activity in the Underdeveloped Economy

In the account of the technology generally prevailing in the underdeveloped country, emphasis was placed on primitiveness in most instances. The technology embodied in the physical capital and organization of production results in a much smaller rate of output from the direct inputs than is the case in rich countries. Also it is abundantly clear that neither the physical capital nor the organizational arrangements embody very much basic technical knowledge relative to that already available. Since the knowledge resulting from basic research is general, in the sense of being independent of man-made environmental factors, the underdeveloped country has access to large quantities of such knowledge without having to create it. The same argument applies to knowledge accumulated through applied research. Part of the problem will be in gaining access to these two categories of technical knowledge.

Furthermore, the description of the nature of pure and applied research suggests additional reasons why committing resources to these types of activity in the underdeveloped country is uneconomic. The "high" degree of uncertainty accompanying these activities *plus* the "long" gestation period required for the outputs to reach a practical form *plus* the necessity of a "high" capital intensity in the production process *plus* the relative scarcity of capital add up to an impressive argument against using investible resources for these purposes. The gestation period is lengthened further because the supply of scientists—the supply of men capable of doing pure and applied research—is so limited that if the effort were made to pursue such activities in the underdeveloped countries, a training program would have to be the first step.

The conclusion seems to be clear. Because there already exists a very large amount (attention is called to the use of quantitative language) of pure and applied technical knowledge not now exploited in the underdeveloped economy, and because the factor endowment in such a country relative to the demands of the process of this type of knowledge accumulation suggest strongly that the use of resources in such activities would be uneconomic, the underdeveloped country should not engage its investible resources in pure and applied research activity. (A qualification to this conclusion appears below.) The arguments that lead to this important conclusion are not applicable to the final stage of the knowledge-accumulating process, development, and blueprinting. In the first place, there is no great untapped inventory of "suitable" (a term to be defined) developed and blueprinted knowledge awaiting use by the entrepreneurs of the nongrowing country. That this is true follows from the fact that this category of knowledge is necessarily so specific, so directly applicable that its exploitation is limited to the general area for which it was specifically designed. In the second place, the inappropriateness of the allocation of investible resources to development and blueprinting is not clearly uneconomic, as it was in pure and applied research. The developing country, if it is to overcome its general technological backwardness, must therefore either apply resources of its own to the task of working up new blueprints that are suitable for its environment, or it must find them to import. The latter is quite unlikely for the reasons just stated, and it is necessary to discuss in further detail the process of the development and blueprinting of pure and applied knowledge in the underdeveloped economy.

II. The Development of the Results of Pure and Applied Research

The final activity in the knowledge-accumulating spectrum is the development of the results of pure and applied research into a form that makes it possible to incorporate these results directly into the production process. In the very last stage this means a blueprint defining a new form of physical capital or a new form of organization. Such a definition can hardly be said to be unambiguous enough to imply precisely what the obvious technique is for accomplishing the objective, but the general idea is surely reasonably clear. The research chemist, pursuing an activity that would be classified at the left end of the spectrum, turns out a research memorandum written in the jargon of his discipline that not only has no direct relevance to the industrial chemist, but may even convey no information to him. The scientist or engineer working at the other end of the spectrum has the task of translating these pure scientific results into a language and form that permits their practical exploitation. The question is how may this latter task be performed in the kind of economy described in Chapter 7?

A. The Production Function

The earlier arguments rested on the assumption that there could be assumed to exist a production function relating direct inputs of scientific and engineering labor and laboratory capital to the output of blueprints. Produced inputs consisted of knowledge from further left on the spectrum. An error term was assumed necessary to show that there was a necessary uncertainty inherent in the relationship. The notion of a production function implies that if inputs are increased, outputs will increase in a predictable fashion subject to the probability distribution shown by the error term. What else can be said about this production function as it exists, or can be made to exist in the underdeveloped country?

1. Quality of the inputs. The input of greatest significance is the trained scientist, the worker trained in the techniques of research and having a working command of the raw materials, i.e., of the knowledge originating in the earlier stages of the knowledge-accumulating process. The quantity of such labor is in any society fixed in the short run, as increments to the quantity require substantial time to be produced. For the underdeveloped country, the quantity available in the short run is indeed small, and the existing facilities for increasing the quantity, for training the labor, are meager. The terms "small" quantity and "meager" training facilities are relative to the number of areas of the economy where the practicing technology is extremely primitive, and relative to the proportion of the labor force engaged in similar activities and total expenditure on these activities in other, richer countries. Neither comparison means necessarily that the underdeveloped country should use its investible resources to create more such trained workers than it is now doing.

Several things are relevant to this supply situation. The fact that the source of supply of trained scientists is severely limited means that any reasonably rapid increase in the net quantity must come through training abroad. To increase the supply by domestic production means not only constructing laboratories and classroom buildings, a relatively small task, it means also training teachers, an immensely difficult and time-consuming task. However, it is possible to achieve a gross increase in this type of labor by use of individuals now engaged in teaching. Can a case be made for the transfer of individuals now teaching others to be scientists and engineers, from this task, to acting as scientists and engineers?

Immediately, one must recognize that using up capital in any form may be sowing the seeds for future difficulties. Suppose, however, the underdeveloped country of Chapter 7 had a teaching cadre of such size and effectiveness that it was just able to turn out the number of scientist-engineers necessary to keep constant the ratio of this segment of the labor force to the total labor force. Suppose further that this cadre of teachers contained men who were well equipped to do the very thing that they were teaching others to do, i.e., to develop the already available (to them) general scientific knowledge into a form directly usable in the production processes in their economy. Teachers embody a form of capital, namely a certain kind of knowledge, that may be used in two different ways: to train additional scientists at a rate sufficient to maintain the prevailing position of this category of resource in the economy, or to develop technical knowledge that will add to the productive capacity of the economy. The capital is also perfectly substitutable between these two uses.

There is no a priori reason to conclude that capital (the already trained teachers) used in one way will always necessarily be the more productive use. One can easily construct a situation in which a concentrated research effort by teachers on a specific engineering problem may result in a much greater increase in capacity than is achieved by using teachers as trainers. Especially might this be true where a specific engineering problem had been isolated that, if solved, would yield major increases in exports. Such increases in exports may then enable the importation of teachers and scientists later to take up the slack created by the reduction of the training function of the currently available teachers. One can, of course, construct examples where continued use of teaching capital as teaching yields the greatest returns as will be shown in the next section. The outcome depends on the estimated gains in productivity from both uses, on the time shape of those gains, on the rate of interest, and on the extent of uncertainty as to the success of both activities. This example is emphasized because trained personnel provides the clearest case of capital that can be shifted from one type activity (teaching) to another (researching), and where it "should" be used is not evident without investigation.

The example also indicates that the varied forms in which capital may be embodied and its varied role in the production process make it necessary to be cautious in using the term "using up capital." In the example here, capital embodied in teachers is being used up in the sense that teachers will not reproduce themselves. A more accurate statement is the one made above having to do with the transfer of the teaching capital rather than its being depleted. Another reason for using this example is the evidence referred to in Chapter 7 that educational capital in the underdeveloped country is underutilized, and opportunities may exist in a number of cases to increase the research activities of the teachers without diminishing their contributions to training.

The upshot of this discussion on the quality of the inputs into the production function consists of two very simple, but important points. First, a net increase in the rate of supply of the necessary inputs is an extremely slow and uncertain process, and consequently the supply of blueprinting personnel cannot be increased except in a very long run. Second, the shifting of teachers from teaching to "blueprinting" may constitute an important means of exploiting unusual opportunities for development of a new technique. In the event that a calculation of the relevant income streams shows such a shift in the use of this kind of capital to be profitable, the capital embodied in this form is not being "used up" in the usual way that this term is applied.

Consider now the total cost of producing the blueprints. Evidence available on costs of development in the United States and Britain suggest that this stage of the knowledge-accumulating process is relatively the most costly of all stages. The high cost is due to a variety of things. The definition of this final stage is in terms of the concreteness and practicality of the results, a heavier use of models and pilot projects is necessary than is the case in previous stages where results are general and frequently involve merely a memorandum or a report. The result is that less nonlabor embodied capital is probably used in the early stages than in the later. One perhaps should include in development costs the costs associated with eliminating the bugs and bottlenecks that are sure to appear after the new process or technique is already installed. If the blueprint is of a new product, then included in the costs of development are those associated with marketing or market testing.

Such suggestions do not show that the costs of the final stage of knowledge accumulation are necessarily higher than those of the other two stages. What is suggested is that the costs of development can be affected by giving attention to the raw material input, the results of pure and applied scientific research. Consequently, some attention should be given to the question of how to minimize the costs of achieving a given increment in output. Two generalizations seem possible. In the first place, the development costs are likely to be lower if the work in the applied stages is more firm and complete. That this should be true hardly needs support. The greater the specificity and completeness of the underlying scientific theory, the less the extent of empiricism, of trial and error, involved in the development and blueprinting operation. Since the state of the underlying theory varies widely from sector to sector, development costs will not be independent of the sector chosen. If development proceeds in areas where the underlying scientific theory is less firmly and completely built, the resources ostensibly devoted to development of blueprints will to some extent be solving or trying to solve applied research problems. Thus the question of the choice of inputs is one of some importance on the cost side, and its proper solution depends on the command of the body of scientific knowledge possessed by the scientists operating in the underdeveloped country.

The second generalization has to do with knowledge that results in a new product. In Chapter 7, the limited variety of the composition of output in the underdeveloped country was noted. Part of the failure of international trade to solve some of the economic problems is due to the inability of the economy to supply the world with products different from the traditional ones. But to introduce new products requires their development and marketing, and this is a nonroutine activity. The evidence suggests that, in many instances, reduction in prices due to input saving forms of new knowledge will not serve to provide as high returns as the same "quantity" of new knowledge that results in a new product will. In international trade, for example, using resources to find ways to reduce the cost of jute fiber production by 2 per cent per year will surely not bring the same return to Pakistan as would be the case if the same amount of resources were used successfully to find a way to manufacture jute into a fabric that looked and felt like silk. It is probably correct to say, however, that costs of accomplishing the latter greatly exceed the cost of finding ways to reduce costs of producing the traditional product.

Further demands are placed on the scientists and scientist-administrators in the selection of areas in which to work. There appears to be no market or other mechanism that leads automatically to the "right" choice for blueprinting activity, in the sense used here, and heavy pressure is therefore on the workers in these sectors to choose their undertakings with understanding of the full implications of their assignment.

2. Returns to scale. The fact that there exists such a large body of idle knowledge available to the underdeveloped country, in addition to the interdependence of much technical knowledge, suggests the possibility of increasing returns to the part of the activity carried on in the underdeveloped country. Increased size of development activity may result in advantages arising from a greater division of labor and additional cross fertilization. The latter is particularly important in this activity as developments in one sector may have direct relevance for other sectors, and a problem solved in one sector may permit a more rapid or more advantageous solution to a problem in other areas. A narrowing down of individual problems made possible by increased size of the development sector may facilitate the solutions of all problems. For these reasons, then, a presumption may exist that there are increasing returns to scale in this sector of the economy. Since increasing returns have important implications for allocation, the question is somewhat relevant to the argument.

There are two reasons to suspect diminishing returns. The quality of the inputs may decline, and this fact increases costs and increases the uncertainty attached to the undertaking. This source of diminishing returns is likely to be especially applicable to that part of the development activity concerned with isolating and identifying those problems that are most economic for the underdeveloped economy to undertake to solve. These were previously identified as areas resting on the firmest scientific base, and consequently requiring relatively little trial and error in the development stage, as well as topics that were researchable in the underdeveloped country. Since this part of the activity requires perhaps a different kind of insight and understanding, as well as a greater command of the results of the research in the two preceding stages, it would be surprising if more scientists also meant more men who could perform this particular task. If it did not mean this, then the "supply of recognized problems" would be a factor increasing less rapidly than the other inputs.

The more important source of diminishing returns to development activity, however, is at the other end of the scale. For investment in knowledge accumulation to be productive it must be applied, and the application of new knowledge requires innovation. If, then, development of knowledge outstrips the capacity of the economy to innovate, the productivity of the resources used to develop new knowledge drops to zero. Since the role of innovation is obviously crucial, all of Section III of this chapter is concerned with the issue. The assumption will, therefore, be made that diminishing returns to scale exist for the two reasons just given.

3. On the suitability of technology. The argument has been made that blueprints designed in a capital-rich country are unsuited for use in a capital-poor country. "Unsuited" referred to the blueprints that were developed in the former countries and resulted in production techniques that called for a degree of capital intensity that was not economic for the capital-poor economy of Chapter 7. The suitability of technology is now explained.

Consider Diagram VI constructed as the other, similar diagrams have been constructed. Suppose operation is now taking place at point *A* where *OR* of capital and *OL* of labor are combined to produce *OA* (equal to 100) of output. Suppose further that *OL* represents "full employment" of the labor force and *OR* the total amount of capital available in the economy, i.e., it is a one-sector economy. In the next period, a blueprint is developed in a capital-rich country that, if used, will shift the isoquant from I to II. The increased productivity on Ray *C* is so great that, if the technique represented by that ray is used, the output of 100 can be produced with a smaller quantity of both capital and labor than is required at point *A*. (It is recalled that Techniques *A* and *B* are made technologically inefficient by the innovation, and that the line connecting the rays after the innovation no longer has the traditional meaning of the isoquant.) However, with the new knowledge applied to Ray *C* the achievement of full utilization of all resources is not technologically possible, as there is not enough capital to employ all available labor if this technique is used. (Full employment of labor and capital could be maintained by using Technique *A,* but output would be smaller than it would be with Technique *C* and unemployment.)

If, on the other hand, the new technical knowledge can be applied to Technique *A* so that it does not become technologically inefficient, all labor can be employed without sacrificing output. The increase in output due to the innovation in this case is greater than in the case where the innovation was limited to Technique *C*. This result holds because the out-

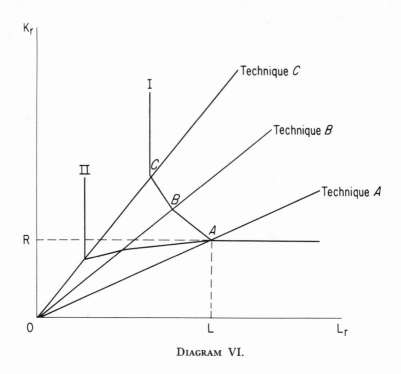

DIAGRAM VI.

put on Ray A, for a given amount of capital, is greater than that on Ray C for the same quantity of capital, unless A is technologically inefficient. These arguments suggest a definition for "suitable" technical change: new technical knowledge is suitable for an economy if it permits continued full utilization of existing resources without sacrificing output. For technological change in a country already experiencing underutilization of labor, one may define "suitable" as meaning that the innovation results in no increase in the extent of underutilization and "very" suitable would refer to an innovation that, without sacrificing output, facilitated the reduction in the degree of underutilization. In the diagram, as drawn here, suitability would mean that Ray A never became technologically inefficient.

A more general criterion of suitability of technology would include other resources—not merely capital and labor—available in the community. That this general notion is necessary follows from previous arguments relative to the limited substitutability between capital and labor, the fixity of some capital equipment, the nontransferability of some labor from one sector to another, the role of natural resources, and the importance of the role of the social environment in permitting the acceptance and introduction of technical innovation. For example, a nation may possess large quantities of a particular natural resource, currently usable only in a few activities, and to find a way of making this resource usable in a wider range of activities may be most profitable. Similarly, the composition of labor skills—not merely the quantity of labor—may affect the suitability of technology. From the discussions of the interdependence of the system it is evident that a technological improvement in one sector may permit a great increase in the rate of output in other sectors. So the unsuitability of nonindigenously developed blueprints arises not only because of the differences in optimal capital intensity from country to country, although this is the most specifically identifiable reason, but also because the range and composition of resources that a technology is meant to exploit differ from country to country. The argument may be summarized by saying that the more suitable the newly developed knowledge is to the environment in which it is to be applied, the greater will be the returns (as defined above) to the resources allocated to the creation of that knowledge.

4. On the financing of the development of blueprints. These two questions are discussed: (1) Will individual firms undertake investment in the development of blueprints or must the activity be undertaken or subsidized by the government? (2) Is there any mechanism that results in these blueprints being of the kind that have been just described as "suitable"? Consider the first question.

Will privately owned firms use investible resources available to them to develop new technical knowledge? Previously, the argument was made that the production function for knowledge development may be considered as similar to that for a more conventional product with the important exception that the former function has attached an error term of significant size indicating that there is an inherent uncertainty in the relationship, while the latter function contains no such distribution term or only a very small one. Similarly, the method of computing returns on the use of investible resources for knowledge development has been established as similar to that for more conventional activity. Under these conditions, a firm would presumably compute returns on alternative uses of its available resources, and choose those uses of resources that were estimated to be the most profitable.

There are, however, several reasons why such an approach may result in the development of technical knowledge being uneconomically slighted.

In the first place, one of the important characteristics of this kind of activity is its effect on sectors other than the one that bore the cost of its creation. The interdependence effect, through which the reduced costs of a product are transferred to the other parts of the economy, places heavy demands on the pricing system if the full possible returns on the outlay creating the new knowledge are to be realized. Thus, a firm might conclude that investment in the development of a new technique would be profitable if the pricing system of the country were such as to result in prices throughout the system reflecting opportunity costs. Thus, the known failure of Expression 11 of Chapter 4 $(P_j = l_j P_l + k_j P_k + a_{ij} P_i)$ to hold may mean that an undertaking that would be profitable to the economy is not tried. Similarly, a new technique that is developed by one firm may be copied by other competing firms in a manner that prevents the originating firm from realizing a profit that is necessary to persuade the firm to commit the resources to this uncertain endeavor. Patents are only a partial solution to this problem, and are less effective in the underdeveloped economy than elsewhere. Indeed knowledge accumulation is perhaps the most—possibly only—important source of the traditional type of external economies, i.e., those economies that are created by a firm that cannot be captured by that firm. Conceptually, a tax and subsidy system could achieve the "correct" reward and payment, but to expect this to be achievable is surely carrying optimism to unrealistic extremes.

Also, of course, the appraisal of the distribution of the error term attached to the production function of the blueprint is of great significance in estimating the profitability of investment in such activity. The variance of the distribution may be kept low if the development scientists are effective in choosing areas for research that rest on the firmest scientific basis, and the degree of empiricism involved relatively small. But even great success in doing this cannot reduce the variance to zero, and consequently the argument holds.

Another side of the uncertainty argument deals with the length of time involved. Thus, given a sufficient time horizon, the variance of the "uncertainty distribution" may be reduced nearer and nearer to zero for the firm. As time elapses, however, another source of uncertainty enters in an important way, namely that another firm will succeed in a profitable development of an identical or similar technique. Even in the absence of a real threat of this nature, the possibility of a long gestation period adds to the cost of the activity, and indeed may add markedly when recognition of the high opportunity cost of capital is introduced.

All of these factors result in an impressive argument against a firm—even a relatively large one—in the underdeveloped economy undertaking the development of new techniques on its own. On the other hand, the general primitiveness of the prevailing technology in such a country and the large "quantity" of unexploited—of idle—pure and applied technical knowledge suggest strongly that the use of some of the available investible resources for such purposes will be the "correct" (correct meaning yielding a higher return than other competing uses, a problem that is examined in Chapter 15) choice. The result would appear to be, then, that this kind of activity is best undertaken by the government where the kinds of problems just discussed do not apply. Such a result does not necessarily mean that government laboratories must be established and scientists become civil scientists. It does mean, rather, that this activity must be subsidized and supported from tax revenues, and—during the early stages of development—the workings of the market cannot be relied on to accomplish the desired objective even if schemes to equate the price of factors with their opportunity costs are successful. Based on reasons developed in Section III of this chapter, it can be stated that the government's programs in this area *should* be in the nature of subsidies to firms, and for this reason in addition to the actual innovating being done by the firm, the question of whether the development of technical knowledge may be expected to result in a technology that is "suitable" is considered.

5. *The mechanism determining the kind of blueprints developed.* In the arguments developed in the previous chapters on growth, reasons were given why the new knowledge developed in the growing economy could be expected to produce a technology reasonably suitable for the factor endowment of that economy. Can reasons be given for a similar expectation in the case of the underdeveloped country just initiating research efforts? The problem may be seen most clearly under the following assumptions: suppose that the government subsidizes an individual firm to conduct research in an area on the firm's choosing, is there any mechanism at work in the system to lead the research effort in the direction of producing the kind of technical knowledge that will result in a "suitable" or "very suitable" new technology emerging?

The firm is interested in the maximum return achievable with its available resources, and in the present context this means that it is interested in achieving the maximum increase in productivity with its research resources. The firm will, therefore, consciously seek the maximum increase in productivity rather than any particular type—favorable to capital or to labor—of knowledge, because it is increases in productivity that affect the potential increases in profits due to the use of new knowledge. So the question really is does the factor supply situation existing in the underdeveloped economy affect the profitability of the various kinds of new knowledge differently?

If the supply of all factors is perfectly elastic to the individual firm, then the answer to the question seems to be negative. For if that were the case, the firm has no incentive to save one input more than it does another. This result holds no matter what the relative prices of the inputs happen to be. For example, if the scheme to subsidize wage payments described in Chapter 9 were in effect, and the effective wage rate to the firm was very low at the same time that the firm can acquire capital at unchanging costs, the firm would still have no incentive to seek knowledge that would permit innovations favorable to labor. The reason is simply that under these circumstances the cost line of the diagrams is taken as a datum by the firm to which it adjusts by its choice of technique. Hence, the output effect is the sole concern of the firm. On the other hand, if the firm recognizes that its increased demand for capital consequent to an innovation favorable to that factor will result in rising capital costs, and an increase in demand for labor consequent to an innovation favorable to labor will have no effect on wage rates, then the firm finds it profitable to take into account, not only the output effect of the new knowledge, but also its effect on the optimal combination of inputs. In general, if the firm has reason to believe that, as a consequence of its actions, a price of one of its inputs will rise, it will seek the kind of knowledge that will facilitate the reduced use of that input.

The argument applies equally well to any input. For example, a particular category of labor skill may be recognized by a firm to be so scarce in the economy that the only way that more such skill can be acquired is to bid workers possessing it away from other firms by offering higher wage rates. If this is the case, then the knowledge-developing firm will seek to find techniques that minimize the increased use of this particular input. If, then, the underdeveloped country does have a large supply of "disguised" unemployed labor available, suitable techniques are those in the area from Ray *A* of previous diagrams to the horizontal axis. To produce an effort to develop these kinds of techniques then would require a capital-rationing policy such that the terms on which increased capital is available is increasingly costly. That this should be the case in the underdeveloped country, even without a specific policy to this effect, would not be surprising. The individual firm has access to few sources of lending, and the likelihood of borrowing increasing amounts on the unchanging terms is indeed limited. To the extent that the market imperfections work in this way or can be made through explicit policy to work in this way, the subsidizing of individual firms to do development research in their own interests will result in the emergence of suitable or very suitable technological improvements—assuming the research is successful—as these terms were defined above.

Further, it should be noted that the cost line shifting as a consequence of a large increase in the demand for capital is not enough to insure efforts of the right kind, since the individual firm does not, in this event, attribute the change in relative factor prices to his application of a specific piece of new knowledge. If the economy or firm had a backlog of blueprints on which it could draw as factor prices changed, then the arguments would not matter very much. Such may be the case in the country with a long tradition of research and development, where a backlog of techniques are available for blueprinting, if and when factor prices change, to make their use profitable. This most assuredly is not the case for the economy of Chapter 7; therefore, it is necessary to find ways to make sure that resources devoted to the development of blueprints produce "suitable" or "very suitable" techniques.

The problem may be solved by issuing edicts along with the subsidy. The edict would read—develop blueprints of technical knowledge that are favorable to labor. Edicts are open to numerous disadvantages, and much more consistent with the general approach developed here are methods designed to secure a set of incentives for the firm that result in its pursuing a policy consistent with economy-wide resource availability. The approach gains merit here because the condition necessary to produce development activity consistent with the design of a suitable technology are conditions likely to prevail anyway. Indeed, the most probable danger is not that economic incentives on the firms will not operate satisfactorily, but rather that these economic incentives will be ignored in favor of research in areas thought to be prestigious. If this is the case, the cost to the economy is sure to be high.

The preceding arguments have been couched in terms of the productivity increasing effects of new knowledge. The same arguments apply to the development of new products. An alternative to the development of knowledge that will lead to innovations favorable to labor is the development of a new product that can be produced by labor intensive methods or, more generally, that exploits the resources available to the underdeveloped country. Thus, the development of new technical knowledge in the form of a new product has the same criteria of "suitability" as has the development of new knowledge to use to produce an established product more cheaply. The argument also has concentrated largely on capital and labor, but "suitability" applies to all terms in the production function. This point is especially relevant in countries where the relative supplies of capital and labor is very similar to that prevailing in countries with advanced technology. Simply importing the technology or the physical capital may be satisfactory, but in general, doing this will create problems, and some adaptation will be necessary because of differing organizational and administrative machinery or different natural resources.

Conclusion. In this section, the accumulation of knowledge has been treated in a fashion similar to the production of a conventional product. A production function was defined with identifiable inputs and outputs and diminishing returns to capital and labor. "Suitable" technical knowledge was interpreted as that in which resulting innovations were consistent with full utilization of factors without sacrificing output. The conclusion was also reached that individual firms in the underdeveloped economy would not generally undertake research unless subsidized in one form or another by the government. The need for the subsidy arises out of the existence of uncertainty in the production function, the long gestation period, and the necessary dependence on developments in other sectors of the economy for full return from the investment in development and blueprinting research. Finally, it was argued that, under circumstances held to be generally applicable, firms doing research would introduce the economy-wide relative factor supply situation into the considerations governing the nature of the kind of research that was undertaken.

B. SUPPLEMENTARY CONSIDERATIONS

The arguments and conclusions just outlined rest heavily on the validity of the production function applied to technical knowledge creation, and to the notion of a spectrum of activities extending from basic research on the left to blueprinting on the right. There are numerous examples of specific new techniques that have proved to be extremely productive, and that have been originated by persons with little command over basic or applied scientific knowledge. What is involved appears to be more of a learning process or intuitive insight than an input-output relationship. To this, one may add that the magnitude of the variance of the uncertainty distribution may cast considerable doubt on the usefulness of the production function notion in that the outcome of an exercise is neither controllable nor predictable. The conclusion would then be that one must look in another place rather than in an input-output relationship for the explanation of the development of technical knowledge. In particular, a strategy to accelerate the development of practical knowledge is different from that required to bring about an increase in the production of bicycles.

In a significant area of endeavor, these sorts of ideas are extremely relevant. One may argue they are especially applicable to the organizational details associated with the conduct of agriculture and small, rural manufacturing activities. The development of appropriate seeds and fertilizers, of water control and use are only part of the story. The other part has to do with insight and imagination and the growth consciousness of the farm population. The policy implications of this argument are that development depends on those environmental factors that affect the way individuals approach their daily tasks.

But these arguments result in supplementing the production-function approach, not in replacing it. If a society commits itself to a systematic effort to replace its primitive technology, that society can do this in an economically rational manner only by formally committing resources to the task. Since there are other claims on resources, it must appraise the returns on alternative uses of its investible resources. And these tasks all require a production function approach.

III. The Demand for Technical Knowledge

The fact that blueprints of new techniques are available does not necessarily mean that the new techniques will be employed. There may be idle knowledge along with idle capital, labor, and other resources. The task now is to study the demand for newly created technical knowledge, i.e., the conditions in which productive units will adapt the new knowledge that becomes available. In Section A, the innovating process that will result in the maximum contribution to the growth process is explained, and Section B is then concerned with the difficulties of assuring that such a process is effected in the underdeveloped country.

A. THE CONDITIONS FOR INNOVATION

Consider now the demand for productivity increasing technical knowledge that has to be introduced in the form of physical capital. In this case, the act of introducing the new knowledge is an act of net or replacement investment.

As a machine ages both the quality and the quantity of the product it turns out are assumed to decline. The quality deterioration relative to quantity deterioration depends largely on the type of physical capital. For example, a building may be expected to experience virtually no quantity deterioration, but its quality deterioration may be quite marked. A machine, on the other hand, may evidence deterioration by its reduced capacity at the level of operating costs prevailing when it was new, or it might turn out a less exact product. The consequence of this deterioration is either rising operating costs—due to increasing maintenance or other charges—or a reduced rate of output. As a capital item ages, therefore, it becomes increasingly less profitable to operate than a new, identical capital item. If other more productive machines (i.e., machines incorporating technical knowledge not available when the existing machine was constructed) are becoming available, then the profitability of the existing machine falls at a more rapid rate.

The simplest case is that in which no new knowledge has been created, and replacement is thereby to be with a machine identical to the one in use. The old machine will be used until the variable costs of producing a preassigned output associated with it exceed the revenue obtained from the sale of that output. At that point, it becomes uneconomic to operate, and a new machine is to be installed. Suppose that this economic life of the machine was precisely foreseen, and the capital costs were exactly written off by the time the operation of the machine became uneconomic. Thus, the switch to the new machine involves no real or imaginary problems as to "capital loss" on the machine being replaced. Capital costs on the old machine are zero, so total costs equal operating costs that exceed revenue because the machine has become less productive as it has aged. The operating costs on the new machine are below those of the old machine, and are sufficiently below them to cover fixed costs on the same quantity of capital. (If this were not the case, the first machine would not have come into existence.) The total cost of producing the given output stream with the new machine is, therefore, less than the operating costs of the old machine. The new machine represents the same quantity of capital as did the old machine.

No modification of the preceding argument is required if new technical knowledge becomes available just as the old machine "wears out." For then replacement will take place at the same time as before, only now the new machine will represent a larger output capacity than did the old and, depending on demand, a change in the quantity of capital may be part of the adjustment process. But blueprints of new technical knowledge are unlikely to become available in this neat, no-problem-creating way. In particular, they are likely to appear at times when they create problems of replacement, at a time when the existing stock of physical capital is yet to be fully used up. Then, the problem arises as to the determinants of the profitability for the firm, and the economy, of the new knowledge relative to that already embodied in the capital in use. The previously stated condition for replacement still holds no matter whether capital costs be positive or zero. If the total costs of the operation of the new machine (equal to fixed plus variable costs) are less than the operating costs on the machine, then the costs of abandoning the old machine and using the new machine (equal to total costs of the new machine plus the fixed costs associated with the old machine) will be less than continued use of the old machine. This statement holds even if the "old" machine is brand "new" and its operating costs are still below revenue. The key point is that capital costs of the old machine—sunk costs—do not affect the replacement decision. This profitability of replacements applied to both the individual producing unit and the economy as a whole, as long as operating costs (chiefly wages) to the firm are economy-wide opportunity costs.

This argument is fairly simple and easily applied. The major source of complexity arises if there exists prospects of additional new and even more productive machines in the future. Consider the following simple example. Suppose average revenue is 30 and average costs are as follows:

	(1) Old Machine	(2) New Machine Available Now	(3) New Machine to Be Available 5 Years Hence
Operating Costs	18	10	5
Fixed Costs	10	6	4
TOTAL	28	16	9

Clearly to replace now is profitable. If the fixed costs on the old machine continue, then total average cost with machine 2 is 26, 2 less than for the old machine. To wait five years to replace with the new machine available then (machine 3) would result in a total cost of 19, but if replacement occurs now and again in five years, the capital costs of machine 2 must also enter, so average costs of using machine 3 would then be 25 (10 + 6 + 4 + 5) until the fixed costs associated with machines 1 and 2 are covered. The choice of cost streams is between:

| Replace now and later | 26 | 26 | 26 | 26 | 25 | 25 | . . . | 15 | . . . | 9 | . . . |
| Replace in 5 years | 28 | 28 | 28 | 28 | 19 | 19 | . . . | 9 | . . . | | . . . |

Which of these series yields a lower present value depends upon the rate of interest used, but evidently, some rate of interest would dictate not replacing until five years hence, when a more productive machine is safely anticipated.

If all costs are opportunity costs, again here, there is no conflict between public interest and the interest of the individual firm. Such a conflict may arise, however, by virtue of the entry of new firms. Suppose, for example, that present value calculations indicate that the second alternative above —replace in five years—is to be chosen. A new firm just entering the field, however, has no continuing costs from past investments to worry about. It would, therefore, use machine 2 and would be able to produce at a lower cost than the existing firm. In this case, the new machine would force the scrapping of the old machine prematurely, i.e., prior to the time that its operation became uneconomic from the standpoint of the economy as a whole. The new firm entering to take advantage of technical knowledge not available when the existing firm built its machine forces capital waste on the economy. On the other hand, entry or the threat of entry is one of the most effective ways to force existing firms to seek out and install cost-reducing innovations, and the complete absence of potential entry is likely indeed to breed laziness with respect to cost consciousness. In general, the assumption that existing firms' profitability calculations made in the previously described manner will be consistent with that for the economy as a whole is correct, always assuming that factor prices equal opportunity costs. The most important qualification to this conclusion is the problem of assuring that firms allocate the "right" amount of resources to development of new technical knowledge.

The preceding discussion dealt with replacement of capital, not additions to capital. In the growing economy, as already described, more and less productive machines exist simultaneously. As new demand develops and capacity is added, the new capacity exploits the most suitable technique available. The old machines are kept in use as long as average revenue is in excess of operating cost (and the new methods do not result in replacement). The arguments could also be complicated by introducing scrap value or site value, but the general form of the argument would not be changed. If the newly available technical knowledge is of the kind previously described as organizational, the problems are much simpler. The change in the organization can—by definition—be imposed on the existing physical capital, and the greater rewards realized immediately. If a new product is involved, the question of whether to undertake the necessary investment to place it on the market is no different from the general question of whether to invest or not.

B. OBSTACLES TO INNOVATION

Unless the new technical blueprints are used at the time that they are first economic for the community as a whole, the return to investment in the drawing up of blueprints is, of course, reduced. Resources used to develop the new knowledge, therefore, produce less than was assumed to be the case when they were committed. Creating those conditions in the economy that will assure innovating in a manner consistent with the degree of exploitation of the new technical knowledge that is economically rational is an essential part of the technical change analysis. The question then arises as to possible obstacles to the creation and maintenance of those conditions in the underdeveloped country.

In the most sophisticated of economies, the urge to protect capital values is exceedingly strong, and where new techniques are occurring as a matter of routine, the effort to protect sunk capital is often a major obstacle to full exploitation of new knowledge. As noted above, entry or threat of entry of new firms is the strongest antidote to such delay, and if entry is impossible, then the tax system is the only hope. In the underdeveloped country where the appearance of new blueprints is not a routinized manner, other obstacles are probably more relevant.

A range of difficulties is easily identified. If investment is required, access to loanable funds may be a handicap. Especially is this difficulty likely in the case where full depreciation has not occurred on the old capital item, and internal funds are not available. The new technique may require a different type of laborer or different quality produced input, and such changes may be difficult or impossible to implement quickly. More generally, a change in technique may require changes from traditional sources of supply of inputs, and this may create additional costs. All of these reasons simply mean that the cost—in various forms—of switching to the new technique may be discouragingly high in the underdeveloped country, while in the more sophisticated, organized economies it would not be. Also, of course, ignorance of new technique and lack of facilities for circulating knowledge and information about new techniques are major barriers. Given the short-time horizon and the generally prevailing attitude that continuous economy-wide growth is not possible, there is reduced incentive to change from the tried and known procedures. Various social arrangements work against quick exploitation of new techniques. These and other general obstacles that one might mention can hardly be attacked by specific policies, but are overcome or reduced as development proceeds. All the obstacles should, of course, be recognized and taken into account in the decision to commit resources to the development of new blueprints. There are two additional obstacles that should be given more attention and that have more specific implications for the whole question of the accumulation of technical knowledge.

The argument was made in Chapter 7 that the majority of the population of the underdeveloped country was willing, indeed eager, to find and use ways of increasing output. Thus, particular segments of the economy are anxious to innovate, are anxious to exploit every idea that is believed to be profitable, but lack the means of evaluating the information with which it is supplied. The key point seems to be to convince the relevant decision maker that a new process really has the effect claimed for it.

The most important example of this point has to do with agriculture. The introduction of new techniques in agriculture, in many instances, requires that individual peasants adopt new methods and adapt their work habits and work routine to the demands of the new knowledge. Thus, the final link in the agricultural knowledge-accumulating and -applying chain is the rural peasant, the least equipped—economically, socially, intellectually, emotionally—of all economic agents to introduce change. The introduction of new seeds, new fertilizers, new watering techniques, new products, and the like depends, then, on an element in the society very poorly equipped to appraise the new techniques, and the least willing and able to risk trying out new techniques and methods. On the other hand, industrial innovations face a more manageable final link. Less reliance need be placed on the individual worker in appraising a new method, and usually greater resources are available for risk taking than is the case for peasant farmers. The urban industrial worker at all levels is probably more flexible and adaptable than his rural counterpart. The result would seem to be that at the crucial innovating stage of the process, the industrial sector may be much stronger than the agricultural sector. Further, where obstacles to acceptance appear, government policies to relieve the obstacles—e.g., subsidies, insurance schemes, and so on—are much easier to devise and apply for the organized, urbanized industrial sector than for the rural sector. The moral would seem to be that at the innovating stage, at least, prospects are brighter in industry than in agriculture. The main point here, however, is not so much that innovation in agriculture may be more difficult than innovation in industry, as it is that the choice of area of blueprinting activity depends on the capacity of the affected agents to use the new knowledge, as well as upon matters affecting the capacity of the economy to supply the new technical knowledge.

The second obstacle that appears to be of great relevance in accounting for innovational activity is the extent to which the firm is cost conscious. Evidence accumulated in Great Britain and the United States suggest that the technically progressive firm is also one that is alive to economizing in all aspects of its operations. Thus a firm is unlikely to follow a strongly progressive sales policy and a backward technology policy. Therefore, a large part of the problem of innovation is the still larger problem of creating a conscious economizing attitude on the part of the firm. For a firm to follow the kind of innovating policy outlined in Section A above requires that that firm have estimates of its various costs and of anticipated demand as well as knowledge of what new things are available. Until a firm begins to be conscious of costs, demand, and technology, the other relevant factors—finance, risk, expectations, and so on—are secondary and do not really matter.

There are several implications of this point. The role of management training and of the development of a managerial class in the economy is evident. Less evident is precisely what policies can be pursued that will attack this very nebulous problem. The subsidization by the government to enable firms to conduct technical research will help create an awareness of the advantages of conscious thought about efficiency and improvements therein. The general notion is that not only will the firm engage in the search for "suitable" knowledge if subsidized, but also that the very search will contribute to making the firm more conscious of economizing and less conscious of its traditionalism. Indeed, the very fact that a firm engages in a conscious effort to develop new blueprints means that it has at least become aware of the notion of efficiency. Again, the difficulties with respect to agriculture seem greater than for industrial activity, simply because the individual farmer cannot do much in the way of technical research, and merely making available new techniques to the farmer does not seem as likely to be effective as in the case where the user himself develops the new technique. The frequently referred to example of United States agriculture is hardly applicable to the underdeveloped country. The farmer in the United States is literate, informed, and very conscious of profit-making opportunities, and where new developments are made available through the United States Department of Agriculture or through companies that produce agricultural implements, they are eagerly snapped up. In those parts of the United States where agricultural workers are less educated and less informed, agricultural productivity has lagged behind the national average. The rural farmer of the economy of Chapter 7 is much more akin to the latter group of United States farmers than to the first group.

Other methods that have been found potentially fruitful are demonstration or pilot projects of various kinds. The chief difficulty with such devices is that often advantages are available to the pilot project that cannot possibly be made generally available. In this event, the project really is not a pilot project, but rather an enclave with no demonstrating impact at all. The utilization of technical experts from abroad, of foreign managers, of government ownership and operation, and the like may be included. All such devices are important and useful, create problems and have major limitations, but in the "right" conditions can make contributions. Of greater and more far reaching importance, however, is discovering ways to create an economic environment in which the firm will find it to its own advantage to develop and apply technical knowledge, and the chief tools available for this purpose are the tax and subsidy systems previously discussed.

IV. Conclusion

The process by which an economy changes from one where technical change is virtually absent to one where it is a matter of routine can hardly be said to be well established. The process as outlined in this chapter rests on admittedly disputable assumptions, and where efforts to reach down to specific empirical conclusions were made, great caution is required. For example, the tentative argument that technical development in agriculture faces a greater hurdle than it does in manufacturing activity is one that is surely open to many doubts. In general, however, the process as described here seems worthy of understanding and further study, and possibly to represent a useful approach to the problem.

Several things are evident. In the first place, the argument that allocating research resources to basic and applied research activities is uneconomic is convincing. Further, great importance must be attached to the selection of areas of endeavor that are as firmly grounded in the earlier stages of the knowledge-accumulating process as possible, and are researchable. In the second place, the argument also seems convincing that if investment in technical knowledge accumulation is left to the firm on its own, this area of activity is likely to remain uneconomically slighted. Therefore, a subsidy or other form of government sponsorship is necessary. For a variety of reasons, a subsidy to firms seems more likely to be effective than does a government laboratory that develops findings and passes them out to the general community. The major qualification to this conclusion deals with problems that seem to be too large or otherwise unsuited for individual firms, and, of course, such instances may be important. Finally, the conditions that will lead producing units to use the new knowledge are of great relevance. Formal criteria can be established, but their implementation depends heavily on the existence of a cost-conscious, efficiency-minded firm, as well as a market structure or subsidy tax system that assures the equality of social and private profitability. The chief obstacle to innovation seems to be the nature of the organization of the firm, rather than market organization, misinformed ideas on replacement policies, shortage of finance, and the like. Finally, a reminder is necessary that the production-function approach must be supplemented by the acknowledgment that rapid technical progress depends on the climate of opinion and attitudes prevailing in the society, as well as upon the formal allocation of resources to the search for new techniques.

The nature of the process in combination with the resources available to implement it, suggest a final conclusion that also is convincing: to achieve the objective in the underdeveloped country of a continuous flow of new blueprints of "suitable" technology, speedily adopted is a long, slow process.

Bibliography

Perhaps the best place to begin additional study of the unwieldy subject of this chapter is with two articles by Richard R. Nelson, "The Economics of Invention: A Survey of the Literature," *Journal of Business, XXXII* (April, 1959) and "The Simple Economics of Basic Scientific Research," *Journal of Political Economy, LXVII* (June, 1959). The volume, *The Rate and Direction of Inventive Activity: Economic and Social Factors,* a report of the National Bureau of Economic Research (Princeton: Princeton University Press, 1962) contains a series of papers covering most aspects of the problem discussed in this chapter, including some very interesting empirical studies. The article by William Fellner, "Does the Market Direct the Relative Factor-Saving Effects of Technological Progress?" in this volume was relied on very heavily in the discussion of the mechanism determining the kind of blueprints developed, pp. 294–99 above. Three general books on the subject are John Jewkes, David Sawers, and Richard Stillerman, *The Sources of Invention* (London: Macmillan & Co. Ltd., 1958); and C. F. Carter and B. R. Williams, *Industry and Technical Progress,* (London: Oxford University Press, 1957) and the same authors' *Investment in Innovation* (London: Oxford University Press, 1958). The most interesting endeavor to nail down costs and returns on a specific research project is Zvi Griliches, "Research Costs and Social Returns: Hybrid Corn and Related Innovations," *Journal of Political Economy, LXVI* (October, 1958).

Richard S. Eckaus's paper, "Technological Change in the Less Developed Areas" in Robert E. Asher (ed.), *Development of the Emerging Countries* (Washington, D.C.: The Brookings Institution, 1962) is a useful survey of the technology problem in the developing country. Fritz Machlup, *The Production and Distribution of Knowledge in the United States* (Princeton, New Jersey: Princeton University Press, 1962) is chiefly concerned with the United States, but has some general discussion that is also helpful in a broader framework. See also John Jewkes, "How Much Science," *Economic Journal, LXX* (March, 1960). On the spread of techniques, see Edwin Mansfield, "Technical Change and the Rate of Imitation," *Econometrica, XXIX* (October, 1961).

On a somewhat higher level of abstraction see A. P. Usher, *A History of Mechanical Inventions* (2nd ed.) (Cambridge: Harvard University Press, 1954) Chaps. 1–4 and H. G. Barnett, *Innovation, The Basis of Cultural Change* (New York: McGraw-Hill Book Company, 1953).

On problems of technical research on an international level, see Arthur T. Mosher, *Technical Co-operation in Latin American Agriculture* (Chicago: The University of Chicago Press, 1957). A series of case studies on efficiency in business organization in Iran prepared by George Fry and Associates, Management Consultants, Tehran has a lot of interesting material on conducting a reasonably efficient business enterprise in a developing country. On research in a developing area see Bruno Leuschner, "Technological Research in Latin America," *Economic Bulletin for Latin America, VIII* (March, 1963).

CHAPTER 12

THE TRAINING OF LABOR

The argument in the preceding chapter examined the issues associated with the accumulation of new technical knowledge and its introduction into the production process. In this argument the assumption was made that such knowledge was either incorporated into the physical capital of the producing unit or into the organization of production. Explicitly excluded were changes in the quality of labor input. However, in Part One, the argument was made that changes in the labor input were also relevant in accounting for the growth of output. This chapter examines in some detail the role of labor in the achievement of the economic objectives of an economy. Section I establishes the framework of the analysis, and the remaining sections explore the specific issues pointed up by this framework.

I. The Problem

Tables I and II of Chapter 4 show that a required primary input in any activity is a particular complex of labor skills. Thus to produce a unit of commodity 2 in Table II requires l_2 units of labor, and these l_2 units are different in quantity and quality from the labor input requirement for the production of commodity 3. The table, therefore, emphasized that the labor input is not a homogeneous mass of productive power, but rather it is a structure of skills, and the nature and extent of the various skills affect both the level of output and the composition of output. To increase the rate of output, therefore, requires not merely more men, but rather more men in whom are embodied certain skills. If all skills were endowed by nature—i.e., were free—then the economist would have little to say. However, skills are not costless to acquire, but are created through education and training and both of these require scarce inputs to produce. The problem then may be conceived in the following way: At a given interval of time, an economy has a specific number of individuals able to work. These workers have certain skills that have been acquired either by formal education or by on-the-job training, and what the economy can produce in this period depends in part on the skills that are available. The economy may choose to produce in one period new skills embodied in the work force so that in future periods the composition and level of output may be different from what they are in the present period. The question of relevance to the economist is what kind of training and education yields the highest returns to the economy, and how much training and education should be produced relative to other commodities.

A. The Array of Skills

The analogy with physical capital and technical knowledge is clear, though not complete. An individual laborer is assumed, at the outset of his career, to possess no skill (except some intelligence to learn skills), and some education and training is required before that individual can perform a productive function in the economy. Just as it was assumed that physical capital embodies technical knowledge, so it is assumed that labor embodies training and education. Further, the assumption is made that by introducing more training and education into labor, its productivity rises. But training and education, like the accumulation of technical knowledge, require the use of scarce resources. Also skills, like physical capital, may be made obsolete by development of new skills and new physical capital, and people, even more so than machines, are difficult to push aside and frequently are equally difficult to teach new skills as the worker ages. These ideas may be further developed by considering several skill categories separately.

Some skills require so little training that their acquisition requires merely a few minutes observation of someone who is employing the skill. Swinging an ax, pulling weeds by hand, or carrying messages is such an easily acquired skill that it does not seem very helpful to consider that its acquisition is a process that demands the use of scarce inputs for training. Unskilled labor, in general, refers to individuals possessing no special skills, and able to perform only those tasks that are simple enough to be learned by short observation. In the economy described in Chapter 7, most of the work force is in this category. If the development process imposed no demands for skills beyond this, then there would be little objection to equating the labor supply problem to the explanation of population growth, and no need to discuss the skill problem.

There are also skills that require rather limited training—for example, one year—to acquire, and usually the most effective form of such training is on-the-job training rather than attending any educational institution. In this category of skills would be the operation of simpler machines, truck driving, various aspects of construction activity, and possibly jobs imposing a little literacy. Once full literacy is required, the one-year limitation is almost sure to be inadequate, and formal educational institutions are in general necessary. Thus, the change or attempted change in an economy from one requiring largely illiterate workers to one where the performance of most jobs requires literacy may be an extremely expensive change. More on this later.

There are also skills that can be acquired with little or no specialized training, but do require considerable general training—at least secondary school and possibly college. Such skills are those associated with many administrative and organizational jobs, with jobs requiring judgment and initiative as well as general background knowledge, and jobs that impose a great variety of demands on the jobholder. The production of these skills requires more formal academic training than the previous category, and experience becomes a relevant factor in explaining the effectiveness with which the individual performs the job.

All three of these categories are characterized by a lack of specificity, and by considerable substitutability among the skills within and between each category. This fact has great importance in forecasting the composition of skills called for by the development effort.

However, there is a wide range of skills that seem especially relevant to the newly developing economies that do require specific training and among which there is very little substitution. Most professional activity—medical doctors, engineers, craftsmen, college teachers, chemists, and the like—are in this category. In almost all instances, persons possessing such skills have gone through from ten to twenty years training, and have "embodied" in themselves a large "quantity" of very specific skills. The result is a skill that has been created at great cost, and the productivity of which depends very much on the pattern of development in the economy as a whole. If such skills are not substitutable among themselves, then evidently the consistency problem defined in Chapter 4 must be expanded to include labor training. This large category of skills thus creates the greatest problems for manpower projections, as well as requires the greatest commitment of resources for training purposes. It is also in this category that the notion of a production function for skills is most pertinent, and on which most attention will be focused in the following sections.

As already noted, the underdeveloped country is dominated to a very marked degree by a large labor force (relative to other inputs) possessing only the most primitive of skills, i.e., those acquired by observation and the talents with which they were endowed by nature. At the same time, the argument has made clear that changing the economy of Chapter 7 into a continuously growing one requires not only more capital than the underdeveloped economy has in its initial conditions, but also physical capital that embodies new technical knowledge and thereby demands new skills for its operation.

B. The Role of Labor in Development

There are several ways of viewing the role of skill supply in development, and it is useful to examine each in some detail. The assumption may be made that the appropriate set of new industries to be established (or old industries to be expanded) are determined by considerations of factors other than specific labor inputs, e.g., natural resources. Then the complex of labor skills—the L_r of Table 1—must be forthcoming or the activity is simply not possible, just as it would not be possible if a required produced input were not available. The economy, then, must allocate resources to producing the required skills (or to producing exports in order to import the skills) if the projected industrial structure is to come into existence. In this case, the assumption is that the labor skill input is the adaptive variable or is meant to be the adaptive variable, and other determinants dictate the occupational structure to which the training institutions adapt. It is in this context that the problem of the projections of manpower requirements has its most precise meaning.

Evidently, the greater the extent to which substitution among skills is possible, the less is the relevance of the projection. If no substitution at all among skills were possible, then the accuracy of the forecasted occupational structure becomes crucial in decisions as to what kind of skills should be created. For example, if an economy has large quantities of oil deposits that it seeks to exploit and its educational plants produce only lawyers, accountants, and poets and no petroleum engineers, the effort to establish an oil industry must necessarily be abortive (unless the country can export poetry and import petroleum engineers.) On the other hand, if substitutability among the skills were quick and easy, then whatever skill was produced could be adapted to whatever requirements emerged, and the projecting or forecasting problem would cease to be crucial. Since there is evidence that substitution is far from perfect among skills, the accuracy of the projection is usually regarded as of great relevance when labor's role in development is viewed in the manner described in this paragraph.

The assumption that the skill complex is the adaptive input variable is not the only approach to examining how the creation of skills enter into the development process. Under certain circumstances, a situation may exist in which the rest of the system adapts to or takes advantage of a flow of particular skills that are being made available to the economy. This process is somewhat the opposite of that described in the two preceding paragraphs. Here the argument is that the particular skills that are produced determine or help determine the set of activities that are created or are expanded. If, for example, the educational system turns out a large number of engineers relative to chemists, then it is to be expected that the labor costs to an employer of the former will be less than those of the latter, and consequently industries requiring engineers will be favored relative to those requiring chemists. Obviously demand is relevant too, but the cost considerations will play a role. In this case, the labor skills that are created are assumed to provide the points to which the rest of the system adapts.

Neither of these extreme views is realistic nor practically significant. The first approach—labor assumed to adapt to the demands placed on it— assumes that production costs of the variety of skills do not vary sufficiently to affect the profitability of alternative investment allocations. But this is not always true. Ample evidence exists to show that the costs of producing a chemical engineer able to operate independently in this capacity are much greater than those required to produce an accountant or lawyer. Similarly, numerous examples could be cited to show that physical capital has been created or acquired from abroad that requires an operational skill whose production costs clearly make the physical capital uneconomic for the economy.

The opposite approach is likewise one sided. Labor-training costs are not the sole costs of production, and cannot be the sole determinant of the allocation of new investments. Nevertheless, this way of thinking suggests some important points. In any given short-run interval, the flow of trained personnel is more nearly fixed than is most physical capital. Therefore, simply because the gestation period of (some) skill production is so much longer than the gestation period for (some) physical capital, the flow of new workers with particular skills can in some short-run intervals be taken as a datum. In this case, the capital costs of producing the skill are zero, and to build physical capital that is designed to exploit this (given) input may result in extremely low-cost production. Again, demand considerations may indicate that even these low costs do not justify the use of any scarce resources to exploit the skilled labor. However, the point remains that the relevance of skilled labor as a primary determinant of profitable investment opportuntities is much greater in the short run than in a long-run context.

This way of thinking about the role of skill production is also helpful under another set of assumptions, especially applicable to international trade. The usual approach to the question of the determinants of a country's exports is in terms of its factor endowment relative to the factor endowments of its trading partners. Now, it is conceivable that a particular economy may have characteristics that enable it to produce certain skills relatively cheaply. Perhaps the most realistic example would be in terms of an accident of history that resulted in the immigration of a crew of teachers in a given field into a country. Thus, for a long period of time it would be expected that this economy could produce workers in this particular field relatively more cheaply than other countries that happened not to be so fortunate. Similarly, one can find examples where, because of location advantages or because of a more or less accidental establishment of a training institution, a complex of people or equipment has come into existence that makes possible more effective training than is available elsewhere. In this case, training services can even become a major export item.

In general, however, the two approaches must be combined. In a given period the economy has, as has been shown, investible resources to allocate in a manner that will result in the maximum contribution to its objectives. What this allocation is will depend on all costs, of which labor training is one, as well as on demand considerations. The question is whether or not the activity as a whole is profitable not whether the cost of a single input is relatively low or high. Also, in this sense, the "projecting of manpower requirements problem" is part of the solution to the allocation problem rather than a problem added after the question of which new sectors to create or which to expand has been solved. Neither is it a matter of saying simply that the economy can produce certain skills more cheaply than others; therefore, it should seek to create a set of activities to which these skills are inputs. The result is the introduction of skill production as an ingredient in the general allocation problem.

C. How Much Skill?

There is a further question that complicates matters even more. In the activity defined by a column in Table II, the labor input coefficient, l, defines the quantity of a particular labor skill required to produce a unit of output if that activity is employed. It seems clear, however, that in almost all instances variation in the quality of skill is permitted. A minimum level is required to achieve any output at all, but a higher level of skill will, with unchanged nonlabor inputs, result in a higher rate of output. In a wide variety of cases, the extra skill is a matter of on-the-job training, simply the accumulation of experience, but in other instances, it is a matter of the extent and quality of formal training to which the laborer is subjected. Further investment in the creation of skills will then result in an increased rate of output. To answer the question of how much training, therefore, requires consideration of the details of the production function describing the relationship between training inputs and skill output. Such a task—as will appear—is extremely complicated, but also of great relevance to the issues at hand. If first-rate engineers require fifteen years training under the supervision of a group of first-rate engineers who are also first-rate teachers, then there is at least a question as to the appropriateness of producing first rate, as opposed to say third rate, engineers—after the decision has been taken to produce engineers at the expense of lawyers or accountants. The assumption is then made that minimum levels of skills are required to permit the activity at all, and these minima are employed in examining the consistency problem. However, beyond this, further investment in training may yield returns in excess of the costs of this training, and hence the problem of how much training arises.

The argument may be summarized. The development process requires an array of skills ranging from (a) those that are easily and virtually costlessly acquired and among which there is a great deal of substitution, to (b) those skills that can be acquired only after long and expensive training, and among which substitutability approaches zero. The skills—especially those in the latter category—are viewed as being produced by formal training institutions or on-the-job training, and their production thereby requires the use of scarce inputs. The consequence of this argument is that the cost and availability of training facilities and the flow of skills is of relevance in the understanding and specification of the growth path the economy should (and will) follow. From this viewpoint, the way in which labor enters the story, three rather specific questions emerged that require detailed treatment. The most obvious question has to do with consistency requirements. If the educational system is turning out only lawyers, and physical capital is being built that requires lathe operators and machine tool specialists, then difficulties will emerge. These difficulties may take the form of mere delays in realizing returns on the investments, but they may take the more serious form of severe capital loss; i.e., physical capital or human skills may have been created by means of investment that yield no output, because the "wrong" complementary inputs were created. Thus, a major question of concern in the analysis is the availability of a mechanism—market or otherwise—that contributes to the achievement of consistency in this respect.

The second question deals with how much training, once the question what kind of training is answered. The examination of this issue requires some way of measuring the costs of education and training, and of the returns that may be attributed to such activity. The question here is conceptually clear, but, precise measurement of these concepts is not something now possible. Some quantification is necessary on both the cost and the production side; otherwise there can be no claim to rationality.

A final general question that emerges from the framework just established, pertains to the type of training institution. Of particular relevance is the choice between on-the-job training and that done in conventional educational institutions. The choice here will be seen to depend not only on the costs and the effectiveness of the training, but also on considerations having to do with the external effects of on-the-job training on the general overall operation of the firm. Sections II, III, and IV consider each of these questions in turn. Before proceeding to these tasks, some other general aspects of the labor/skill question are discussed.

D. Some Modifications and Amendments

The preceding discussion was based on the assumption that an individual's skill was in effect a produced input in the production process. But skill acquisition and education in general is also a consumer good. Individuals often pursue educational programs for reasons completely unrelated to considerations of skill as an input in the production of further goods and services. Education is then a final good, as well as the means of creating an input. The rationale of investing in education as a consumer good is, of course, quite different from that of investing in it as a means of creating an input. As a consumer good, education must compete for resources with other consumer goods, clothing, food, entertainment, and so on.

For many skills created by education, this fact introduces few difficulties, but for others the line between a production input and a consumption good is not easily drawn. Particularly is the line dim with respect to literacy training and in most areas of education that fall under the heading of social studies. In these areas, expenditure on education may be both a consumption and an investment expenditure, and the cost of the investment may therefore be nil. Despite the difficulties involved in an empirical distinguishing between education as a consumption and as an investment good, the conceptual difference is clear enough, and enables the policy maker to understand much more effectively the role of education in his economy.

A more troublesome point is that individuals are not only possessors of skills, they also are members of society, voters, heads of families, and so on. Education affects the effectiveness with which they perform in these capacities, and no one would argue that their role here is not as important as their role as the possessor of skills. But, here, the issue seems clear enough: the economist seeks to understand the way in which investment in education affects the economic system as defined in Part One of this book. From the standpoint of the society's larger objectives, more education than is optimal from a purely economic standpoint may be needed, but this in no way reduces the significance of the economic question.

As the skill is embodied in the human being, it cannot be separated from him, and sold or used independently. This fact has a number of implications, the most important of which has to do with the sources of funds to invest in the formation of human capital. Private firms face an added risk in such commitments because they have no way (or rarely have a way) to assure themselves that they will be the recipient of the returns due to the creation of new skills. This characteristic also limits the trade that can take place due to skills. An economy cannot package some skills and ship them to other countries where production would be more costly.

The framework described above is merely complicated, it is not undermined, and policies have to be devised with these characteristics as constraints. The constraints do not mean that rational policy is impossible.

Finally, the point should be made that the labor input considered here does not include the entrepreneurial function. The entrepreneur problem seems best considered in the context of the social and institutional matters to be discussed in Chapter 13.

II. The Consistency Problem

The stationary section of Table IV shows the inputs for the production of the intermediate goods, the final demand column consisting entirely of consumption items, and the inputs for the primary inputs, capital and labor. As already discussed both primary inputs are assumed fixed as to quantity and quality in the current period, and if there were no dynamic section in the table, the static problem of allocation would be to use these resources so that the largest possible output is achieved. The dynamic section of the table shows the various activities of the economy whose operation results in additions to the capacity of the system. Attention has already been given to the activities in this section of Table IV that include both the production of new physical capital and new technical knowledge. If there is a dynamic section in such a table describing a given economy, then in period two more physical capital items will be available for use in the production of both maintenance and capital goods. Also some of the new physical capital items will embody technical knowledge not available at the time the capital existing in period one was produced. Now it has just been argued that the production of skills is a resource using activity that adds to the capacity of the system, and is, therefore, to be included in the dynamic section of the table. In the language used in Chapter 4, the activities in the dynamic section result in the output of new primary inputs to be available in the next period.

In a growing economy, resources allocated to producing primary inputs are great enough to result in net physical and human capital formation and in the creation of new technical knowledge. The consistency problem to which attention is now directed can be defined in terms of Table IV: the use of investible resources allocated to the production of skills must be such that the flow of new skills—embodied in workers—will serve as complementary inputs with available physical capital. "Inconsistency" would be evidenced by the appearance of particular skills that are not usable because of the lack of complementary primary inputs.

An examination of this consistency issue is made by explaining very simple education problems and working slowly into more complicated ones.

A. A Single Skill

Suppose that the human race was so endowed (or the demands placed on it were such) that any skill required as an input into a productive activity could be acquired within ten minutes by anyone who had completed seven years of schooling that consisted of a particular schedule of courses. Suppose further that these courses have no consumer satisfying characteristics at all. In this event, the educational activity would be made up of the one set of courses, and the consistency problem becomes quite simple. Suppose that from a stationary, maximum position, infant mortality declines abruptly and in a few years the labor force begins to grow by 1 per cent per year. The economy must then expand its educational capacity in each year of schooling by 1 per cent in each of seven successive years. At the end of seven years, the total activity must be expanding by 1 per cent per year.

The initial year increase in the capacity of the education activity represents an investment that will yield a return only if resources are available to be allocated to increasing the activity in the following six years. The gestation period of the skill-producing operation is seven years, and the amount of the investment is whatever the cost of expanding the education amounts to. (The expanding of the education activity involves more instructors and *their* production is also a time-consuming process that adds to the complexity of the problem. To avoid spelling out all this in useless detail, it may be assumed that the new teachers are imported.) At the end of the seventh year, the economy is supplied with 1 per cent more workers possessing the capacity to learn the required skill. What happens now?

Whether the new skills produce anything at all in the eighth year depends on whether new physical capital is available as a complementary input. (If there is no net increase in capital, the increased supply of skills may depress the wage rate, but this alone will not result in the employment of the new labor until replacement-capital formation can sufficiently change the form of the physical capital to enable the employment of a more labor intensive technique.) If *all* available investible resources were necessary (and were used) to expand the education activity and none was available to expand physical capital, evidently, a simple kind of inconsistency would emerge. There would be "too much" of one resource and not enough of another, and the economy would realize nothing (at least for some time) on its investment in human capital formation. If the rate of saving was inadequate to enable the expansion of the education activity to the extent required by the higher population growth rate *and* to build sufficient physical capital to complement the labor, then, evidently, to earn any return on the investment in education, some resources must be diverted from expanding the education activity and be used to build physical capital. The consequence is that all of the persons becoming of school age cannot be trained, and hence will not (under present assumptions) be employable. The rate of saving must be increased, the population growth reduced, or the productivity of investible resources used in the education activity must be increased if consistency is to be achieved along with full utilization of available labor.

Another issue to be noted is the timing of investment. Ideally, just as the individual completes his training, the physical capital with which he is to work is also completed and an increased flow of output begins promptly. The gestation period of a skilled worker is assumed to be seven years. If the physical capital requires three years to build, then these facts impose on the decision maker this question: when to begin the investment in the various projects.

The assumptions underlying the preceding example are admittedly very simple. They are also realistic for a wide range of education problems in the kind of economy described in Chapter 7. In a number of instances, the product of the formal education activity is not a man embodying a skill directly usable in production, but a man capable of learning such a skill. The skill itself may then be acquired in on-the-job training. As will be argued in Section IV of this chapter, on-the-job training may be an important source of training activity in the underdeveloped country for this very reason. The chief point here is that under present assumptions a major source of inconsistency—namely, the wrong kind of education—is not present.

B. MULTIPLE SKILLS

The problem is immensely more complicated if the education requirement is such that it cannot be met by a single educational program. There are necessarily several activities in the manpower training category, and the consistency problem for expanding skill production now requires consideration of various types of education rather than simply one. The issue arises most clearly when education beyond elementary school is undertaken. Until then, the purpose of education is concerned with literacy training plus more or less general background material such as history, arithmetic, government, and the like that introduce no specific skills to the individual. As education continues beyond this elementary, general stage, further training does result in an increasing commitment to the acquisition of particular skills, and consequently, the task of deciding which skills becomes especially acute.

To appreciate the problem more fully, consider a case where education and formal training of a rather specific sort are prerequisites to the acquisition of a given skill, and many skills are currently in use in the system. To what extent does a failure of skill production, to mesh with the production of other inputs, create difficulties? There are several sources of adjustment. If the substitutability among skills is very great, few difficulties arise, and if substitutability were infinite no difficulties could arise. Thus, the greater the substitutability among skills, the less the economy suffers from lack of consistency or rather the less the possibility of inconsistency occurring. (A distinction might be made between substitution among skills and that between men possessing different skills. The latter would mean simply that one man could perform several jobs, while the former would mean that one skill could be used in a variety of ways. In a more detailed analysis, such a distinction would be helpful, but it does not seem necessary here.) A similar source of adjustment is the possibility of substitution not between labor skills, but between labor skills and other inputs, either capital or produced inputs. Thus, if a labor skill can replace physical capital, then evidently the task of planning in order to assure consistency between human and physical capital, is greatly reduced. Finally, if nonlabor inputs can be substituted among themselves so that the composition of output can be essentially determined by the complex of skills that emerge, the penalty for *ex ante* inconsistency is reduced by adjustment in the composition of output. The extent of this source of adjustment depends also on the price elasticity of demand for the commodity or service whose supply is increased as this adjustment is effected.

Three sources of adjustments to correct for emerging inconsistencies are available: substitution between skills, in the input mix, and in the product mix. The effectiveness of the last source depends also on the elasticity of demand of the product whose supply increases in consequence of the adjustment. If these three sources of adjustment provided enough flexibility in the system, the failure to achieve *ex ante* consistency may not result in underutilization of available resources in future periods. However, even if sufficient substitutability did exist to prevent underutilization due to this inconsistency problem, there are several reasons to believe that losses on the investment that created the skill would not thereby be prevented.

Evidently, a worker possessing a skill acquired by a costly training program, can also perform a task requiring no skill at all. In general, it would appear that there is a high degree of substitutability downward—i.e., highly trained people can perform tasks that can also be performed by unskilled workers—but a very low elasticity of substitution in an upward direction. But obviously, to invest in human capital formation, and then employ the skill thereby created in a task that could be performed by someone with no produced skill, results in a situation in which the economy receives no return on its investment. Arguments have already been presented as to why substitution between inputs is an acceptable concept only in an *ex ante* sense. Adjustment through changes in the product mix imposes less penalty on the system due to *ex ante* inconsistency. However, this source of adjustment requires either input substitution (which is not possible in the short run) or requires that nonlabor inputs be available that are also adaptable to the production of a product other than that for which they were originally designed. Both requirements are quite strong, and this source of adjustment cannot be a reliable solution to the consistency problem. It is evident, therefore, that an assumption of sufficient substitutability is not a satisfactory means of solving the consistency problem.

Substitutability does have a helpful role. The assumption that there is a high degree of substitution among skills that require little specific training is realistic and important. It means that in seeking to bring about consistency in manpower training, a very large category of skills can be grouped together as requiring either no training or only elementary school training. The problem is simply the total of these. It may be assumed that all high school academic (as opposed to vocational) courses result in no specific skill, and such individuals are easily adaptable, at virtually similar productivities, to a wide range of jobs that the system may devise, nevertheless, the highly trained, specific skill consistency problem, does not lend itself to such an easy solution.

When some education is a prerequisite for further education or training, then an additional complication is introduced. If secondary school is a prerequisite for advanced training, then the maximum number of people eligible for advanced training is determined by the size of the secondary school activity. This observation is not without difficulty in implementation not only because of the high costs involved in producing men with advanced training, but also because of the misplaced prestige value that seems to attach itself to the establishment of universities. The general point, however, is simple: effective utilization of available resources requires consistency between the flow of skills and the flow of complementary inputs, and it also requires that consistency be achieved within the various categories of education.

It is to be kept in mind that at least part of the educating activity can be imported.

C. Means of Achieving Consistency

There is abundant evidence attesting that most underdeveloped countries of the Chapter 7 category have failed to achieve even an approximation to consistency. As previously emphasized, there is a great deal of unutilized and underutilized physical capital in almost all underdeveloped countries as well as unemployed "intellectuals." There are lawyers, accountants, engineers, and scientists who are underemployed at the same time that there are machines that remain idle because the appropriate labor inputs are lacking. There are many cases where medical doctors are more numerous than nurses, and engineers more numerous than technicians, although the evidence suggests that for a doctor or engineer to work full time in that capacity requires that there be two or three nurses and technicians, respectively, available to help him. If such help is not obtainable, the highly trained specialist must do things that lesser trained people could do, and consequently, the social return on the investment that produced the specialist is well below what it might otherwise be. Even more in evidence are large scale undertakings—the building of multipurpose dams, steel mills, chemical factories, and so on—whose operation will require a particular set of labor skills, and no such skill complexes are under construction. Indeed, one can easily find examples of a planning commission that is successfully proceeding with a development program that calls for technicians, for engineers, for chemists, and for agronomists while the education policy is to turn out lawyers, sociologists, and historians. There can be little doubt that the solution to this particular form of consistency problem is not readily available to the developing country.

A major part of the explanation of this set of difficulties springs from the many noneconomic aspects of education, and the fact that it is a consumer durable as well as a production input. Pressures for universal literacy, so prevalent in the new countries, can hardly be attributed to purely economic calculations. There are also bureaucratic difficulties. Ministries of Education are rarely intimately linked with Planning Commissions; hence, they tend to proceed more or less independently of each other. Furthermore, there is a reluctance amounting to downright refusal on the part of those with a skill that is in excess supply to accept either a job in which that skill is not employed, or to be willing to work for anything below the going-wage rates paid to workers currently employed using that skill. Now, however, the more analytical problems associated with achieving consistency are discussed.

1. A price mechanism. In a perfect, timeless market where aggregate supply was a homogeneous mass that could be squeezed in such a manner that made possible the production of anything at a moment's notice, inconsistencies would not appear. If, for example, there is a shortage of nurses relative to the number of doctors, the latter would bid for the services of the former, thereby pushing up the nurse wage rate. As the nurse wage rate increased relative to other wage rates, more people are encouraged to become nurses rather than something else. Demand for nurse training rises, and the aggregate supply glob is so squeezed that more nurses emerge immediately. In a country with general educational institutions in existence, and a built-in growth process functioning, the above argument is not so unrealistic as to be useless. However, in a Chapter 7 type country where efforts are being made to move the economy from its underdeveloped stage, the argument cannot be reliable for two general reasons.

One of the most far-reaching ways in which the price system fails in the underdeveloped country is with respect to the determination of wages. Particularly, but not exclusively, in government employment does there appear great discrepancy between wage rates and productivity. This discrepancy is most clearly illustrated in agriculture. The evidence is quite convincing that a major obstacle to increased productivity in the agriculture sector is the individual farmer, and there can be little doubt that effective extension workers reaching the individual farmer have extremely high productivity. Yet the wage rates in most agricultural advisory work are such as to encourage people to seek urban desk jobs. Often such urban desk jobs require—by legal edict—the holder to have a high school or perhaps a college degree. Thus, not only are wage rates higher for the less productive worker, but he is also required to have more training as well. The economy is twice the loser. The problem is intensified because the rural life in most of the underdeveloped countries is less exciting than urban life. There are, for example, many instances where agriculture advisory training facilities are underutilized, and a major explanation seems to be this type of wage discrepancy.

Reference has already been made to other examples: doctors and nurses, engineers and technicians, and so on. Perhaps an accurate general statement is that wage rates in many instances are based on the cost of acquiring the training necessary to meet the legal requirements for the job, rather than on the productivity of the job. This, of course, would not be possible in competitive markets, but as emphasized in Chapter 7 and elsewhere, few markets—and certainly not labor markets—are dominated by competitive forces. The generalization, therefore, seems accurate that in a wide range of activities and especially in those requiring skilled labor inputs, a perverse wage-setting mechanism creates a major difficulty in relying on wage signals to achieve the consistency in the production of skills. Any approach to the consistency problem must certainly include an alteration in this wage-setting machinery, but that alone is not enough.

Even if the wage rates were related to productivity to a satisfactory degree, the possibility of external economies associated with training and the certainty of a long gestation period required for the production of most skills, would cause difficulties. The latter, particularly, is troublesome. Long gestation periods mean that some fortunate people earn large rents, some unfortunate ones suffer severe capital loss, but the signals provided thereby are unreliable allocation clues because by the time a fresh quantity of currently profitable skills is produced, the roles may be reversed. The extent of risk varies and, in some areas, is so small that it has no consequence. The risk element, however, probably means that the individual will underinvest in his own education unless it is subsidized. The external economies effect means that the productivity of a particular skill is greater than the return the owner of the skill can acquire. Although such economies are not easily identified, some are surely present in a developing economy. An example perhaps would be that parents, who themselves are highly trained, frequently spend time training their children, or if not actually training them, creating in them a set of values that in turn, makes the children more easily trained. This is a service for which the parents receive no reward in the conventional economic sense.

If all these arguments are valid, then ways of supplementing the price mechanism approach to the consistency problem must be found.

2. A Planning Approach to the Production of Skills. The preceding argument leads to the conclusion that an explicitly formulated education and training plan is necessary, and such a plan necessarily involves a projection of the skills that are to be used as inputs in the future. The essential problem is: how to project. It has been noted that attention is concentrated in those areas where the acquisition of skills requires a long period of training and where substitution without loss of productivity is limited. There are a variety of methods available for making such projections, and a detailed review of all of them is unnecessary here. By discussing only a few of the techniques of projection, it will be possible to establish some general principles that must underlie any technique.

Beginning with some rather specific knowledge of the existing skill vectors, it is recognized that the existing labor supply of the underdeveloped country will be largely unskilled, and illiteracy more the rule than the exception. The existing formal education activity (including teachers and students with prerequisites, of course) is therefore quite small, and the quantity of educational services that can be supplied domestically in the short run is also necessarily small. This point is similar to that made earlier that the total amount of capital formation is limited by the size of the domestic capital goods sector and the capacity to import.

In the medium and long run, the size of the education and training activity is subject to change, and the projecting problem essentially is in what way to change it.

(a) Given Final Demand. The simplest approach is along the following lines. On the basis of a variety of considerations, a planning authority announces a final demand column—a target—for a year, e.g., fifteen years hence. Then, given this final bill of goods and current or expected technical coefficients, including the labor coefficients, the complex of labor skills necessary to produce this final bill of goods can be determined, and the education activities expanded in whatever manner required to produce these skills. This approach has the disadvantage that no optimizing or maximizing notion is involved that explicitly includes the cost of producing skills. In particular, it means that no explicit consideration is given to the fact that costs of production of various skills are neither zero nor the same, and therefore that they should enter into decisions on which final bill of goods is the best choice for this particular economy.

A step closer to including the cost of production of skills as an element in the maximizing process rather than as a constraint would be to set the targeted final bill of goods on the basis of some consideration of the education requirements as well as other requirements. To the extent that this can be done, it eliminates the disadvantage that was just noted. Either approach assumes a planning agency whose authority extends over most of the economy, whose control of the economic system is quite rigid, and that has a great deal of technical information at its disposal. Such planning authorities are rare, but the discussion does emphasize an extremely important point: planning which skills to produce must necessarily be done in the context of the kind of economy that is emerging. Failure to do this is almost sure to result in wasted skills, wasted physical capital, or both.

(b) *A Growth Path Assumption.* To proceed without economywide, comprehensive planning with a great deal of technical data, some sort of guide or leader may simply be followed. For example, suppose one particular underdeveloped country, Country A, had a resource endowment very similar to Country B, but the latter had a 25 per cent higher per capita income which lead it had recently acquired. Further, suppose that Country B showed evidence of growing fairly steadily. Country A may then assume that its growth path will be very similar to that actually followed by Country B, and then seek to establish the same kind of educational activities or the same set of skills that are observed in the richer country. For this approach to be acceptable, several assumptions as to the extent of the "similarity" are necessary. The demand for all goods in both countries must be similar at the relevant level of incomes, in the sense that as A's per capita income rises, its composition of demand—the final demand column of its *optimal* programming matrix—will be identical to the actual final demand for Country B. Such an assumption would mean either that income was the chief determinant of demand for various goods and possible price effects were small enough to ignore or that relative prices moved similarly in the two countries.

Similarity must also include technology. Thus, it must be assumed that the input coefficients of the activities included are the same for Country A as the ones in effect were for B when the latter country passed along the successive levels of income. This similarity implies that the rate of capital formation is also the same over the relevant growth periods in the two countries. Finally, the similarity in foreign trade must also be assumed. This similarity may be either no foreign trade or so little that it can be ignored or that both countries had access to the same markets at the same levels of income.

If all of these assumptions are true or approximately true, then the occupational structure of Country A would follow along the path once traversed by Country B. These are strong assumptions indeed, and few people would be willing to argue that they held in a general way among all countries for all times. It may be, however, that any particular country could find a guide that is reasonable to follow. A great many development policies are based on what is happening or has happened in other richer countries. The great difficulty is usually that the wrong country is chosen as a guide, particularly one that achieved its richness many decades earlier. A cautious conclusion then might be that a projection of skills that a country should have in order to maximize output ten or so years hence might rest in part on the skills being used in a similarly endowed country with a higher level of income. The term similarity applies to the aspects referred to above. Since the assumptions necessary to make the analogy hold exactly are surely quite unrealistic, an analysis of the factors specific to the country must also be made.

(c) *An Analytical Projection.* Suppose that all activities except those involving education were conducted in a free market, and the Ministry of Education had the responsibility of devising the "right" training and education activities. If analogy with other countries were ruled out, how might the Ministry proceed? Clearly, some sort of projection of the economic system—conceived of as a programming matrix—is required. To do this exactly for a period 10 or 15 years hence is probably a meaningless exercise, but approximations are surely feasible. If one can assume a fairly assured rate of growth of total product, then projections of the growth of broad categories of activities can be done with some degree of accuracy. Construction (residential and nonresidential), various sources of power, and transportation facilities are in this category. Assuring a flow of skills consistent with these activities should, therefore, be possible on the basis of simple forecasts. The same assertion would apply to certain other broad categories of specific activities. Also certain extremely large projects may have a long enough gestation period themselves that trained personnel can be produced within the period of the construction of the physical capital. The projecting problem is thereby reduced in complexity. Finally, certain training and educating activities can be eliminated with some degree of confidence. Perhaps the most obvious of these activities is the esoterica that one finds on the frontiers of many disciplines (including especially economics).

The area where the greatest difficulties emerge is also the area where it is perhaps most important not to be wrong. This has to do with assuring the supply of skills required for the development of activities not now existing in the economy, or present now only to a very small extent. The achievement of consistency here is important because, as shown earlier, it is new activities that are most likely to provide the major source of dynamism to an economy of the kind described in Chapter 7. It is especially difficult because of the great role that assumptions as to productivity changes play in any projection, and that technological data in these sectors are less available than in those activities that are common in the economy. A foolproof projection method does not seem to be available in this kind of situation, and perhaps the only thing that can be said is that education and training activities should be provided on the basis of knowledge of and consultation with the chief dispensers of loanable funds. Because of this projecting problem and of cost problems to be discussed later, reliance on the importing of training services and on-the-job training is an important source of adjustments that will help to produce consistency without sacrifice of productivity.

In practice, of course, the education planners will combine different approaches, and actual decisions may emerge from a consideration of all or most all the issues mentioned above. Once decisions are made, the final link in the process is the problem of how much resources are required to produce the quantity and composition of skills decided on as optimal. Conceptually this task is easy enough. Evidence is available as to what the education and training facilities (including teachers) currently available will produce in the forecasted year. These figures are then compared with those decided on as optimal, and investment in education must be sufficient to close this gap. And, as already emphasized, this investment figure cannot be "too large" or there will not be enough investible resources left over to produce the inputs complementary to labor. In this event, the decisions reached on what the appropriate skill output should be in the forecasted year are faulty. It would then be necessary to start all over again on the projection task with lowered ambitions.

3. Conclusion. This section has concentrated on defining the problem of consistency between skill production and the production of other "primary" inputs, and then examining the methods of achieving that consistency. The conclusion was reached that any method chosen necessarily involves an explicit projection of the skills that are expected to be optimal (and hence consistent) for the forecasted year, as a market mechanism did not seem applicable. Further, it was argued that substitutability of skills among activities that could be accomplished without loss of productivity would facilitate solving the problem, although it seems that the greater the skill, the more likely is downward substitutability rather than that possibly yielding no capital losses. At the other end of the skill spectrum, unskilled labor or skills requiring only general knowledge, are likely to be easily substitutable among themselves in a manner that involves little or no capital loss. Two final points are to be emphasized: to the extent that education takes the form of merely providing general background material that prepares an individual to learn a specific skill in an on-the-job training exercise, the difficulty of solving the consistency problem is greatly reduced. Hence, on-the-job training deserves considerable attention for this reason, and (as discussed later) for other reasons also. Finally, any approach to consistency must necessarily include policies that will result in a wage-rate-setting mechanism that relates wages to productivity rather than to education, title of job, or any other extra economic considerations.

III. How Much Skill

The distinction between the consistency problem just discussed and the problem of how much training may be illustrated by reference to the diagram that has been employed in previous discussion. Consider Diagram VII. The consistency problem was concerned with allocating resources so that the flow of ΔL_r and ΔK_r would be such that movement along the optimum ray was possible. In this problem, the emphasis was on the complementarity of the inputs in the activity. The definition of a ray in the diagram implies that the labor coefficient, l_r, is precisely fixed for that ray. Thus, the consistency problem could be clearly defined.

In the discussion of Part One, the argument was made that an improvement in the quality of the labor input would result in an increase in output with a given quantity of K_r, given technical knowledge, and an unchanged number of workers. Therefore, when Diagram VII is drawn, the assumption is made that L_r represents a particular level of skill just as K_r represents a particular level of technology.

To fix the argument as clearly as possible, assume that the rays drawn in Diagram VII represent the rate of output achievable with the minimum level of skills necessary to bring the activity into existence or to increase its magnitude. Then the question arises as to the profitability of

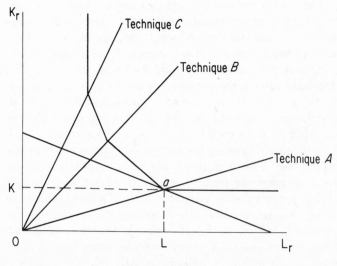

DIAGRAM VII.

increasing the level of skills above this minimum. This problem is of interest to the economist because, as already discussed, to increase the quality of the labor input requires resources allocated to training programs, and this cost must be weighed against the increased output that would result from the improved labor.

In this situation, the emphasis is placed on the substitutability of various levels of labor skills rather than on the complementarity between labor and nonlabor inputs. That such substitutability is possible seems both empirically evident and a priori reasonable. A given complex of machinery can be operated more or less skillfully, and in consequence the rate of output will be affected accordingly. Trains can be run by more or less qualified people, and they will be run more or less on time, with fewer or more accidents, and more or less economic routings. Irrigation facilities can be used in many ways some of which will contribute to production much more than other ways. Or economic policy can be made by men with high school education or by men with advanced degrees in economics, and the growth of the economy will reflect the difference. The general point is simply that the rate of output obtainable from a given complex of physical capital depends not merely on the quantity of labor used with it, but also on the quality as well.

There is a final link in the argument. As noted above, the problem is relevant because of the assumption that the creation of more productive labor inputs requires training. If this were not true, if labor could not be made more effective by some sort of explicit training or educational program, the argument fails. Level of skill must, therefore, be related in some way to level of training, and the analysis must include reference to the productivity of education in creating skills.

The problem now is this: The level of skills is assumed to be a function of the level of training or education the laborer has received. A minimum level of skills and hence of education is required to make an activity technically possible with given complementary inputs. Additional training produces greater skills, which in turn enable the achievement of a greater output from the same complex of physical capital. With these assumptions, the question arises as to how much training the economy should undertake. The answer requires examination of the costs of education and training, and an examination of the education "production function" including an analysis of the extent to which more skills do result in a larger rate of output with given nonlabor inputs.

It is useful perhaps again to caution the reader that results can hardly be called definitive.

A. The Costs of Education

Suppose a firm is in the equilibrium position represented by position *a* in Diagram VII. The labor input is shown by *OL* and, as emphasized above, this quantity of labor is assumed to have a particular level of skill. The capital inputs are represented by OK. Evidence is available to the firm that if it ceased operation for a year, and sent all of the workers to a training program, the rate of output from the given sized plant and given sized labor force would be increased. This would mean that interval Oa would then represent a rate of output that is $t_l \cdot MP_l \cdot L$ greater than that represented by the original interval.

Here the costs of the increment of education to the economy are easily identified. They include the direct costs of the training program—i.e., the cost of the resources used for training purposes—and the value-added forgone by the closing of the plant for one year. Who pays this cost is to be discussed in Section IV of this chapter, but now it can be stated that these constitute the costs to the society of having the workers in this plant engage in a training program. This cost would then be compared with the present value of the increments in the output stream due to the extra training to determine if the resources used in this fashion yielded a positive return.

This simplified example isolates the components of the cost of education as the resources used directly for training and the output sacrificed by having people in training rather than producing. The same costs are present when the general problem of the costs of education are considered. The first component is easily understood and is briefly discussed. The chief difficulty is to find ways of valuing the resources used, especially teachers. Teachers vary greatly in effectiveness, and salaries paid them often misrepresent the opportunity costs to society of having these individuals teach. This particular difficulty is, of course, common in allocation problems (see Part One), but is especially troublesome when applied to work where effectiveness depends as heavily on personality characteristics as does teaching. Problems of arriving at estimates of shadow wage rates (and other shadow prices) are treated in Chapters 15 and 16.

The second component, value-added forgone, is much more difficult to manage, especially in the context of a developing economy. If the individuals undergoing training would otherwise be unemployed, then presumably there is zero output forgone in having them in training. For the education of children under ten or twelve, the assumption of zero opportunity costs seems safe enough. For older persons, even though ostensibly unemployed, seasonal jobs may be so important that to sacrifice them would impose a real loss on the economy. This is especially true in rural areas where many elementary school terms are built around the seasonal duties in the fields. With respect to older persons, those attending advanced education programs may have a positive marginal product even though there is unemployment in general. This means simply that for the opportunity cost of labor to be zero, general unemployment is not a sufficient condition. This point has particular relevance concerning advanced training for individuals who already have some training. Finally, where the unemployment is due to the failure of the pricing mechanism to function effectively enough or due to misconceived economic policies, the apparent opportunity cost-free labor may in fact be very expensive in the sense that alternative policies could result in the labor becoming productive without further claim on resources. This last complication makes exceedingly difficult any sort of verifiable conclusion as to whether labor for training could contribute to output were it not in training. Indeed, in any discussion of labor's opportunity cost in a situation where unemployment exists, it is necessary to arrive at a decision as to whether or not that unemployment can be eliminated without claims on additional resources. Usually, but not always, this claim on resources would mean capital formation. The discussion in earlier chapters stresses that much of the idle labor in the underdeveloped economy is due, not to inadequate supplies of complementary inputs, but rather to inadequate policies.

Consider this brief illustration. Suppose that the minimum skill level (as defined earlier) is reached on the completion of seven years of schooling. Suppose further that because of defective factor pricing, firms are operating on Ray C of Diagram VII while true scarcity values would dictate Ray A, and consequently there is unemployment because, with Technique C, there is not enough capital to employ all the available labor. Institutes are set up or expanded to provide further training for these unemployed workers on the assumption that the extra training will make them employable. At the close of the last paragraph, it is suggested that valuing the output forgone by having these seventh-grade-school dropouts continue with their education at zero may understate the costs of education to a significant degree. If factor prices were accurate measures of opportunity costs, seventh-grade-trained labor would have a positive marginal product. If the policies to effect the change in factor prices can be implemented without a claim on scarce resources, then output can be increased (see Chapter 9) from existing resources. Whether this increase in output exceeds the return to the economy due to the additional training is another matter, but where there are unemployed laborers with some training already accomplished—a situation quite common among the underdeveloped countries—there is some presumption in favor of attaching a positive value to the output-forgone component of the costs of higher education. This point seems worth emphasizing because of the abundant evidence that the costs of education are (implicitly) underestimated in the development plans in many countries.

If the opportunity cost of having the labor in training is not zero, then methods must be found to estimate the output sacrificed. In the simple example above this was easy to do as the forgone output was simply one year's value added of this particular firm. In most instances, however, the estimation will not be so easy. A common practice is to assume that the wage rates of individuals in schools would equal the wage rates of those in similar age groups that are in fact working. For this to be an acceptable measure requires that wages be a reasonably accurate measure of labor's productivity, and that productivity would not have been affected even if all students were in fact in the labor force. This method is probably as satisfactory as any rough approximation can be. It obviously makes more sense in a highly developed, fluid economy with full employment than in the type of economy described in Chapter 7. For such an economy, the chief qualification is that associated with unemployment as discussed in the preceding two paragraphs.

B. THE EDUCATION PRODUCTION FUNCTION

The notion underlying the approach to manpower training developed here is that education is an activity in the matrix of activities with inputs (teachers' services, laboratories, buildings, and so on) and outputs—knowledge embodied in the individual that makes that individual more skillful in working with the complementary inputs at his disposal. The ultimate objective of the education and training activity, therefore, is the increase in the rate of output resulting from the produced increment in labor's productivity. It is this relationship between educational activity and increased output through increased skills that is now to be explored.

1. The Return to Investment in Education. In the example built around Diagram VII, the output of the additional training was identified from assumed knowledge about this diagram with two different qualities of labor used. After the training, OL of labor and OK of capital could produce not merely Oa of output but rather $MP_l \cdot L \cdot (t_l - 1) + Oa$. Needed now, however, is a general relationship between t_l, and some kind of a measure of the quantity of training. Conceptually, such a relationship could be found in the following way. Suppose there were twenty firms known to have a capital plant identical to or very similar to the K_r of Diagram VII, and that each of the firms employed a labor complement with varying educational qualifications. Plotted on a two dimensional chart with output per worker or per month on one axis and number of years in school on the other, the relationship between education and output could be measured.

The relationship obtained in this way is not likely to be distorted by a consumption effect, whereas relationships between levels of GNP and average educational attainments (on a time series or cross-section basis) measure the demand for education as a consumer good as much as they do the contribution of education to output. The assumption that firms do not consume education, i.e., do not hire employees simply because they are educated, does, however, seem to be a realistic assumption. Other differences among firms—market power, management ability, and the like—

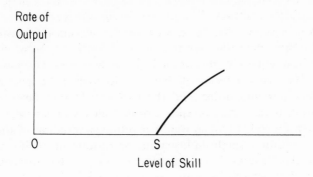

may distort the relationship, but still the data would provide a rough guide to the productivity effects of increasing education.

What can be said about the shape of the curve describing this relationship? Obviously much depends on the activity for which the labor is being trained, but in the more conventional types of activities, the curve may be expected to look like that shown here. The interval *Os* measures the skill level (number of years training) required to achieve any output at all. Beyond that point, further training will contribute significantly to output at the outset, and then the curve levels off. The argument described by the curve seems reasonable on several grounds. The extent to which skills can be substituted in the production process is not infinite, and as the "easy" ways to use a machine more effectively are exploited, the substitutability that is technically possible decreases. At the point where the curve becomes horizontal, substitutability has become zero and further training yields no results.

Independent of technical substitutability, available evidence also suggests that the aptitudes of an individual are such that continued exposure to the same education process does not result in increasing understanding. This suggests that increased learning requires contact with new processes and new ideas rather than continuous repetition of the same process or simply going over the same material again and again. The evidence implies that human beings have a limit on what they can learn about a process or phenomenon.

The length of *Os* will vary widely from activity to activity. It will be very large for some—e.g., atomic physicists, medical doctors, university professors—and virtually zero for others. Similarly, the curve will turn horizontal very quickly for some activities, and only after long years of study for others. Although there is less assurance here, the particular experiment described by which the curve was derived is a feasible way of estimating the increased output arising from increased education. The underdeveloped country will doubtless have to include firms in other countries in its analysis, but if done carefully, this is not a major handicap. Some major advantages of comparing foreign firms are to be discussed.

The curve derived in this way to measure the relationship between education and output does not take into account contributions of education of workers in one activity to output in other activities, i.e., possible externalities. Most such effects will have to do with more general social arrangements, law and order, and the like, which have been excluded from attention here. Other possible external effects might be traced directly, but, in general, to do so would require examination of the education process within a single industry in the context of an interindustry model. There is little evidence, however, to suggest that external effects of education that have a direct impact on output in other sectors are very important. To assume them to be zero would not introduce significant error into the allocation decision.

Simpler means than the approach outlined here have been suggested to estimate the contribution of education to output. The most obvious of these is to compare lifetime incomes of individuals with different amounts of education or training. This approach has many pitfalls. Lifetime income—or variations thereon—are invariably poor measures of productivity as family connections, job category, ambition, intelligence, and the like have an impact that cannot be ignored. With sufficient data and imagination these difficulties can be surmounted to a degree that make the results interesting. The major problem that defeats this approach is that in a wide variety of instances—especially having to do with on-the-job training —the profitability of undertaking the education requires that labor's wage not rise by the extent of its rise in marginal productivity. This point is developed in Section IV. Attention has already been directed toward the difficulty of interpreting results obtained from relating measures of aggregate output to the average education of the work force.

2. Some Problems of Implementation. The greatest difficulty with the approach taken toward the role of education in the development effort has to do with the exact nature of education and training. In the discussion of the costs of education, the inputs were listed simply as teachers, laboratories, buildings, and so on. Inputs into educational activity do not assure the output of an individual equipped to perform any function. Quality of education is a nebulous notion about which little beyond rather truistic generalizations are known.

For almost all underdeveloped countries the evidence is convincing that the quality of education is generally extremely low. Such an assertion means that individuals attending law schools do not learn law, men studying engineering do not learn to be engineers, and children studying reading and writing do not learn to read and write. The single most important reason for this situation seems to be the attempt to do more training than there are resources available with which to train. Part of the problem arises because of political pressure for education for everyone with no analysis of the economic consequences; part of it is also due to the lack of knowledge about effective teaching techniques. For example, little is known as to the effectiveness of size of class, of reliance on television, of type of examination, and the like on the student. The evidence suggests that confidence placed in manpower training by development policy makers as a means of overcoming the obstacles to development rests more on hope than on understanding.

The uncertainty surrounding the outcome of the educational activity is similar to that discussed in the chapter on the production of technical knowledge. This uncertainty is probably less where the job specificity can be quite exact. For training for these kinds of jobs, the introduction of a distribution notion into the preceding argument is about all that is needed to meet the uncertainty problem. However, in the occupations that are not rigidly defined, the difficulties are much greater. Particularly in regard to management skills and other "high level" manpower inputs, the difficulties involved in a direct application of the framework established here are severe.

The consequence of these remarks, however, is not the abandonment of the approach. Rather, it is the using of the approach in a manner that recognizes the need for flexibility and adaptability. It does seem especially important to probe carefully into the costs of any educational project, and to try to accumulate understanding—if not quantitative data—of the economic returns generated by training in excess of that necessary to bring the activity into existence.

IV. What Kind of Education

Before now, no analytical distinction has been made between on-the-job training and that provided by formal educational institutions. The distinction is, however, of great relevance in educational planning in the newly developing country, and it is helpful to explore some of the implications arising from these alternative forms of training. First some general considerations, and then a more detailed account of the economics of on-the-job training.

A. GENERAL CONSIDERATION

The preceding discussion has isolated a number of problems, the solution of which seems to lead toward a heavy emphasis on on-the-job training to meet the educational requirements of the country just beginning to grow. The problem that is solved in the most convincing manner by on-the-job training has to do with the consistency issue. In those cases where skills are specific to an activity or to a firm, reliance on on-the-job training greatly facilitates the achievement of consistency as that notion was defined earlier. This seems true for a variety of reasons. Firms supply training only for slots that are already in existence or are virtually certain to come into existence, while in an educational process that operates independently of specific job demand this directive force is absent. For example, there can be little doubt at all that if lawyers were produced only via an apprentice system in law firms and all law schools abolished, the resource misallocation that is represented by the supply of and demand for lawyers in many underdeveloped countries would be greatly relieved. Similar examples could be cited in other occupations as well.

On the cost side, there are some equally obvious points that seem to suggest on-the-job training may have advantages over institutionalized training. Physical capital can often be used for both training and production purposes, and, more importantly, instructors are equally shiftable between teaching and production. Overhead costs that seem so determined to skyrocket in university education in developing economies may be lower when going concerns supply the facilities. Also, firms in which on-the-job training is part of their routine are more likely to be aware, at least, of the "how much education" problem, and to solve this problem in a more rational manner than are institutions with no links to specific job requirements. Finally, the casual empiricism that is available on the subject suggests that the quality of the training—as defined above—is higher when conducted in plants than when conducted in schools. The reason for this is partly a simple matter of the competence and commitment of the instructors, and partly due to the greater ease with which cost and profit calculations can be introduced into training programs relative to formal educational institutions. An important aspect of this point is that the training takes place in the same environment—same buildings, same machine, same companions—in which work will be done, and this enables a more specific form of training than is possible outside the firm.

It is evident that on-the-job training is necessarily limited to certain types of activities. In general, there are some types of knowledge that can be acquired most effectively when studied in the context of immediate application, while others seem best acquired in a long period of formal academic specialization. It is in the area of vocational work and some professions—law, accounting, teaching, nursing—that on-the-job training and school-room instruction seem most directly substitutable. Also in those tasks requiring knowledge that is specific to a process employed by a firm or to the firm itself, contact with the practical problems becomes an inherent part of training. Indeed, it seems safe to argue that for the underdeveloped country, the required training activities that must necessarily be done in formal educational institutions are limited to the two ends of educational process. On the one hand, literacy (including arithmetic) training seems to be necessarily an academic pursuit, and at the other extreme, the training of men in the more advanced reaches of most disciplines also places heavy demands on institutionalized training.

These arguments will enter in a significant way into the final education strategy to be developed in the last section of this chapter. How on-the-job training may be introduced into the activities of the firm is now briefly examined.

B. The Economics of On-the-Job Training

1. Costs and Profits. Suppose that Diagram VII represents activities in the marginal vectors so that at point *a*, the firm is operating where wage rates equal the marginal product of labor as shown earlier. Suppose also that the firm's management is aware that improving the quality of the labor input will result in greater output with the existing capital complex. Finally, suppose the firm is equipped to do the necessary training itself. Under what conditions will the firm profit from engaging in this kind of on-the-job training?

The costs of the training to the firm are made up of the wages that it must pay during the training period (W_0), direct outlay on the training program itself (C_0), and the output forgone due to having workers training rather than producing (P_0). The subscript zero refers to the period during which training takes place. The return to the firm on the investment represented by these costs depends on the extent of the change in output due to the training, and on the change in wage rates that accompanies that rise in productivity. The higher output rate accrues over several periods, and the return to the firm from this source must be discounted so the interest rate is relevant in the firm's calculations as well. The central issue, however, has to do with wage rates. The firm will be indifferent toward investing in labor training if its outlay is exactly matched by the increased returns due to that training. That is if

$$W_0 + C_0 + P_0 = \sum_{t=1}^{n} \frac{MP_t - W_t}{(1+i)^t} \tag{1}$$

where MP_t is the marginal product of the worker in the n periods after training.

The key thing is that as long as C_0 is positive, wages cannot equal the marginal product of labor in both the training period and period t if the firm is not to suffer a loss on the program. If $MP_t = W_t$, the firm receives nothing for its investment in the training program, and $W_0 = MP_0 - (C_0 + P_0)$ is necessary if the trainees are to pay for their own program. (MP_0 is the marginal product of labor in the training period.) If $W_0 = MP_0$, then, as just noted, $MP_t = W_t$ would mean that the firm was supplying the training program free to its employees. Evidently, to get a firm to supply its own training, the competitive mechanism must be such that the firm is able to get and keep labor when its wages are below the productivity of that labor to the firm.

The chief implication of this result has to do with the kind of training offered by a firm. If the firm provides training to its employees that raises their marginal productivity in a wide range of activities, and if it is operating in a fairly competitive market, it is unlikely to undertake training programs. It cannot get labor by paying wages below the economy-wide opportunity cost-wage rate, and after the training to pay a wage below the new, higher marginal product would also result in losing labor to other firms where such labor had an equally high productivity. This consequence would seem to rule out on-the-job training in such things as reading and writing or general courses having to do with history, government, and so on and such skills as typing, truck driving, and the like.

On the other hand, a firm may train a person to perform a task that only the firm itself demands. In this case, the productivity of the trainee to the firm rises, while his productivity in other firms remains unchanged. If this occurs, W_t will be no different from the wage prior to the training program, and the firm will earn a yield on its investment in training. More realistically, the distribution of the incremental output will be determined by a bargaining operation rather than by an invisible market process. This sort of situation results in a kind of rent being produced, arising out of the fact that a particular skill has a much larger output in one particular firm than in any other firm. Few training programs will be completely specific in the sense that the trainee's marginal product rises only in one firm. There will be many, however, where labor's productivity in one firm rises considerably more than it rises in other firms, and thereby provide a means by which a firm can recoup its outlay on the training programs.

The introduction of on-the-job training into the firm's activities complicates the notion of its equilibrium conditions. Suppose that the cost line shown in Diagram VII represents the opportunity cost of labor, but for reasons just enumerated, the marginal product of labor is higher than that implied by this curve. The most realistic assumption would seem to be that the wage rate paid the trainees must equal what they could get elsewhere, i.e., $W_o = MP_o$. Then for the firm to plan rationally, the rent that it expects to receive due to $MP_t > W_t$ must provide an acceptable return on $C_o + P_o$, the cost of the training program to the firm. Equilibrium of the firm (in this limited context) requires that the marginal product of labor equal wages paid plus an acceptable return on the investment in training. In this case, $C_o + P_o$ is simply an investment, and as such, it must compete (or should compete) for resources in the manner to be elaborated on in Chapters 15 and 16.

Stating the problem in this way suggests two important considerations.

The first is simply the clarification of the point that training is an investment, and as a claim on resources its contributions must be weighed against competing claims on resources. The second has to do with the role of wage rates. If the wage rate after the training program is the same as it was before the training program, then the total increase in output accrues to the firm and, barring external effects, measures the return to the economy as a whole. If the price system functions effectively, this return will be that which compares with alternative uses of investible resources. Suppose, however, that wage rates rise somewhat over their pretraining level, i.e., suppose that labor is able to capture some of the rents generated by the training, what then? Evidently in this case, the return to the firm is less than the return to the economy because this latter is now shared with labor. The problem of measuring the returns on training is complicated as is the problem of assuring that the firm invests the "right" amount in training. It is clear that if wage rates do absorb part of the rents, a subsidy to the firm is necessary to get "enough" investment into training. The problem is further complicated because the wage rate in this kind of a situation is determined by a bargaining process, the outcome of which is exceedingly difficult to predict.

On-the-job training does not necessarily take the form of specific educational programs. Often it means simply that newly employed workers spend much of their time observing and practicing as well as performing modest tasks below their intended assignments. In general, however, this does not modify the argument outlined above, although further measurement problems would be added to those already mentioned. An examination of on-the-job training in government establishments can be conducted along the same lines as just discussed for the firm. The question of subsidy does not arise, of course, and there is no presumption against training that results in the production of skills generally used in the economy. The profitability criterion is the same as for the firm. The question of who gets the rent that is created, in case the skill is specific enough to government employee to produce a rent, is a matter of bargaining and general policy.

2. The Implementation Problem. For firms to engage in training programs in the manner just discussed assumes considerable awareness on their part of the production function of their current activity, as well as the production function of a training program. For the typical firm in the economy of Chapter 7, such knowledge can hardly be assumed. As in the case of the development of technical knowledge, one of the advantages of a subsidy to the firm is that the firm is more likely to examine consciously the profit opportunities of the training of its employees if subsidies are offered than if they are not. This is due in part to the simple fact that the offer of subsidy calls attention to the possibility of training that possibly may not otherwise occur. More importantly, the subsidy may be necessary to offset the uncertainty attached to the two production functions involved, and to the outcome of the wage-rate bargaining after the training. The conclusion would seem safe, therefore, that any broad policy of relying heavily on on-the-job training must also include, at least for a time, a subsidy system to help support that training.

The difficulties are not all solved by simply announcing a subsidy, and, as shall be discussed later, the collecting and paying of subsidies also creates problems. The major problem is simply that most firms in the underdeveloped country are not now using labor that is appropriately trained and that can train newcomers. However, in almost all such countries, there does exist a number of firms that are in a position to supply on-the-job training, and that can be relied upon for this purpose. Therefore, along with the type of training—general vs. specific—the kind of firms that are available in the economy becomes a relevant factor in decisions as to an educational policy, and in some countries the lack of suitable firms to conduct training may be a major factor limiting reliance on on-the-job training. Since the government will be a large employer of skilled manpower, on-the-government-job training is also to be included, and the government is also probably able to perform these training tasks.

V. An Educational Policy

A. SUMMARY

The most important notions developed in this chapter are briefly summarized. Except in the short run, the labor skills that an economy has at its disposal must be considered as produced inputs into the production process. Their production—education and training—requires the use of scarce investible resources, and consequently, the contributions that education makes to the development effort must be weighed against the contribution that the investible resources could make elsewhere. Skills are assumed to have a certain specificity attached to them—men trained as lawyers cannot operate turbines—and therefore the education program must be an inherent part of the general development program of the economy as a whole. The achieving of this consistency between the production of skills and the production of other "primary" inputs, in the manner to achieve maximum growth, was found to require a correction of the tendency found in many underdeveloped countries for wage rates to be more related to position and prestige factors than to productivity. This correction alone, however, is not enough, and some form of forecasting is necessary. The implications of errors in the forecasts are much greater, the more specific are the skills, but for a wide variety of skills there is relatively little problem because transference among skills is easily done. The problem is most acute, and it is most important that it be solved with respect to new activities that are emerging as part of the development process, and for which little data and experience are available.

The achieving of consistency is not the only problem. The assumption was made that an activity could be created with a minimum level of skills, and that the rate of output with a given physical capital complex could be affected by varying the quality of the skills. The further assumption was made that increased skill could be achieved with more training and education. Hence, solutions are needed for the problem of how much education and the problem of the production function of education, or more generally the problem of the rate of return on investment in education. Neither problem lends itself to definitive formulation at this time. Undefinitive formulation, however, does help to point up the issues more clearly than no formulation.

Finally, attention was given to on-the-job training as contrasted to that done in formal educational institutions as a means of solving some of the problems associated with the development of a rational education policy. On-the-job training was found to be an appropriate procedure for some types of training and for some types of firms, but probably would require a subsidy to the firms undertaking it.

From the standpoint of formulating an education policy, the most important characteristics of the underdeveloped country is the small size of the education activity (especially the small number of people equipped to teach), and the difficulty of enlarging it quickly. It is also relevant that the proportion of firms for whom it is profitable to discuss on-the-job training is relatively small compared to a country where most firms were large, well organized, and some of whose employees were equipped to perform training functions.

B. OUTLINE OF AN EDUCATION POLICY

When the role of education in the development process is observed from this viewpoint, what sort of policy—of strategy—would be appropriate for the developing country described in Chapter 7? The following seem to be the most relevant points.

(*a*) Reliance on rules of thumb—e.g., 10 per cent of investment allocated to education, everyone to read and write in ten years, and so on—is misplaced. Decisions should emerge from a complete, formal analysis even when data can only be estimated. Also the distinction between education as a consumption item and as an investment is one that must be consciously appreciated if economic rationality is to prevail.

(*b*) Although the notion of a production function for education is fuzzy, as is the criterion by which the quality of education is appraised, understanding of both notions is sufficient to mention the quality of the product of education. There is little doubt that the efforts made to achieve widespread literacy or general secondary education, and even college-level training, have resulted in the use of resources—chiefly people in teaching slots—that are essentially unqualified, and turn out a product that is essentially useless. This point has its greatest relevance in the short run, but it is relevant in the medium run as well, because of the long gestation period of education capacity.

(*c*) Explicitly formulated development programming models are not available in any underdeveloped country, and the effective use of any sort of optimizing formula, including education costs, does not now seem possible. Certain generalizations, however, can be used safely. Unskilled, illiterate labor has in most countries a very low opportunity cost, and activities that can make extensive use of such labor have at least a preliminary advantage over those that call for a minimum skill of, for example, five years education. It is especially evident that new activities calling for widespread literacy are certain to be costly undertakings.

(*d*) Some generalizations about the overall forecasting problem are possible. The rough make-up of the economy over a decade or two in the future will, in most instances, be reasonably clear, and some occupations are in such widespread demand—power plant workers, construction workers, and so on and are sufficiently substitutable—that there is little likelihood of significant error. The biggest problem in this area, as has been noted, will be relating to new activities.

(*e*) The major effort with respect to formal educational instruction in most countries probably should be at the secondary school level. In most instances, the objective of this level of education should be a thorough grounding in basic tools—mathematics, technical training, reading comprehension, and so on. Then maximum use should be made of on-the-job training in both private and public activity. Reliance on training programs in the government rather than setting up artificial academic qualifications is perhaps the most effective way to reduce the prestige of and demand for college training. The argument is strong that such training is much more efficient than university training. With the qualification stated below, the most important use of foreigners is in on-the-job training programs.

(*f*) The role of universities in the early stages of development seems definitely much more limited than is implied by the numerous buildings classified as universities in these countries. Only in very specialized areas of training and research does it appear that university training has a place in a purely economic calculation of appropriate educational policy.

(*g*) Finally, careful attention should be given to the use of foreign "experts" and to sending students abroad. The latter practice, extremely helpful in many instances, is not without pitfalls. The most obvious such pitfall has to do with training abroad in different environments that often does not equip the student to be very effective at home. The simplest illustration of this is the training of engineers and scientists in large, lavishly equipped laboratories in a major western university, and who upon their return must work with much less capital. Often they are helpless. This is also true for doctors, economists, chemists, businessmen, and other disciplines. The great advantage of indigenous education is that it is indigenous. Education, like technology, can be effective in one environment and not in another, and that aimed at the labor of an underdeveloped country must, in most instances, be quite different from that designed for persons holding similar tasks in rich countries. Again, however, attention is called to the fact that in specific activities, reliance on foreign education—especially at the advanced level—is surely economically appropriate. Perhaps the single most important area in the education activity that the underdeveloped country can profit from reliance on foreign help is in the technique of teaching. Productivity increases in this area would yield huge returns in the developing country, and there is virtually unlimited room for improvement in the technique of teaching in these countries.

C. CONCLUSION

The preceding analysis of the education problem is approached from a rather narrow point of view. From a broader point of view, one might argue that the overriding purpose of education is to equip individuals, as workers and citizens, to affect the economic and socal environment in a way that yields maximum returns. Consequently, emphasis on consistency, types of training, and so on is misplaced. The emphasis should be on quality education, and the more the better. Certainly it is correct to argue that educated, brilliant men can shape their environment in many varied ways, and if strong assumptions could be made as to the flexibility of a society and the general ability of the population to absorb knowledge, then a chapter on education might simply advocate more effective training for everybody. Available evidence does not support the usefulness of such a chapter, and the obvious failure of education to produce desired results in virtually all countries suggests that a very formal approach to education policy making is in order. This chapter has outlined such a formal approach.

Bibliography

The general approach of this chapter owes much to H. Correa, *The Economics of Human Resources,* (Amsterdam: North-Holland Publishing Company, 1963) especially Chaps. 8–9. The special supplement of *The Journal of Political Economy,* LXX (October, 1962) is devoted to "Investment in Human Beings" and contains a number of useful papers. In my discussion of on-the-job training, I have followed quite closely the approach used by Gary Becker in his article "Investment in Human Capital: A Theoretical Analysis" in the *JPE* supplement. Another general treatment of education is Frederick H. Harbison and Charles A.

Myers, *Education, Manpower and Economic Growth: Strategies of Human Resource Development* (New York: McGraw-Hill Book Company, 1964). See also the papers in Selma J. Mushkin, (ed.) *Economics of Higher Education* (Washington, D.C.: United States Department of Health, Education, and Welfare, Office of Education, Government Printing Office, 1962). The papers by Mary Jean Bowman, Richard S. Eckaus, T. W. Schultz, and Alice M. Rivlin are especially rewarding.

On the forecasting problem itself see Herbert S. Parnes, *Forecasting Educational Needs for Economic and Social Development* (Paris: Organization for Economic Co-operation and Development, 1962). On the same subject see the excellent paper by R. G. Hollister, "On the Economics of Manpower Forecasting," *International Labour Review*, XC (May, 1964). I have also profited from many conversations with Professor Hollister on this subject. Also see *The Challenge of Aid to Newly Developing Countries* (Volume III of the papers presented at the Policy Conference on Economic Growth and Investment in Education) published by the Organization for Economic Co-operation and Development, 1962. This volume contains papers by W. A. Lewis, F. H. Harbison, and J. Tinbergen. *The International Social Science Journal* No. 4 (New York: UNESCO, 1962) also has a series of helpful papers on the economics of education.

On the problem of the returns on investment in education begin with any of the publications of T. W. Schultz. See especially his *The Economic Value of Education* (New York: Columbia University Press, 1963). A convenient survey of the various methods of measuring the return on education is a mimeographed paper by William G. Bowen, "Assessing the Economic Contribution of Education: An Appraisal of Alternative Approaches" (Paris: Organization for Economic Co-operation and Development, 1962).

One should also look at studies of education in particular countries. The most famous such study is probably *Investment in Education*. The Report of the Commission on Post-School Certificate and Higher Education in Nigeria, Sir Eric Ashby, Chairman (Lagos: The Commission, 1960). A more general study is John Wilson, *Education and Changing West African Culture* (New York: Bureau of Publications, Teachers College, Columbia University, 1963).

Then for additional information, there is an annotated bibliography, *Human Resources and Economic Growth* (Menlo Park, California: Stanford Research Institute, 1963) with over eleven hundred entries.

CHAPTER 13

THE SOCIAL ENVIRONMENT
OF ECONOMIC DEVELOPMENT

In the production function developed in Chapter 2, a term for "social environment" was included as a position variable. The content of this concept was said to refer to those social and organizational characteristics of an economy that affect the productivity of the direct inputs, i.e., allocation decisions, entrepreneurial activity, labor's work habits, and so on. Then in Chapter 7, those aspects of the social environment that seemed most relevant to understanding the existing underdevelopment problem were described. Two general characteristics were emphasized: first, the social environment that prevails in the nongrowing economy is not only consistent with the existence of that nongrowth, but has emerged in part as a means of easing the hardships imposed by mass poverty. Second, the society was characterized as a traditionalistic society in contrast to a conscious, choice-making one. At the same time, the point was emphasized that the choice making—traditionalistic distinction was an oversimplification. The evidence is strong that economic agents in these countries do react—i.e., do make choices that lead to economic advantage—when they are given the opportunity to do so and are convinced that change will produce improvement. Thus, there is something for the economist to work with from the start.

The problem in this chapter is to explore a bit further the role of the social environment in the development problem. To do this in a few pages is both dangerous and necessary. It is dangerous because even a cursory look at the environment reveals such a large number of relevant issues that a considerable degree of arbitrariness is necessary in selecting those to be examined. Since the theoretical underpinnings are just now beginning to be worked out, it is difficult to make sure that one is not concentrating attention on the least important social characteristics. But

241

to ignore the role of these factors is, as already emphasized, to give a misleading impression of the development problem. The point is not merely that "noneconomic" factors affect the performance of the economy, and hence must be included in an analysis of the "economics" of development, but rather that the production of economic goods takes place within a particular social and institutional environment, all parts of which affect, in one way or another, the capacity of the system to turn out goods and services. Therefore, to understand the functioning of an economy—particularly the underdeveloped one—environmental considerations must be introduced. In Section VII of Chapter 7, the apparent relevant features of the social and institutional environment of the nongrowing community were stressed. Now the question is which characteristics of a social environment can make the most contribution to the achievement of the development objective, and then how might formal policies contribute to the achieving of this environment. The discussion here gives only some suggestions as to how these questions might be approached, and does not give a definite *answer*. The following section examines the nature of the social environment that seems to facilitate the development process, and leads up to those specific environmental characteristics that are to be explored further in succeeding sections.

I. On the Meaning of Social Environment

That social environment that would contribute the most to achieving the development objective would be one that encouraged full exploitation of all "objective" economic opportunities. Perhaps its most important characteristic would be mobility, not only of factors of production, but also of legal arrangements, of property rights, of consumer goods, and of techniques. The discussion in all of the preeceding chapters has emphasized that growth of output imposes on the economy the necessity to adapt to new situations, indeed to create new situations to adapt to.

A major part of the conditions for mobility and adaptability have to do with the flexibility of prices of factors and products. The issues associated with this element in the mobility picture have been analyzed in detail in preceding chapters. Now suppose that prices do accurately reflect social opportunity costs, there can still be aspects of the social environment that impede or completely prevent economic agents from responding in the way that would contribute to the economy realizing the maximum return from its available resources. It is these non-price, non-cost elements that affect mobility and adaptation in the environment that are the concern of this chapter. There are many ways to illustrate the point. For example, strong village ties may impede the shifting of labor in response to wage rates and employment opportunities. More subtly, the social prestige attached to various occupations may result in certain activities attracting resources in excess of that dictated by price and cost calculations. One could also mention a variety of institutional arrangements ranging from the extended family system to institutionalized, built-in (and hence accepted) financial and personal dishonesty that limit the extent to which the resources of the system move in response to price incentives. Thus, any institution, organization, mores, or values that impede recognition and exploitation of new economic opportunities or the creation of new opportunities, thereby impede achieving the development objective.

There are, however, difficulties. Any society, by its very nature, has some resistance to change and to the kind of mobility referred to above. To the degree that a society has existed for some time without significant change, and patterns of behavior have become established and are internally consistent, then any mobility not sanctioned by these patterns will meet with resistance. A society, therefore, that is not characterized by anarchy has built-in resistances to economic (and other) changes, and these resistances arise in part from the very fact of adaptation to some previous economic and social situation. Traditionalism in the underdeveloped country is, therefore, both an impediment to the mobility of relevance to the development effort, and also a source of social stability that is essential to development. A major issue, then, is how to provide sources of security and control that traditional arrangements have long provided in a manner that facilitates the evolution of a new economy and does not lead to social chaos, which itself prevents the emergence of the new economy. The daily newspaper suggests that not much success has been achieved in pursuit of these objectives.

This brief discussion leads to one rather obvious, though important conclusion. Merely destroying some element of the social environment that is alien to mobility without providing either for the elimination of the problem that gave rise to that element, or for an alternative way of meeting the problem is sure to create a degree of instability that is possibly as harmful as was the obstacle destroyed. For example, the extended family system, noted frequently, has many aspects that are alien to the kind of adapting and exploiting activity essential to growth. At the same time, it provides an answer to many difficulties that an individual faces in an economy dominated by mass poverty. To destroy the extended family system without providing alternative solutions to the problems it now solves, leaves the society vulnerable to a damaging instability.

One might argue that the causal sequence is in the other direction. The upsetting of a particular social arrangement may force changes in the way that the economy operates. For example, it may be argued that the static hand of traditionalism is so great in agriculture that, until it is lifted, nothing can be done, and the possibility of subsequent anarchy or near anarchy is a necessary part of the development process. In this kind of argument, it is the change in some part of the social system that induces change in the economic system. This way of approaching the problem, though perhaps applicable in some instances, would appear unnecessarily harsh. If the assumptions made earlier—that the social organization does have a rationality and that economic agents do respond to economic incentive when convinced that it is profitable to do so—are correct, then it seems possible to devise alternative social arrangements that are compatible with a successful attack on the development problem, and that are acceptable to those who are affected.

The task, then, is to examine what social arrangements or organizations contribute to or are at least compatible with development, and to consider by what means or formal policies such elements of the environment may be made effective. The discussion is based on three main headings: institutions, the labor force, and entrepreneurship, but it should be recalled that a considerable degree of arbitrariness is inherent in any such selection of topics to discuss.

II. Institutions for Development

The term "institution" refers to consciously planned or at least consciously recognized organizations or arrangements for accomplishing particular objectives in socially acceptable ways. As such, they define rules to govern behavior in certain circumstances. For example, the price system may be considered as an institution that, if firmly established, dictates rules of behavior of economic agents over a wide range of activity. The land tenure system in a country is also an institution, one that contains rules for the distribution of agricultural produce and the sharing of costs of production. Similarly, the family, however defined, may be thought of as an institution that provides society the rules by which another important aspect of life is ordered. It is quite evident that certain institutions, or, more accurately, the rules of conduct that make up an institution can determine to what extent a society takes advantage of its economic opportunities, i.e., how free of social restraints the economic agents are to respond to economic opportunities. Institutions may thus have a variety of incidences that are of relevance in explaining the existence of underdevelopment and the problems of getting growth under way. One way of examining the role of institutions in the context of development is to consider their incidence on a number of the aspects of the growth process as that process was outlined in previous chapters.

Institutions may exist or be devised that affect the costs and profits associated with a particular activity. For example, in some countries where unemployment is widespread, attempts to alleviate the suffering caused thereby have lead to a number of laws that make it very costly for a firm to employ temporary workers. Laws as to leave pay, termination allowances, provident funds, and the like have been devised as a means of income transfer, and have the effect of distorting the costs of the firm in a manner that works against the long-run solution of the problem. Evidently other arrangements—other institutions—could do the task in a manner that has much less adverse effect on firm efficiency and growth. Public or possibly private insurance schemes or unemployment allowances are alternatives, as is an arrangement whereby public works programs are available. In most countries, these alternative arrangements for meeting the difficulties associated with unemployment are not expected to be adequate in the short run, but neither are the laws designed to make the firm violate rational costing.

Similar institutional arrangements that may facilitate a more satisfactory costing system, especially for investment in innovation, training, or other uncertainty filled activities, are insurance schemes. Thus rather than outright subsidies to firms undertaking research or innovational activities, a general insurance program may be established that simply protects the investor from loss on his undertaking (more accurately spreads the loss among the taxpaying population). Such an arrangement may have particular advantages for small peasant farmers for whom new investment in new seeds or fertilizers may pay handsomely if their crop is not washed out or eaten up by insects. Insurance against such catastrophes could well be the encouragement needed to get the farmers to experiment. The burden of the argument here is not to describe specific and detailed proposals, but rather to show that in setting up institutions to meet very real problems, considerable care is required to prevent these arrangements from affecting costs in a way that keeps output below the level it might otherwise reach.

Institutions may also affect the extent to which reward and effort are related. Generalizations about motivations are extremely risky, but most observers seem to accept the argument that incentives for economic action are greatest when the return from that action accrues to the actor or someone the actor accepts as a legitimate claimant. Perhaps the most obvious area where this point is relevant is in agriculture. In many countries there is evidence that peasants with idle time are reluctant or unwilling to engage in output increasing capital formation simply because all or most of the increment in output accrues to the landlord. This result is, in a general sense, a consequence of the failure of the price system to function adequately, but a quick correction may demand more than an attack on pricing methods. Land reform programs often recognize this possibility by making the peasant the ostensible owner of the land, but less frequently do they recognize that the landlord's other roles (other than a collector of rents) have to be met by alternative institutions. The appropriate institutional arrangement for this kind of job varies widely from country to country. For example, a cooperative may be a satisfactory arrangement in some areas, but it too may run into difficulties as the incentives must be such as to keep each member not only working, but believing he is receiving a "fair" share of the total product. Similar remarks can be made about technical innovations, about saving campaigns, about tax laws, and about other aspects of development that are facilitated by working without receiving an immediate reward.

One arrangement that is worth specific attention is the extent to which the development effort and plan are generally understood. An institution devoted to advertising a development plan and providing information to the population regarding economic development may yield great returns by inducing people to save or not reduce their effort when taxes are levied, or not to press for wage increases if profits are being invested. Propaganda cannot carry a heavy load, but it is correct to argue that if there is some insight on the part of the population into the nature of the development process, claims on resources by capital accumulators may be acceptable to the population where, in the absence of such insight, the same claims would not be. Using propaganda that is convincing for this purpose is no simple matter since—as previously emphasized—the possibility of development is alien to such a large proportion of the community that demonstration of this possibility is probably a necessary prerequisite to an effective advertising campaign. The propaganda also must be true, i.e., claimants of resources must in fact use them for capital formation. For example, a government tax program sometimes runs into difficulty because taxpayers do not accept as legitimate the uses to which tax receipts are put.

The central point here is that continued effort demands that the fruits of that effort accrue to a claimant recognized by its supplier. In the underdeveloped country, the assurance that this demand is met may require new formal institutions to replace existing ones, e.g., cooperatives for landlords. Also information services may help to induce the supplier of effort to recognize claims—e.g., pay taxes or work on certain projects for nothing—that they would not otherwise do. That a war against poverty does not generate the national fervor to the extent that a war against a neighboring country does, is either an indication of the superior propaganda value of the latter war, or a rather sad commentary on human nature. Perhaps there is still reason to assume that if development efforts were given the widespread propaganda that war efforts are, they would also generate the same national fervor.

Social institutions may have great relevance for the growth process by affecting the freedom of the individual to respond to economic incentives in a manner commensurate with his ability. If, for example, the social arrangements in a given community are such that only members of the *existing* elite may hold certain high positions, the quality of man serving in the position can be expected to be generally lower than if there were no barriers except competence to holding the slot. The most obvious form of this type of barrier has to do with the various categories of caste systems that are observed in many parts of the world. The most damaging characteristic of a caste system, from the point of view of development, is that it tends to allocate labor, or at least affect the allocation of labor, by reference to the origins of the worker. Evidently, any such allocation will conform to that dictated by economic rationality only by accident. But formal caste systems are not the only source of interference with full exploitation of the talents available to the community. Geographic, racial, religious, color, and family considerations are also frequent sources of institutionalized obstacles to vertical labor mobility.

Along with man-made obstacles to the freedom of individual laborers to move as high as their talents will take them, there are also frequent interferences with the free access to markets by individual firms. One condition of equilibrium growth has been defined earlier as a situation in which prices of all products equaled the cost of the primary inputs used directly and indirectly in their production in the marginal vector. But strong monopolistic positions in some markets may make this pricing difficult to achieve by any sort of subsidy or tax system. In economies where a wide range of direct controls exist, monopoly positions are often created simply by the way that the controls function. Thus import controls may create a monopolistic position for firms that are allowed access to foreign exchange, and the power of this position may be difficult indeed to counteract by monetary or tax policy.

The freedom of access to the market, however, may be inhibited by more general social characteristics than direct controls, size, or financial resources. There are social arrangements that dictate that certain groups in the society are banned from entry into specific activities. Also, institutionalized behavior may impede the spread of knowledge about market opportunities. This has to do not only with customary secrecy surrounding business information, but social arrangements as well. For example, in some societies certain groups have business dealings with each other, but do not eat together or attend social events together. In this way, an important channel of economic communication is cut off that is available in more fluid societies.

Social stratification is present in all societies, and "perfect" fluidity is probably not a meaningful concept. It does, however, appear meaningful to examine a social system to isolate those institutions or social arrangements that impede the freedom of the economic agents from making their maximum contribution to the development process. Once these are isolated—be they castes, tribes, ethnic jealousies, secret societies, or what—then some effort may usually be made to modify them in such a manner that they are less damaging to the development effort. The mere recognition of their existence and the general acknowledgment that they are impediments to development will itself help to reduce their strength. It may be added that social and institutional obstacles to the freedom of labor is much more important than those that are expressed in the form of monopoly. Further aspects of the labor issue are discussed in the next section.

There is some evidence that "values" (defined as the attitudes or behavior that a society has designated as acceptable or desirable) may be affected by institutional arrangements. Charles Wolf, Jr. in his paper on the study of institutions, "Institutions and Economic Development," suggests that the high place that leisure holds in some underdeveloped countries is due not to any motivational or value characteristic, but rather to the fact that increased earnings must be shared with near and distant relatives. Since such sharing is undesirable, little or no effort is made to gain further income, and announcements are made that the "good" life is one of leisure and not of work. A change in the extended family system—made possible, for example, by a publicly supported system of unemployment insurance—would, therefore, result in a change of values. More accurately, a change in this institution would permit the "true" values to dominate behavior. This argument is consistent with the assumption made in Chapter 7 and earlier in this chapter that the nationals of poor countries are as economically calculating as those of rich countries, and, given the opportunity, will act accordingly.

Other examples supporting this point could be cited. Some evidence exists to suggest that the occupations that are in greatest demand are in part determined by prevailing institutions. The great value placed on economic security is one of the reasons for the appeal of government employment, but security consciousness itself arises out of the failure of the economy to generate continuing employment opportunities, or to develop alternative institutions to help relieve the misery caused by unemployment. Attachment to land is often similarly explained. Also it is frequently noted that industrial leadership carries less prestige than does religious activity or landownership. This is surely due in no small measure to the fact that industrial leadership has, by and large, failed to produce results. Where industrialization has caught hold, however, the prestige of those who participate is very high indeed. Thus, in part, what activity carries high value—high prestige—depends not on its intrinsic characteristics, but simply on the success of its practitioners. This argument is slightly modified in the discussion on entrepreneurial ability.

These examples suggest the general argument that one task that development policy makers must concern themselves with is the extent to which growth impeding social arrangements do reflect particular economic conditions, and the extent to which such arrangements reflect genuine values. In the latter case, not only may the impeding institution be difficult to change, but more importantly society's consensus may dictate that it not be changed. The development effort must then take place around (in spite of) the conflicting institutions.

The preceding examples were of social institutions or arrangements that had their incidence in a rather indirect way on mobility, adaptability, or fluidity of the economic agents within the society. One can also mention more specific forms of institutional arrangements that are equally relevant. These are organizations such as banks, schools, religious groups, agriculture cooperatives, labor organizations, political clubs, saving clubs, and so forth. As specific organizations, they are much more susceptible to change, modifications, and establishment than those previously discussed. In a variety of instances, using specific organizations may be an effective way of accomplishing an objective that does not lend itself to other policy tools. For example, attacks on the population control problem (see Chapter 14) may be made through family planning clubs. Labor organizations may be used as a means of effecting knowledge of job opportunities, of designing wage policies, and of explaining the development process. Financial institutions are discussed in Chapter 17.

These brief remarks suggest simply that by utilizing some of the kinds of institutional arrangements, a government may be able to enlist support for the development effort that would otherwise be lacking. Especially as a means of spreading information and facilitating movement of labor, establishing formal institutions that seek to institutionalize economic responses may be an effective device to attack various aspects of the traditionalistic behavior patterns. But their establishment requires the use of scarce inputs, and one must always ask, is the return worth the cost?

III. The Supply and Productivity of Labor

The previous chapter contained a rather detailed account of the production of labor skills, and the way that skills affect the development effort. In the following chapter, attention is directed toward population growth, and the consequent rate of growth of the labor force. Now the problem is labor's social attitudes and responsiveness to new economic opportunity, how such attitudes and responsiveness affect development, and, finally, the sources (if any) of change in these characteristics that are of concern to the economic policy maker.

Why is this question of relevance? The discussion of the growth process in Part One imposed a continuing commitment on the labor input to adapt itself to new techniques, to new work habits, and to respond to changes dictated by economic incentives. There the assumption was that labor's productivity depended on available complementary inputs, the level of skills, and the state of technology. But, evidently, if labor is unreliable, if absenteeism is high, if wage demands are inflationary, if labor does not respond to wage incentives, if laborers throw sand in machines, then the labor input problem is greatly complicated. These characteristics of a labor force have been known to exist in the kind of economy described in Chapter 7, and there is no difficulty in appreciating the limitations that such characteristics impose on increasing output. The problem is further complicated by the fact that, in countries where incomes are very low, increasing wages may lead to an increase in the productivity of labor due to the favorable effects of higher wage rates on diet, housing, and clothing. If this is the case, the formulation of a wage policy is more difficult than in the case where there is no such relationship beween wages and productivity. Both of these characteristics of the labor force are briefly examined.

A. LABOR'S MOTIVATION

The characterization of labor as "traditionalistic" suggests that workers in the underdeveloped country do not respond quickly and easily to mere wage incentive. Thus, the labor mobility demanded by development must be achieved by something more than a wage incentive. In any society there are, of course, a multiplicity of motives for working or for changing work, and the difference between developed and underdeveloped economies is likely to be one of degree rather than kind. Perhaps the safest and most helpful generalization is along the following lines. In the low income country—especially in rural areas where the use of money is not widespread—there is less distinction between the economic and other aspects of social life than in richer countries where use of money is universal and work specialization very great. Thus, in the former country, the social context in which work is performed is the source of its meaning, and work that is alien in that context is either rejected completely or accepted only under heavy pressure. The consequence of a close link between the economic and non-economic aspects of social life is that labor mobility and adaptability are impeded, unless the changing demands on labor are also accompanied by changes in other aspects of the social structure. A wage incentive may not be enough to induce workers to commit themselves in the manner commensurate with achieving their maximum output, and an attack on the labor mobility problem must then be more general. More accurately, projects that are more nearly consistent with existing patterns of behavior and social organization will be more effectively implemented, at least as far as the labor side of the issue is concerned.

In those instances where labor has been a bottleneck (because of social factors, not skill factors), the explanation in terms of this strong relationship between mobility demands and a social framework uncongenial to change is much more convincing than an explanation in terms of fundamental differences in personality or attitudes between workers in rich and poor countries. Consider two examples. A backward-bending supply curve of labor was suggested as a possibility in the economy described in Chapter 7. If the labor supply curve turns back after a modest increase in wage rates, this might imply a high valuation of leisure relative to additional income as some sort of deepseated personal characteristic of the workers in underdeveloped countries compared to those in rich countries. On the other hand, it may mean simply lack of knowledge of alternative uses of income, of unacquaintance with the use of money, or the job may be one that imposes burdens on the worker—a long walk to and from location of work, unpleasant atmosphere or working hours, and so forth—that are equally relevant to any worker in any country. The type of capital employed in new activities may also violate traditional behavior. For example, in many countries, workers are accustomed to squat for hours as they work, and a machine that to be operated requires the worker stand or sit on a stool or chair may result in reduced productivity and a reluctance to work regularly. The policy aimed at straightening out the labor-supply curve may then be development projects that fit in with the existing social organization and work habits, or, at least, force only modest changes on it rather than increase production of consumer goods.

A second example is the source of labor available for new activities. There is little evidence of people with firm positions in the economic and social hierarchy moving out into new and more remunerative jobs—even when they are available. Labor recruits for new activities are much more likely to be from the landless groups, from those who have no political power, or from social outcasts. To find effective managers, supervisors, or quick learners among such a group is not something that can be relied on. A possible qualification to this argument has to do with educated unemployed in some countries, but as noted in the previous chapter, there are additional difficulties here. The key point, however, is simply that the hold that the social complex has on the worker who is a part of that complex is strong enough that mere wage incentives are not adequate to pull him into new, untried activities. The new then must be accompanied by attributes other than wage incentives, and in particular, attention must be given to maintaining the worker in a social complex and in a work routine that he recognizes as valid.

These labor force problems are particularly relevant with respect to new activities that have as yet no established place in the social system. In economies that are predominantly agricultural and rural, most industrial, urban-centered activity is in this category, and labor difficulties associated with the building up of new industries may be real bottlenecks. Thus, a new industry may have a problem finding a group of laborers willing to commit themselves fully to the regimen imposed by modern factory work. The consequence is frequent work stoppage, high injury rate, and generally inefficient deployment of labor. It is important to recognize that the problem is not one of learning to perform a task. There are examples to the contrary, but, in general, the barrier is not likely to be an inability to learn the mechanics of the new job as such. Rather, it is a reluctance to commit oneself to enter a way of life quite different from that that has been acceptable in the past.

The most overt form of the lack of commitment is the worker who aims simply to accumulate a given amount of cash by industrial work, and then return to his village, tribe, or general area. Often, he never does return permanently, but the attitude itself is a handicap to his job performance and his interest in learning and advancement. Also factory managers complain a great deal about absenteeism to attend weddings and funerals, to help with seasonal plantings and harvesting, and simply to visit. All of these factors make the achievement of factory discipline and control extremely difficult.

These arguments suggest that the barriers to mobility inherent in this kind of social complex are so great that the mere number of workers does not measure the real labor supply situation. To appraise the profitability of a new activity, therefore, requires examining the extent to which it fits in with existing social arrangements. Furthermore, where reliance is placed on a push of labor out of agriculture or other traditional activity due to unemployment, no land, social unacceptability, and so on, the quality of the labor is likely to be low, with the consequence that the labor input for new activities may, therefore, be a bottleneck independent of the commitment problem.

The recognition that these characteristics of the labor force may be of relevance in' the development problem has a number of implications for the policy maker. First of all, projects whose construction and operation require large, sweeping changes in work routines and work environment will tend to face labor problems to a greater degree than new projects that impose relatively modest adjustments on the worker's living habits. Considerations due to this point may affect location decisions, form of organization of the enterprise, choice of technology, and so forth. Attention may have to be given to institutional arrangements that may help the worker to commit himself, and to apply his full effort in a work situation in which he feels alien and insecure. The arguments also suggest that incentive to change must include more than wage incentives, and that simple assumptions that equate available labor to existing unemployment or underemployment are likely to yield unworkable policy positions—even where no skill obstacle exists. The issues considered here may also affect tax policy, the content of education, and the form of technical advice that is sought. Perhaps most important of all is the burden that these particular attributes of the labor force place on management. To the extent that the atmosphere of a firm can be made congenial to the personalities and social instincts of the workers, they are less likely to be dissatisfied with their lot and less determined to make such work purely temporary. This is not a very encouraging conclusion, however, because the foreman or manager-level worker is perhaps the most difficult productive resource to acquire. There is no obvious training program that will produce one, and the social system is not one that encourages the natural development of a personality suitable for such jobs.

Along with these in-plants characteristics that affect the quality of the labor input there are also other factors having to do with the environment in which the worker lives that are relevant. A brief discussion of these will help to reveal another side of the issue.

B. The Relationship Between Wages and Productivity

The labor and wages problem is further complicated by the fact that in many low income areas, labor's productivity is not independent of wage rates. This relationship may exist because at very low wage rates, nutritional standards, housing conditions, medical services, and the like are such that workers are not able to work as effectively as they could if they enjoyed better food, better housing, and so on. The difficulties may be reflected in frequent illnesses or in an inability to maintain a desired work pace. Perhaps the simplest example would be the case of a machine that was operated more slowly than it was designed to because of the demands the higher speeds placed on workers. Similarly, the poorly fed worker may be unable to cope with particular difficulties—e.g., land reclamation—because he is poorly fed and housed. Independent of the health effect on the worker, there is also what may be called an environment effect. The difficulties of commitment, just noted, may be reduced or overcome by making living conditions more pleasant than generally available, or by making them convenient to place of work or by providing schools.

The empirical relevance of these arguments is difficult to assess. Clearly, as income rises well above subsistence, they lose much of their importance. There is, however, evidence that the arguments are applicable in enough cases to make them worthy of recognition. For example, there are specific instances where workers eating and living together in mining camps have had their diets changed with marked effects on their productivity. Also, comparisons of labor productivity among firms often suggest that firms paying higher wages get a greater output from their workers. Assuming that there is a relationship that is worth recognition there are two questions of interest at this point. What are the consequences of this relationship between wages and productivity for wage policy in the developing country, and what are its consequences for the allocation of investible resources?

Suppose that a firm is operating at an equilibrium position for given factor prices, and is realizing a satisfactory rate of return on its operations. Suppose further that the firm knows that if it raises its wage rate, labor's productivity will rise. If the increase in wage rates exactly matches the increase in output, the firm's profits are unaffected because the value of the total increase in output accrues to labor. The increase in wages will result in an increased demand for consumer goods (including housing), and this increased quantity of consumer goods must be forthcoming, or there will be no increased labor productivity. The cost, then, to society of the increased labor productivity is the resources used to increase the output of these newly demanded consumer goods.

The yield from the use of resources for the purpose of producing these extra consumer goods must then be compared with alternative uses to which the same resources might be put. Suppose the firm mentioned above is engaged in producing capital goods, then the output of capital goods may be increased *if* the output of consumption goods can be increased. But if resources are available to produce the consumer goods, the output of capital goods might be increased directly by using those resources to produce capital goods directly, rather than to produce consumer goods that are (in effect) an input in the production of capital goods. This type of argument would seem to have greatest relevance in a situation where the capital goods sector is so small that a larger number of workers cannot be absorbed, but more productive labor could be used to good advantage. In this case, making the workers in the capital goods sector more productive is the only way to increase the rate of capital formation in the short run, independent of foreign trade.

To determine the wage policy that will result in the maximum contribution to the development effort in these circumstances involves a quantitative estimate of all these variables: an estimate of the productivity effect of a rise in wages in a given activity, and an estimate of the effect on the rate of capital formation of the increased consumption due to the higher wage rates. Of course, such estimates are extremely difficult to make with any degree of confidence, and the argument may easily be misused to get higher wages when there is no productivity effect. Despite these difficulties and dangers, the argument is important if for no other reason than the simple one that it emphasizes the complexity of the labor and wage problem in the context of the developing economy. These complexities are often missed by the assumption of large scale unemployment, and it is quite clear that failure to recognize the peculiar features of the labor supply can easily lead to misplaced policies. When the problems noted here are added to the training and skill problems examined in Chapter 12, it is easy to see that the simple assumption that labor is free has limited application.

IV. The Entrepreneur

In Chapter 7, the argument was made that the supply of entrepreneurial talent relative to the labor force was less in the underdeveloped country than in richer countries. This fact was explained in terms of the traditionalistic environment in which the personality and attitudes of individuals were formed. It was also argued that where entrepreneurial talent was present, the most profitable forms of its expression were often in areas that contributed little to the development process. The economy was doubly harmed: the social environment was such as to discourage the appearance of entrepreneurial talent, and if it appeared, economic rationality often dictated that it be applied in activities that made less than maximum contribution to the social product. The entrepreneur may be defined very generally as the source of the investment decision, and as such requires the attributes previously enumerated: open-mindedness, imagination, self-confidence, detachment from immediate milieu, access to investible resources, and some degree of recognition that it is possible to modify a prevailing situation. The absence of men with these attributes or the existence of a social environment that effectively smothers or misdirects their activities can greatly impede the development process. In particular, the emergence of new activities and new techniques are slowed down relative to an economy where "objective" economic opportunities are similar, but entrepreneurial talent is in more abundant supply. A word of caution is in order. The term "objective" profit opportunities is hardly unambiguous, and must necessarily depend on who is doing the viewing. Also, as just noted, an entrepreneur with strong enough attributes can create his own opportunities for exploitation. Despite this danger of circularity, it is helpful, and not illegitimate, to distinguish between the opportunities that are easily seen by any member of the community, and those whose isolation and exploitation depends on the appearance of an individual who is unusually fortunate to possess the entrepreneurial talents just discussed.

These arguments suggest two things; the first suggestion is that increasing the supply of entrepreneurial services can be expected to result in an increase in the rate of capital formation. This is due in part to the greater capacity of the system to carry out investment activity if more entrepreneurs are available, and in part because more entrepreneurs mean more projects that merit exploitation. In the context of the assumption that the level of investment in a given period is determined by the government as a matter of social policy, the "supply" of entrepreneurship would be a variable that entered into that decision. Having more entrepreneurs this period than last would mean that a higher level of investment may be feasible. One can also imagine a situation in which other variables relevant to the investment decision—saving, supply of quality labor, and so on—were such that entrepreneurial talent was in excess supply, in which case, of course, to increase its supply would not increase the capacity of the economy to invest.

The second point suggested by the preceding arguments is that entrepreneurial talent is not something given or withheld from the society by an outside force. This is to say that it is helpful to look upon entrepreneurial talent as a dependent variable, related in some way to the other characteristics of the social environment. If this is accepted, then the final question would naturally be, can formal policies be devised that affect the capacity of the system to generate entrepreneurial talent?

A. THE SOURCES OF ENTREPRENEURSHIP

The definition of the entrepreneur as the source of the decision to invest is a very broad one. It includes not merely the innovator, the producer of something new, but also the person who is responsible for committing resources in a situation where the outcome of this commitment is necessarily uncertain. The attributes of open-mindedness, detachment, confidence and the like are necessary characteristics of such an individual since without them he would not rise above routine, and routine, by definition, involves little or no uncertainty. But investment, be it to increase existing capacity, to establish a new activity employing a technique used elsewhere, to establish a new activity involving the use of a completely new technique or resulting in a new product, or to search for a new technique, does necessarily involve an element of uncertainty. It also involves seeing a *new* economic situation in place of the one that currently exists. The "better" the entrepreneur, the clearer he can see the new situation that would emerge as a consequence of investment, and consequently, the more carefully he can narrow down and appraise the uncertainty.

One of the reasons, then, that entrepreneurial activity appears in "short supply" or is directed into activities whose social yield is minimal is the high degree of uncertainty associated with investment in those activities that lead into new areas in the newly developing country. The statement could be turned around to read that the purchase and holding of land, the building of luxury housing, and the engaging in trade or finance are more clearly understood and involve less uncertainty than does the building of a fertilizer factory or investing in an agricultural machinery plant. Part of the difference in uncertainty is due to the quick turnover in the former activities relative to the latter. This sort of argument implies that the entrepreneurial problem is not that there are no (or only a few) individuals who are mentally and emotionally equipped to initiate and carry through the investment decision, but rather that the "objective" profit opportunities are severely limited, and are concentrated on activities unessential to the development process.

To a large degree this is an acceptable argument. The description of the underdeveloped country in Chapter 7 emphasized the point that the search for economic gain and economic rationality, in general, were as characteristic of the nationals of a low income country as of a high income country. Consequently, one would expect the distribution of individuals with the entrepreneurial talent to be about the same in the two categories of countries. It was, however, also emphasized that a social environment had emerged in the former country that was consistent with a lack of economic change, as well as very low incomes. As noted, such an environment works against the appearance of individuals who can look beyond the existence of the prevailing situation and not only see a different one, but also recognize that they can do something to effect the change. This argument clearly implies that the entrepreneur problem is that of the supply of the right individual, not that of creating a profit situation in which the readily available entrepreneurial talents are given an opportunity to function.

There can be little doubt that the general environment of the underdeveloped country in which most people are reared and live discourages the appearance of the entrepreneurial personality. Consequently, a number of observers have emphasized that the change-leading individual must be, in some significant way, deviant or outside the society. If this means simply that the entrepreneur is necessarily a small minority group, it is correct, because in any society the number of people possessing the qualities listed as those of the entrepreneur will be relatively few. If it means that outsiders initiate change, then there is a major difficulty, because the task of the entrepreneur is that of a change producer. Outsiders, however, rarely lead insiders, and the more likely outcome of the existence of deviants is a permanent enclave within the society, rather than the source of investment decisions that impose change on the entire society. The existence of enclaves is indeed evident in a number of countries that are seeking to pursue development programs at the present time. In general, it seems safe to argue that if entrepreneurial action is going to set the economy in motion, it must be performed by individuals who are an essential part of the society, or the response of the rest of the economy will be to ignore or condemn, not encourage and follow.

This way of thinking then leads to the conclusion that if more entrepreneurial talent will lead to more rapid growth, that talent must come from within. If the social environment does militate against the development of such talent, then the solution of the problem requires that it be modified in one way or another.

It is appropriate to mention that there are explanations of the entrepreneur personality that rest on psychological considerations. These considerations usually relate to childhood experiences of one kind or another, and, while not inconsistent with the social environment argument just stated, are usually much more specific. Such explanations may be profitable at some time, and their study can reveal the personality characteristics of the individual who performs as an entrepreneur. In general, however, such theories amount to saying that entrepreneurial talent is independent of current social variables, and, therefore, beyond the reach of policies. Thus, these personality arguments are not obviously wrong, but they do not tell much about the policy issue, and to act one must rely on hypotheses relating entrepreneurship to the prevailing environment.

B. Toward an Entrepreneurship Policy

The first argument above asserted simply that the distribution of individuals with entrepreneurial talent in one country was little different from what it was in another. To get it functioning in a way that contributed to the development effort would then require changes in the economic environment that affected uncertainty and profit expectations. To a large extent, much of the argument in the preceding chapters was aimed precisely at this objective. The pricing of inputs, the effort to get the accumulation of technical knowledge routinized, the concentration of attention on labor training, the control of aggregate demand, all have the effect of contributing to the creation of a milieu in which the exercise of entrepreneurial talent is facilitated, and is directed in a way that yields high social returns. In this respect, the policies to "unleash" and redirect entrepreneurship place no demands on decision makers different from those already acquired by virtue of other aspects of the development process.

The social environment side of the argument is not so simple. Two ingredients of a policy to attack this problem may be emphasized. In the first place, the idea that growth is possible is crucial. Independent of the effects on "objective" profit opportunities in one sector of investment in another due to the type of interdependence described in Chapter 4, the precedent-setting nature of successful investment is important. In several places in this book, attention has been called to the fact that in the underdeveloped country the idea that progress is possible is lacking among the population. The only way that this attitude will change is for development to become evident. Thus, investment projects carried through to successful completion and operation will have some impact on the generally prevailing notion that escape from mass poverty is simply not a meaningful notion. Government and international aid policy can seek to contribute to supplying information and data that are generally unavailable to the individual entrepreneur. The accumulation of knowledge and experience by actually accomplishing investment activities not only tends to lessen the uncertainty attached to investment in the future, but also makes it increasingly clear that socially profitable investment can succeed. Further, it was noted in the section on institutions that one reason that social prestige does not—or at least has not—attached to industrial entrepreneurs is simply that they are generally unsuccessful. As they succeed, it is expected then that the prestige problem will disappear, i.e., prestige will attach itself to the successful industrialist—if (this is the qualification previously announced) these successful men are an integral part of the social system.

The second ingredient of the attack on the entrepreneurial problem has to do with creating a social structure that permits "new men" to appear in positions of economic leadership. If an economy has long been stagnant, then by definition its leaders are not providing the kind of talent required to produce change. Also it is not difficult to understand why men in positions of prestige and affluence look with some apprehension on change. Landlords, some religious leaders, bankers, and civil servants are often lumped together as an entrenched group obstructing change in the traditional society. The argument is not that new men will be broader and more socially minded, but rather that a social environment that permits anyone competent enough to rise to positions of economic leadership to do so, will never have an entrenched, obstructionist elite. New men, then, become carriers of economic change and sources of continuous disruption to the economy's becoming stagnated.

A social environment that poses no artificial barriers to the emergence of economic leaders appears to be a more meaningful approach to the entrepreneurial talent problem than concern with particular personality traits as such. One of the important consequences of contact with other societies and other cultures is a loosening of the hold that an entrenched group may have. Similarly, such things as education, elections, and nation-wide radio, may serve to open an otherwise closed society.

These arguments and conclusions should not be interpreted to mean that "entrepreneurship" is not an obstacle worthy of much attention. They do, however, suggest that within a very broad framework, what is needed is not peculiar personality types. Rather what is called for is an understanding of the economic opportunities and social environments that develop entrepreneurial behavior in normally alert, active individuals.

To say that the government is not a substitute for effective private entrepreneurship may bear repeating. Government officials are nationals of the same environment as the private individual, and although the civil servant may have a broader outlook and a longer time horizon than the private citizen, that is probably the only difference between the two. In general, if a society is in such shape that there is an entrepreneurial talent problem, the civil service will be equally moribund. This observation, of course, does not argue anything about the role of the government in the development process.

V. Conclusion

The issues raised in this chapter have been in the little known area of the relationship between the characteristics of the social environment of a community and its economic performance. A social environment that encourages or facilitates the mobility and adaptability of economic agents to the extent necessary to take full advantage of economic opportunity was found to be the most helpful from the standpoint of the development effort. Any society has, however, resistance to change, and consequently a major policy objective must be to find ways to enable new features of the environment to replace old without creating anarchy in between. No such concept as equilibrium or smooth or painless environmental change is meaningful, nor does any specific *modus operandi* of such change present itself. Nevertheless, recognition of the difficulties involved in this sector, and some acquaintance with even a few of the issues present, helps to show the development process somewhat more clearly than would be the case if the topic were ignored.

Attention was directed to institutions, labor, and the entrepreneur. An attempt was made to examine the incidence of various institutions on how the economy performed. It was argued that institutional arrangements could act on a variety of aspects of the economy, and that outlining their impact might enable the development of policies that would tend to make the economy perform more, rather than less, effectively. The labor problem was analyzed by considering the question of the commitment of the labor force to new, different activities, and with the implications of a relationship between wage payments and labor's productivity. The first point emphasized that labor bottlenecks might be avoided (or lessened) if attention was given to the social context in which the work was performed. Such attention might affect the composition of investment and the type of new activities introduced. If there is a relationship between wage payments and productivity, then further explorations into the returns and costs associated with exploiting that relationship is necessary. Finally, with respect to the entrepreneur, emphasis was placed on trying to get the idea of progress commonly accepted, and to the creation of a social system that permitted a continuous flow of "new men" to move into positions of economic leadership, rather than on the appearance of particular personality types.

To repeat, there is need for caution here. Not only is it necessary to limit somewhat arbitrarily the number of issues considered, but also it is easy to be misled in this area by one's own observations. Furthermore, there is a strong temptation to look at the social environment in the rich countries, and conclude that the underdeveloped country must have the same or it is doomed. This is surely wrong. Just as there are a variety of technologies, so there are a variety of social arrangements that can contribute to the development effort. It is correct to conclude that no single environmental feature is either essential or is an insuperable obstacle to the achievement of the development objective. The strategy of successful attack on these problems is no different from that in other parts of the problem, that is for the society to learn to exploit the opportunities that are made available to it. A society that can do this will always lead the society that depends on copying from a rich country ten thousand miles away.

Bibliography

Bert F. Hoselitz has written extensively on the social environment of economic development. See his *Sociological Aspects of Economic Growth* (New York: The Free Press of Glencoe, 1960), Chaps. 1–4, and his "Tradition and Economic Growth" in Ralph Braibanti and Joseph J. Spengler (eds.), *Tradition, Values, and Socio-Economic Development* (Durham: Duke University Press, 1961). In this same volume, the papers by Spengler and Wilbert E. Moore are also quite helpful. See Bert F. Hoselitz (ed.), *The Progress of Underdeveloped Areas* (Chicago: The University of Chicago Press, 1952) noting especially papers by Linton, Herskovits, and Gerschenkron, and also refer to Everett E. Hagen, "A Framework for Analyzing Economic and Political Change," in Robert E. Asher, *Development of the Emerging Countries* (Washington, D.C.: The Brookings Institution, 1962).

On institutions, Charles Wolf, Jr.'s paper, "Institutions and Economic Development," *American Economic Review*, XLV (December, 1955) was very helpful to me. Chapter III in W. Arthur Lewis, *The Theory of Economic Growth* (London: George Allen & Unwin, 1955) is also excellent. For a general discussion of forms of public organization and institutions see A. H. Hanson, *Public Enterprise and Economic Development* (London: Routledge & Kegan Paul, Ltd., 1959), Chaps. 6–13.

On the aspect of labor discussed in this chapter, Wilbert E. Moore, *Industrialization and Labor, Social Aspects of Economic Development* (Ithaca: Cornell University Press, 1951) is very good for both theoretical and empirical material. See also Moore and A. S. Feldman (eds.), *Labor Commitment and Social Change in Developing Areas* (New York: Social Science Research Council, 1960). E. H. Phelps-Brown, *The Economics of Labor* (New Haven: Yale University Press, 1962) has some helpful discussion on this problem, especially in Chapter 3. On labor (and the entrepreneur), *Industrialism and Industrial Man* (New York: Oxford University Press, 1964) by Clark Kerr, John T. Dunlop, Frederick H. Harbison, and Charles A. Myers is also relevant. A careful empirical study, Peter Kilby, "African Labor Productivity Reconsidered," *Economic Journal,* LXXI (June, 1961), gives some helpful information on labor's attitudes and motivation in one culture. See also Walter Galenson (ed.), *Labor and Economic Development* (New York: John Wiley & Sons, Inc., 1959) especially the introduction by Galenson and Chapter 3 (on Japan) by Robert A. Scalapino.

The possibility of a relationship between wages and the productivity of labor is discussed by T. W. Schultz, *Transforming Traditional Agriculture* (New Haven: Yale University Press, 1964), Chap. 12 and Jacob Viner, *International Trade and Economic Development* (Oxford: The Clarendon Press, 1953), Chap. 6. Harvey Leibenstein uses such a relationship to explain unemployment in underdeveloped areas in "Underemployment in Backward Economies," *Journal of Political Economy,* LXV (April, 1957). See also Paul Wonnacott, "Disguised and Other Unemployment in Underdeveloped Economics," *Quarterly Journal of Economics,* LXXVI (May, 1962).

For additional references on entrepreneurs see the Hoselitz volume listed at the beginning of this bibliography. Also John Habakkuk, "The Entrepreneur and Economic Development" in *Lectures on Economic Development* (Istanbul: The Faculty of Economics, Istanbul University, 1958); Charles A. Myers, *Labor Problems in the Industrialization of India* (Cambridge: Harvard University Press, 1958), especially Chaps. 1–3; Frederick Harbison, "Entrepreneurial Organization as a Factor in Economic Development," *Quarterly Journal of Economics,* LXX (August, 1956); and (especially) Henry G. Aubrey, "Investment Decisions in Underdeveloped Countries" in Moses Abramovitz (ed.) *Capital Formation and Economic Growth* (Princeton: Princeton University Press, 1955); Harvey Leibenstein, *Economic Backwardness and Economic Growth* (New York: John Wiley & Sons, Inc., 1957), pp. 121–35. For more specific approaches see Gustav F. Papanek, "The Development of Entrepreneurship," *American Economic Review*, LII (May, 1962), and Everett E. Hagen, *On the Theory of Social Change*, (Homewood, Ill., The Dorsey Press, Inc., 1962).

CHAPTER 14

THE ROLE OF POPULATION GROWTH

In Chapter 1, the change in real *per capita* income was accepted as the measure of economic development. The argument to this point has been concerned with the determinants of the growth of national product, and now population growth is discussed in order to have a complete picture of how the developing country can affect *per capita* output. The chapter might be made very short by arguing simply that the growth of population is unrelated to the economic system, and that the growth of total output is unaffected by changes in population characteristics. In this case, the economist would have nothing to say about population growth, and would merely introduce into his analysis of the growth of total output whatever population figures were given him by noneconomists in order to get *per capita* output results. Until the post-World War II concern with economic development, most economists of the last hundred years generally did consider population changes to be outside their spheres of competence. On the other hand, population issues were a strategic part of the economics of the British classical economists. As presented in this chapter, the evidence is completely convincing that the economics of the development of currently poor countries must again include explicit concern with population. This means not merely that population growth is the denominator in a ratio that measures the success of the development effort, but, more importantly, it means that an analysis of the consequences of economic policies must include possible effects on population growth. More specifically, it means that decisions on the use of those available resources not required to maintain the economy must consider the effect on population growth, as well as the effect on total output. Finally, it means that some attention must also be devoted to the relationship between population change and other economic variables, e.g., saving rate, composition of demand, and the like.

This chapter is divided into three main parts. The first part defines the population issue that most immediately affects the success of the development effort, the likelihood of a country finding itself caught in a population trap just as it begins its development effort. The second part is concerned with possible approaches to preventing the trap from permanently deterring the achievement of a successful development program. In the third part, a brief description of some of the more obvious ways in which population affects other variables in the system is given.

I. The Population Trap Problem

The problem can be explained most effectively with the aid of a simple diagram. In Diagram VIII, *per capita* income is measured along the horizontal axis and percentage changes in income and population are measured along the vertical axis. The two curves show the response of output and population, respectively, to changes in the *per capita* output. A defense of these relationships is to be given later; consider, first, what the curves as drawn show.

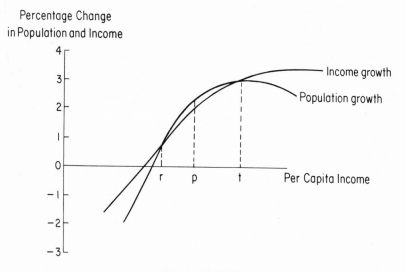

DIAGRAM VIII.

Suppose income per head is now at r, a very low level, where aggregate income and population are growing at the same percentage rate (e.g., ½ of 1 per cent) and *per capita* income remains constant. Now, suppose that for some reason or other *per capita* income suddenly rises to p. At p, population is growing more rapidly than output, and in subsequent periods *per capita* income will move leftward toward *r* again. If for some reason income per head falls below *r*, the rate of population growth drops below that of income growth and *per capita* income moves back to *r*. The level of *per capita* income represented by *r* then identifies a stable equilibrium from which escape by small movements is not possible.

If, however, the economy can make the jump from *r* to *t* in one big effort, then it again is in an equilibrium position. But *t*, unlike *r*, is an unstable equilibrium. If the economy slips slightly and *per capita* income falls—due, e.g., to an adverse change in the terms of trade—the diagram shows that population growth will again exceed income growth and *per capita* income tumbles to *r*. On the other hand, if *per capita* income can reach a point to the right of *t*, the economy will grow indefinitely as income growth levels off at a rate in excess of population growth.

The "population trap problem" in development is how to get from *r* to slightly to the right of *t*. Two general arguments are suggested. The economy must make a "big push" and leap from *r* to *t* in one massive move. The second argument asserts that policies must be taken that result in a shift in the curve measuring the population growth. The latter approach rests on the assumption that population growth is subject to some control by the national policy maker, while the former approach implies that the shape and position of the curve describing population growth cannot be changed by conscious policy. Before considering these alternative approaches in detail, the shape of the curves in Diagram VIII is considered.

The economy of Chapter 7 was described as having a population with a high growth potential that arises in the following way. Currently a high (over 40 per thousand) birthrate exists along with a death rate only moderately lower so that growth of population at the outset of the development effort is probably less than 1 per cent. The high growth potential stems from the possibility of a sharp, quick reduction in the death rate that can accompany even nominal increases in *per capita* income. These reductions are due to public health measures that permit control of epidemics—e.g., vaccination, spraying DDT, elimination of famines, establishment of law and order, and so on. With more significant rises in income, improved housing, sanitation facilities, diets, clothing, and medical help are made possible, and these, in turn, also make possible the reduction in the death rate. The technology of death rate reduction is thus known, and is easily transferable from the rich countries to the poor. Finally, there is rarely any difficulty at all in getting people to accept measures that prolong their lives and the lives of their children. The absence of any significant cultural, social, or psychological barriers to innovations in this sphere further simplifies the reduction of the death rate. That this argument is valid is borne out by mortality rates for a great range of countries over long periods of time.

The effect on the birthrate of a rise in *per capita* income does not lend itself to such a simple statement as that just made about the death rate (international migrations of significant size may be ignored as a relic of bygone days). The available evidence suggests clearly that the birthrate will not fall promptly with an upsurge in *per capita* income. As discussed below, most hypotheses as to birthrate changes depend on far-reaching structural changes in the economy, and changes in the attitudes and values of the population. Obviously such changes do not occur overnight. The assumption underlying Diagram VIII to the left of point *t* is that the birthrate remains at its high level for some time, and this assumption plus the death rate argument yields the sharp rise in population growth, shown in Diagram VIII, as income rises from its level at *r*.

The decline in the population growth after *per capita* income has risen beyond *t*, again depends on the birthrate assumptions. Evidence from currently rich countries has led many observers to conclude that the structural and motivational changes previously referred to will occur and will produce the downward trend in birthrates. Therefore, after *per capita* income has reached and maintained, for a given length of time, levels sufficiently high to produce the changed structure, birthrates and hence population growth rates fall. The leveling off of the birthrate takes place at a rate sufficient to maintain population growth at about the rate achieved prior to the beginning of the whole experience. Further attention is given to the determinants of the birthrate in the next section. The point here is that the population curve in Diagram VIII rests on assumptions as to changes in the socioeconomic environment that accompany changes in *per capita* income, and not upon any assumptions as to the working of an explicitly formulated population policy.

The income curve in Diagram VIII requires less defense in the present context. To make the rate of growth of income dependent on the level of *per capita* income as in the diagram, an assumption about saving rates and the productivity of newly created capital is necessary. If, as *per capita* income rises, the saving rate also rises for a while and there is no decline in capital's productivity, then the rate of growth of output will rise. The leveling off can be explained in terms of a leveling off of the saving rate or possibly a decline in capital's productivity. The only requirement is that income growth between *r* and *t* in Diagram VIII be less than population growth, and not fall at all or not enough to put it below the growth of population after *t*. Other arguments to support the shape of the income curve could be presented, but this seems adequate for the argument here. The assumption will be made in what follows that the income curve represents the maximum rate the economy can achieve, and therefore is not subject to manipulation.

To repeat: the population trap possibility in the development problem arises from the likelihood of sharp increases in the population growth rate swamping increases in output, and thereby preventing the establishment of a sustained growth of *per capita* output. The objective of development policy in this context then is to reach the point where—for whatever reason—the birthrate begins to drop. In terms of Diagram VIII, the problem is to leap from r to slightly right of t or to move the entire population curve in a manner that removes the problem, i.e., pulls the curve below the income-growth curve.

Perhaps it is important to note that another population issue is often the concern of growth economists. This has to do with the consequences of any positive rate of growth of population on levels of achievable welfare. The extrapolation of current rates into the future for 50 to 100 years can easily produce huge problems as to food, living space, education, and so on. This problem, though of great significance, is not discussed here. The trap problem just defined is the immediate problem for the developing countries, and unless immediate problems are effectively solved, concern with what may happen 50 or 100 years hence seems to be of little purpose.

II. Approaches to a Solution

Describing the problem is much easier than finding an answer. It is clear, of course, that the key to the solution is to be found in the extent to which the determinants of the birthrate can be understood and affected. To seek to solve the problem by consciously delaying the implementation of measures known to reduce the death rate is obviously unacceptable. It should be stated, however, that some decisions are taken that do adversely affect the death rate. For example, resources used to build steel mills and chemical plants could be used to build hospitals and infirmaries, and surely the latter would, in the short run, reduce the death rate somewhat more than the former. In general, however, policies are not made that are aimed specifically at preventing a decline in the death rate, and no one would seriously advocate such a policy.

One further preliminary observation is that the historical evidence for a great number of modern rich countries shows no case where substantial rises in population were accompanied by secular declines in *per capita* output. The possible explanations of this evidence are many, and the data are not adequate enough to permit a satisfactory testing of alternative hypotheses. One important element in the explanation is that, with the possible exception of the United States, the birthrate in the currently rich countries was never as high as it now is in most of the underdeveloped countries. Similarly, the decline in the death rate in these earlier years was, in general, much less rapid that it can be now. Thus, there was not the high growth potential in the early period that there is now for the countries just initiating development plans. Also in most of the currently rich countries, population density was much below what it is in many modern poor countries. Although high population density is not an insuperable handicap to growth, it seems reasonably clear that countries that have considerable unused fertile lands have one less hurdle than those that have long since occupied all readily available lands. For example, most Latin American countries are much less crowded than Asian countries; though the former have, in most instances, a higher population growth rate than do the latter. On strict *ceteris paribus* assumptions, one would expect that the smaller density in most Latin American countries would make the achievement of a given income growth rate somewhat easier (i.e., requires less capital, fewer institutional changes, and so on) than would be the case in Asian countries. All of this means that the population side of the development problem in the United States and Western Europe a century and more ago was much less acute than that confronting the contemporary underdeveloped country. This result will be examined later. Consider now various approaches to the solution of the population problem as it has been defined.

A. An Economic Approach

In explaining the level of the birthrate in a given society, one possible approach is in terms of an application of conventional demand analysis. In societies where knowledge of birth control devices is very general and their use acceptable, a married couple is assumed to decide consciously on how many children to have. Children provide a stream of pleasure and possibly revenue to parents, but also impose a cost. Decisions to have children are then taken by weighing the satisfactions (or revenues) against the cost and acting accordingly. In this sense, children are considered as a consumer or producer good, and decisions to have children would then be analyzed in the same way as demand for consumer or producer durables.

This approach to the birthrate explanation has a number of drawbacks. The major one is simply that there is little evidence to suggest that parents apply any sort of profit calculations to decisions in this area of their actions. More generally it would appear that in instances where it makes any sense at all to speak of a "choice" being made, that choice is dominated by social and cultural factors. One may say then that the freedom permitted the parents on family size decisions is so constrained by institutional factors that applying any sort of formal decision model is not likely to help much. This seems to be true in any society, but especially so in the low income country, where—as already emphasized—choice is much more constrained by social factors than it is in rich countries. At the same time, something does emerge from this way of thinking about the birthrate problem. Costs of children are surely not completely irrelevant in decisions about family size. The observed differences between family size in rural and urban areas in most parts of the world is due in part to the fact that children are less of a financial burden in rural areas than in urban centers. Also the attractiveness of new consumer products and the recognition that they could be possessed if there were fewer children has doubtless caused some parents to recognize that some element of substitution does exist. The point then seems to be that although costs, especially, and returns, to a lesser degree, enter into the birthrate explanatory apparatus, there is need for a much broader analysis than that permitted by the demand analogy.

B. Some Socioeconomic Considerations

Consider again the question: Why is the birthrate higher in underdeveloped countries than in developed countries at the present time? With respect to this question, several things may be noted. First, the age distribution of the population is relevant. If, rather than a comparison of crude birthrates, the comparison is between age specific fertility rates, the differences between rich and poor countries are smaller, but still quite significant. Similarly, in low income countries a larger proportion of women marry and do so at a younger age than is the case generally in the richer countries. Statistical data, however, do not show that these differences are sufficient in their impact to account for the observed differences in birthrates. There are religious differences as well between the rich countries and the poor countries, but they are not such that systematically favor high birth rates in the poor countries and low ones in the rich. Knowledge of birth control is also more widespread in rich countries than in poor, but again the data do not suggest this difference is of great explanatory value. As already noted, few societies are without any means of contraceptives, and in some poor countries, the most modern devices have been made available with little or no effect on birthrates. Then one can always mention France where the birthrate began to fall long before modern forms of contraception were available. All of these possible explanations of the differences between the birthrate in rich and poor countries are reasonable and doubtless relevant, but neither singly nor collectively do they provide a convincing argument or one that is consistent with the data. To every argument, a conflicting argument could be easily produced that severely qualified the original explanatory hypothesis.

Greater care must be taken with arguments relating the birthrate to economic and social structure. The chief components of structure that are usually thought to be of relevance include degree of urbanization, family unity, status of women, social and geographic mobility, education, and occupations. To some extent urbanization covers parts of the other items. The relevant thing is the urban mentality, not mere residence in the city.

Family life in cities is usually less cohesive than in rural areas, and contacts are much less limited to family members than on farms. Also—as mentioned earlier—children are certainly less of an earning asset in the city than on the farm. In industrial centers, as opposed to religious or government centers, the weight of tradition in the determination of behavior is less than in isolated villages, and individuals may more rationally appreciate the consequences of their own acts. The same type argument applies to the other components of the changing structure argument. As the mores of the community permit more women to work outside the home, they become much less bound by tradition (and by their husbands' wishes) than previously. The effect of education may be assumed to operate in a similar fashion. It induces a more conscious appraisal of the consequences of one's actions, and results thereby in more rational decisions. Mobility also opens up new horizons that encourage both the man and his wife to appreciate (or at least recognize) the advantages of change from the established routine of childbearing. All of these developments seem to work in the direction of the married couple—especially the wife—having greater freedom from tradition, and gaining competence in appraising the values and institutions that had been accepted without question. The origin of the decline in the birthrate, then, is a changed attitude toward childbearing, and not the availability of effective contraceptives.

Data on birthrates are better than those on investment or capital stock, but in almost all underdeveloped countries now and in rich countries in earlier years, such data are most unsatisfactory. Nevertheless, it is important to note that cross section and time series data for a wide variety of societies are consistent with the arguments in the preceding paragraph. Indeed, it is appropriate to consider these arguments as the general explanation of why the population growth curve, in Diagram VIII, turns down.

Now, consider this question: Why did the attitude that led to a high birthrate develop in the first place? The most convincing answer seems to be, because the death rate was so high. In a society where the death rate is 30 to 35 or more per 1000, the birthrate must approach 40 or more (which is not far from the biological maximum) or the propagation of a race of people is threatened. Consequently, large numbers of children in a family are regarded as a national, as well as family blessing, and honor and prestige are allocated accordingly. One of the explanations of why the wife is so sheltered in many societies now and in earlier years is that she was to be allowed maximum security for successful childbirth. Recently, a monarch from an ancient and underdeveloped country answered a question as to the role of his Queen as that of having children. This effect of the high death rate is readily apparent to individual households as it is evident that a wife must give birth to several more children than she expects or wants to raise to adulthood. The result of all this is the development of a set of attitudes, values, and institutions that encourage, even demand, a very high birthrate.

Despite this argument, a drop in the death rate alone is not sufficient to induce an immediate drop in the birthrate, because it alone will not automatically change the attitudes and motivations that lead initially to the high birthrate. The decline in death rates and a continually rising *per capita* income will, however, set in motion the forces that will, at some point, not only convince society that large families are not necessary for the preservation of the race, but also alter the governing mystique of the society in such a manner that that society is permitted to do what its rationality tells it is right. This body of thought seems to work rather well when discussing the economic history of most of Europe and northern North America over recent centuries. As emphasized earlier, their population trap problem was minor or even nonexistent. In terms of Diagram VIII, this would mean that the entire population growth curve lay to the right and below the income growth curve. For the modern underdeveloped country, the trap problem surely is a very general phenomenon, and the necessary lag between the fall in death rates and a comparable fall in birthrates must occupy the attention of the policy maker.

Can one say that the only possible policy is to leap from *r* to *t* in Diagram VIII, leaving population growth to its own doings? The general difficulties associated with the Big Push strategy of development are discussed in the final chapter of this text. The difficulties associated with the particular application of that strategy implied here have to do with measurement problems and resource availability problems. Knowledge of the specific shape of the curves of Diagram VIII is so completely lacking that to assume one could put values to the *per capita* incomes corresponding to *r* and *t* is misleading. There is no empirical evidence of a country that has made the jump successfully to serve followers as a guide. More damaging to the Big Push approach is the fact that the preceding arguments, which explain why the population curve turns down, imply not merely a significantly higher level of *per capita* income, but they also imply a series of time-consuming structural and social changes, which by their very nature cannot be compressed into periods short enough to solve the lag problem, at least when unaided by specific policies. Finally, the quantity of resources available to make the Big Push would appear inadequate for the job even if the time difficulties and measurement problems—mentioned above— did not exist. Whatever the actual magnitude of the leap from *r* to *t*, it is surely much larger than any developing country since the war has achieved, and there seems little prospect for these resources to be significantly increased in the near future. For these and other reasons to be summarized in Chapter 18, the conclusion is accepted that the Big Push is not the solution. This means a specific population policy is necessary.

C. Toward a Population Policy

A population policy means measures designed to effect the position and shape of the population growth curve of Diagram VIII. For reasons already discussed, a population policy is essentially a policy designed to reduce the birthrate concurrently with falls in the mortality rate. The policy issue gains in relevance if there is a conflict between policies that favorably affect the growth of aggregate income and those that favorably affect the growth of *per capita* income. This would mean, of course, that by transferring investible resources from increasing physical capacity to activities that resulted in reduced birthrates, the gain from the latter activity more than offset the loss from the reduced capacity creation activity. For example, suppose that the population policy consisted of supplying to all newly married couples birth control devices and instructions on their use. Resources used for this purpose would mean fewer resources were available for building factories, dams, fertilizer plants, or training farmers where, in most cases, the effect on total output would be greater than if the resources were used for birth control purposes. If the allocation decision were correct, it would mean that both the income and population curves in Diagram VIII moved rightward (in the relevant range), and that the population curve moved by a proportionately greater distance. The question, then, is a further aspect of the general problem of how to use available investible resources.

1. The Role of Birth Control Devices. The preceding arguments have not placed much confidence in merely making available contraceptives. They do, however, enter the picture, and, as just noted, making them available and encouraging their use is not a costless operation. The available evidence—chiefly some hit and miss surveys—suggest that both peasant and urban women strongly wish to be rid of long and unpleasant years of childbearing. For example, a survey reported by Kingsley Davis, in his study of population in India and Pakistan, shows that less than 5 per cent of rural women in the sample wanted to use contraceptives and less than 40 per cent of women living in upper-class urban areas wanted to use them. At the same time, most women expressed the opinion that three or fewer children were a sufficient number to raise to adulthood. Despite the evidence against reliance on the use of contraceptives, two points are worth emphasizing. In the first place, a simple, safe, oral contraceptive taken by the woman is much more likely to succeed than other types, especially other types that depend on the male. There is little doubt that women are much more interested than are men in reducing the birthrate in virtually all societies. Also, women are more likely to seek medical help and, therefore, make themselves available for advice and encouragement in the practice of birth control. The little experience with oral contraceptives suggests that they are less objectionable not only because they are simpler to use, but also because they can be taken independently of the sex act and do not appear to be directly associated with it. Clinics and "training programs" in the use of contraceptives are an essential part of this method of attacking the problem, and preparing effective teachers and advisors is also part of this approach. Very little data are available on the use of the pill, however, and any sort of general statement must be viewed with considerable caution.

A second relevant point is that there has been relatively little all-out campaigning in behalf of birth control in the developing countries. Some countries that have formal development plans have allocated funds for study or for advising on family planning, but in no country has it been given full backing and wide publicity by the government leaders. There is some evidence that this lack of commitment is changing slowly, and also that objections of leaders of religions whose teachings traditionally opposed the overt practice of family planning are also reexamining the appropriateness of these teachings in the modern setting. Perhaps the single most important element of a population policy, designed to enable a country to avoid the trap, is the full and open advertisement that government and social and religious leaders are in full support of the practice of family planning in an environment in which the mortality rate is declining rapidly. To persuade national and local leaders to so commit themselves is not an economic problem, but the economist in presenting his analysis may help to convince the leaders of the necessity of such action.

2. Changing the Social and Economic Structure. Evidently, a society cannot build cities simply to try to lower its birthrate, but some policy guidance can be gained from what was said earlier about the effect of the cultural and economic milieu on decisions as to family size. This guidance would take the form of isolating those categories of investment that seem to be relatively unfavorable to natality. It is evident that they are complementary to, not replacements for, the approach suggested in the discussion above. The following are suggested by the preceding arguments.

(*a*) Investment that results in the price of goods and services that are used in the rearing of children rising relative to the price of alternative claims on consumer's income may be expected to affect the birthrate. The element of truth in the child-durable good analogy should be exploited. The making available of consumer goods—bicycles, electricity, a watch, colorful cloth—at prices that make it possible to buy them if sacrifices are made will help. As already emphasized, it is not adequate to do the job alone.

(*b*) Investments that tend to open up hitherto isolated regions or that result in redistribution of the population are likely to affect the birthrate adversely. Thus communication (e.g., newspapers and radios) and transportation facilities that bring new contacts and new ideas to regions long sheltered may be expected to shake up all the traditional behavior patterns including those that dictate a high birthrate.

(c) For somewhat similar reasons, large scale investments that make over an area rather completely are more likely to affect the birthrate adversely than are numerous small investments that result in piecemeal changes in existing arrangements. The former type investment will impose more modifications in behavior than the latter, and will thereby be more likely to change those attitudes and goals that have some bearing on family size.

(d) Investments in education may have some effect, but the reasoning is even less clear cut than in the previous arguments. The evidence is inconclusive, but there are some reasons to think that training programs for adults aimed at explaining the consequences of population growth would have some effects. In particular, one may argue that a short annual training program of this sort would yield greater returns than trying to teach all six- and seven-year olds to read and write.

The greatest difficulty in these approaches has to do with measurement of the effects of the birthrate of the various types of investments. To make the population growth an explicit policy variable leaves the way open for justifying particular investment projects in a manner that is difficult to dispute. Thus steel mills and highways surely have an effect on the birthrate in some roundabout way, but it is unlikely that they could be supported on this ground alone. This general difficulty is discussed in Chapter 15. The conclusion here would seem to be that investment projects that do not act on the birthrate in a firm, predictable way should not have such an effect added as an externality in evaluating its impact on the economy. Surely supporting "industrialization" on the grounds that it will reduce the birthrate is not an acceptable argument in its favor.

3. *The Use of Tax and Subsidy Instruments.* One of the most direct approaches to the birthrate problem is a system of financial rewards or penalties that encourage family planning. Again, here no very adequate evidence is available on the effectiveness of such approaches simply because they have not been tried in a systematic way. The acuteness of the problem suggests that some experiments might yield large returns especially in small countries where administrative difficulties are not so overpowering.

There are several rather obvious approaches, the most likely of which would be progressive subsidies. For example, a payment would be made to a couple if the wife had not had a baby during the year and was not pregnant at the time the payment was made. At the end of the second year, if the same conditions were met, the couple would receive a larger sum, and after the third year if no babies or pregnancies, a still larger sum, and so on. Perhaps the system would apply only after the couple had two or maybe three children. Such a program has several advantages.

First of all, it makes explicit that there are advantages to be gained from limiting births. In a similar fashion, the subsidy would give the couple an incentive to acquaint themselves with birth control devices. The proposal also makes explicit the full support of the government for family planning.

The subsidy payments would be used largely for consumption by the recipients, so the proposal would doubtless reduce total saving and hence physical capital formation. Its financing would be accomplished from general tax receipts. Evidently a tax on subsidy recipients would defeat the purpose of the scheme. Financing could also take place through foreign aid or foreign loans, the repayment of which would be made possible from the growing *per capita* income resulting from the reduced birthrates. There are alternative forms of the subsidy to which attention could be directed, but they would all have the general characteristics of the scheme just outlined.

A tax on large families eliminates the problem of financing, and thus has advantages over the subsidy approach. This advantage is probably more than offset by the difficulties of administering such a tax. If family size reaches the point where the family is to be penalized but cannot pay, there is not much that can be done. Although there would probably be some deterrent effect if a progressive tax were levied on all children after (say) the third one, the population would be expected to recognize that the collection of such a tax would be a virtually impossible task. The "tax" might be levied by a plan that called for sterilization after the third child, but this kind of tax is again difficult to enforce, and is even more unpleasant to contemplate (or enforce) than the other tax and subsidy system just mentioned.

The use of subsidies or taxes to affect decisions as to family size is not likely to have great appeal to anyone. Such decisions are about as personal as one can imagine. There is little doubt, however, that in many underdeveloped countries, the population trap problem is of such immediate relevance that these personal matters become the concern of the national authorities. All measures that bear on the issue then become part of the development planning effort.

4. Conclusion. The picture that emerges from these discussions of a population policy cannot be described as hopeful. Knowledge of specific factors that act on family size is limited indeed, and, consequently, it is necessary to attack the problem on a broad front. When this is necessary, one can be sure that there will be waste and misallocation even with the most sincere and dedicated administrators. The policies outlined above are not really alternative approaches, they are rather complementary and would—if it were possible to introduce them simultaneously—reenforce each other. The problem is of such acuteness and such complexity that to rely on a single policy is to plan on hopes rather than on evidence and careful analysis. It is perhaps appropriate to add that studies of the time path of birthrates in given localities might lead to more specific policy measures in which considerable confidence could be placed.

III. Effects of Population Change on Total Output

In Sections I and II of this chapter, attention was directed toward the role of population growth as the denominator of the ratio that measures the success of the development effort. This meant, in effect, that population growth as such was assumed to have no effect on the growth of total output (though, of course, the use of resources to seek to effect the rate of growth of population may result in a smaller quantity of resources being available to increase total capacity). This is not an entirely acceptable assumption, and some attention as to possible relationships between growth of total output and population change is necessary. The discussion is based on three population characteristics: its absolute size, its rate of growth, and its age distribution.

A. Size of Population

The effect of size of the population on total output may be mentioned and dismissed easily. One can easily imagine an economy where with given nonlabor resources, *per capita* income would be higher if the population were larger. This would mean that the larger population would permit greater exploitation of economies of scale, greater division of labor, or possibly have a favorable effect on the composition of output. Similarly, one can imagine a situation in which a larger population would result in a lower *per capita* income due to a traditional diminishing returns argument. This kind of reasoning has led to the notion of an "optimum-sized population" as one in which, given everything else, the population is just the size to maximize *per capita* output. The optimum-population notion is not a very helpful guide to policy as the argument is of a particularly static variety. Suppose the policy maker were rightly convinced that with a larger work force, under present conditions, *per capita* output would be higher than it is now. An innovation may change the situation tomorrow, and by the time a larger work force has become available, the quantity and quality of complementary inputs will certainly have changed. Indeed, the change in the size of the population can be expected to induce a change in the complementary inputs. Thus, the optimum-population argument reveals very little as to what should be done now.

Of greater significance than this argument is the fact that almost any of the advantages that can be gained from an increased population can also be gained with a larger income, by fiscal and tax policy, or by international trade. Economies of scale and division of labor are largely functions of the size of output, not the size of population. Unless one assumes little or no international trade, then for a country to seek to exploit technological advantages through an increased population is to misunderstand the sources of these advantages. One can devise technological situations that require that this statement be qualified, but such situations do not seem important enough to introduce here.

The size argument does mean that some countries may not have a trap problem or have only a very minor one. This would be true if the rise in population facilitated (or did not hinder significantly) pushing the income growth curve of Diagram VIII leftward and upward. In most instances, such countries will be those whose population density is considerably below that prevailing in the more crowded low income areas. Relatively low density is not, however, a sufficient condition for avoiding the trap problem.

B. RATE OF GROWTH OF POPULATION

The role of the rate of growth of population on the level and growth of output is usually analyzed in terms of its effect on aggregate demand. The various forms of the stagnation hypothesis flowing from the Keynesian analysis were (and are) frequently explained, in part, by the effect of a declining rate of growth of population on the profitability of investment. To argue in this way—even if correct—does not mean that the most effective way to correct the difficulty is to seek to raise the rate of growth of population. In the economy of Chapter 7, an insufficiency of aggregate demand may also be a problem, but here neither the explanation nor the solution is found in the population area. The rate of growth of population in some countries may affect the wage rates, but since widespread unemployment is a common characteristic of the underdeveloped economy, a possible wage effect seems generally irrelevant, at least for a considerable period of time. In summary, it seems safe to say that almost any positive effect on the growth of output that can be accomplished by affecting the growth of population can also be accomplished through fiscal and monetary policies or by direct controls.

C. THE AGE DISTRIBUTION

The age distribution of the population has greater relevance for total output than either its size or the rate of growth. If international migration and the immediate consequence of wars are ruled out, the chief determinant of the age distribution of a population is the birthrate. A high birthrate over an extended period results in an age distribution shaped like a tower, very broad at the base for very young and tapering rapidly toward the top as age increases. A look at the age distribution of virtually any low income country will show this kind of age distribution. The low birthrate country will have a much less broad-based age distribution, and will be much less tapered in higher age groups. If the fertility rate is quite low, and has been for some time, the largest age group may not even be the youngest. Changes in mortality rates will have little effect on this age distribution pattern.

The immediate consequence of the age distribution characteristic of the underdeveloped country is a higher "dependency ratio" than in lower birthrate areas. If the ages 15–65 are assumed to be the working years of most people, then the ratio of the number of people in this age group to the total population is significantly smaller in high fertility areas than in areas that have had a much lower birthrate for long periods of time. Unless one assumes that even with a more favorable dependency ratio, no more workers would be employed than is now the case, the age distribution patterns of the underdeveloped country adversely affect *per capita* income. If the dependency ratio could be suddenly changed, the employment problem would, in most instances, counter any beneficial effects that might accrue. In a longer-run situation where conscious policies were being pursued to use all available productive resources, the changed ratio can surely facilitate the achievement of the development effort.

More important than simply reducing the number of dependents to be supported by the working groups, is the possible effects on saving rates and on the composition of investment. Not only may it be expected that the saving potential of an economy with a high dependency ratio is less than that of an economy with a low dependency ratio, but the composition of expenditures is also different. Saving rates may be assumed to be affected simply because of the demands placed on households by the need to support large families. Even if saving rates were the same irrespective of the size of families, the composition of investment is affected. Pressure for education and health facilities is increased as it is for a great range of child welfare expenditures. Since the pressure is great and the need so painfully obvious, the heavy weight of the high dependency ratio is sure to direct resources into such welfare activities even when a cold, economic rationale dictates otherwise.

The element to be emphasized in the analysis is that the age distribution—and hence the dependency ratio—is more or less independent of changes in the mortality rate of the kind that usually occur. A reduction in mortality of the usual kind will, of course, increase the proportion of the population entering the working age group, but it will also increase the proportion of the population capable of being parents. Demographic tables show that the upward effect of the latter on the dependency ratio outweighs the downward effect of the former. On the other hand, a reduction in the birthrate has immediate negative effects on the numbers in the below-15 age groups without immediate effect on the numbers entering the working age groups. One may then conclude that if the employment problem is solved—or is increasingly solved—a reduction in birthrate will tend to facilitate the achievement of an acceptable rate of growth of total output because of its effect on the dependency ratio. Reduction in mortality rates will not have this effect.

IV. Conclusion

The primary emphasis in this chapter has been on the prospective population trap into whose clutches most developing countries can so easily slide. Brief attention was paid to the possible effects of population characteristics on the level and growth of aggregate output. In both instances, the importance of the control of the birthrate overrides any other aspect of the population issue of an underdeveloped economy. The escape or prevention of the trap depends very heavily upon the extent to which a society can and will reduce the birthrate as the mortality rate goes rapidly downward. If this birthrate reduction does not take place, the economy will find itself experiencing not only a rapid rise in population but also increasing difficulty in generating an acceptable growth of *per capita* output. Some of the harder pressed countries may even find their death rate creeping back up as population shoots up so rapidly that adequate health, medical, and sanitation facilities cannot keep pace. A mere short-run increase in *per capita* income in a country with relatively little density cannot be taken as proof that the trap has been permanently escaped. For that to be the case, the birthrate must have turned down, and analysis show that it is reasonable to assume it to be falling as a regular affair.

With respect to the relationship between population and output, the most relevant issue is the age distribution, and this, in turn, is most directly the result of the level of the birthrate. A declining birthrate lowers the dependency ratio, tends to permit an increase in the saving rate, and reduces the pressure to use investible resources in sectors where their productivity is below that that could be achieved in other sectors. Any possible advantage accruing from a high population growth rate can be supplied in alternative ways—growth of *per capita* income, tax of fiscal policy, or international trade.

These arguments add up to the need for a conscious population policy —i.e., conscious policy aimed at reducing the birthrate—as part of the development program. The knowledge of the determinants of the birthrate, gleaned largely from a survey of developments in countries where the birthrate has fallen, is imprecise and rudimentary. Consequently, policies flowing from these relationships are not likely to be instantaneously and strongly effective. Despite this, the population issue is critical enough to require that formal attacks on it be undertaken.

Bibliography

The most lucid discussion of the trap problem is Richard R. Nelson, "A Theory of the Low-Level Equilibrium Trap," *American Economic Review,* XLVI (December, 1956). The diagram used in the text is from Nelson. On the same theme see Everett E. Hagen, "Population and Economic Growth" *American Economic Review,* XLIX (June, 1959) and Harvey Leibenstein, *A Theory of Economic Demographic Development* (Princeton: Princeton University Press, 1954) and the same author's *Economic Backwardness and Economic Growth* (New York: John Wiley & Son, Inc., 1957), Chap. 10.

For a more general treatment of the relationship between population and development see Ansley J. Coale and Edgar M. Hoover, *Population Growth and Economic Development in Low-Income Countries* (Princeton: Princeton University Press, 1958) especially Parts I and V and M. L. Qureshi (ed.) *Population Growth and Economic Development* (Karachi: Institute of Development Economics, 1960). Joseph J. Spengler has two excellent survey articles on population: "Population Theory" in Bernard F. Haley, *A Survey of Contemporary Economics,* Vol. II (Homewood, Ill.: Richard D. Irwin, Inc., 1952) and "Demographic Patterns" in Harold F. Williamson and John A. Buttrick (eds.) *Economic Development* (Englewood Cliffs, N.J.: Prentice-Hall, Inc., 1954). See also Spengler and Otis Dudley Duncan (eds.) *Population Theory and Policy, Selected Readings* (New York: The Free Press of Glencoe, 1956) and the vast survey, *The Determinants and Consequences of Population Trends* (New York: United Nations, Population Division, 1953).

For an economic approach to the discussion of birthrate see Gary S. Becker, "An Economic Analysis of Fertility" in *Demographic and Economic Change in Developed Countries,* A conference of the Universities—National Bureau Committee for Economic Research (Princeton: Princeton University Press, 1960). The discussion of Becker's paper by James S. Duesenberry and Bernard Okum is equally helpful. On this same point see also the two papers by Spengler previously mentioned.

Two excellent studies on specific populations are Irene B. Taeuber, *The Population of Japan* (Princeton: Princeton University Press, 1958) and Kingsley Davis, *The Population of India and Pakistan* (Princeton: Princeton University Press, 1951). Also useful is P. K. Whelpton and Clyde V. Kiser (eds.) *Social and Psychological Factors Affecting Fertility,* Vol. II (New York: Milbank Memorial Fund, 1950).

In approaching the policy question a useful model is found in Kingsley Davis and Judith Blake, "Social Structure and Fertility: An Analytical Framework," *Economic Development and Cultural Change,* IV (April, 1956). See also *Approaches to Problems of High Fertility in Agrarian Societies* (New York: Milbank Memorial Fund, 1952). Stephen Enke has a number of papers on population policy. See for example "The Economics of Government Payments to Limit Population" *Economic Development and Cultural Change,* VIII (July, 1960). A most optimistic attitude about population is held by Albert O. Hirschman; see his *The Strategy of Economic Development* (New Haven: Yale University Press, 1958), pp. 176–82.

Part Four

ON THE ALLOCATION
OF INVESTIBLE RESOURCES

The problem to be considered in this part may be stated in the following way: resources are available in excess of the quantity required to maintain the economy at some acceptable level. These resources—labor and skills of various kinds, physical capital of a variety of sorts and types, foreign exchange, and so on—are available to add to the capacity of the economy to produce a flow of goods and services. The question that must now be answered is how do we use these investible resources in order to make the maximum contribution to converting the underdeveloped economy of Chapter 7 to the growing economy described in Chapters 2 through 6. More specifically, it is the question of how to allocate these resources so that they result in the largest increase in the capacity of the economy to produce goods and services.

In Chapter 15, the first task is the establishment of a general criterion to guide the allocation decision. Then with this criterion established, problems associated with its implementation are examined under a variety of situations as to the impact of the investment project.

Chapter 16 considers a number of special aspects of the criterion issue having to do with choice of discount factor, length of life of capital item, timing of investment, and the like. Also in this chapter some policy conclusions on the allocation problem are discussed in the final pages.

CHAPTER 15

A GENERAL APPROACH
TO THE ALLOCATION PROBLEM

Read also chapt 8

Investible resources can be used in a great variety of ways. They can be used to construct school buildings, to train more teachers, to increase research activity, to build a steel mill, to build a multipurpose dam, and on, and on. Since all the demands for investment cannot be satisfied, it is necessary to choose among them. The objective of this chapter is the development of a means of making this choice in an economically rational way.

This general problem may be divided into three separate though closely related, subproblems. The first is the question of the total amount of capital formation to be undertaken from current income. This issue was discussed explicitly in Chapter 8 and implicitly in the other chapters of Part Two. Nothing more will be added in this chapter. The second question has to do with the allocation of these investible resources among different sectors of the economy. The third component of the general problem is that having to do with the choice of technique to be used in the newly created sectors. In almost all instances, choice of technique refers to the combination of inputs employed, or in terms of the diagrams of Part One, the selection of the ray to be used in the production process. That these latter two questions in particular are not independent of each other will become clear as the discussion proceeds, as will the advantages of keeping them conceptually separate.

Section I sets out the criterion of allocation of investible resources that seems most appropriate for application in the underdeveloped country. The criterion question has received a great deal of attention in the literature, and in no sense is Section I a survey of this literature. It is rather the development of the criterion that a study of the problem suggests has the most relevance for the investment problems of interest here. The three following sections deal with problems associated with the implementation of this criterion under a variety of assumptions. The following chapter is concerned with an elaboration of some specific issues associated with the general investment allocation problem.

I. The Criterion Problem

It was just stated that the objective of the allocation of the limited investible resources is to achieve the largest possible increase in the capacity of the economy to produce goods and services. But more needs to be said on the exact content of such an objective before it can serve as a guide to policy or as a source of illumination of the development problem. To get the maximum returns from a limited quantity of resources appeal can be made to marginal productivity, and since interest is centered on the returns to the economy as a whole, the appeal is to social (as opposed to private) marginal productivity (*SMP*). As the investment project yields a stream of output over time, something must also be said about the time pattern of the income generated by a project.

There is a predetermined amount of available investible resources, and a series of prospective investment projects. The present value of the output stream produced by a particular project is the annual net contribution of that project over its life to the national product—all discounted to the present period. Let V_{it} be the gross value of output of the ith project in the tth year, and the project have a life of n years. Then let C_{it} be the corresponding total cost of producing that output in that year with the ith project. Then the net income of the project in year t is the difference between gross output and input, so $Y_{it} = V_{it} - C_{it}$. The present value of this net income stream for project i is

$$Y_i = \frac{Y_{i1}}{(1+r)} + \frac{Y_{i2}}{(1+r)^2} + \cdots + \frac{Y_{it}}{(1+r)^t} + \cdots + \frac{Y_{i3}}{(1+r)^n}$$

where r is "the" rate of discount. The problems surrounding the choice of discount factor are discussed in the next chapter. The *SMP* criterion is to choose the projects in such a way that the sum of the present values of all projects is a maximum. More exactly, choose m projects such that

$$Y = \sum_{i=1}^{m} \sum_{t=1}^{n} \frac{Y_{it}}{(1+r)^t}$$

is a maximum subject to the limitation on the quantity of investible resources available in period one and the production functions. Thus the *SMP* of a project consists of the ratio of the present value of returns minus operating costs to the amount of capital invested, i.e., the *SMP* of project i is

Y_i/K_i where Y_i is computed as above and K_i is the quantity of capital. Frequently the discount issue is ignored and the formula is written $SMP = \dfrac{V}{K} - \dfrac{C}{K}$ where V and C are defined as above. (C is total annual costs including interest and amortization.)

The *SMP* criterion is applicable to private firms as well as government agencies. One can imagine investment funds being made available to all proposed projects with an *SMP* of a specified value throughout the economy as the simple allocation rule. The big problem is to create the economic environment in which the cost and revenue figures used by the firms are those that measure the cost and benefits to the economy as a whole. To examine the various issues involved with this question, it is convenient to begin with very simple investment opportunities and work slowly toward those more likely to appear in the real underdeveloped world. The next section considers investing units that are completely independent of each other, then Section III looks at possible side or indirect effects, and Section IV examines the implications of interdependence among several sectors.

II. Direct Effects of Investment

Consider an economy made up of independent firms that produce only final goods and use only primary inputs. This is the same kind of economy that was discussed in Chapter 3. Assume further that investments have only the consequence of increasing the capacity of the economy to produce a single product or set of products. There are no side or indirect effects on saving, social structure, labor training, or what have you. Also assume that there are constant costs in each sector, and alternative projects all have the same expected length of life. Finally, assume that the prices of factors that are operative are equal to opportunity costs as that term was defined earlier. This equality is assumed to be accomplished by a tax and subsidy system along the lines already discussed. Under these assumptions, present values of all projects can be summed to get an economy-wide total, and individual firms' investments will be consistent with the maximization of the increment in national product. These assumptions make the allocation problems about as simple as they can be made, but still there are major difficulties.

Forecasting the revenue stream under these assumptions means forecasting a physical output stream, presumably technologically determined, and a price series. Similarly, forecasts must be made for costs other than the fixed costs. Obviously, a large element of uncertainty must necessarily be introduced into empirical estimates of these series. The problem is less difficult for a small firm in a growing economy than it is for large projects, the operation of which must necessarily affect the prices that are being forecast. Any sort of formal uncertainty model or probability distribution assumed for costs and revenues is not likely to be of practical relevance to the underdeveloped country for some time. Recognition of uncertainty is part of the story, however, and some effort to introduce it into the calculations is essential. The simplest approach would be to estimate a range—from optimistic to pessimistic—of values for each forecasted value, but such a procedure seems logical only if some sort of decision can be reached about the degree of risk involved in each. At any rate, some "uncertainty factor" is helpful, if it is not merely pulled from a hat. There is a temptation to introduce the uncertainty element by making the discount factor larger than it would otherwise be, but there are enough questions with the interest rate without introducing another foreign component into it. Neither does it seem appropriate simply to shorten arbitrarily the period over which revenues are expected as a means of introducing uncertainty. Considerations of uncertainty may mean that the future revenue stream drops off rapidly, but this is not the same thing as ignoring all income after, say, the third or fourth year as a rule of thumb.

If the project will yield more than one product, not only is the uncertainty problem further complicated, but the very identification of all sources of benefits and costs may be difficult. In large multipurpose dams, for example, the full effect on the capacity of the economy of increased power, of clean water, of regular irrigation, and so on should be valued and included in the receipts stream. In most instances, an accurate valuation is impossible and rough approximations must be used.

The impact of projects aimed at producing technical knowledge, labor training, or the practice of family planning are—as discussed in previous chapters—still more difficult to measure *ex ante*. Although few government planning offices formally estimate returns arising from investment in these areas, it is a major theme of this book that such attempts should be made. The present value expression quoted earlier is as applicable to this type of project as it is to that yielding an increase in capacity to produce a physical product.

For example, suppose that a private firm or government agency seeks to set up a research unit to try to find a seed that is more suitable for the soil in a given area. What is the present value of the contribution to national product arising from such an investment? An estimate must be made of the costs of the research, of the production of the seeds, and of persuading and teaching farmers to use them once they are researched and produced. Then an estimate must be made of the increased yield due to the new seeds and to prices of the increased quantity of output. Finally, this net income series must be discounted to the present by "the" interest rate. All of these steps are extremely precarious ones, but having the formal model as a guide is surely better than rules of thumb or allocation decisions based on the debating skills of the several ministers.

The same set of arguments applies to education projects, population control, and other projects where output is in the form of a service that indirectly affects economic capacity rather than a physical product. As emphasized in the preceding chapters, the uncertainty surrounding the projection of the productivity of all such investment is very great indeed.

Along with uncertainty associated with estimates, there is the further problem of identifying total costs. For example, a particular investment project may require that current nutritional, housing, or clothing standards be raised if workers are to be able to perform the new tasks associated with the projects. In this case, the *SMP* criterion should include, as a cost, the resources required to achieve the higher living standards. Similarly, any extra social overhead required by the project should be included as a cost. These costs may be significant to the economy, and their omission from the cost side of *SMP* of a project may give it an unduly high value when, in fact, it is imposing a burden on the economy. Also the nature of some of the costs—e.g., extra police, fire prevention, or housing—may be such that the private firm does not include them in the calculation of its *SMP,* and a risk is incurred that the private sector projects will underestimate the costs associated with some of their undertakings.

In the case of government enterprises, a further difficulty arises. Suppose that the *SMP* of the research unit, previously mentioned, was such that it merited funds from the investment kitty. Suppose further that the projected net income stream materialized. Finally, suppose that the government for any of a number of reasons was unable to sell the new seeds to the farmer, and simply gave them away so that the research unit as such received no revenue. Thus, even though the project had an *SMP* high enough to justify a claim on investible resources, difficulties may rise for continued financing in an economy with an inadequate taxing bureaucracy and limited borrowing capacity. This is a type of difficulty usually associated with external economies, but it is also applicable to government and private undertakings that produce a product that traditionally is not sold on the market. Some attention may, therefore, have to be given to the problem of financial feasibility, as well as to economic feasibility.

The assumptions that no firm creates any external effects, and that all input prices have been made equal to their opportunity costs by government policy eliminates the major reasons why private profitability might deviate from social profitability. The former assumption will be omitted in Section IV, but the latter assumption will not, and as noted in earlier chapters, the implementation of policies designed to equate input prices with opportunity costs in an underdeveloped economy is extremely difficult.

The ruling out of any side effects simplifies the problem of the choice of technique. If there are no indirect effects on any element in the economy due to the particular combination of factors employed, then, evidently, economic rationality dictates the choosing of that technique that permits the production of a preassigned flow of output at minimum costs. This will be done by the maximizing firms under present assumptions. As emphasized in Chapter 3, what that technique is depends very much on technology, and changing technology may affect the least cost combination of inputs.

The discussion of the implementation of the *SMP* criterion under the present rather unrealistic assumptions illustrates a number of the difficulties associated with choosing the investment pattern that will add the greatest possible increment to the economy's productive capacity. All arguments mentioned here remain applicable as more complicated effects of the investment process are explored. And, of course, the *SMP* criterion itself is not dependent upon the assumptions of this section, although its measurement in any specific instance may well be.

III. The Role of Side Effects

In the preceding section, the assumption was made that the only effects of a particular investment project were an increase in the capacity of the system to produce one or more products or services—e.g., bicycles, tractors, new knowledge about seeds, birth control propaganda, and so on. In almost any project, however, there are other effects that are of consequence to the development process, and hence of relevance to the allocation problem. For example, two particular projects may result in net income streams of the same size, but out of one, the saving rate is twice as high as from the other. Obviously, such data are pertinent to how the investment funds are used. Thus, some attention must be given to the "side effects" of projects, as well as to the "direct effects" noted in the previous section. Side effects are most important when they run counter to the direct effects. Saving may again provide an example. To get the maximum direct effects from a given investment project, the least cost combination of inputs is chosen. However, another combination that calls for higher immediate costs of production of a given output will also yield a larger saving rate. In this case, it would be necessary to weigh the lower costs and lower saving rate of one technique against higher costs and higher saving of another.

There are many possible side effects that could be considered, and a major difficulty in any specific analysis involves isolating those that are relevant enough to warrant investigation. Three specific side effects—saving, population growth, labor training—will be considered individually here, along with some brief, general comments on other possible effects; the section will conclude with a discussion of how side effects may be introduced in the *SMP* criterion as it was previously worked out. The assumption that each sector produces only final goods is retained until Section IV.

A. THE SAVING EFFECT

The side effect most frequently noted has to do with the effect of the choice of technique on the marginal rate of saving. Two hypotheses may be identified. On the one hand, it is sometimes argued that the saving rate from profits exceeds that from wages, and, therefore, the greater the share of profits in a given income stream, the greater will be the rate of saving from that income. The rationale of this hypothesis rests—as noted earlier— on the assumption that the level of income of profit earners is enough above subsidence that a high rate of saving involves no physical hardship, and (more importantly) that recipients of profits have a stronger incentive to save than do wage earners.

On the other hand, a more general argument states that for a variety of reasons, one choice of technique may produce a higher rate of saving than another. The variety of reasons include the government's ability to tax certain groups relative to others, different groups (e.g., skilled and un- skilled workers, urban and rural residents, various age groups, various in- come groups, and so on) have different saving propensities, and possibly the degree to which income recipients are within or beyond the monetary sector of the economy.

There is sufficient evidence to suggest that both hypotheses merit re- spect. As has been noted earlier, it is particularly clear that profit earners save relatively more than other income recipients (including others whose income is equally high, e.g., land owners). Also surveys of saving and con- sumption habits show that factors, such as those mentioned above, are relevant explanatory variables in accounting for variations in saving rates. But to accept this empirical generalization does not necessarily imply that the least cost technique not be chosen. Profits are, of course, maximized by following the dictates of the market in choosing the input combina- tion, i.e., the use of the least cost combination will result in maximum profits, and hence—if the hypothesis about saving out of profits is accepted —maximum saving.

The more general hypothesis stated above—that different income recipi- ents have different saving propensities—is more appealing conceptually, but imposes severe problems of implementation. Thus, it is necessary to have a very great deal of data on saving propensities of various groups, and, in particular, on the groups affected by the new investment under- taking. Given these data (which would have to be accumulated by using resources that have very high opportunity costs), there remains the task of determining exactly how each available technique affects the distribu- tion of income among these groups with varying saving propensities. Even with this information, the problem is not completely solved. Since a pos- sible saving effect will not be reflected in the cost or income streams of individual producing units as conventionally measured, it will be entirely fortuitous if the least cost technique to the producing unit results in an exploitation of the full saving potential. So a final step would still be necessary to bring about the desired techniques. These practical difficulties still do not exhaust the range of problems.

The government via its taxing and fiscal policies affects the rate of saving. Indeed, those who advocate using the choice of technique as a method to affect the saving rate usually explicitly assume that the government is unable to affect the rate of saving by fiscal measures. At the same time, it is necessary to assume that the government does have the policy instruments to affect the choice of technique and the empirical material by which to decide what technique will yield what result. It is clear, however, that these assumptions are inconsistent. If the government tax bureaucracy is sophisticated and informed enough to lead producers to a particular input combination, it is surely sophisticated and informed enough to affect the level of saving to a significant degree via taxes and fiscal policy. Furthermore, it is this latter kind of taxation effectiveness that in other areas of the development process—e.g., control of inflation—is more relevant, and thus is the kind of talent that the government is more likely to acquire— and must acquire—if it is to contribute in a significant degree to the development effort.

Given the technique, similar arguments and conclusions can be applied to the choice of product. For example, there is evidence that suggests the general conclusion that persons who live in rural areas save a larger proportion of their income than do people living in urban areas. From this evidence, one might conclude that investment in the agricultural sector may produce an ultimately higher rate of growth for the economy than investment in manufacturing due to the higher saving rate in agriculture. The same difficulties of implementation and measurement arise here as with respect to choice of technique.

The conclusion seems rather clear. There are not only major practical problems in exploiting whatever saving effect arises from different techniques or different sectors, there is also considerable advantage in concentrating the energies of the government on improving its fiscal and taxing instruments as a means of affecting saving. Despite this conclusion, in a given context it may be important to introduce the saving effect into the calculations of the social profitability of a project, and some comments on how this may be done are in a later section.

B. Side Effects on Population

In Chapter 14, the possible ways that investible resources could be used to affect the birthrate directly were discussed. From that discussion certain hypotheses emerged as to variables that may have value in explaining changes in the birthrate in a given community. And now the problem is whether or not choice of the technique of production or the choice of the area of the economy to expand can have side effects on the birthrate.

The chief hypothesis of current relevance emerging from the arguments of Chapter 14 is that new technique by modifying the living routine and work habits and by acquainting the affected groups with new ideas and new ambitions may have an effect on the birthrate. For example, there is some evidence to suggest that the birthrate among families engaged in cottage industry activity producing cloth is higher than among families whose breadwinner works in a factory producing cloth. It is probably a safe generalization to make that the technique of the cottage industry is more suitable, *ceteris paribus*, to the underdeveloped country than is the technique of the factory. The explanation of this apparent side effect on the birthrate would seem to be in terms of the argument just stated: the factory system creates a different environment from the cottage system and this new environment by upsetting the routine, by imposing new values, and so on, may produce a downward effect on the birthrate. The hypothesis is, of course, tenuous—as all hypotheses explaining the birthrate are —but does seem worth consideration in particular circumstances. If the hypothesis does hold, then it might mean that with a given quantity of investible resources, the *ceteris paribus* least cost combination of inputs will produce the largest total output, but a second technique generating a smaller total output stream may so reduce the rate of growth of population that *per capita* output is greater than with the first technique.

The kind of argument most frequently implied as to the possible effects of the choice of technique results in a more capital intensive technique than the *ceteris paribus* least cost combination would dictate. Thus, if the birthrate effect were significant enough to affect the choice of technique, then it would be necessary to adjust market prices to permit the private sector to choose the "right" technique. Evidently, for the individual investor the fact that the technique he chooses may affect the birthrate will not enter into his calculations of the profitability of his investment. A further difficulty is also relevant. It certainly cannot be said that in *all* instances will the birthrate effect dictate a combination of inputs other than the least cost combination. A general policy that subsidizes and taxes so that a higher capital-labor ratio than would be chosen on the basis of prevailing opportunity costs is selected would not, therefore, assure the maximum birthrate effect. Not only must the government decide where a higher capital-labor ratio will be profitable to the community, but it must also design its taxes and subsidies in such a manner that only these sectors are led to the use of this technique.

Again the awkward situation emerges that an argument that may be applicable imposes such major measurement and implementation problems that its practical importance is severely dampened. What does seem clear enough, however, is that the possibility of gain flowing from a side effect on the birthrate is real enough to be explicitly considered in particular instances. Some attention then must be given to how it can be introduced formally into the *SMP* criterion. Strong emphasis, however, is to be placed on the conclusion of Chapter 14 to the effect that the population problem is not one that can be solved by relying on side effects. A direct attack on the problem is essential.

C. LABOR AND MANAGEMENT TRAINING

The possible side effect of the choice of technique or of product on the training of labor and management rests on two hypotheses. The first is that introducing labor and management personnel to new processes will subject them to the necessity—as opposed to the opportunity—of learning new ways of doing things. In learning new methods, both categories of agents are equipping themselves to develop their capacities in such a manner that a more rapid rate of technological progress and of innovation becomes possible. A simple illustration may be found in agriculture. The agricultural worker in the low income country must not only learn to farm differently from the way his grandfather did, he must also learn to farm differently in virtually each year relative to the way in which he farmed in the previous year, if he is to realize the full value of newly available knowledge, or even to be interested in acquiring that knowledge. A training effect requires contact with new techniques and processes by the work force. Workers must be confronted with the necessity to learn how to adapt to new situations. Although it is not a priori impossible that new techniques be consistent with the least cost combinations, there is no necessity that they should be.

The second hypothesis has to do with the sources of technological improvement. The major inventions and innovations that increase the effectiveness of labor independent of capital are—as was discussed in Chapter 11—largely organizational and administrative in nature, while technical improvements most frequently involve physical capital. Also, most technical improvements emerge from a study of the production process and an awareness of the advantages and possibilities of increased efficiency. Thus, the more capital intensive process may produce more rapid technical improvement than the less capital intensive process, both because the use of physical capital lends itself much more to technical change than does the use of labor, and because the use of a machine may make the management more cost-conscious than the use of labor. The latter reason is especially relevant in societies where labor is relatively abundant, and where social pressure obligates the paying of many persons quite irrespective of their contribution to output.

If external consequences of such training are temporarily ignored, this side effect would be reflected in the cost or income streams generated by the several available processes. This side effect would generally be reflected in declining operating costs for several years due to the effect on labor training. The present value of these cost reductions will measure the returns attributable to these side effects, as the costs for the other techniques that produced no such side effects would be unaffected. The cost of this effect would be the increased initial outlay associated with the technique producing the side effect relative to the initial outlay of the technique producing the same direct effect. To the extent this side effect is significant in magnitude and is foreseen and correctly measured and hence included in estimating the costs attributed to the several available techniques, it will be included as a relevant consideration in the choice of technique by the profit-seeking firm. Thus, here, the problem is not to devise a tax or subsidy that leads to a particular input combination, and there is no necessary conflict between the least cost process and one that exploits the training and innovation effect imposed and taught by a particular process. The task is rather to make these effects understood and quantified, and therefore included in the estimates of output and cost streams. But this objective in no sense arises out of the peculiarities of the training and innovation effect, but is again an essential part of the environment in which rational decisions may be made. It may then be concluded that the implications of a possible training effect arising from the choice of technique are not that actions must be taken that are contrary to those to be employed if the least opportunity cost combination of inputs is sought. Indeed, the exact opposite seems to be the case. A full recognition and quantification of the training effect will lead to the correct choice, and the policy objective then should be to provide knowledge and data on the implications of the training impact and the achievement of the equality between the prices entering into the decision-making and economy-wide opportunity costs.

D. FURTHER SIDE EFFECTS

One of the difficulties of introducing side effects is to know where to begin and when to stop. A whole series of possibilities readily present themselves. One could, for example, mention a possible effect on the ability of the economy to attract foreign capital as a potentially significant side effect of any number of investment projects. Similarly, considerations as to the quality of the product may be brought into the picture especially with respect to foreign markets. Or possibly an effect on the flexibility of plant (i.e., ability to adjust to a changing demand or to an increased demand in the future) should be recognized. If one includes such things as effect on morale, on political stability, then a virtually unlimited number of effects could be traced down and given some sort of value. A reasonable case can be made for the inclusion of any of these possible effects, as well as others, that might be mentioned, and in a specific case, the inclusion of such effects would not only be reasonable, it would be accurate as well.

There are, however, severe dangers in an indiscriminate inclusion of side effects in the appraisal of various projects. All of the problems mentioned in Section II of this chapter with respect to projecting output and cost streams are multiplied when applied to side effects. As the brief survey above of types of side effects indicates, their magnitudes are probably beyond secure measurement, and, in many cases, their very existence is open to legitimate question. It is especially important to recognize that no simple rule has emerged that may be followed that will enable all effects to be realized. For example, there are no arguments, and certainly no empirical evidence, that lead to the conclusion that maximum capital-labor ratios will always (or ever) lead to the "right" techniques and projects. Nor can it be said that minimization of the use of capital—even in the economy of Chapter 7—will always be "right." Nor are there convincing arguments or data that point to manufacturing and away from agriculture as the rule to follow. The absence of the possibility of such rules means that the empirical question remains a most strategic part of the whole problem.

It is equally important to recognize that all of the side effects mentioned can be sought directly. The role of tax and wage policy and of investment opportunities will surely have a much greater effect on the saving rate than will the choice of project or the choice of technique. Similarly, direct approaches to population control, to labor training, to technological change, and all the rest are likely to be much more rewarding than is reliance on the side effects.

Despite these warnings and disclaimers as to the importance of side effects, they cannot be completely ignored. A brief word on their introduction into the *SMP* criterion is therefore necessary.

E. An Expanded *SMP* Criterion

The possibility of side effects does not mean that the *SMP* criterion is inappropriate. It means merely the measurement of the output and cost streams must be expanded to include their impact on the projected streams. To do this in a rigorous fashion is more awkward than difficult, but will not be attempted here. The following simplified approach is suggested.

The *SMP* is to be divided into two components. The first is the measure, as applied in Section II, when side effects were not considered. This measure should always be computed separately. The second component, simply added to the first, shows the impact of the side effects. The side effect component also should always be computed separately. The side effect must be converted to an income stream (or a *per capita* income stream) in order to be introduced into the *SMP* criterion. For example, one must estimate not only the differential saving rate associated with a given project, but the income associated with the additional saving as well. The same holds for labor-training effects, technological change effects, and all the others. These side effect income streams must also be discounted by the "appropriate" rate of interest. Some of the side effects have a life much longer than the project that generates them, and presumably should be discounted over this longer period. To do this seems an unnecessary refinement and little is lost, in most instances, by assuming that discount period for the project itself applies to all components of the *SMP*. The expanded version of the *SMP*'s of the potential projects are ranked as before, and the investment funds allocated to the highest ranking projects to the extent possible.

IV. The Interdependence Effect

The argument to this point has rested on the assumption that the various sectors of the economy in which investment may take place could be considered independent of each other. With this assumption, it was possible to compute the *SMP* of each potential project without reference to what was happening in other sectors. The argument of Chapter 4 showed that such an assumption could at best be only an initial step. In general, investment in Sector j will have repercussions on Sector i of such a kind that decisions as to the allocation of investment funds are affected. It is the purpose of this section to examine how recognition of the type of interdependence introduced in Chapter 4 does affect the investment decisions.

The major assumptions of the previous sections remain. There is a given quantity of investible resources for investment, determined independently of the profitability of available investment opportunities. These resources are available at constant cost until their supply is exhausted. There is also a "given" rate of discount whose origins are discussed in the next chapter. Finally, prices of primary inputs equal their opportunity costs also given from outside though something more on this matter can be said in the context of the current discussion. Also some remarks on the different effects of constant and decreasing costs is introduced here.

Look again at Table II in Chapter 4, as it will serve as the basis for considering the present side of the allocation problem. The table shows three productive sectors, the export sector, and the corresponding import sectors. Each productive sector is assumed to have three techniques of production currently known to it. The techniques are shown by the three activity columns for each sector. Thus the product of Sector I can be produced domestically in one of three possible ways, or it can be imported. Two types of primary inputs are isolated, capital and labor. The prices of the primary inputs are given at the outset, and are equal to prevailing estimates of opportunity costs.

Suppose that Expression 11 of Chapter 4 holds, i.e.,

$$P_j = \sum_i a_{ij} P_i + l_j P_l + k_j P_k \tag{1}$$

where P_j is the price of the jth output and is made equal to the cost of all produced inputs (P_i) and primary inputs, labor and capital, used in its production. The a_{ij}, l_j and k_j are the coefficients describing the inputs required for the production of one unit of output of j for a particular activity. In equilibrium the profit in each sector as computed earlier is therefore necessarily zero.

The question now is how does this interdependence of sectors affect the allocation decision.

The *SMP* criterion remains valid. In terms of the system defined by Table II, the *SMP* of a particular activity is

$$SMP_j = \frac{P_j - (\sum a_{ij} P_i + l_j P_l)}{k_j} \tag{2}$$

This is, of course, identical to the *SMP* of projects as computed in Sections II and III so long as all prices of inputs are equilibrium prices. And the same argument holds as to ranking projects by their *SMP*'s and allocating all available investible resources among those projects with the highest *SMP*. What then is gained by introducing interdependence? In general, the answer is very easy: investment in Sector i affects the *SMP* in Sector j because of the possible impact on the cost and revenue streams of the latter sector. For example, investment in Sector i may reduce the price of its product relative to other prices, and if product i is used by Sector j then the *SMP* of the latter will rise. Therefore, whether the SMP_j ranks high enough to merit a claim for investible funds may depend on whether investment is also concurrently taking place in Sector i. Or if expansion of Sector i requires inputs from the jth Sector, investment in i will thereby affect the demand for j's output and so affect its *SMP*. The possibility of decreasing costs in any sector increases the importance of these interindustry links. These remarks mean simply that it is inappropriate to rank *SMP* of individual projects without specifying the total investment composition.

A. PRICE EFFECTS

To maintain the competitive equilibrium as defined in an economy where net investment and technological change are occurring, prices must either reflect future as well as present costs and demand, or all investors must know what prices in the future will be and invest in such a way that their expectations prove correct. But this is to place a burden on prices that cannot be carried in any economy, and certainly not in the economy of Chapter 7. The point does, however, suggest that one important attack on the problem is not only a quickly responding price system, but also widespread knowledge of the composition of current investment. Knowledge of the composition of current investment, if acted on, would serve as a sort of future's pricing market, which is discussed later.

There are two separate questions: on the one hand, the question of the sector in which investment should take place in order to meet the *SMP* criterion, and then the more difficult question of how much investment should be allocated to the sectors that are selected.

To answer the first question, consider a very simple illustration. Suppose that there are two sectors, steel production and automobile production, that are related in that the production of one automobile requires .5 tons of steel as an input. Both products are currently imported in amounts of 1,000 tons of steel and 2,000 automobiles. Now a new technique becomes available that enables the domestic production of steel at a cost below the imported price. So a domestic steel plant becomes profitable, and is built to supply 1,000 tons of steel, the present domestic demand. Is this large enough? Probably not, because if steel prices are reduced as a consequence of the lower costs of producing it, then investment in automobile production may become profitable. If 1,000 cars are produced domestically, then 500 tons of new demand for steel is added to the already existing demand of 1,000. Indeed with several sectors using steel, demand for steel at the new lower price will increase by more than the 500 associated with the investment in the automobile industry.

In this example, the investment may be presumed to have occurred in the "right" sector, but was not of the "right" amount. The inadequate amount of the investment would soon evidence itself by excess demand for steel, and presumably investment in the steel industry would catch up in the next period. This lag may be costly, and if an unpredicted increase in demand for steel occurs in the next period also, the size of the investment in that period will again be inadequate.

Prices alone may never do the job if there are economies of scale. In the example used here suppose that at an output of 1,500 tons of steel costs were low enough to warrant investment, but this was not the case at a rate of output of 1,000. The failure to appreciate that the demand would in fact be 1,500—for the reasons stated in the previous paragraph—means that an investment in a profitable sector is overlooked. In this case, investment would not take place in the "right" sectors, and the increment in output would be less than would be the case if the scale and interdependence effects were both recognized.

Other examples could be developed, but the simple ones just discussed illustrate the way price effects in the interindustry model affect the allocation question. Before trying to appraise the importance of such effects, a brief comment is necessary on non-price forms of interdependence.

B. NON-PRICE EFFECTS   External Economies

The examples and analyses just concluded were all in terms of the effect of a particular investment project on the prices of inputs or outputs. There are, also, other interdependence effects that cannot, or in general, are not transmitted from one sector to another through price changes in inputs. The most frequently cited example has to do with inputs in the production function of one activity from another for which no payment can be secured. A simple (and frequently used) illustration is the making of honey in one sector and the growing (e.g.) of peaches and oranges. The peach and orange producing sector has no way to impose payment on the beekeeper for allowing his bees to use the peach and orange blossoms to make honey. Evidently, however, the destruction of the peach and orange orchard would impose major difficulties on the honey-making sector. The importance of this type of external effect is probably quite limited, but there are two other types of activities—educational and technical research —that are highly relevant and must be introduced formally into the allocation model in a manner different from that described in the previous section.

Consider education first. The shadow price of trained labor (equals its marginal product) measures the contribution that one more unit of this resource can make to the economy when it is used in the most productive sector. Thus the profitability of allocating investible resources to producing trained labor depends on the productivity of such labor in the economy, and this determines its shadow price. If the cost of training a unit of labor is less than the shadow price of the labor, it is profitable for the community to allocate investible resources to increasing the supply of labor. Whether or not resources should be so allocated with a limited quantity of investible resources, depends upon the *SMP* of this investment relative to alternative uses of the resources. It is perhaps worth repeating that an educated populace has additional effects that cannot be appropriately described in an interindustry model, as well as being itself a final good, but still the primary question to ask about outlays on education in a developing economy is simply whether such investment pays.

The second type of activity that deserves a special comment in the present context is technical research. The result of such research, if successful, would be a reduction in the input of capital and/or labor per unit in some activities at all rates of output. The consequence of these reductions on the performance of the economy provides the source of the profitability of such investment. To measure the full impact of the reduction in the input coefficients—and hence to measure the profitability of the technical research activity—requires comparing the output of the system with the new coefficients with that of the system for the previous set of coefficients. The profitability of using investible resources for technical research—e.g., finding a new production activity for bicycles, devising a new fertilizer, and so on—is the difference in the output between the new and the previous matrix with the same quantity of primary inputs. It is perhaps appropriate to recall the emphasis placed on the uncertainty that surrounds the outcome of research activity, as well as that placed on the existence of likely lags in the realization of the impact.

With respect both to manpower training and technical research, the objective of the activity is to modify the matrix or to increase the available resources rather than to work through a given matrix with a given quantity of investible resources. Their impact on the system then arises almost entirely from their interdependence effects with few if any direct or side effects. Hence, the necessity to use a more complicated approach to measuring profitability. Also, education and research are rarely purchased in the way that iron ore is purchased in order to make steel, but the mere fact that an activity is not effectively identified and measured in the market may complicate the problem for the public authority, but in no sense does it alter the underlying arguments.

C. The Relevance of the Interindustry Model for the Allocation Problem

Failure to recognize the links that one sector has with another in deciding where and by how much to expand capacity may lead to investment in the wrong sector, and is almost sure to result in an incorrect amount of investment in the sectors. This is true even if primary inputs are valued at their opportunity cost. The difficulty arises from the fact that investment in one sector affects the prices of its output and those of the producers of its inputs. And the price changes then affect the pattern of *SMP*'s that would be eligible to merit investment funds. Only if prices remain unchanged as investment takes place or if future prices are all universally and accurately known, would it be appropriate to ignore interdependence.

One can then imagine a giant Planning Office that planned and carried out all the investment activities, and that had all the necessary data on inputs, technology, technical change, demand curves, and the like (and a giant electronic computer) at its disposal. This office could then turn the allocation problem into a programming problem, and obtain a solution in the manner described in the bibliographical references for this chapter.

Despite the satisfaction of arriving at a formal solution in this way, it is doubtful that it provides a practical answer to the problems involved. There are great demands for data that cannot be met satisfactorily in the foreseeable future with such an approach and, of course, projections with large elements of uncertainty attached to them must always be made. Also, although the evidence is not completely convincing on this point, it is probably correct to say that resources used in this way—i.e., to collect data, invert matrices, and so on—have higher productivity elsewhere in the economy. At the same time, it is surely grossly misleading to assume that no interdependence exists (that all the a_{ij} are zero) in making allocation decisions. The practical problem then is to insure consideration of the interdependence effects in the allocating process without solving formally a programming problem. Two approaches may be suggested.

All investment decisions may be made by the public authority. In this event, knowledge of how much investment is in which sector would always be known and directly controllable, and, with some data on interdependence, the allocation pattern and magnitude of investment could be adjusted to approximate the ideal. The great difficulty with this solution is in terms of the administrative cost of such control, and the almost certain fact that if no investment were permitted outside the public sector, total investment would be sure to suffer.

Alternatively, and of more practical relevance, the government may assume the task of accumulating as complete data as possible on investment projects under way in the economy in addition to information on supply and demand developments in as many markets as is feasible. Data on investment projects are available from a wide variety of sources, e.g., banks, development corporations, government lending agencies, corporation reports, and so forth. And a requirement that prospective investors report their intention to a public authority is a modest bit of red tape, the return on which is sufficient to justify its existence. These data would then be made readily available to the general public.

Armed with these data, the next task would be that of forecasting future prices to the extent that prices are affected by the investment programs. Such price information would then be made as widely known as possible to lenders, borrowers, and potential investors. Given that this information is made available to all interested persons, it may be assumed that the market, applying the relevant discount factor, will choose its investment projects in a manner that approaches the ideal, assuming these future prices. In a general way, this sort of arrangement serves as a surrogate futures market. This arrangement does not mean that the government sector would not undertake any investment activity, but only that it would not be the sole investor in the community. One might, for example, be able to define certain areas of activity where the external effects are particularly far reaching, i.e., many sectors are affected by their expansion. It would then be especially important that the correct level of investment in these sectors be achieved. Consequently, a case might be made that the government—with its presumed greater information on the interdependence network of the economy—should assume primary responsibility for investment activity in these sectors. Social overhead capital is frequently in this category, and of course government control of these activities is very common. The same might also be true of large industries where economies of scale were significant.

How effective this approach is to the problem of determining and reaching the optimal pattern and magnitudes of investment depends on the effectiveness of the government agency charged with accumulating, analyzing, and distributing the relevant data, and the extent to which entrepreneurs—government and private—respond to predicted future prices. But the risks appear less than those attached to alternative methods, and for most of the low income countries, the task appears possible to undertake.

V. Conclusion

The objective of this chapter has been to establish a general model within which an examination of the impact of investment projects could be explored. The criterion by which such an examination is conducted is that conventionally designated as *SMP*, the social marginal product of an investment project. The *SMP* is defined as the ratio of the present value of output minus the present value of costs over the required amount of capital. The choice of discount factor is crucial, and is discussed in the next chapter. The *SMP* criterion is applicable in all stages of the examination although the measurement problems associated with its use may vary.

In the simplest stage of the analysis, only the direct effects of the investment were considered. Even here measurement problems were severe and heavy with uncertainty. Uncertainty was increased when education or technical knowledge were considered or when a project might yield a number of different categories of products—irrigation, clean water, flood control.

In the second stage of the examination it was recognized that projects may have "side effects" that are of relevance to the development problem. Special emphasis was given to possible effects on saving, on population growth, and on labor training and management, although it was recognized that a great variety of other side effects could be isolated, and at times may be quite relevant. The side effect stage raises new problems of measurement and new sources of uncertainty, and is made more difficult by virtue of the fact that no general rule on the exploitation of side effects emerged. It was found clearly incorrect to assume that maximum favorable side effects are associated with high capital-labor ratios, or with industry as opposed to agriculture, or any other simple guide line. Finally, all side effects can be attacked directly through fiscal policy, population policy, education, and so on. The conclusion, however, remains that some attention must be given to the possibility of side effects in appraising certain projects.

Finally, in the third stage the interdependence of the *SMP*'s of various projects was recognized and illustrated, and its role in the allocation process elaborated. The major conclusion here was that projects affect the *SMP* of other sectors, and thereby affect the cost and income stream that would be generated were investment made in the affected sectors.

Throughout, the assumption was made that the price of primary inputs always equaled their opportunity cost. This equality was assumed to be brought about by government fiscal and tax policies. This is a key assumption of the whole story, and cannot be modified without requiring a complete modification, even alteration of the criterion. The other assumptions were made to simplify the exposition, and are not believed to be of great importance for the analysis.

Bibliography

A rather complete survey of the literature on the criterion problem is the United Nations, *Manual on Economic Development Projects* (New York: United Nations, 1958), Pt. 2. Less comprehensive surveys are *Economic Bulletin for Asia and the Far East,* VI (June, 1961) and Hollis B. Chenery, "Comparative Advantage and Development Policy" *American Economic Review,* LI (March, 1961).

Part One of the United Nations *Manual* is a useful review of the direct effects of investment, and also contains a number of revealing illustrative cases.

Many important articles have been written on the side effects of investments. See especially Walter Galenson and Harvey Leibenstein, "Investment Criteria, Productivity and Economic Development," *The Quarterly Journal of Economics,* LXIX (August, 1955); Hollis B. Chenery, "The Application of Investment Criteria," *Quarterly Journal of Economics,* LXVII (February, 1953); Otto Eckstein, "Investment Criteria for Economic Development and the Theory of Intertemporal Welfare Economics," *Quarterly Journal of Economics,* LXXI (February, 1957); A. K. Sen, *Choice of Technique* (Oxford: Basil Blackwell, 1960); and K. A. Bohr, "Investment Criteria in Manufacturing Industries in Underdeveloped Countries," *Review of Economics and Statistics,* XXXVI (May, 1954). The argument in the text owes much to these studies.

On the interdependence effect almost all of the material originates with Hollis B. Chenery. See especially his paper in the *Economic Bulletin for Latin America* (March, 1958) and his "The Interdependence of Investment Decisions" in *The Allocation of Economic Resources* (Stanford: Stanford University Press, 1959) and the article in *The American Economic Review,* LI (March, 1961) cited above. See also Tibor Scitovsky, "Two Concepts of External Economies," *Journal of Political Economy,* LXIV (April, 1954) and J. A. Stockfish "External Economies, Investment, and Foresight," *The Journal of Political Economy,* LXIII (October, 1955).

A number of references on the general criterion problem are supplied at the end of Chapter 16.

Chapter 16

FURTHER ASPECTS
OF THE ALLOCATION PROBLEM

The previous chapter reviewed the allocation problem within the confines of very rigid assumptions. It is now necessary to consider a variety of other aspects associated with the arguments already developed. The most important issue to be considered is the choice of discount factor. This question will be discussed in Section I. Section II considers very briefly a number of specific points that are—or might be—relevant in the decision on the use of investment funds. Here, timing of investment, length of life of projects, possible alternatives to the SMP criterion, and other similar questions are noted. Then some further attention must be given to the specific role of the government in assuring the "right" allocation of investible resources. In the final section, some very broad generalizations about the use of investment funds in the developing economy are formulated from the content of this chapter.

I. The Rate of Discount

The computation of the social marginal productivity of investment projects in the previous chapter required a rate of interest in order to discount future cost and income streams. In Chapter 15, the interest rate was assumed known, and now its source is to be considered. Some of the issues relevant to this question were discussed in Chapter 8 on "The Optimal Saving Problem," and frequent reference is made with that chapter in the present discussion. There the question had to do with the distribution of income and consumption toward the future, and the chief variable in that problem is the level of saving and investment, not the rate of discount. The question asked of the discount rate is that of the weight to be attached to consumption at different times in the future. Attention in

Chapter 8 was, therefore, centered on how much investment, and the answer was in terms of a value judgment made by political leaders acting in response to what they conceived the long-run public interest to be. In particular, the assumption was made that the level of investment was independent of the productivity of investment. The rate of interest is also considered to be a value judgment derived from an understanding of the development process. It is helpful, however, to outline the considerations that make this conclusion plausible.

A. THE MARKET RATE OF INTEREST AS A NORMATIVE CONCEPT

In a perfectly competitive economy, the firm that maximizes profits employs each factor up to the point where the present value of the "certainty equivalent" of the net income stream created by the marginal outlay is zero. The interest rate used to compute the present value is determined in the capital market by the interaction of the supply of saving and the demand for investment funds. The supply of saving is based on the community's valuation of future goods relative to present goods—its time preference—and the demand for investment funds on the productivity of capital. An interest rate, so determined, is assumed to equate the disutility of postponing the marginal "unit" of consumption with the utility of the increment in income obtained from the marginal "unit" of capital. Thus, the utility enjoyed by the economy is maximized.

The assumption of perfect competition throughout the economy rules out a number of complications, especially those having to do with external economies, decreasing costs, and factor price-opportunity cost inequalities. The term "certainty equivalent" implies either perfect foresight about supply and demand of factors, products, and technology or knowledge of a probability distribution of the relevant income and cost streams by both saver and investor. Also, the size distribution of income must be assumed optimal in some sense. With these assumptions, the argument concludes that an interest rate, which equates the marginal productivity of capital and marginal-time preference of income recipients, has normative significance. Here, of course, both the level of saving and the interest rate are simultaneously determined.

B. AN ALTERNATIVE APPROACH

There are two general reasons why this argument is of little help as a guide to public policy in the context of the developing economy.

The first and most obvious reason is simply that the assumptions of perfect competition do not apply, and the required amount of information on technology, income streams, and the like is not available. The capital market is sure to be quite imperfect and all kinds of factors—ignorance of alternatives, irrational biases against particular forms of financing, long lags, and so on—prevent the market from functioning in the manner required to give normative meaning to the market rate of interest as a price. The large number of rates observed in the various markets in the underdeveloped economy cannot be explained simply in terms of risk premiums, but must be accounted for by the failure of the market to function in accord with the competitive model.

A second objection to the normative argument is more fundamental, especially in the development context. A case can be made that the time preference of the society is not some kind of an average of the time preferences of the individuals making up that society. More specifically, it may be assumed that individuals have two different time-preference maps, one that determines market actions and one that governs actions in essentially political or national matters. Earlier, the point was made that one of the reasons that levying and collecting taxes in the underdeveloped country is so difficult is that everyone is convinced that no one else will pay taxes. If, however, the members of the community were convinced that the collection of taxes was general and the revenues devoted to the announced purposes, tax payments would be more nearly consistent with the demands of development. In the time preference context, it is quite clear that individual time preferences expressed in the market are extremely high, i.e., an increase in consumption tomorrow is valued much higher than a similar increase three years from tomorrow. This is explained in terms of the extremely low level of current consumption, and the not insignificant probability of not being alive three years from tomorrow.

Despite this obvious market attitude, it is also correct to argue that "development" is a widely and sincerely accepted goal of economic and political policy. Projects that contribute to that goal are thus acceptable even though they violate the individual time preferences revealed in non-development, market phenomena. Development projects then take on the nature of a public good (even when done by the private sector) traditionally defined as "psychically consumed simultaneously by all members of society." The reward from the investment in the projects is not measured in terms of increased future consumption relative to present consumption for yourself on your heirs, but rather in terms of the immediate satisfaction derived from recognizing and contributing to the development effort. This attitude, one of the most important ways in which "nationalism" enters directly into the development process, is not to be confused with the argument that the government must look after the interests of the future generations because of the myopia of the market. The point is rather that, just as with the level of investment, the members of a community have a different frame of reference when considering national development schemes from the same individuals when pursuing private gain.

The validity of this argument varies, of course, from country to country, but seems to be generally applicable in the type of economy described in Chapter 7. Perhaps the chief difficulty, which was mentioned earlier in another connection, is the problem of convincing people that development is possible. This latter problem is magnified in countries where corruption in the government is an established and well-known routine.

/ These two reasons—the gross imperfections in the capital market in the underdeveloped country and the peculiar properties of development expenditures—suggest that the choice of interest rate is a matter for public decision making, rather than for market determination. The second argument is of great relevance, for if the difficulty were only that of imperfect capital markets, the job confronting the policy maker would be that of trying to estimate what the rate would be in a free, perfect market. With the introduction of the second consideration, however, an argument justifying a particular discount rate cannot be made in these simple terms.

C. THE CHOICE OF DISCOUNT RATE

1. General Considerations. The main consequence of the preceding argument is that the discount rate chosen by the planning authorities should be lower than that suggested by market evidence. The alternative project's *SMP*'s are ranked on the assumption of a given interest rate. A reduction in that interest rate from a given level will raise the *SMP* of all projects because of the effect on fixed costs, with the greater effect on the projects or activities with greatest capital intensity, i.e., greatest capital-labor ratio. Also, projects that have a large yield in the more distant future are benefited relative to those whose yield is realized earlier and then falls. If, then, the discount factor is below the market-time preference indicator, the investible funds will be used in projects whose characteristics are similar to those that would be chosen if more saving were available. In this sense, the lower interest rate is something of a substitute for increased saving.

The argument is most relevant when two income streams from alternative projects cross each other. Consider the simple diagrams below. On the left, two projects *A* and *B* both have the same capital cost and net income streams as drawn. In comparing these two projects, the choice of discount rate is irrelevant. Project *A* always wins. On the other hand, the choice between *C* and *D* (assuming their capital costs the same) depends very much on the discount factor. A "high" discount rate would rule out *C*, while a "low" one would result in its being chosen.

/ The main reason that considerable confidence can be expressed in the view that the "social" time preference is less (i.e., dictates a lower discount factor) than the "private market" time preference, emerges from the view of the development process outlined in the preceding chapters. Those chapters placed great emphasis on (*inter alia*) the creation of an indigenous source of supply of new applied technical knowledge. More capital,

NET INCOME
FROM PROJECTS

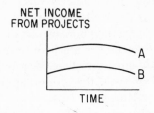

TIME

NET INCOME
FROM PROJECTS

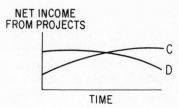

TIME

suitable for the underdeveloped country, means neither more wooden plows nor the huge ground-covering farm machines of Iowa or the Ukraine. Rather, it means more capital embodying a technology that is "suitable"— as defined in Chapter 11—to the economy of Chapter 7. Resources must then be allocated to the kind of technical research already discussed. The same is true for educational activities, for birth control policies, and the wide range of other factors that have emerged as part of the development process. Commitment to development means commitment to these projects. The *SMP* of such projects are thus not lower than alternative uses resources, but they do, in most instances, require a longer period for their full fruits to be realized. Indeed, the arguments above, especially in Part Three, suggest quite strongly that unless resources are used for technical research, labor training, and the like, then resources used in the more direct product-yielding activities may find their *SMP*'s falling embarrassingly low in the developing country. All of the problems associated with measurement, uncertainty, external effects, and the like, of course, continue to plague the estimating of the contribution of investing in these position variables.

What these various arguments assert may be summarized as follows: A general community desire for development suggests that the social-time preference of the income recipients in the underdevelopd country cannot be appropriately represented by either the market rate of interest, nor the latter corrected for market imperfections. It must, therefore, be determined by the government on the basis of an understanding of how the development process works, i.e., of how the economy of Chapter 7 can be converted to that described in Chapters 2 through 6. To do this requires innovations, production of skills, control of the birthrate, and the like. Investment in these activities is essential, but their yield is likely to be long in maturing. Hence the conclusion that the social rate of time preference is below that figure suggested in the private markets.

Can something more specific be said?

2. Specific Considerations. To be much more specific would require a level of detail about a particular economy that cannot appropriately be given here, but some suggestions may be given. One approach might be to try manipulating the interest rate in the market through fiscal and monetary policy in order to reflect the desired level, and whatever level was obtainable consistent with price and balance of payments stability would be the "right" rate. In an economy where the taxing bureaucracy and fiscal system are firmly established, such an approach has much to recommend it. In the type of economy that is under discussion here, to follow this approach would probably mean to forget all about the considerations that underlie the selection of the "right" rate of interest.

Another approach would be to choose the interest rate that would result in the last project included having an *SMP* of exactly zero. This would apparently mean that the interest rate did in fact equate the supply of saving with the demand for investment. The appraisal of the current status of the development process in a given environment would reveal strategic areas of investments—areas in which investment must currently take place if the development effort is to move on from the position already reached. Suppose this area is technical research or possibly some educational activity. Such areas, as already noted, are likely to require a longer period for their yield to be realized than are alternative investments in directly productive activities. Now choose the discount factor that makes these "development" projects just marginal, i.e., makes their *SMP* just positive, with all due regard to uncertainty, side effects, interdependence effects, and the like to which attention has already been called.

Such an approach has advantages and problems. The chief advantage is that all projects with higher *SMP*'s than the strategic "development" projects would be included. This would tend to counteract any resentment and dissatisfactions among the population with too heavy emphasis on investments the yields of which were far away. The fact that the social-time preference is less than the private-market-time preference does not mean that the latter can be ignored, and this seems to be an effective way of doing it. (Another possibility would be to have two discount factors, one for all development projects and one for "other." This is not completely impossible, but seems to introduce even more complications than the present method.)

（ There are two difficulties of some magnitude. First is achieving firm enough insight into the development process to gain a secure view on which "development" projects are currently crucial and merit the marginal classification. This point could presumably be satisfied with sufficient study and analysis. The second involves simply the fact that with such a discount factor there is no assurance that the level of investment is suitable; it may be too large or too small. The approach indeed amounts to arguing that certain projects must have a present value sufficient to be included in the investment program, and all others with a higher *SMP* must also be included. Therefore, the level of the investment program must be large enough to accomplish this. It would mean that the level of investment was related to the productivity of the investment, and for reasons outlined in Chapter 8 this does not seem possible in the context of the underdeveloped economy. ||

All of these approaches are relevant and their consideration reveals certain aspects of the problem that will enable the policy maker to be somewhat better informed to approach his task. But none solves all problems. Finally, it appears necessary to select the discount factor used to rank *SMP*'s at the time that the level of investment is estimated, and to adjust and modify as the results of these decisions begin to unfurl. That is, the selection of the discount factor must rest entirely on the understanding and insight of the development authorities into the functioning of the economy with no simple rules to follow. And the more specific something that can be said is simply that the greater knowledge the decision maker has of the development process, the more likely he is to choose the "right" rate.

The lengthy consideration given here to the choice of discount rate is merited not merely by the fact that it is required in the *SMP* criterion. When the investment allocation problem is expanded to include research, education, and so on—as it must be—as well as multipurpose dams and textile mills, the particular rate chosen can make or break the effectiveness of a development program at a given time. These sections have pointed up this important role. The role of the interest rate as a tool of monetary and financial policy is considered in Chapter 17.

II. Some Further Aspects of the Allocation Problem

There are any number of aspects of the allocation problem that have not been explicitly included in the discussion to this point. It is useful to call attention to some of these in order to give a more complete picture (or at least enumeration) of the issues involved in this important problem.

A. LENGTH OF LIFE OF THE NEW CAPITAL

When the project considered takes the form of physical capital, alternative projects may have different lengths of life. For example, alternatives for the increased production of electricity may include a conventional and nuclear power station where the former will last for thirty years and the latter twenty years. The *SMP* of the conventional power plant may be greater than that of the nuclear one simply because of the additional ten years of life that it has. But the extra life also involves a cost in that it precludes the taking advantage of any new technology that over the extra ten years may become available. (This is true unless the new technology is so effective that, if it were used, total costs on the new power plant would be below variable costs on the old.) The shorter lived project does not have this cost.

To make the two projects comparable as of the present time, it is necessary to add to the present value of the twenty-year project the expected present value (for a ten-year period) of a specific investment that can be made at the end of twenty years. The income accruing from this new project would, of course, be discounted all the way to the present period. To do this requires a great deal of information, and adds significantly to the uncertainty already inherent in the project selection problem. Some such approach is necessary, however, and is particularly relevant in decisions to commit resources to very large, long lasting projects.

The argument also points up again the technology problem. Not only is availability of information about current technology part of the allocation problem, but so also are data about future technology. In some cases, such data are lacking completely, but in others—e.g., use of nuclear power, desalination of sea water, effective oral contraceptives, and so on—there is information that should be available to the decision maker.

B. Timing of Investment

A problem similar to the one just stated has to do with when to undertake a particular project. For example, a particular project may have an SMP high enough to merit its inclusion in the investment program of the current period. The question may still be asked whether the same project would have enough higher SMP at a later time to warrant postponing its construction. A higher SMP could result from changes in demand, changes in operating costs (for example, due to wage-rate changes), or changes in technology so that the same project three years hence may have a quite different impact on the system from the impact that it now has. The costs of a postponement must also include the foregone benefits of the postponed project relative to the one included in its place. Again, in this case, complete evaluation of a project involves looking ahead to see the factors that a few years hence will determine the SMP of a similar project.

This particular point has its greatest relevance with respect to social overhead projects—highways, railroads, power plants—and to large scale multipurpose projects such as dams, educational plants, and the like. The relevance arises out of the fact that the contribution to the capacity of the economy of such projects depends so heavily on what else is happening or is about to happen in the economy. Suppose that a large scale dam that will supply both power and irrigation is contemplated. The latter requires a great deal of ditch digging and other things on the part of the individual farmers in order to have any effect on the economy. Farmers may for any of a great variety of reasons be unable to build their part of the undertaking for some time after the construction of the dam. The SMP of the project may still be relatively high due to the increased output of power, but it might be much higher ten years from now after the farmers have had some training and extension service help. A question would then arise as to whether postponement was profitable. A similar argument would apply to research. The development of a blueprint for a new technique contributes to growth only if it is widely employed. And postponement of research might be in order, if anticipations are such that the wider acceptability of a new technique in a few years will add enough to the *SMP* to warrant its postponement.

The point cannot be emphasized very much for purely practical reasons. The *SMP's* of all projects obviously cannot be computed for each point of time in the future. For the great majority of projects ignoring the timing problem does little harm, but it does loom large and should, therefore, be considered in the larger projects where so much depends on the responsiveness of other parts of the system to the creation of a new capital item.

C. ALTERNATIVE CRITERIA

The criterion on which the preceding chapter and this one were based is that referred to as the *SMP,* defined in a rather broad way to include both side and interdependence effects.

There are a number of other possible criteria, but there seems little need to review them in detail. There are several such reviews, and the reader interested in studying alternative formulations may consult the sources listed at the end of this chapter. A satisfactory criterion that did not depend on a discount factor would be desirable indeed. The internal rate of return is independent of an outside interest rate. It is defined as the discount rate that would just equate the cost and income streams, i.e., make the present value of the net income stream of a project zero. Projects could be ranked according to this rate, and investible funds allocated among the projects with the highest internal rate. For a variety of reasons, the internal rate has been shown to be unreliable, and in recent years has lost most of its appeal. The *SMP* as computed above is much more reliable despite the great difficulty that the choice of discount factor creates.

A number of other criteria have been suggested that try to take advantage of a particular characteristic of underdevelopment. For example, the evidence that there is widespread unemployment in the developing country has led some people to use the gross output/capital ratio as the *SMP*. The assumption underlying this approach is that the opportunity cost of all inputs except capital is zero. This *may* be a correct assumption but—as already discussed—is unlikely to be, and to proceed to use such a ratio indiscriminately will surely yield misleading results. Similarly, the great importance of foreign exchange in the development process has led to a criterion that places full weight on a project's capacity to produce for the export market. Again, this criterion may be appropriate in a given context, but it is not a satisfactory general criterion. Indeed, one can say that these—and other—alternative criteria are satisfactory only to the extent that special conditions make them reasonably close approximations to the *SMP*. In a similar vein, one can say that the appropriate criterion varies with the specific conditions in which it is applied. What was attempted here was an examination of the criterion problem under assumptions that seem generally realistic for the underdeveloped economy, but this is not meant to imply that there are no circumstances in which alternative formulations of the guiding criterion are not acceptable.

III. The Role of the Government

The preceding discussion has made little distinction between investment in the public sector and that in the private sector. The criterion was set up in a manner that, if followed completely, would be equally applicable to both private and public investment. The role of the government is complex, and it is worthwhile to try to summarize what seems to emerge as the key functions that it must play in the allocation problem.

The primary function is that of achieving equality of the prices that guide investment decisions and social opportunity costs. Brief mention of subsidy and tax schemes was made earlier, but the fact that detailed attention was not given to how this objective could be achieved is not to be interpreted to mean it is easy. It is impossible, but attempts can be made. Included in this pricing problem is the decision on the discount factor.

If this objective were fully achieved, and there were no side or interdependence effects, the problem would be virtually solved. If side effects are believed to be important, then the question arises as to whether the maximizing firm includes them in its computation. In some cases it will, in others it will not. For example, a side effect on saving or on the birthrate would not enter the firm's calculations, while an effect on labor training might well be included. Since the equality of factor price with social opportunity cost cannot ordinarily include the side effects, some additional measures are necessary to make sure they are considered. This may take the form of a subsidy, a tax, or possibly some more direct inducements. To exploit such side effects is, as shown above, a delicate and risky operation, the rewards of which are easy to exaggerate.

Then there is the more conventional type of external economy, the creation of a good or service, the disposal of which cannot be controlled by the creator. Where these are part of a project, then government action is again called for to make sure the economy does not miss out on them. What these are is difficult to say. In Chapter 11, the argument was made that firms should undertake the type of research called for in the developing economy, but a subsidy may be required. Some form of education may be in this category, and the textbook examples of bees and apple orchards, and dams and a clean water supply in particular areas should at least be noticed. The usual answer to this problem is either government ownership and operation, or a subsidy.

Finally, sectors of the economy produce not only final goods, they also produce inputs for other sectors to use in production, and, in turn, demand the products of other sectors as their own inputs. Therefore, when one sector expands, there are repercussions on others that must be taken into account in appraising investment projects. The role of the government in this task is to provide as much information on investment plans as possible to all the economy.

With all of these complications and difficulties, would it not be appropriate to conclude that a centrally planned and implemented investment program is superior to the kind analyzed here? Both approaches, of course, have major defects. A centrally planned investment program has an advantage on the interdependence problem, but is certainly much less equipped to appraise conditions as to demand and supply in local areas, and to project cost and income streams in individual sectors of the economy. Also, it seems safe to assume that the market pressure to proceed with economic rationality in almost any underdeveloped economy is greater or can be made greater than any corresponding pressure on the planning agency. Furthermore, total investment is sure to be less if limited to the public sector. A tentative conclusion then is that the government's role is that of creating the market environment so that the allocation of total investment funds conforms as nearly as possible to the *SMP* criterion. It will be argued later that this role is more nearly compatible with the resources available to most governments in underdeveloped countries than is direct control of economic activity.

IV. Conclusions on the Allocation Problem

There are so many sides to the allocation issue that firm conclusions are difficult to formulate. The following remarks are not so much "conclusions" as they are suggestions as to what conclusions might be if they could be made.

A. INVESTMENT PATTERN

Can any sort of generalization be made about the ranking of *SMP*'s of projects? Can one say that a sequence of investment beginning with agriculture, then light industry, and on to heavy industry is a general pattern? The answer is surely no to both questions. One of the conclusions that can be made is that what constitutes the right allocation depends very much indeed on the particular circumstances of the moment. More accurately, it depends on the opportunities that an economy has at any given time. With these limitations in mind, the following remarks still seem appropriate.

While no industry sequence can be generalized, the arguments of Parts One and Three suggest clearly that sustained growth depends on the continuing availability and application of new "suitable" technical knowledge in addition to a cadre of skilled workers. One can then say with some assurance that resources must be allocated for these purposes along the lines discussed in Part Three. Research on birthrate determinants is also to be included in this necessary category.

Recent efforts to measure the contribution of the various sources of growth in western countries—mainly the United States and Great Britain —show that merely more physical capital per laborer is much less important than other sources in accounting for rising *per capita* income. Measurement difficulties do not permit a very firm view on which other sources —e.g., technical knowledge, skilled labor, economics of scale, environmental factors, and so on—are most important, but the evidence does lend support to the view that technical knowledge and skilled labor are very significant. One should note that because such evidence is available for the United States and Britain does not automatically mean that it is applicable to the economy of Chapter 7.

The underdeveloped country does not have the broad base of existing capital stock with a high rate of replacement each year that the United States and Britain have. It does not then have the built-in method of introducing new knowledge via replacement that these two rich countries have. At the same time, merely making available more of the kind of physical capital that the underdeveloped country now has is no answer at all, neither is importing machines and organizational techniques from abroad. So the emphasis on the research for new blueprints and the production of the "right" skills seems merited.

The preceding discussion and available empirical evidence lend support to the view that returns on huge, multipurpose projects are often quite low. The chief reason for this was stated earlier in the discussion of the timing of investment. The real impact of such projects depends so heavily on how complementary factors in the economy respond. Part of the emphasis on these projects results from the foreign loans that are frequently available for them, but not for other things, and countries tend to feel that their opportunity cost is very low. To some extent this is not wrong, but it should mean greater efforts to get lending authorities to review their loan criteria rather than simply taking what is offered.

Any use of investible funds that contributes to the economy becoming more responsive and more adaptive to change has a high *SMP*. This includes not only the price policy discussed above, but also the use of funds to encourage mobility, to increase contact among various groups in the community, to improve taxing methods as well.

A further generalization that is appropriate has to do with the "side effects." Although it is admitted that in a given situation they can be extremely important, concentration on direct effects and the problems of interdependence will be much more rewarding. As noted already, virtually all side effects can be attacked directly.

Perhaps repeating that "good" allocation decisions must arise out of the specific knowledge of the economy available to the decision maker is in order. Relying on generalizations or on rules of thumb is not an acceptable approach to this problem.

B. IMPLEMENTATION

The arguments in this and the preceding chapter place a heavy burden on all economic agents. One can well ask whether, in an economy where the capital market is very imperfect, where there is a large non-monetized sector, where the saver and the investor are often the same individual, where price—opportunity cost equality is a dream, where political and social considerations inundate economic arguments, any effort at the establishment and implementation of an allocation criterion is worth the effort. The answer must be yes. The problem is, of course, extraordinarily difficult. If it were not so, the problem would have been solved long ago. But the very description of the underdeveloped economy in Chapter 7 shows that strong action is required. The difficulties of measurement, of projections, of identifying all the effects of a project must be recognized, but must not be allowed to lead to reliance on hunch, intuition, or politicians. Finally, the use of funds for further investigation into the effects of projects, after they have been constructed, may be expected to yield good returns. This question has been surprisingly neglected.

Bibliography

On the rate of interest problem see Otto Eckstein, *Water Resource Development* (Cambridge: Harvard University Press, 1961), pp. 94–104; Richard A. Musgrave, *The Theory of Public Finance* (New York: McGraw-Hill Book Company, 1959), pp. 86–89; Stephen A. Marglin, "The Social Rate of Discount and the Optimal Rate of Investment," *Quarterly Journal of Economics* LXXVII (February, 1963); M. S. Feldstein, "The Social Time Preference Discount Rate in Cost Benefit Analysis," *Economic Journal,* LXXIV (June, 1964); and Irving Fisher *The Theory of Interest* (New York: The Macmillan Company, 1930).

On the range of general issues involved in the whole allocation problem see Eckstein's *Water Resource Development* just mentioned and also his "A Survey of the Theory of Public Expenditure" in *Public Finances: Needs, Sources, and Utilization,* A conference of the Universities-National Bureau Committee for Economic Research (Princeton: Princeton University Press, 1961). Also Jack Hirshleifer, James C. DeHaven, Jerome W. Milliman, *Water Supply* (Chicago: The University of Chicago Press, 1960), Chaps. 6 and 7; Jack Hirschleifer, "On the Theory of Optimal Investment Decision," *Journal of Political Economy,* LXVI

(August, 1958); and M. S. Feldstein and J. S. Flemming, "The Problem of Time-Stream Evaluation: Present Value versus Internal Rate of Return Rules," *Bulletin Oxford University Institute of Economics and Statistics*, XXVI (February, 1964).

Empirical studies of the effects of projects are difficult to find. One of the most useful is K. N. Raj, *Some Economic Aspects of the Bhahkra Nangel Project* (Bombay: Asia Publishing House, 1960).

Part Five

SOME SPECIAL TOPICS

The discussions in the preceding chapters have been concerned primarily with the real aspects of development, and little attention has been directed toward financial aspects. In Chapter 5, the discussion of the role of demand in a growing economy involved some reference to financial and monetary matters as did the analysis of inflation as a means of raising the rate of capital formation in Chapter 10. But financial matters may play a strategic role in the development process, and a systematic, though brief treatment is a necessary part of the development story. In Chapter 17, therefore, an examination of some of the aspects of the financial side of development is undertaken.

Chapter 18 presents a review of a variety of development "strategies." This review will permit not only calling attention to a number of approaches to the development problem not specifically reviewed here, but also it will provide an opportunity to fill in some gaps in the development process as outlined in the preceding chapters, as well as an opportunity to sum up the policy issues in a more cogent manner than has yet been done.

Chapter 17

MONEY AND FINANCE
IN THE DEVELOPMENT PROCESS

The present chapter is concerned with an examination of the role of finance and related money matters in the developing country. Although there are a great variety of ways in which finance enters the development story, the discussion here will be concentrated on two broad issues, the role of finance in the saving-investment process, and the problems of maintaining control over total demand. The saving-investment question will be discussed in terms of the effect of finance on the level of saving and investment that the community achieves, and its effect on the allocation of investment. The consideration of the stability issue will be limited to a brief review of the effectiveness of the various policy weapons at the disposal of the monetary and banking authorities.

The discussion is necessarily limited to general principles, and particular institutional arrangements can be treated only incidentally. This is unfortunate because, in a way, the most important question is precisely what institutions are best suited to help the economy of Chapter 7 begin to move. The bibliography contains a list of some excellent studies on the effectiveness of various types of financial institutions in serving the needs of development.

I. The Role of Finance in the Saving-Investment Process

Consider first a very simple model of a closed economy. Suppose that all saving were done simply by depositing money in a "savings bank," and all investing were done with funds borrowed from the same bank. Savers would deposit their money and receive a financial asset—a claim on the savings bank—in return, borrowers would receive money and incur a financial obligation—an obligation to repay the loan. In this case, the accumulation of physical capital would be accompanied by an equal accumulation of financial assets and of debt. In this case, also, the bank could line up potential investors (including the government) in order of the rank of the *SMP* of their respective projects, and hand out the money deposited by the savers until the total available was exhausted. If this equality of saving and investment occurred at maximum use of available resources, and if the level of saving were "optimal," then this economy would be in a very favored position relative to its development effort.

Of course, all saving is not done in this manner, and all finance for investment is not channeled to investors in this way. Savers may lend directly to the investors, in which case the former receives a claim on the latter rather than on a bank. Here too, financial assets and their debt counterpart are accumulated along with physical capital. So also may the saver and investor be the same individual (or business unit), in which case there is no accumulation of debt or financial assets involved in the investment program. In both of these cases, whether the right allocation of investment is achieved requires additional specification of how the money and capital market function.

A general model may then be established along the following lines. The saving of a particular decision unit—household, firm, government—is its income minus its expenditure on current consumption. If a household saves, it is not using all of its current income for the purchase of consumer goods. The household would then accumulate either physical or financial assets in one form or another. The same principle holds true for the firm or for government. Similarly, if an import surplus is achieved, the "rest of the world" is doing the saving. In consuming less than their income, such units are thereby releasing resources for other purposes, i.e., for investment. Deficit units, on the other hand, acquire command over resources in excess of their income. If all investment were financed in this way, the problem of financing investment would be that of transferring the command over resources from saver to investor. Some investors are also savers, of course, and there is no transfer problem in this case. In general, however, it is helpful to think of the financing problem as that of making available to the investors the finance by which they can gain control over the available real investible resources. The investment that is financed by borrowing also results in the creation of financial assets and debt instruments. An equality between saving and investment, in the usual national accounts sense, must therefore also mean an equality between the supply of and demand for investible (loanable) funds, and an equality between the willingness to issue debt obligations by deficit units and willingness to hold such obligations by surplus units. Except in the unusual instance where all income receivers spend all their income themselves for consumption or investment purposes, capital formation is, in this way, necessarily accompanied by the accumulation of financial assets and debt obligations.

Now consider the question of whether or not this financial side of the capital formation process has any impact of its own on the development process, or is it simply the shadow of the "real" side.

A. EFFECT ON TOTAL SAVING AND INVESTMENT

The process just described emphasized the way in which capital formation results in financial asset and debt accumulation. If there were no way that an economy could create financial assets and debt instruments, saving and investment would have to be done by the income recipient who did not spend all his income on consumption. No one could save independently of the accumulation of physical capital, because such assets would be the only available way in which saving could be accomplished. This arrangement for financing or rather this lack of financing arrangements would surely impose major bottlenecks for the capital formation process, and in such a situation the mere establishment of a mechanism for the creation of financial assets may be expected to increase the rate of saving and investment.

The economy described in Chapter 7 is not as devoid of financing facilities as that just described. There is, of course, a monetary system—and money is a financial asset as well as a means of payment—although a significant proportion of the economy is beyond its limits. There are commercial banks too, but to a very large degree their lending operations are concentrated on short-term loans for internal and foreign trade. Medium- and long-term loans for industrial and agricultural production assume a very small portion of a commercial bank's loan portfolio. Other than commercial banks there are only a small number of financial institutions, although such organizations as insurance companies and pension funds are beginning to loom large in some of the developing countries. In general however, it is correct to say that "financial intermediaries" are not yet common in the economy of Chapter 7.

"Financial intermediaries" may be defined as institutions whose function is to serve as the middleman between saver and borrower. Their role is to convert the kind of securities that investors wish to sell into the kind of assets savers wish to buy. As just noted, the mere creation of such institutions in an environment in which none existed will surely increase saving and investment. Furthermore, where they already exist, increasing the form and variety of both asset and debt instrument may also increase the willingness of the members of the community to save. It is, therefore, useful to examine the nature of such intermediaries.

It is customary to distinguish three main ways of getting the saver and borrower together. In the first place, the investor may sell his security directly to the lender. This may be done directly or through a stock market, or in less formal ways. The lender then acquires a direct claim on the

borrower, and the borrower a claim on current output that has been re-
linquished by the lender. Second, the investor may sell his security to the
banking system, and receive a newly created demand deposit in a bank.
These deposits are then spent on current output and eventually accrue to
the savers in the community as deposits, i.e., as financial assets. If there
are no savers, or if the monetary system creates deposits in excess of the
amount savers are willing to hold, this process leads to inflation unless
there is excess capacity in the system. Finally, the investor may sell his
security to non-bank financial institutions such as insurance companies,
pension funds, post office saving clubs, credit unions, savings and loan as-
sociations, and similar institutions. These institutions in turn sell claims
on themselves to the saver. Thus the non-bank financial intermediary is
able to supply a debt instrument particularly suitable to the needs of the
borrower independent of the kind of asset that the lender wants. Similarly, it can offer financial assets to the lender independent of the kind of
debt instrument the borrower is prepared to issue. It may, then, be argued
that these financial intermediaries by liquifying and diversifying the
securities issued by lenders may thereby encourage saving or discourage
dissaving. It may also be argued that a firm may invest more if it can sell
exactly the kind of security it feels is suitable for it, than it will if it is
forced to tailor its securities to a limited market.

1. Effect on Saving. There are major difficulties in appraising the importance of these arguments on total saving in the context of the development process. The creation of the most satisfactory financial institutions
will not result in an economy changing from a 5-per-cent saver to a 10-per-
cent saver. The factors mentioned in Chapter 10 continue to be of much
greater importance than the kind of asset available for the saver to buy in
determining the level of saving. Despite this fact, the particular financing
arrangements are of some relevance, and it is worthwhile to examine *how*
very briefly.

In the economy described in Chapter 7, the chief available assets were
money and physical goods. Even money was not available to significant
segments of the community. The accumulation of physical items as a
form of saving has often been noticed. Gold and other precious metals are
widely held in Asia and elsewhere, as are carpets in Iran, cattle in some
countries, and other things in still other countries. This practice weighs
against a development program, as it has the same effect on the availability of resources for capital formation as does consumption. It seems
clear, however, that the motivation leading to the purchase of gold orna-
ments or expensive carpets by households whose income is just above subsistence is quite different from the motivation that leads to the purchase
of food, clothing, and housing. It is the same motivation that prompts the
more sophisticated individual living in a country with a highly developed
capital market to buy a bond or an equity. The physical assets, partly be-

cause they serve the function of saving instruments, have a degree of liquidity that is significantly greater than the same object in other countries. To the extent that households become willing to switch from the purchase of physical assets to financial assets to serve as their instruments of saving, resources are released for development purposes, even though the household does not consider that its consumption is reduced.

What is the process by which savers become willing to shift from holding physical assets to holding financial assets? The explanation is most certainly institutional. It has already been suggested that the development of financial intermediaries—e.g., savings banks, insurance companies, and so on—may increase the willingness of a household to hold down its consumption, or at least to hold down the rate of increase in its consumption. Similarly, the existence of such intermediaries may encourage households to hold financial assets, instead of resource-using physical assets. But the required institutional changes are, of course, deeper and more subtle than merely establishing savings banks. Rather far-reaching changes in the attitudes of most households toward the government and the government's development program are also required. Perhaps the key monetary-policy implication is to seek to make sure that the switch in the composition of the asset portfolio does not result in losses that would not have occurred had other (physical) assets been held, and this objective may possibly be in conflict with other objectives of monetary policy.

A change in institutional arrangements is paramount in bringing about such a switch in the type of asset, but the more conventional considerations are also relevant. The main motive for holding physical assets is precautionary, not with respect to changing interest rates or price levels (though the assets held are almost always a good hedge against inflation), but against economic disaster. The advantages of liquidity that such assets have in a particular environment outweighs the mere fact that they yield no return (other than psychic income resulting from a feeling of security). But once the saver is convinced that a piece of paper represents a legitimate and recognizable claim, he may become more interested in yield. The effect on saving of changes in interest rates has been largely written off in western countries, but in some low income countries it may be relevant. The fact that savers often receive 3–4 per cent yield, while rates of return on investment of 25–50 per cent are observed, suggests there is room for trying. Frequent changes in the rate of interest may cause difficulties because of the effect on the capital value of fixed yield assets. For if the rate of interest is changed often, surely at some time, it will force a significant capital loss on people who purchased bonds assuming they were immune to such things.

The first type of financial asset held by a new saver is likely to be money. Hoardings can, of course, be compensated for by issuing new money, i.e., by creating demand deposits as mentioned above. This has the advantage of facilitating control in the hands of monetary and planning authorities over the direction in which investment funds flow. It has the great difficulty of creating a situation in which control over aggregate demand may be difficult. The practice also increases the complexity of the problem of determining the appropriate changes in money supply from period to period. The chief explanation of the appeal of money is largely in terms of familiarity and protection from capital loss, i.e., high degree of liquidity. Increased sophistication by savers may be expected to lead them to examine the advantages of diversification of their asset portfolio. When this point is reached, the failure of the system to provide alternative forms of assets may possibly lead the saver into inventories, a bank account in London, or back to gold or rugs.

Along with precious metals, inventories, and capital flight, the purchase of land is also attractive to individuals seeking liquid and safe assets. It is important to recognize that buying land out of current income does not result in a claim on the investible resources of the community. Such a purchaser of land has abstained from using all of his income for consumption, i.e., he has saved. What happens in the economy as a whole depends on how the seller uses the receipts from the sale. If he uses it for consumption purposes, then the sale of land is simply a transfer. If he uses it for capital formation, then the sale of land has served the same purposes as the sale of financial assets. All this does not mean that land speculation does not matter to the development effort. It usually does, but in a more roundabout way than simply usurping saving potential. Land speculation frequently uses up entrepreneurial capacity, frequently affects interest rates adversely, and has some effect on the distribution of incomes. Of these possible consequences, the effect on entrepreneurial activities is the most difficult to counteract.

Does all this mean that savings are elastic enough with respect to availability of financial assets to make it worthwhile to consider financial intermediaries an essential ingredient of the development process? Two considerations suggest the answer is yes. First, the preceding arguments seem especially applicable to a significant group whose income is well above subsistence, but who do little saving (and pay virtually no taxes). This group is usually reasonably literate and is able to appreciate some of the advantages associated with life insurance, investment funds, savings accounts, and so on. With good advertising and good experiences in terms of yields, protection of capital values, and suitability of type of asset, the demand for such securities may be expected to merit the cost involved in making them available. Several countries have experimented with a variety of government bonds in an effort to reach this small saver. Results have been inconclusive (see references at end of chapter), but the record of many governments on bond redemption, rate of return, and liquidity has caused many potential investors to avoid buying their securities. Even less evidence is available on the effect of attempts of private firms to vary the form of security in an effort to reach new savers.

The second reason why the development of financial intermediaries seems important enough to warrant emphasis is the problem of "mobilizing saving." This term is somewhat misleading, and is often used to refer only to the hoarding problem mentioned above. As noted, there is no problem of "mobilization" in such a case, because credit creation can easily compensate for hoardings. There is, however, a real mobilization problem to the solution of which financial intermediation may make a contribution. There are underutilized resources in the economy of Chapter 7 that need to be "mobilized," i.e., need to be made available to potential investors. Most attention is placed on labor, but as argued earlier, physical capital is also allowed to remain idle a great deal of the time. *One* of the reasons for this situation is the failure of the economy to supply a network of finance that brings all of these resources into the view of potential users. In a very general way, what the development of a financial system (beyond simply supplying trade credit) can contribute is the linking together of potential suppliers of investible resources with potential demanders of such resources in a much more effective way than is possible without such a system. This point suggests that the job of the financial middleman is not simply to sit in his office and wait for customers. This means that the financial middleman's main job is exactly to provide the link that would help to take advantage of the potential slack in the system. In this sense, the financial middleman acts on both the saver and the investor, and it is helpful to examine his role in the demand for investment funds more systematically before developing this argument further.

2. Effect on Investment. The possible effect on the total amount of private investment of the state of financial intermediation is as difficult to estimate as the effect on saving. In the developing economy, new and small firms particularly may have their growth inhibited by the absence of a suitable mechanism for the marketing of their securities. This is due in part to risk problems, and to the fact that potential purchasers of these securities have no way of knowing or learning about the existence of such securities. A financial intermediary may then serve as a means of spreading the risk of such investment, as well as of providing the borrower with a market for the particular security he prefers to sell. The great bulk of private investment in almost all underdeveloped countries is from retained earnings and depreciation reserves, and relatively little from general sale of equities or bonds. Such an arrangement constitutes a major handicap for new, untried enterprises that often are a potential source of dynamism for the economy. Financial intermediaries may have their greatest impact on investment if they serve as an agent for the investigation and isolation of new men with new ideas and new techniques that merit exploitation.

The major difficulty in this context is the high cost of servicing and investigating small loans, and probably no financial institution could survive on the basis of buying securities from the small borrower and selling its own securities to the small saver. The total effect of small investments would, however, seem to warrant a subsidy to support this kind of operation, at least in specific cases. The discussion of entrepreneurship, in Chapter 13, emphasized the absence of an environment in which entrepreneurial activity resulted in productive activity. Part of this environmental difficulty is the absence of effective lending institutions. The observation that it is often easier to borrow 50 million dollars to build a steel mill than it is to borrow $1,000 to build a machine shop is a relevant part of the explanation of the sluggishness of private investment. Just as the financial intermediary seems more likely to help the individual whose income allows just a little saving than the extremely rich groups, so also it seems that such institutions may be expected to help the small firm to a greater degree than the large, well-established firm with access to retained earnings and foreign capital markets.

These arguments add to those discussed in connection with saving. The role of the financial institution is partly that of buying securities of one type from borrowers and selling securities of another type to lenders, and thereby contributing to an increase in the willingness to save and the inducement to invest. Also, and more importantly, their job includes finding investment opportunities and facilitating their exploitation. This latter task is especially relevant with respect to small, new enterprises in the developing country. In this sense, the term "mobilization of saving" is a relevant notion in the development picture.

3. Type of Institution. The exact type of institution that most effectively serves these purposes varies from country to country, and generalizations are dangerous or truistic. Attention has already been called to the limited role that commercial banks play in the capital formation process in the economy of Chapter 7. It is also probably correct to argue that seeking to expand the activities of the commercial banks is not a very rewarding approach. New institutions seem to be necessary.

The most frequent type of bank tried is the Development Bank, and these have, in a number of instances, proved a major source of investment finance for the private sector. For the most part, however, they have not aimed at small savers, but have relied largely on government or international sources for their loan funds. Also they have not been very successful in small scale lending, and many of them have legal or customary limitations that prohibit loans below a certain level. (Their loans are, of course, well below those made by the very large international banks and aid agencies. In some instances the Development Bank has come into existence largely to serve as a middleman between these larger lending agencies and the smaller borrower. The point here is that probably the

Development Banks are still too large to exploit fully the possibilities for saving and investing discussed earlier.)

Qualified workers for the financial intermediary are relatively expensive in most countries, and the problems associated with effective supervision are also important obstacles to their development. Embryonic stock exchanges have also been tried, and in some cases worked well. Perhaps one way to attack the cost problem is to concentrate attention on intermediary activity that can serve as a by-product of other activity. Withheld earnings, postal savings, compulsory insurance schemes would be in this category. The essential issue would remain however; namely, whether the contribution of the financial intermediaries to the capital formation is sufficient to warrant a public subsidy to support them. In some instances the answer to this question is definitely yes.

B. EFFECT ON THE ALLOCATION OF INVESTMENT

In Chapters 15 and 16, the problems associated with the allocation of investment were discussed. Even if all the conditions there specified were in effect, investment might still be misdirected for reasons connected with the availability of finance. In the simple case given at the beginning of this chapter, where all saving is done by making deposits in a bank and all investment is financed by obtaining loans from the same bank, meeting the *SMP* criterion would easily be accomplished (once all the *SMP*'s had been computed). At the other extreme, in an economy that has no financial assets at all, the composition of investment would certainly be far from that defined earlier as appropriate. A ranking of investment projects by their *SMP*'s may be expected in virtually every instance to call for investment by some firms in excess of their saving capacity, and investment by others to be below their saving capacity. As shown above, this allocation would not be possible if there were no financial assets. The availability of money balances helps a great deal, but except in the case mentioned at the beginning of the paragraph will probably not be enough to assure a satisfactory solution to the allocation problem.

In a situation where the government monetary or planning authorities have complete control over all sources of investment finance, they can, of course, announce that no finance is available for projects with an *SMP* below the cutoff point. Control over *all* sources is difficult as it must include internal financing also. Direct controls on private investment are always possible, but pose major implementation problems for the bureaucracy of any country, especially the one described in Chapter 7.

What nonmonetary financial intermediaries can do that is of great relevance in the allocation context is to bring more projects into the competition for investment funds. This may be a major contribution in an economy in which most private investment has been customarily financed chiefly with retained earnings. Financial institutions, though concerned with the safety and earnings of their loans and equities, are more likely to be aware of and to consider the economy-wide implications of a given form of investment than is a single producing firm. Also financial institutions are more likely to consider that an investment project that is consistent with and contributes to the achievement of the broad outlines of the entire development effort is thereby a safer investment than is a project possessing neither of these characteristics. These remarks suggest that financial middlemen may help achieve recognition of interdependence effects and the implications of deviations of market prices of factors from social opportunity costs. But, evidently, they cannot carry the whole burden, and the task of achieving a reasonably satisfactory pattern of investment in the private sector is in no sense solved by the evolution of financial institutions.

II. The Control of Aggregate Demand

In Chapter 5, two aspects of the aggregate demand problem were noted. The first considered the difficulty of gauging the capacity of an economy to absorb expenditure without price level repercussions. These difficulties are compounded in an underdeveloped economy with frequent underutilization of resources, inadequately pervasive monetary system, along with immobilities, supply inelasticities, bottlenecks, and the like, and consequently, the problems associated with determining how much expenditure were serious problems. The second aspect had to do with what was called the micro problem of price level stability, and was concerned with how relative price adjustments may affect overall price level stability. Then in Chapter 10, inflation was introduced as a possible means of increasing the rate of capital formation. Also in that chapter the dangers of spiraling inflation were emphasized. Finally, the policy objective was defined as maintaining firm control of aggregate demand in the hands of the monetary authorities. The task now is to make a more detailed examination of these various issues. The central objective of the discussion remains that of examining the effectiveness of the tools at the disposal of the monetary and fiscal authorities to accomplish the general objective of maintaining control over total spending.

A. THE INSTRUMENTS OF CONTROL OF TOTAL SPENDING

In the context of the developing economy, the component of total demand to which prime importance is attached is the level of investment. Earlier, the assumption was made that the level of investment was determined by the government as a matter of social policy, but since it is also assumed that the private sector does considerable investing, this assumption involves an estimate of what the community will—or can be induced to—save and what the private sector will be induced or be allowed to invest. Therefore, the decision-making authority must have some notion of the determinants of private investment, and, of course, some way to affect its level. Attention is directed toward investment, and consumption is considered as a residual and will not be explicitly considered.

In Chapter 10, the loanable funds model of monetary equilibrium was introduced as part of the inflation story. Consider this model now from a slightly different point of view. The customary formulation of the loanable funds argument is along the following lines. The net supply of loanable funds during any given period is equal to planned saving in all sectors of the economy plus the increase in the quantity of money. This is equivalent to the increase in demand for securities by direct lenders, the monetary system, and nonmonetary financial intermediaries. The net demand for these loanable funds is planned investment plus increases in the demand for money to hold as an asset.

The level of these four components of the supply and demand for loanable funds are assumed to depend primarily on the size of national income and the rate of interest. Expectations, institutional restraints on credit creation, and a miscellany of other things are also relevant. Equilibrium in this part of the economy requires that saving plans and investment plans be equal, and that the supply of money to hold and demand for money to hold also be equal. The equilibrating mechanisms are changes in the level of national income and the rate of interest. If this equilibrium occurs at full capacity of the economy, then further analysis consists simply of spelling out the details of the argument. If the equilibrium occurs at less than full utilization, there remains the great problem of whether or not forces are thereby unloosed to drive the economy to full utilization. The policies to affect the level of demand for loanable funds include changing the money supply to raise or lower the rate of interest and changing the government's saving and spending levels.

This simple loanable funds model provides a helpful format for examining the effectiveness of the instruments for the control of the level and the composition of investment in the underdeveloped country. At the same time, there are important difficulties in its application, the notice of which will help to reveal the range of problems that must be attacked if the "right" level of investment is to be achieved and financed in a manner consistent with the price level objectives.

1. Control of Credit by Commercial Banks. The conventional policies of open market operations, changing the discount (bank) rate, and varying reserve requirements are of little use in the developing country. The size of the market for government securities is very narrow, and commercial banks are reluctant to buy them as alternative commercial paper is much more lucrative. Consequently, when the Central Bank tries to sell government securities, bond prices tend to fall sharply. About the only examples of open market operations have been on the buying side, and here the purchases that have taken place have usually been directed at affecting the price of securities rather than the credit situation. Also the reserve and liquidity position of most large commercial banks in the developing country is such as to make them more or less unaffected by any variation in discount rates or reserve requirements. The practice of maintaining excess reserves springs from considerations about the inadequacy of suitable liquid assets for secondary reserves, frequency of sudden currency withdrawals, and a tendency to seek to avoid dependence on the central banks. The frequency of sudden currency withdrawals is especially pertinent in countries where the banking habit is limited and demand deposits make up a relatively small part of the money supply. There are a wide range of variations on these traditional tools that can and have been employed by Central Banks that may increase the control over the supply of credit, but, in general, it is correct to say that destabilizing short-run fluctuations in the credit to the private sector must be attacked by more direct means than is common in the highly developed money markets.

Central Banks or other monetary authorities may, for example, be able to establish rates of interest that commercial banks may charge on various securities, and may exercise some control over the supply of credit in this fashion. Or some control may be exercised by regulations that permit monetary authorities to limit the type of securities that the banks may buy. In many countries the central bank is not only a banker's bank, but also a commercial banker itself. Such Central Banks are usually large relative to competing commercial banks, and by their own actions may affect significantly the volume of credit. The difficulties of controlling credit creation by the commercial banks are increased in a country that has a large foreign trade sector subject to major fluctuations. An abrupt change in exports has direct effects on the money supply that are usually beyond the control of the Central Bank, and may be difficult to compensate for as well. The flow of foreign aid has similar effects on the control of the money supply by conventional means. Especially does commodity aid—e.g., United States aid in the form of agricultural surplus commodities—impose problems of the timing of changes in the money supply, as well as the amount of such changes.

All of these arguments suggest that control over private credit via control over its availability is more likely to succeed than are attempts to affect its price. But even control by the monetary authority over availability is far from complete, and once cost is abandoned or subordinated as the rationing device, problems arise not only as to quantity of credit but also as to its allocation among competing claims. As already noted, the commercial banks of the underdeveloped country concentrate their lending operations very heavily on short-term, "self-liquidating" loans to finance foreign and domestic trade. Although such loans can be destabilizing, they are not likely to be the source of continuing inflationary pressure unless fed by note-creating activity on the part of the Central Bank. So the fact that the monetary authority has only a very imperfect arsenal of weapons to control commercial bank operations is not a serious problem in most developing countries. It is important, however, to recognize that interest rates serve only in a very indefinite way as an equilibrating mechanism in this sector.

2. *Development Credit.* Suppose that commercial banks' activities could be written off as a source of finance for developing projects or as a significant destablizing force. If this assumption is reasonably realistic, then the finance for development projects must come from financial intermediaries —development banks, agriculture banks, insurance companies, and so on,— from the government, or from retained earnings.

If all sources of finance for development projects were under the direct control of the planning authority there would be no more difficulties than those already explained. There are, however, two other significant sources of finance of investment projects, internal financing and (in some instances) nonmonetary financial intermediaries, to which some attention must be given.

(a) Internal financing of new investment is a very common means of financing private investment projects in the underdeveloped country, and there is no very orderly way that its level or its allocation in a given period can be controlled. The effectiveness of the rate of interest as a means of pulling these funds into the market is unlikely to be very great simply because the other factors surrounding the investment and liquidity decisions swamp any effect that interest rate changes may have. In countries where it is believed that the use of internal funds to finance investment results in a serious deviation from the *SMP* criterion, or in undesirable inflation, direct controls are the customary answer. These controls may take the form of requirements for permits issued by the government to do any investing by anyone, or possibly controls on strategic investment materials, or (more likely) on imports. A longer term solution is in terms of improvement in the capital market, but this is not a meaningful policy objective in the short run for the economy described in Chapter 7 as so much depends on the responsiveness of investment decisions to the interest rate manipulations, and such responsiveness by large firms with their own funds can hardly be expected.

(b) Non-government supported financial intermediaries are, as already observed, of relatively minor importance in most developing countries. It has, however, been argued that an encouragement of their expansion will contribute to the achievement of a higher level of saving and investment, and may help in isolating unusually productive investment activity. If these intermediaries are to be encouraged, then the question of how their actions can be controlled is relevant.

The development of nonmonetary financial intermediaries means that another source of loanable funds becomes pertinent over which the monetary authorities' usual weapons have no direct effect. For example, a large insurance company may affect the supply of loanable funds at a time and in a way that complicates the achievement of a desired monetary policy or a desired allocation of investment. If the monetary authorities exercise their most direct effect on the stability of the system via control of the money supply, the increased role of such intermediation means that another source of complexity on the determination of the right money supply emerges. In an economy with a large-scale-development program under way, any arbitrary rule of thumb on money supply increases is certain to cause trouble at one time or another even if money is the only financial asset available. In the early stages of development, the extent of the monetization of trade increases gradually, but may decline in years of bad harvest. Transactions demand alone does not lend itself to simple prediction, and, of course, money to hold will be particularly susceptible to variation as the members of a community gain in economic sophistication. And, as already emphasized, the interest rate may be an unreliable guide to what is happening to demand for money.

What nonmonetary financial intermediaries do in this context is to add greatly to the complexity of analyzing the demand for money as well as the supply of loanable funds. One can, of course, build models that relate the portfolio demand for money to a variety of factors in a specific way. This is a useful exercise, and may provide a clue as to appropriate policy. But in general, the approach has to be in terms of a constant contact with the economy on the part of the monetary authorities, and in adjustments made on the basis of current evidence.

Perhaps this increasing complexity can be adequately summarized by saying that as the financial system develops, the range of choice to lenders and borrowers, to savers and investors, to households and firms greatly increases. As the area of choice relative to assets to be purchased and sold widens, so evidently does the complexity of the task of explanation and prediction. And so too will the task of devising a monetary policy that contributes to the achievement of a given objective increase in complexity. The policy area must also widen in the sense that it is no longer possible to limit attention to commercial banks, the Central Bank, and Treasury. These difficulties are accentuated in the case of a developing economy where there is no experience to guide. As the financial system progresses and new opportunities emerge, their effects have to be considered more or less from scratch. Institutional characteristics of an economy change slowly, but the impact of change may well make itself felt suddenly. A monetary policy that fails to foresee these suddenly appearing changes is then likely to fail to achieve its objectives. But it is exactly this increasing choice that produces the major contribution of the financial system to the development program.

It may be repeated that only in a few currently developing countries are there non-government controlled financial intermediaries of significance. But their evolution is part of the development process, and their contribution to this process, and the problems they create must be acknowledged.

(*c*) Government activity has been most frequently accused as the major source of destabilization. Central Banks are usually not able to withstand demands placed on them by the government, and it is easy to find historical examples of a government pursuing a deficit spending policy that made it impossible to avoid undesirable inflationary increases in the money supply. Where such deficits have been created with either malice aforethought, or abject ignorance, they represent difficulties for which the economist cannot prescribe. The preceding discussion has emphasized the difficulties in gauging what expenditures the economy can absorb, and a government deficit policy designed to make absolutely sure that price level stability was maintained may impose a heavy burden on the economy in the form of underutilization of available resources. This is especially true where the taxing capacity is as severely handicapped as it is in most underdeveloped countries. The real problem is not a naive note-printing exercise, which everyone recognizes to be harmful, but rather devising a government spending policy that is consistent with control over aggregate demand and the making of the maximum contribution to the development process.

Before trying to reach a conclusion on the general issue of stabilization policy, a further consideration of the problems of relative price adjustments is given.

B. RELATIVE PRICE ADJUSTMENTS

In Section B, Part II of Chapter 5, the "micro aspects" of the aggregate demand problem were discussed. The issues discussed there had to do with how the changes in relative prices that accompany economic development might result in the monetary authorities losing control over the level of money income. Two sources of difficulties were isolated. The first was the creation of inframarginal vectors of activities as growth proceeded. The second source was the possibility of factors pushing up their returns independent of changes in productivity or demand. In both instances, much stress was placed on the flexibility of prices and of returns to factors in response to the changing markets that accompany growth. As the underdeveloped economy begins to grow, the burden placed on the adjustment of relative prices is likely to be severe indeed. It is, therefore, useful to say something more about this adjustment process in the context of the stability problem.

1. The Burden of Adjustment. If an economy grew in accordance with the "expanding circular flow" model described in Chapter 4, the burden placed on relative price changes would be quite light. In that model all sectors are growing at the same pace, and all activities of the economic process simply repeat themselves on an ever larger scale. But the development process, as outlined in the preceding chapters, does not resemble the expanding circular flow, because the heart of that process involved doing new things and doing old things differently. Furthermore, the price system does not cover the entire economy, and where it is used, it is rarely employed to its maximum effectiveness. Therefore, the burden on price adjustments is expected to be particularly heavy, and both sides of the micro aspects of the aggregate demand problem, mentioned earlier, become relevant to the monetary authorities.

The success of the subsidy or tax schemes designed to bring about the equality of factor prices and social opportunity cost may be able to reduce the strength of the wage problems described in Chapter 5. That such policies can be completely effective is not to be expected, and wage pressure on costs is likely. In particular, a situation may emerge in which unskilled labor is unemployed or underemployed at the same time that there is excess demand for skilled and semiskilled labor. And situations may also emerge where the only way to keep the real wage of the category of worker whose marginal product is very low or zero from rising is by inflation.

But the problem is not limited to the wage-rate problem. It also includes the adjustments imposed on lagging sectors in a growing economy. Unless one is prepared to assume that increments of output occur in the "right" sectors as a result of expectations, then excess demand is likely in the leading sectors. This excess demand may, in turn, be expected to produce rising prices. Firms will find themselves falling behind in meeting orders, and respond by raising their prices. The concentrating of an increment of demand (equal to no more than the increment in total capacity) on a few sectors will create excess demand in these sectors and push prices up. In sectors where excess capacity emerges, the tendency for prices to fall will be significantly counteracted by rising costs (including, but not exclusively labor) plus a possible reluctance to lower prices due to market position, or to the expectation that observed increases in money income will eventually alleviate the need to reduce prices.

It was emphasized earlier that if the kind of situation described in the two previous paragraphs and in greater detail in Chapter 5 presents itself, inflation would not continue indefinitely without an increase in the money supply. For if money income is held constant, labor and commodities whose prices are pushed up will price themselves out of the market, and underutilization will result. Increasing money income then is necessary to prevent the appearance of unemployment. Suppose that exactly the "right" level of investment is determined, and that methods of financing are such that no inflationary pressures due to the macro side of the problem are present. Suppose further that the micro side causes problems for the reasons discussed, i.e., wages rise in some sectors above the productivity of the relevant labor input, or that some other prices do not adjust downward despite falling costs or demand. One of two results must follow: if the price level (and money income) remains constant, fewer resources than expected and than are available (by hypothesis) will be used, or if all resources are to be used, the macro conditions of price level stability must be violated and the price level goes up. Under these conditions an important conclusion is obvious: the development program moves significantly slower with stable prices than with rising prices. But this is not the end of the story.

2. *The Development of a Price System.* The point has been made earlier that the price system does not seem to work as well in the underdeveloped economy as in the richer economies. Also it has been argued that the advantages of the price system had to be learned, and were certainly not self-evident. The purpose here is to develop a very tentative hypothesis having to do with the learning of the use of a price system.

A price system is usually thought of as functioning within a broader set of economic and social institutions. Among the institutions that are relevant for the understanding of how the price system works are not only those that operate directly upon the efficacy of the price system—e.g., the banking system, the width of the money economy relative to the total economy, the priority of profit making as a guide to action, labor unions, cooperatives, anti-trust laws, and so on—but also those that are part of the general social system of the country—e.g., landlord-peasant relationships, family system, attitudes toward leisure, strength and content of prevailing religious doctrine, prevalent form of economic organization, extent of minority groups, ease of vertical mobility, methods of rewarding effort, and so forth. The existence and form of these institutions then limit or facilitate the extent and speed of response to price incentives. Perhaps the most appropriate summary statement on these matters (discussed in detail in Chapter 13) would be that institutions permit or encourage more or less freedom to respond to price incentive. That the price system works less well in some countries than it does in others, results from the fact that the institutions in some countries not only permit freedom but positively encourage response to prices, while in other countries such freedom is not only inhibited, but existing institutions are alien to effective response to these incentives.

In the previous section one way in which institutional arrangements affected the price level was discussed. Now turn the argument around and examine to what extent (if any) price pressure may force alterations in the institutional arrangements. The following hypothesis may then be defended: price pressure strong enough to produce resource mobility, changed economic routines and habits, and a forced rethinking of prevailing social and economic arrangements, will thereby contribute to a loosening of institutional obstacles to the price system performing more effectively. More specifically, it is suggested that price incentive and pressure are ways to induce institutional change of a kind that facilitates more effective utilization of the price system in the future.

There is, of course, pressure on such barriers from a number of sources. A rising labor-land ratio has resulted in a movement away from agriculture into urban areas on a significant scale in recent years in many countries. And there can be little doubt that an urban environment produces a different behavior among economic agents from that prevailing in rural areas. Similarly, an increased literacy rate or increased contact among people of diverse characteristics probably contributes to a reduction in the strength of the prevailing routines. The same is true of improved health standards and so on.

It is now suggested that one way for a society to learn how to use a price system reasonably well is for a situation to develop where price directives are so strong that they "have" to be obeyed. For as long as economic behavior is definitely dominated by institutions that are unrelated to effective economizing, price incentives will play a minor role. One way to make them much more relevant is simply to increase their relative weight, and this can be done most easily by adding to the price incentive. Given the price mechanism as it functions in most newly developing countries, it is unlikely that heavy pressure in certain areas of the economy will be offset in other sectors, i.e., net upward pressure on the price level will result.

In the previous section, it was argued that for reasons arising out of the necessity for the many sectors of the system to grow at many different rates and because of the likelihood of price rises in growing sectors not being counteracted by declining prices in stagnant sectors, an increase in money income such that the macro conditions of stability are violated would be necessary if full utilization of the resources available for development were to be achieved. Now added to this is the hypothesis of this section: because of the important contribution that an effective price system can make to economic development, its creation is an important objective in the early stages of growth. Its creation is facilitated by making sure that price incentives are strong enough to outweigh non-price effects, and to give thereby an opportunity for the population to respond to price effects, i.e., give them a chance to "learn by doing." Since prices are not flexible downward, we may conclude that in order to make any significant contribution to the establishment of an effective price system, money income of a level to produce price level rises will have to be generated. This result is consistent with but somewhat more general and inclusive than the result of the previous section.

III. Conclusion

One conclusion can be made with confidence: the problems of finance in the development process are not the kind that solve themselves. Beyond this, however, conclusions are necessarily precarious in keeping with the spirit of development economics. Two areas of inquiry were investigated in this chapter: the financing of development projects, and the control over aggregate demand.

That capital formation also involves the accumulation of financial assets is necessary in all but the most primitive economies. The quality and variety of financial assets that are available affect not only the ease of financing, but probably also affect the level of saving and investment that is feasible, and the degree to which a satisfactory allocation of investment is achieved. It seemed then correct to conclude that in a wide variety of cases a conscious policy of encouraging the development of financial intermediaries would yield acceptable returns.

As for control of total spending, conclusions were even more tentative. Central Banks' ability to use traditional indirect controls—open market operations, discount rate changes, and so on—are severely limited, and reliance is placed chiefly on influencing supply of currency and the availability of credit rather than its cost. Control of credit is further complicated when and if non-monetary financial intermediaries become important enough to affect the supply and demand for loanable funds.

Finally, an examination was made of the implications for price level stability of a sputtering price system in a developing economy where major structural changes are occurring. Reasons were advanced why price flexibility and adjustments would be slow and limited, and how this fact could defeat the twin objectives of maximum utilization of resources and price level stability. Also a tentative hypothesis was advanced that suggested that, in view of the inchoate nature of the price system and the institutional obstacles inhibiting the exploitation of economic opportunities, price-pressure-forcing change must often be much heavier than in countries where response to price incentives is less impeded by social and institutional arrangements. If, however, price pressure were heavy enough to force economic agents to respect its signals, a process of learning about the advantages of a price system may be helped along, but price level stability would probably be impossible.

Any argument that finds something meritorious in a rising price level must be hedged very carefully. The evils of inflation were detailed in Chapter 10, and these evils are not withdrawn by what is argued here. Inflation does feed on itself, and a price level rise can easily get out of hand. Central bankers are certainly right in emphasizing that allowing price level increases *and* keeping full control over total spending is not only difficult, but history can be used to suggest it is impossible. One can agree to all this, and still argue that the demands placed on the financial system and on the price system by the development process are such that a policy of making certain that no inflation occurs probably means a degree of underutilization of available resources. If then price level rises can occur without the monetary authorities losing control of the situation, a modest inflation may be expected to serve the development effort. Hence, the development of effective monetary instruments and fiscal and tax policy become an integral part of the development program.

Bibliography

Begin with the important paper by John G. Gurley and Edward S. Shaw, "Financial Aspects of Economic Development," *The American Economic Review*, XLV (September, 1955). The analysis in the text owes much to this article. The same authors' *Money in a Theory of Finance* (Washington, D.C.: The Brookings Institution, 1960) especially Chapter 4 and their "Financial Intermediaries and the Saving-Investment Process," *Journal of Finance*, XI (May, 1956) are also helpful. See also John G. Gurley, *Liquidity and Financial Institutions in the Post-war Period*, Study Paper No. 14 of the material prepared for Joint Economic Committee of the United States Congress—Study of Employment, Growth, and Price Level (Washington, D.C.: Government Printing Office, 1960) and H. J. Bruton, *Inflation in a Growing Economy* (Bombay: University of Bombay Press, 1961).

More general surveys of the financing of development are the following: R. S. Sayers, *Central Banking after Bagehot* (Oxford: The Clarendon Press, 1957), Chap. 9; A. R. Prest, *Public Finance in Underdeveloped Countries* (New York: Frederick A. Praeger, Inc., 1963); and Edward Nevin, *Capital Funds in Underdeveloped Countries* (London: Macmillan & Co., Ltd., 1961). Two useful studies with the title *Development Banks* by William Diamond (1957) and Shirley Boskey (1959), both published by the Johns Hopkins Press (Baltimore) for the International Bank for Reconstruction and Development, give good accounts of the work and organization of this type bank. A. K. Cairncross has some general, but pertinent comments on banking problems in development in Chapter 10 of his *Factors in Economic Development* (London: George Allen & Unwin, 1962). A very good survey of all aspects of banking in the development problem is S. N. Sen, *Central Banking in Underdeveloped Money Markets* (3rd ed.) (Calcutta: Bookland Private Ltd., 1961). A good, specific study of finance is found in George Rosen, *Some Aspects of Industrial Finance in India* (New York: The Free Press of Glencoe, 1962).

CHAPTER 18

STRATEGIES OF DEVELOPMENT

In the preceding chapters, an effort has been made to consider the various aspects of the development process in as systematic a way as possible. The arguments have perhaps suggested the great complexity of formulating and implementing policies that enable a low income country to enjoy a rising level of *per capita* income over a long period of time. The great complexity inherent in the development process has, somewhat understandably, led to the search for rules of thumb to follow or to the isolation of one or two obstacles that seemed especially crucial or strategic. The clear implication of these arguments is that if this one obstacle were hurdled or that one rule of thumb were followed, the development process would proceed with considerable regularity. Given the previous discussion of the *modus operandi* of development, it is now necessary in this concluding chapter to examine specifically some of these "strategies of growth." Of course, much of what has already been said concerns them, but there are several reasons why it is useful to bring them explicitly into the picture. The first and most obvious reason is simply their importance in shedding more light on the development problem, and the fact that anyone interested in development must know them. While the following discussion will find much to criticize about each strategy, and none is accepted as adequate, it will also be evident that many of the arguments developed in earlier chapters make use of some part of the particular strategy discussed. Second, such a discussion will provide a framework around which to draw some loose ends of the development story of preceding chapters together, and in effect, to outline an end to that story.

The literature is vast, but it seems useful to note each of the following strategies: (1) Stages of Growth, (2) Import Substitution, (3) Industrialization vs. Agriculture, (4) Big Push, (5) Capital-Output Ratio Approach, (6) The Planning Problem, (7) The Relevancy of Economics, (8) Some Strategic Odds and Ends.

After all this, a one-paragraph conclusion should meet needs for a summing up.

I. The Stages of Economic Growth

Walt W. Rostow's book, *The Stages of Economic Growth,* which appeared in 1960, created a great deal of interest among both laymen and professionals. The book is explicitly a presentation of "an economic historian's way of generalizing the sweep of modern history" (p. 1), and has relevance therefore for placing the modern underdeveloped country in an historical context. If this were done in a satisfactory way, there is no doubt that the understanding of the problem of underdevelopment would be greatly increased. An approach to a study of history by establishing stages has been undertaken by a number of people. The approach was especially popular with German historians and economists in the nineteenth century, and some British and American writers have also found it fruitful in the first half of the twentieth century. It does, however, seem accurate to state that the stage approach to a study of economic history has lost most of its appeal, and the approach employed by Rostow was something of a revival of a technique generally believed to be obsolete.

Rostow divides the growth process into five stages: a traditional stage is the beginning, and forms the point of departure of the growth sequences. Next are the preconditions period, the take-off period, the drive to maturity, and finally the age of high mass consumption. The traditional society is defined as one "whose structure is developed within limited production functions" (p. 4), and as one in which a ceiling exists on the level of output per capita that can be reached, chiefly because of low saving rates and the unavailability of modern science. It is an economy very much like the one described in Chapter 7 of this book. The preconditioning stage is a period of transition during which the society breaks the ties of traditionalism and heads toward the take-off. The key characteristic of this period, says Rostow, is the change in attitude from that of accepting the economic environment as beyond control to a belief that by systematic examination and action, man is able to improve his economic lot. But in this period, other things must happen as well: the rate of investment must rise, entrepreneurs must appear, the population must be willing to accept training and to operate in an economy with constant change, social overhead capital—railroads, power, and so on—must be built, and agricultural productivity must rise. So, too, must the building of an effective national state be accomplished. The preconditioning stage is characterized by a long, slow process of change, and is heavily influenced by external contacts that provide the incentive to change and the knowledge of how to change.

The take-off is a decisive, sharp stage characterized by three main events: a rise in the rate of investment from about 5 to about 10 per cent, development of at least one manufacturing activity, and the appearance of "a political, social, and institutional framework which exploits the impulses to expansion in the modern sector" (p. 39). It is a stage when the "scale of productive economic activity reaches a critical level and produces changes which lead to a massive and progressive structural transformation in economies—and societies of which they are a part" (p. 40). It is also characterized by one or two large industries acting as leading sectors, chief among which in the past has been the railroad. The take-off is a short period, perhaps no longer than two or three decades, unlike the preconditioning stage that may take a century. The fourth stage is the drive to maturity or period of sustained growth during which modern technology is extended into all parts of the system and growth becomes more or less routinized. The final stage, mass high consumption, is just as the term implies, a stage of high living and gadgetry of all sorts. This stage will not be considered in what follows.

Rostow insists that the stages are not mere descriptive characterizations, but have an "inner logic" and continuity that reveal the process of growth. This would mean that not only was each stage distinctive, but, more importantly, it would mean that by examining the characteristics of one stage, one can not only identify it, but also can predict its completion and the emergence of the following stage. To do this, it would be necessary to demonstrate the analytical relationship among successive stages, i.e., to show precisely the mechanics by which the functioning of the system in the preconditioning period produces those developments that bring on the take-off. The stage theory would then be primarily concerned with establishing those behavioral and technological relationships governing the performance of the economy during a particular stage, and accounting for its emergence into the following one. It would also be concerned with demonstrating the sequential nature of the stages, e.g., with showing that the preconditioning stage was not only different from the take-off stage, but also that it was necessarily prior to the take-off and also would necessarily lead into the take-off.

The unambiguous implication in Rostow's *Stages* that this material was provided is probably the major source of the book's appeal to the layman. The argument not only provides order to the growth process, but has an adequate degree of optimism as well. Once the economy moves into the stage sequence, then economic growth proceeds unilaterally, and, despite Rostow's emphasis on choice, virtually inevitably. As such, the argument would also contain much that was relevant to the problem of development. It would, for example, reveal a great deal about how investment should be allocated in the early stages. Unfortunately, as with all stage theorists before him, Rostow has not succeeded in meeting these demands. To discuss briefly how he fails does, however, reveal some relevant things about the problems facing the modern underdeveloped country.

For Rostow's traditional society, and the one described in Chapter 7, the most pertinent stages are the preconditioning and the take-off. Consider first preconditions. The term implies that some things must come before others. Rostow's list includes social overhead capital and increased agricultural productivity. Neither history nor a priori argument suggest that these events must come before other sectors can expand. Both require a considerably higher rate of investment than found in most traditional societies. Indeed as one analyzes the process by which such activities are accomplished, it is difficult to see how that process is different from growth itself, i.e., why is it preconditioning, not growth? A number of historians (see especially Habakkuk and Gerschenkron) have noted that in several countries the events listed by Rostow as necessary preconditions occurred alongside events he described as the take-off.

The argument in the preceding chapters revealed no reason why one particular activity or activities necessarily preceded growth. This statement applies also to the development of the belief in the possibility of growth, as well as to specific economic activities. As already noted, Rostow has used general terms in his discussion about behavioral and technological relationships, but it seems quite clear (as argued above) that the way to create the idea of progress is by growth itself. Rostow is surely right in emphasizing the importance attached to the society believing growth to be possible, but he must show that such a belief can emerge in the traditional society prior to growth, if he makes that belief a precondition, rather than a part of growth. Finally, the emphasis Rostow places on external forces in initiating the stage of preconditions offers little help, because external forces are always at work. The real issue is the understanding of the response of the society to the external forces.

The take-off is equally difficult to explain. To specify "a political, social, and institutional framework which exploits the impulses to expansion" can be done only at a level that makes it virtually a tautology or so concretely as to make it devoid of general interest. It is also not clear how it differs from the political requirement for the preconditioning stage. Nor is there any reason why a manufacturing activity as opposed to an agricultural one must lead the take-off spurt. But more importantly, there is no way to define a successful take-off independently of its occurrence, and consequently it is necessary to wait until growth has sustained itself for a substantial period, to know if an economy has in fact taken off and reached self-sustaining growth before one can conclude that take-off has in fact occurred.

As for the self-sustaining growth stage (the drive to maturity) the picture is similar. In this stage, Rostow argues that growth is not smooth, automatic, and easy, but rather that the technological, social, institutional bases of growth are not likely to wither away to the degree that they have to be reestablished from scratch. But the take-off cannot occur unless growth is sustained, nor can the changes that are preconditioning occur without sustained growth. Presumably one could argue that during the preconditioning and take-off stages the obstacles were greater than in the sustained growth stage. But this in no sense is necessarily true, and there is no evidence to support it. So here again one finds difficulty in appreciating the characteristics that distinguish this stage from others, and consequently the meaning of the whole stage sequence.

If the Rostow approach is as unsatisfactory as the preceding paragraphs assert, why bring it up at all? First of all, Rostow has great insight and perception, and the book is important despite the failure of its most glamorous aspect. But there is a more important reason.

To try to put history into a sequence of stage reveals an important element of the growth process. Any economy that has been stagnating for centuries, and then begins to grow must experience change and transition. The approach employed in this book involves just such a notion, but stages are another matter. The recognition that there are many paths to growth is a key notion, and what may in one society be identified as a precondition of growth (or better as part of early growth) may in another be the *consequence* of a long period of growth. The railroad may be the initiating factor in one community, but to build it in another may wastefully use up limited resources. There is no doubt that corrupt and inefficient government in many countries hampers development, but this does not mean that honest officials are a precondition to development. They could well be a result. There is a wide range of possibilities of institutions, and to get a necessary sequence, one must not simply ignore what the histories surely show. Careful analysis—perhaps even simply careful searching or groping—can lead to solutions of specific problems that are consistent with the general conditions prevailing at the moment in an economy. For this reason, one would prefer that *precondition* and *take-off* were less ubiquitous terms than they have become, and *study* and *understanding* could replace them.

II. An Import Substitution Strategy

Throughout the preceding chapters the foreign sector was treated as simply another sector with no specific peculiarities. The basis for doing this was the assumption that the price of foreign exchange was made equal to its social opportunity cost either by changes in the exchange rate or by some other method. Exploitation of infant industry possibilities could be done through subsidies or various forms of taxes, but the general position was that the optimal pattern of foreign trade could be determined in the same way that allocation within the economy was determined. There is, however, a body of thought that contradicts this approach, and places great emphasis on the hypothesis that an important difficulty confronting the underdeveloped country is precisely its trade relations with the richer countries. From this hypothesis, it is easy to conclude that an essential part of the development strategy is to modify the prevailing trade patterns. Usually, this takes the form of an import substitution policy aimed at a rather quick change in the output composition of the economy.

A. THE LONG-RUN TRADE PROBLEM

The chief variable in the story is the long-term behavior of the terms of trade. In Chapter 1, it was shown how changes in the terms of trade affect real output. If the ratio of the price of exports (P_X) to the price of imports (P_M) falls, the economy must export a larger quantity of its goods and services to obtain a given quantity of imports, than was the case in some earlier base period. The extent to which a decline in P_X/P_M handicaps the growth depends on a variety of factors, the most important of which is increases in productivity. If P_X declines because of an improvement in technology, then fewer resources are required to produce the exports, and the fall in P_X does not mean that more of the economy's resources are required to maintain a constant level of imports. It would still mean that the rest of the world was getting more of the country's goods for an unchanging quantity of their goods, and, consequently, that some or all of the fruits of the technical change were transferred abroad. If P_X had remained constant despite the rising productivity of inputs, then the trading partners would have received none of the returns due to this new technology.

There is considerable evidence supporting the view that the terms of trade have experienced a long-term decline for all or most of the countries usually classified as underdeveloped. This evidence suggests that the secular decline has been going on for several decades, in some instances for a century, and has been interrupted only by wars or threats of war. As with any long-term index, it is easy to dispute the validity of the series that show these price changes. Quality changes in the products are necessarily ignored, weighing systems in the computing of the index are almost always defective, price data are often average values not really prices, and many products and many countries are omitted from the calculations. Despite these difficulties on the empirical side, the evidence has convinced a number of observers that there is something inherent in the operation of the international economy that results in the low income countries being at a serious disadvantage in their trade relations with the rich countries.

There are two general arguments explaining the apparent deterioration in the terms of trade. In the first place, it is argued that, although technical progress has been more rapid in rich countries than in poor countries, price behavior has not reflected this fact. Thus, rather than prices falling in response to technological change, money wages and profits rose, thereby keeping the full fruits of the new technical knowledge in the rich, industrialized countries. The other argument refers to Engels Law that asserts that household expenditure on food does not rise as rapidly as income, after income reaches beyond subsistence. This would mean that a country producing food products for export would find demand for its products growing less rapidly than the income of its markets, and consequently, if food exports continued to rise, food prices must fall. The fact that underdeveloped countries supply raw materials as well as food is countered by another assumption about technology. Technical change has been "import saving" in the rich countries in the sense that it has resulted in the appearance of synthetics and new ways of reducing raw material inputs. The conclusion from this discussion is that the underdeveloped countries must isolate themselves from the rich countries and industrialize, if they hope to avoid permanently subsidizing the rich countries.

Things are further complicated by an obvious argument that leads to the opposite conclusion: the terms of trade must turn against the industrialized countries. Such an argument rests on the ancient assumption as to historically diminishing returns in agricultural activity. If this assumption were in fact accurate, then costs of increasing agricultural output would rise as output expanded, and the industrialized country would find itself having to pay higher and higher prices for its food.

These various arguments suggest several things. Whether or not the terms of trade did in fact move against the underdeveloped in any meaningful sense over a long period of time, probably, cannot be finally ascertained. Indeed, because of index number difficulties there is not much to be said for computing the terms of trade over very long time periods. It is even more dangerous to seek generalizations on this point that apply to underdeveloped countries as a group. Jute, tea, oil, tin, rubber, coffee, cocoa, cotton, tobacco, and the like are surely not all facing similar cost and demand curves. Of perhaps more relevance is that extrapolation of terms of trade cannot be done with any confidence. So much depends on technical change and changes in the composition of demand that extrapolation beyond two or three years can be no more than a hunch. The hypotheses explaining the presumed deterioration of the terms of trade of the underdeveloped country, noted above, can also easily be questioned both as to their appropriateness in the past and their applicability in the future. Finally, and most important, these remarks, as well as the argument in preceding chapters, suggest quite clearly that the terms of trade are not very important in the development story, except possibly as a symptom of a deeper issue. It is important to appreciate this point.

Begin by noting that a decline in the terms of trade of a country means simply that the prices of some of the commodities that it exports have fallen relative to the price it pays for the commodities that it imports. When some prices fall relative to others, while costs remain constant, this is a signal to resources to move out of the sector where prices are falling. To say that a country's terms of trade are declining over a long period, then, means one thing more clearly than anything else: namely, that the economy lacks the flexibility and adaptability to move its resources in response to changing profit opportunities. Flexibility and adaptability, however, are no more or less relevant for the foreign trade sector than for any other sector. An analysis of a particular problem in this connection will help to make the point clear.

1. Saving and transformation capacity. It is sometimes asserted that the primary constraint on a development program is not the capacity to save, but rather the supply of foreign exchange. A simple income model would show, however, that a distinction between saving and foreign exchange earnings is not valid. With no change in domestic investment or in the government deficit, an increase in saving cannot occur without an increase in exports, i.e., an increase in saving is an increase in exports. The distinction however, can be made valid, and to do so reveals some characteristics of the role of trade in the development problem.

Suppose the developing country can produce only agricultural products, all of which it now consumes. Suppose further it decides to pursue a development program, and seeks to acquire capital in the form of agricultural machinery. It has no capital goods (agricultural machinery) sector so its only option is to reduce its consumption of agriculture, export the quantity not consumed, and use the foreign exchange to buy the machinery. If the demand curve for the country's agricultural products is perfectly elastic, the rate of capital formation is limited only by the capacity of the economy to save (and by total output). If the elasticity of demand is declining as the quantity exported rises, then the last unit increase in exports will buy less farm machinery than did the previous unit, i.e., the terms of trade between agriculture and farm machinery are turning against agriculture. And, of course, if the elasticity falls to unity or below, then no matter how much the economy saves, it cannot accumulate any more foreign exchange, and hence acquire any more capital. In this case, foreign exchange is the prior constraint, not the saving capacity.

In this last case, resources are available for capital formation that are not used for that purpose because of the inability of the economy to transform the resources into capital goods either through international trade or internally. From this point, the problem of the economy is to increase the transformation capacity of the economy, i.e., the capacity of the economy to transform its primary inputs into products that it or some other economy wants. In this simple example, the economy would have to develop the capacity to produce capital goods itself, or other products for which there was an export market, or produce consumer goods currently imported if it wished to continue to raise its rate of capital formation. It would seem, then, that more revealing terminology than saving or foreign exchange as constraints on the rate of capital formation would be saving or transformation capacity.

Since the capital-goods-producing sector is often small in a developing country, much of the development program hinges on the capacity of the economy to export. If the world demand for traditional exports is inelastic or the demand curve is moving leftward due to innovations or changes in tastes abroad, then the country will face declining terms of trade. The solution, however, is to be found in increasing the transformation capacity of the economy, and to do this the arguments of all the preceding chapters of this book are relevant. The economy that is flexible and adaptable then has little to fear in the terms of trade in the long run. As noted in an earlier chapter, the transformation problem is a reason for foreign borrowing, even if domestic saving is fairly good.

2. *Some Qualifications.* The above arguments are very general; and there are a great variety of ways that foreign trade can affect the development effort, and specifically can affect the achievement of the flexibility and transformation capacity so essential to avoiding the long-run terms-of-trade problems. An arbitrary ruling out of various categories of commercial policy is, of course, inappropriate, but at the same time care must be taken to avoid policies that tend to prevent the adjustments required. In this latter category, the most important item is an overvalued exchange rate.

A great deal can also be learned from studying the terms-of-trade data, and trying to appraise their accuracy and the explanation of their changes. It is, however, not possible to go into these matters in the present long-run context, but it is to be emphasized that, in the development setting, the central point having to do with the terms of trade is transformation capacity, and not that there is something inherently damaging to the underdeveloped country in its trade with the world's rich countries.

B. THE SHORT-RUN TRADE PROBLEM

The development strategy that calls for considerable independence of foreign trade rests partly on the fact that foreign trade is often subject to marked year-to-year fluctuations. These fluctuations arise largely from short-run changes in demand in the world economy, and from weather hazards that face many of the agricultural countries. In the short-run context the transformation argument is hardly applicable, and the problem is essentially to find ways to iron out the fluctuations or ways to eliminate their impact on the regularity of foreign exchange earnings. Short-run problems (or windfalls) may arise also from sharp and unexpected changes in technology that impinge directly on foreign exchange earnings. Adjustments to such events take time even under the best of circumstances.

There are numerous schemes extant designed to eliminate or smooth over these fluctuations. The chief problem is an obvious one, how to accomplish this smoothing out, without at the same time discouraging the mobility of resources in response to long-run changes in supply and demand. The likelihood that any effective scheme that will function in the international community will be devised is remote, and to a large degree dependence must be placed on the maintenance of high and growing demand in the rich countries. Again, here, one finds generalizations clear and easy, but an examination of all methods designed to meet the requirements contained in the generalizations is difficult and lengthy.

"The trade problem" then may be summarized in this way: the limited variety of exports of most underdeveloped countries means that short-run fluctuations in world demand for these products have major repercussions on foreign exchange earnings, and, consequently, on the continuity of the development effort. Solutions to this problem, in terms of international marketing schemes, have shown little prospect of success, and heavy reliance is, therefore, necessarily placed on the maintenance of internal stability in the buying countries. This reliance has proved false in a number of instances, and the search for more reliable means of ironing out such fluctuations should, of course, continue. Another part of the trade problem has to do with the import policies of the rich countries, especially those dealing with the importation of manufactured products. On this score, the immediate approach is a continuing attack on restrictive trade practices among the rich countries. In a longer run context, the correct policy may be in the terms of custom unions or other forms of economic integration.

The transformation argument above undermines much of the import substitution argument. Short-run fluctuations and restrictive trade policies among rich countries remain, but even these do not now seem potent enough to justify a very narrowly conceived import substitution strategy as the heart of the approach to the development problem.

III. Industrialization vs. Agriculture

A point of view that merges with the terms-of-trade argument has to do with the role of manufacturing vs. agriculture in the development process. In the discussion of allocation problems, the general criterion was formulated that investment should be made in those sectors where it yielded the greatest return to the society as a whole. Whether a country expanded its agricultural sector or its manufacturing activity, or built up its research efforts, depended on what the situation was at the time the investment was initiated. Those who advocate concentration of investment in one specific group of activities must then make assumptions or gather data that lead them to the view that those activities are the ones that will yield the greatest returns to the community. To do this in specific cases is not only legitimate, it is imperative, but there is real danger in seeking generalizations on investment allocation applicable to all developing countries.

The most frequent generalization has to do with either agriculture or manufacturing, but even for these wide areas, it seems clear that no generalization can be valid. It is reasonably safe to assume that the income elasticity of the demand for food products is going to be high in all developing countries over the next decade or so (at least). But, unless one hypothesizes that no foreign trade is possible, a high income elasticity of demand for food products is not a sufficient condition for a given country to invest in agriculture. The discussion of the accumulation of technical knowledge and its application and the development of a labor force capable of using new technical knowledge in agriculture suggests that expanding agricultural output may be an extremely costly operation. But, of course, so may manufacturing. So, it all depends on how the cost and income streams of the various projects appear at investing time.

The only reason for repeating this argument at this point is simply to emphasize that development strategies as to agriculture and manufacturing built around generalizations of the *SMP* of certain activities is not a satisfactory process. At the end of Chapter 16, some observations were made on the possibility of establishing some sort of general theory of a sequence of investment allocation, but the conclusion was that no such sequence was possible, which still holds.

A further argument that is relevant to the agriculture vs. industry issue has to do with the notion that "marginal" changes are inadequate guides. The development planner must rather stand back and ask the effect of "major structural" changes on the effectiveness of the economic performance. Thus one might argue that an industrialized economy would yield a greater output than a predominantly agricultural one, and the development objective should, therefore, be to achieve such an economy as quickly as possible. Furthermore, the *SMP*'s of a limited set of projects in one investment period now may not show this, because the evidence depends not on a single project, but rather on the change in the entire system. Two things must be recognized about this type of argument. First of all, it implies a particular discount factor, i.e., a particular social-time preference, and a *very* low one at that because of the *very* long "gestation period" for the creation of an industrialized economy out of an agricultural one. This would mean, as already shown, that the present population is asked to bear a heavier burden than it would otherwise be asked to bear. Second, the power of the *SMP* approach (as outlined in

Chapters 15 and 16) to effect structural changes must not be underestimated. Once such things as technical research, education, institutional change, and the like are included in the investment criterion model, then the application of the *SMP* criterion does not necessarily mean merely enlarging the economy along existing lines. These two arguments suggest that the formulation of the *SMP* given above is a satisfactory guide even when "major structural" changes are thought profitable.

IV. Big Push and the Question of Balance

One of the most widely discussed strategies of development is that known as the Big Push argument. Reference was made to this argument in Chapter 14 in the context of the population problem. The problem now is to examine it in more general terms. The argument has been built around a variety of points, and the approach employed here will be to begin with a general statement of the argument, and then move on to specific issues having to do with indivisibilities, demand, and decision-making.

A. The Meaning of the Big Push

The clearest statement of the Big Push argument is that made by Harvey Leibenstein in his *Economic Backwardness and Economic Growth.* Leibenstein, in effect, seeks to generalize the argument concerning the population trap. To do this, he argues that the development effort is a struggle between income-raising and income-depressing forces. Among the latter is population growth, already discussed, but it is not the only depressing force. He suggests, for example, as another case that a small increase in output in agriculture would simply be consumed, while a large increase would lead to saving and to a rate of investment that would permit continuous growth. His argument is summarized in a series of diagrams, of which one is reproduced below. The curves marked D and R measure the income-depressing and income-raising effects of the variety of forces that became operative as *per capita* income rises. Suppose *per capita* income equals $o\ m\ (= o\ p)$ in period one. At this level of *per capita* income, income-raising forces would result in an increase of income equal to *na* for period two, but if *per capita* income were at that level, income-depressing forces would be so strong that income would fall by *fb*, forcing a *per capita* income below *om* to *os*. At *os* again, the depressive forces on *per capita* income outweigh the upward effects, and the economy moves downward eventually to equilibrium at E. As was the case with the population argument, E is a stable equilibrium and at any point between the income level represented by E and that by G, the depressing forces win the war and the economy must fall back. Beyond G, however, the income-raising forces win permanently, and the economy grows indefinitely. Hence, again

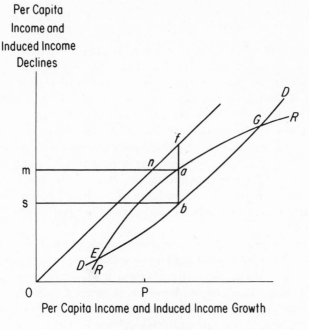

Per Capita Income and Induced Income Growth

DIAGRAM IX.

the conclusion that it is not possible to inch along the way between E and G. The economy must make the full distance in one leap or it does not make it at all. Leibenstein recognizes that one can draw the D and R curves in positions such that the problem disappears (or that it is impossible of solution), but argues that the historical evidence suggests that the juxtaposition shown in the diagram best describes the problem facing the developing country. In Leibenstein's own argument, population is the most important depressant, but other observers have emphasized other sources of difficulties for which the diagram is helpful in understanding.

B. LUMPY CAPITAL

Capital is not infinitely divisible, and the argument is often made that a "minimum" size of investment is required to build any type of capital equipment. The argument is given greater relevance by the added assumption that social overhead capital—railroads, power facilities, and so on—must be built prior to other, directly productive capital. The minimum size of such capital is considered to be quite large, and hence, right at the outset of the development effort, initial investment must be made that requires an outlay greatly in excess of the usual level of investment. The difficulty is increased by the fact that additional investment in activities using the social overhead facilities is necessary before the latter have any-thing to contribute to the economy. In terms of the diagram, the big leap from E to G is made necessary by the assumptions regarding the composi-tion of capital and the lumpiness of the investment projects.

There are two assumptions involved here, one having to do with the necessary priority in time of investment in overhead capital relative to other forms of capital, and the necessary lumpiness of that form of capital. It is difficult to find convincing evidence that either assumption has much to justify it historically or analytically. In the discussion of the Rostow stages, the point was made that no necessary sequence of investment can be justified, and the same arguments apply here too. The argument that investment in textiles, steel, chemicals, bicycles, and the like is not profit-able, unless it is preceded by the building of roads and power facilities, is no more valid than its converse. Freight trains are not profitable, unless there is freight to carry.

Then, it might be argued that investment in social overhead capital and the directly productive capital are both essential to getting a new, higher stream of output. If one views the situation in this way, there are surely divisibilities. More importantly, however, is to emphasize that forms of social overhead capital themselves are divisible. The frequently used argument that one half a railroad track cannot be built is not a helpful way to think about the divisibilities issue. Other forms of transportation are available, railroads can be built with different ratios of initial cost to operating costs, railroads of different size locomotives and wagons can be built, and so on. The same is true of other types of overhead capital.

Capital, of course, is not "perfectly divisible," but this fact alone is hardly enough to justify the Big Push. As long as there are ways of using the resources available for investment in a way that increases output, then the indivisibility argument loses most of its content. The attitude that a developing country can do nothing until it builds a network of railroads and power plants equivalent to those in the United States or Germany is a very effective way to remain underdeveloped.

C. COMPLEMENTARITY OF DEMAND

Along with indivisibilities on the supply side, attention has also been given to difficulties that might arise on the demand side. The late Profes-sor Ragnar Nurkse attached a great deal of importance to the possibility of this difficulty, and concluded that the solution to the problem was "balanced growth." It seems best to avoid this term, however, as its mean-ing has become so vague as to make it almost useless as a means of com-municating ideas. There is however an issue here.

Suppose from a situation of stationary, general equilibrium, a single enterprising entrepreneur found a way to build a new factory to produce a single consumer good. The new income—when the factory was completed—would be equal to the value of the output from the factory. If income increased in no other part of the economy, the only source of demand for the products of the new factory is that created by the income generated by their own production. It is, however, most unlikely that all the new income will be spent on these products, and if this is not the case, the enterprising entrepreneur will find that he cannot market his product at cost-covering prices. On the other hand, if a large number of new activities were initiated simultaneously, all of them combined would generate enough income that each activity would have no demand difficulty of this sort. Thus Nurkse (and others) concluded that a little investment would face at least one problem that a lot of investment spread over several activities would not face. In terms of the diagram above, the argument says that the jump from *E* to *G* is necessary in order to prevent this type of demand problem from appearing. It is evident that strong assumptions as to indivisibilities on the supply side may make this demand problem more difficult for solution, unless investible resources are in great abundance.

This problem would also be present in an advanced economy, but is more acute in the underdeveloped country because single investments are more likely to be a larger part of the low income economy than is the case in a rich country. Also in a rich country, total investment is a larger part of total income, and consequently, this specific demand problem is less likely to appear as long as there is no aggregate demand problem. Does all this add up to a legitimate reason why a Big Push is essential in the early stages of development? There is good evidence that low purchasing power among the majority of the population has caused some entrepreneurs to be reluctant to invest, but there are several reasons to think that the Big Push is not the way to overcome this obstacle.

1. In the first place the argument falls—even under present assumptions—if international trade is admitted. Foreign trade, of course, is an unreliable source of expansion—as discussed above—but still to ignore it is even more dangerous. And markets can, in most instances, be created by import restrictions, if not by export expansion.

2. More importantly, one must ask why expansion in the one sector took place. If it were initiated in response to a cost-reducing innovation, then a decline in price may not be damaging to continuing investment decisions.

3. Also it is necessary to ask what happens in other sectors as investment proceeds in one. As shown in Chapter 15, in the section on interdependence, expansion in Sector One may also induce investment in Sector Two either by increasing demand for Sector Two's outputs, or reducing the price of the same sector's inputs. In this way, one sector expanding for whatever reason may lead to others following along in rapid enough succession that the initiating sector has no demand problem. As

shown in Chapter 15, problems may arise as to allocation of investment funds due to this interdependence effect, but the same effect will tend to help solve the kind of demand problem outlined above. The further conclusion reached in that chapter as to the importance of the spread of information about ongoing and planned investment projects in the economy, as a means of facilitating a satisfactory solution to the allocation problem, will also help to solve the demand problem noted here.

4. A stationary general equilibrium is, of course, most unlikely to prevail in any actual situation. So, in no case would the enterprising entrepreneur face exactly the stagnant situation described by the assumptions that produce the zero profits. And, in no sense should the development problem be thought of as superimposing on top of the traditional, stagnant economy another separate economy where supply must create its own demand independently of what is going on in the older economy. Even population growth alone puts some source of variety into the system. At all times, then, the investor in the underdeveloped economy (indeed in any economy) is facing a disequilibrium situation, and some profit opportunity may thereby be presumed to exist. This argument cannot carry a great deal of weight, however, because in large sectors of the economy of Chapter 7, one is not far wrong to describe it as in equilibrium.

These comments should not obscure the point that there are or may be marketing problems in the developing country. The chief concern in the chapter on allocation was to get capital created in those sectors where it yielded the greatest return to the community. And part of this problem was to trace the effects of the investment in one sector on profit opportunities in another. The market problem is relevant in this allocation problem as well as in trying to understand the sources of demand for investment funds. What is surely not valid, however, is to conclude that for demand reasons a "large" investment program will work where a small one will not. Again here—as was the case with indivisibilities on the supply side—limitation on the availability of investible resources may force the economy to pursue a "little push" policy, and to conclude that a little push is futile is surely to give up too easily.

D. THE DECISION-MAKING PROBLEM

Professor Albert O. Hirschman, in *The Strategy of Economic Development,* argued that the strategic shortage in the underdeveloped country is not the supply of investible resources, but rather the ability to "perceive" and appreciate investment opportunities. If the investment opportunity is recognized then, Hirschman believes that saving will generally be forthcoming to allow the exploitation of the opportunity. From these assumptions, Hirschman argues that the proper development strategy is for the government to create disequilibria, because it is disequilibria that create the most obvious profit opportunities. His approach is to find those sectors of the system that have the greatest "linkage" (contacts with other sectors via the input-output coefficients) with the rest of the system. Then, his argument continues, invest in these sectors in a way that places pressure on other sectors to increase their capacity that is so heavy that it cannot be denied. The pressure is not only price pressure, but political and social as well.

The difference between *heavy* (or demanding) pressure and light (or permissive) pressure is illustrated by reference to social overhead capital and directly productive investment. The former simply reduces costs of some inputs of other industries, and may thereby encourage investment in the affected industries. On the other hand, if investment occurs before there is, e.g., power and transportation, the importance of increasing the supply of such services will be so great that further investment will be demanded, not merely permitted. Thus, the mere appearance of positive profits in certain sectors is not enough, there must be such obvious profit opportunities that even weak decision makers are motivated into action. Rather than a market problem, Hirschman sees a decision-making bottleneck, and hence rather than seeking complementary investments, the government (or someone) should create a series of disequilibria to spur on additional decisions to invest still further. No matter how balanced growth is defined then, Hirschman is opposed to it.

It is extremely difficult to establish evidence of the existence, not to mention the quantitative significance, of the Hirschman argument because there are several problems. How does one define the minimum level of incentive to overcome the perceptive ability problem? Also there is a necessary lag before the induced investment gets under way. How long a lag is consistent with the hypothesis? The lags not only may be so long that they cast doubt on the argument, but so long that the returns from induced investment are discounted away. The continued existence of considerable unused productive capacity in many underdeveloped economies due to shortages of specific inputs suggests that lags may be of a duration so long that the pressures are not really working. Hirschman's emphasis on psychological and sociological barriers to investment is *one* important element in the development picture. And there is little doubt that investment in roads and similar activities is excessive in many countries. But Hirschman's solution to this problem can well be costly. While the first industries are making their excess demand felt and are waiting for the bottlenecks to be broken, investment incentives are dampened and resources wasting away. Also one cannot simply ignore the supply side. One reason why the lag may be a long one is that investment cannot be carried on at a level high enough to exploit the profit opportunity. This is especially true when the skilled labor and management inputs are introduced. Finally, the question must be asked, are there cheaper ways to solve the

problem Hirschman pinpoints? Wider information about investment activities, insurance schemes, greater incidence of use of money, use of taxes
and subsidies, and management training can all be effective. Hirschman, in
effect, says to allow the obstacle to stand and build your strategy around
it. One must also ask, can you attack the obstacle directly? The chapter on
social environment suggests that such an attack may be more effective in
the long run than relying on creating capital known to be unproductive,
because it is believed that this is the only or most effective way to solve the
entrepreneurial problem.

Again, however, the Hirschman argument helps to show the development problem in one of its many-sided aspects, and one can imagine that
in some cases, the Hirschman strategy is the one needed to break a bottleneck. It is, however, even more helpful when seen in the context of the
whole development problem, rather than pointed up as the exclusive
approach.

E. Conclusion

Because the preceding discussion did not lead to an unqualified acceptance of the Big Push strategy does not mean that such a strategy is of no
interest. Indivisibilities can cause problems and their recognition by the
policy maker is important, so too are considerations relating to the market for individual commodities. These issues (among others) prevent the
system from following closely and neatly the adjustment process outlined
in previous chapters. If Big Push meant simply that the economy that
goes all out in its development effort is more likely to succeed than the
one that makes a half-hearted effort, then it is correct. It must mean more
than this, however, and especially does it imply that an economy cannot
do anything unless it does a lot, and this is a dangerous implication. To
repeat, there is much to be gained in the attack on underdevelopment by
recognizing that a country must spend energy using what it has, rather
than simply trying to get more. It is also appropriate to repeat that the
characteristics of the system that determine the shape of the curves in
Diagram IX are themselves subject to manipulation, and this too must be
part of the development picture.

It is clear too that Professor Hirschman has called attention to an important aspect of the development problem, but it is only an aspect, and
it must be fitted in with a great variety of other aspects. The cost of the
Hirschman strategy must also be very carefully recognized. Both the Big
Push and the Hirschman strategy make assumptions about supply conditions that are—to be optimistic—questionable. One may also add that
understanding of the development process would certainly be enhanced if,
along with "take-off" and "preconditions," "balanced" and "unbalanced"
growth were removed from the vocabulary.

V. The Capital-Output Ratio

Although there is no capital-output ratio strategy of development, this ratio figures so prominently in the plans and literature of development that some mention of it here seems necessary. The average economywide capital-output ratio is defined as the ratio of the total stock of capital in existence to the flow of total output in a given period of time, e.g., one year. Thus if total capital available were 300 and the flow of output was 100, the average capital-output ratio is 3. The marginal or incremental capital output ratio is the value of net investment in a period over the addition to net national income. The incremental capital-output ratio (*ICOR*) may, of course, be quite different from the average. A sectoral *ICOR* is the value of net investment in a given sector of the economy over the increase in net value added in the sector.

The usual use to which *ICOR* is put is the determination of the level of net investment required to achieve a targeted rate of growth of income. Suppose saving is a constant proportion of income, *s, Y* is current income, $\overline{Y}$ is targeted income, and *k* is the *ICOR*. Then, since saving must equal investment and

$$sY = k\,(\overline{Y} - Y)$$

$$\frac{s}{k} = \frac{\overline{Y} - Y}{Y}$$

that says simply that the percentage rate of growth of income is equal to the saving rate divided by the *ICOR*. The expression suggests that the lower the *ICOR*, the more rapid the rate of growth that is achievable with a given level of investment. This model was originated by Sir Roy Harrod as a tool with which to examine short-run stability and growth problems in economies with well-developed, functioning money and banking systems, disciplined and trained labor forces, a regular flow of new technical knowledge, no significant structural changes, and an adequate supply of entrepreneurial talent. For this purpose, the approach is quite rewarding, and its study has revealed a great deal about the difficulties of achieving stable growth in the more highly developed economies in a given short-run interval.

For the kind of economy described in Chapter 7, the story is different. The *ICOR* can have little meaning if changes in output are significantly affected by forces other than changes in the stock of physical capital. In the British or United States economy, which Sir Roy Harrod had in mind, it is reasonable to assume that the flow of factors other than capital stock that affect output is fairly constant over short intervals of time. (Even so, efforts to compute the *ICOR* for the United States have shown it to vary widely, but this is due in significant part to changes in the degree of utilization because of changes in demand. The average capital-output ratio behaves a bit more reliably.) The same is not true for the underdeveloped economy. The burden of the content of much of the arguments in preceding chapters has been to point up the varied ways that output in such economies can be increased.

The usual practice is to use as an estimate of the *ICOR*, similar data from other countries or from previous periods for the same country, and to derive investment needs in this way. It is easy to see how this can lead one astray in the kind of economy described as underdeveloped. If estimates from other economies are used, then the major question has to do with appropriate factor combinations, but other issues arise also. Such things as degree of utilization, extent of difference between marginal and inframarginal sectors of activities, mobility and skill of labor supply, availability of new technical knowledge, and quality of management may all be so different as to make the use of such data quite misleading. The same factors are only slightly less relevant when extrapolation of an *ICOR* into the future on the basis of past data for the same country is done. Part of the appeal of the *ICOR* arises out of the temptation to assume that unemployment means that labor inputs can be ignored. The arguments of Chapters 12 and 13 make clear that such an assumption is valid only in very special cases.

However, measurement is not the main difficulty. The concentration of attention on the capital-output ratio implies a particular view of the development process that seems misleadingly narrow. Development does, as already shown, require that resources be made available in excess of those required to maintain the economy. Such investible resources are to be used in a great variety of ways to add to the productive capacity of the system. One can then presumably sum these resources, call the sum investment, estimate the increase in income flowing from it, and have an aggregate *ICOR*. But even if this included investment in education, research, on-the-job training, and so on (which in practice is rarely if ever the case), it still excludes other sources of change, especially those connected with a more nearly optimum use of resources by changes in relative prices, by increasing recognition of possibilities of growth, by economies of scale, and so on. Attention should also be called to problems raised by intermediate goods. Sectoral *ICOR*'s frequently yield wrong results as an estimate of capital needs, because of the failure to probe into the capital used in the production of intermediate goods.

One can still argue that the careful analyst will look at all of these elements before arriving at his estimate of the *ICOR*, and that the final figure actually employed is simply a summary of the whole range of issues considered in previous chapters. This is not necessarily impossible, but if it is actually followed in practice, then there is not much need for the concept itself. More damagingly, the use of the *ICOR* places misleading emphasis on "capital requirements." The simple expression above shows that if the *ICOR* is 3.5, a growth rate of 5 per cent requires a saving rate (or capital imports) of 17.5 per cent of income. Again this is not necessarily wrong (it is necessarily right, *ex post*), but it does detract attention and energies from adjustments, adaptations, substitutions, and institutional and motivational changes that are also part of the development story.

The analysis of development is so complicated that the search for simple parameters around which to build is the major task of the growth theorist and practitioner. And the very purpose of theory is to simplify reality in a manner that reveals the major forces at work without a lot of unimportant detail cluttering up the argument. The *ICOR* approach is simple, to be sure, but its use tends to cloud rather than reveal, and to lead away from rather than toward the strategic factors of the development picture. Perhaps it too should join take-off, preconditions, balanced growth, and Big Push as part of obsolete language, at least, as far as the development problem is concerned.

p 354-5

VI. Planning Strategy

The question of the role of the government in the development effort is immensely complicated, and hardly lends itself to strictly technical analysis. The problem is difficult because the exact nature of the most effective role of government depends on such a variety of factors that generalizations are always questionable. In one country, the private sector may be relatively strong, while in another it may be quite weak. Similarly, a country may be fortunate to have a large group of well-trained, dynamic civil servants, and another country has virtually none at all. Many development plans call for the government to make virtually all investments and to operate all capital goods activities. And many plans call for a wide range of direct controls, the application of which places an extremely heavy burden on government officials. In general, there appears to be a tendency to equate "planning" with the levying of direct controls and the actual carrying out of investment projects. Such a view is unnecessarily limited, and planning may take a great variety of forms and employ a great variety of techniques. One of the more important "strategies" of development then is developing various ways in which government action, in general, can affect the operation of the economy. The discussion of the following points seeks to identify areas of government activity that appear to be strategic in most countries, although it is recognized that in a variety of cases, more specific action than here suggested will be necessary.

1. In general terms, the most important role the government has is the creating of an economic and social environment in which saving and investment are encouraged. Part of this role is performed by maintaining—or seeking to maintain—law and order in the community. More directly, it

involves attention to costs of its own activities, both routine and investment, and to seeking to minimize its own outlays on noncapacity creating
activities. Also, the government must necessarily do a great deal of direct
investment. Such investment includes not only traditional areas—railways
and highways, communications, and so on—but also possibly other activities—e.g., education, some research, unusually risky projects—as well. The
exact content of the government's own investment and operations depends
very much on local circumstances, and, as noted, generalizations are
dangerous. In most specific instances, however, reasonably satisfactory conclusions can be reached as to what the government should do in the way
of direct investment.

2. Perhaps the most important single component of the investment environment that requires concrete policies to achieve is the bringing about
of the equality of factor prices and social opportunity costs; this point has
been repeatedly emphasized in the preceding chapters. The key point is to
assure that the developing country use its resources in a manner that produces the greatest output, and to do this requires "right" factor prices. It
has also been emphasized that to achieve *exact* and continuing equality
between factor prices and opportunity costs is obviously impossible. A start
in this direction can be made, and tax and subsidy schemes can be devised
and implemented that do contribute to this end. Also, included in the environment picture are the various insurance schemes, subsidies, and the
like mentioned earlier that encourage investment, especially in areas where
direct returns are slight, but side effects or interdependence effects quite
large.

3. The government also can take actions that affect private investment
directly. These include all of the things just cited, in addition to the finance point to be mentioned below. Also, important in this regard especially is the full effect of direct controls, which governments are likely to
have to rely on in many instances. One of the major burdens of much of
the preceding argument has been to emphasize how indirect controls
might be used in a way that lessens the need for direct actions, but it is
probably inaccurate to argue that indirect controls can do the whole job.
Thus, it becomes imperative to understand the full impact of any direct
controls used. It is easy to find examples of controls established for one
purpose—e.g., control the use of foreign exchange, prevent exploitation
of labor, prevent the building of "luxury" housing, and so on—that have
other, less desirable, effects on the development effort. Direct controls are
often a very powerful tool in the development effort, but their use must
be tempered by as complete an understanding of their effect as can be
achieved, and the government must bear the responsibility for achieving
this understanding since it is the source of the controls.

This emphasis on private investment and indirect controls seems justified on a number of grounds.

(*a*) It is believed that private investment will, if encouraged along the lines just indicated, respond favorably relative to the magnitude and direction of investment. This does not mean that private investment will jump to 20 per cent of national income overnight, but simply that the economy will get significantly more investment in this way than if the government assumed full or almost full responsibility for investment.

(*b*) Private investors are assumed to have more detailed knowledge and understanding of technical production possibilities than is generally available to the government. If factor prices are in the general vicinity of social opportunity costs, this would mean that production costs would be more likely to approximate their minimum than if government did most of the investing or if heavy reliance were placed on price controls, licensing, and other direct controls.

(*c*) It also seems clear that correct pricing and heavy reliance on private investment is the most effective way to solve the problems created by the interdependence of the various sectors of the economy. No planning board is going to make linear programming models every other year (or if it does, its director should be fired), but the bottlenecks that arise due to the various linkages can defeat a major effort. This is a very important point. Much of the underutilization of capital so painfully evident in many developing countries could be prevented in this way.

(*d*) It is also believed that conscious encouragement of private investment is an effective way to open the way—at least a little—for the "new men" of Chapter 13 to have a better shot at the top.

(*e*) Finally, one may argue that the tasks imposed on the government by this approach are more consistent with its abilities, than would be the case if government investment is the only major source of investment activity.

4. The government has two major responsibilities with respect to finance. The first is to make sure that finance flows where *SMP* dictates its flow. As discussed, this objective may be difficult to accomplish with respect to small projects because of the high costs of investigation, but a variety of financing intermediaries will help (see Chapter 17). The second responsibility in this area is the maintenance of control over aggregate demand. This means especially assuring that no slack appears in the system that can be eliminated by increased spending, as well as preventing inflation. The possibility of a slack occurring due to the inability of inducing a high enough rate of private investment is a good reason for the government to undertake investment projects that it would not otherwise.

5. For reasons examined in detail in Chapter 14, the government's role in development must include a commitment to a birth control policy.

6. Government officials are part of the society, and are, therefore, no different from other people in society. To keep this in mind is important simply because it is tempting to impose on governments tasks far beyond their capacity to implement. The government official does have a favored position to view the economy as a whole, and to take a longer view than an equally competent person in a private firm. This is one reason why he is in a good position to try to design indirect controls to push the economy along its most advantageous path. It may also be that a few men of high talent and vision in positions of great authority in a government have a higher social product there than they would in the private sector. But this is probably not true of the average individual on whom the development effort rests so heavily.

The preparation of a planning document has the advantage of making public the government's programs, especially what it intends to do with its own investment. There are also other advantages: a plan document makes clear the government's commitment to the development effort, the setting of targets is often an effective psychological tool, and the discussion of the various aspects of the plan often reveals characteristics of the economy that are useful to many elements in the community. Perhaps the most important accomplishment of a good plan is that it puts the development effort in a perspective that makes it possible for everyone interested to view the economy within a comparable framework. In general, however, the extent to which it is profitable to draw up a formal plan depends on a variety of local circumstances, and it is easy to find cases where concentration on a formal plan document has had little or no impact. It is also easy to find evidence that plans are defective and built on insubstantial evidence, but this is inevitable and hardly a reason for not preparing a planning document. Whether a plan document is prepared should not be confused with the need for formal analyses and policy making. The government must have the machinery to make its policies known, and then implement them, and to do this involves a great deal of insight and understanding of how the economy works.

If the government could perform the tasks (items 1–5 listed above) without a plan document, then the contribution such a document can make is probably not significant enough to warrant its preparation. If, on the other hand, a published plan does facilitate the carrying out of items 1–5, then it may make an important contribution.

VII. The Relevancy of Economics

The concern of this text has been with the economic principles of the growth of *per capita* income. In Chapter 13, some attention was given to what was called "Social Environment," but even here concern was with only a few characteristics of the society, and they were those that acted directly on the performance of the economy. As noted in the preface, in analyzing the economic development of a particular country, one must pay heed to a wide range of factors not included here—military, political matters of a great variety of kinds, sociological and cultural factors, and so on. Then one may go further and conclude that the simple economics of development is the least of the problems, and hardly merits attention. The problem is not essentially an economic one, and the tools of the economist are consequently of little use in getting at the *real* difficulty.

The most thoroughgoing development of this view is found in Professor Everett E. Hagen's *On the Theory of Social Change*. Professor Hagen is concerned with how growth begins in a traditionalistic society, and he finds the source in personality characteristics that encourage innovational or creative activity. He further argues that it is the change in personality from that usually found in traditional societies that is the necessary first step to innovation and to growth. His extraordinarily interesting book is devoted to explaining how personality characteristics affect the behavior of economic agents, and how and why various personality characteristics emerge. Briefly, Hagen finds that the creative individual usually comes from a group that once enjoyed high status in the traditional society, but then had lost it for any of a number of possible reasons. A son, for example, may be aware of his father's or grandfather's fall from status and, because of a desire to vindicate or avenge the family name, seek through new and untried ways to reestablish the family position. Most important, the attitude of the deposed family is such that the manner in which the children are raised, affects their (the children's) personality in a way that encourages them to be creative, to seek and find new avenues to position and prestige. Indeed, Hagen seems to think that most entrepreneurs are made by the time they are six years old and after that there is not much hope for them. In the latter part of his book, Professor Hagen examines a group of countries in an effort to test his arguments.

Hagen has an early chapter on the inadequacy of economic theories of growth. This is a chapter that reads as if it were added as an afterthought, and is a most unconvincing discussion. The origin of bright men, men with high I.Q.'s, or of entrepreneurs is of great interest in understanding economic change, but isolating that origin does not thereby solve the growth problem. Other approaches that play down the economics of development are equally limited. That social psychology and psychiatry eliminate, or even reduce, the need for understanding problems associated with investment allocation, labor training, controlling inflation, increasing saving, and the like can hardly be taken seriously. What is self evident is that the problems the developing country faces encompass a wide range of disciplines. One of the purposes of the present book is to widen the economic analysis in a way that makes it more useful as a policy guide for the kind of economy described in Chapter 7. To widen it so much as to make it inclusive of every discipline is to destroy its effectiveness in any discipline. Similarly, to solve the narrow economic problem by encompassing it in other disciplines is probably to leave the economic and development problem unsolved.

Professor Hagen's is only one approach that makes notable contribution to the understanding of the economics of development by analyzing a social factor usually left outside the sphere of economic policy. (In Hagen's theory, apparently, the only policy that will work involves the training of children, or more accurately, the training of parents on how to train children.) All can be studied with profit, but there is no evidence that any will make the study of those variables considered in this book unnecessary.

VIII. Strategic Odds and Ends

There remain a number of points that are pertinent and are briefly discussed.

A. FOREIGN AID

This is the age of international aid, but it has become a truism to say that much the greatest part of the burden of development must be borne by citizens of the developing country. Still, aid may mean the difference between success and failure of a development effort. Aid has entered the preceding story in a number of ways. First and most simply, the inflow of foreign aid means more investible resources, i.e., it permits a higher rate of internal investment. Questions concerning the ability of a country to use foreign aid—usually called "absorptive capacity"—refer in general to the *SMP* of investment made possible by foreign aid. Often it is asserted that absorptive capacity of a country is "low." Such a statement means then that complementary inputs are such that the productivity of new capital is "low." This is a meaningful statement, but it is not a complete one, as long as *per capita* income in the developing economy is very much lower than in the rich countries.

What are the complementary inputs? The answer most frequently heard is skilled labor and management. If this is correct, then expenditure of investible resources on the training of various categories of labor would yield higher returns. Thus, absorptive capacity is often limited because the range of projects included for consideration is limited. It is, therefore, important in appreciating the role that foreign aid can play to include all those aspects of the development process that can be attacked by making investible funds available. Included would be not only various forms of education, but also technical research, housing, supplying funds to financial institutions to lend to very small investors, and the like. Foreign aid does not have to result in big projects producing a large physical capital item, and one of the important ways in which the effect of aid can be greatly increased is by extending the range of projects for which grants and loans are made. Loans for general support of the balance of payments rather than for specific projects would accomplish this result, but this may be more difficult to accomplish than would arranging for loans to be made for a much wider range of activities than is common now.

A second point that has been noted in regard to aid is also worth repeating. Aid might be used to support some of the subsidy programs to which attention has been directed in the previous chapters. To use aid in this way is simply another, wider activity than usually considered, but it is helpful to cite it here for individual notice. The carryng out of some government projects that have high *SMP*'s is made difficult because of problems of tax collection. A foreign grant that enabled the government to conduct some of these undertakings—subsidize firms to get them to value inputs according to their social opportunity costs, or to exploit external economies, or to get more research in the "right" direction, and so on—would, therefore, be part of the foreign aid strategy. Similarly, aid or loan funds could be used to investigate various projects that might be suitable for further aid or loans. Finally, considerable attention could very profitably be spent on studying the ways and means of carrying out effective advisory service. Technical assistance has not generally been a great success, and it would seem that further study of this important possibility might yield high returns.

B. Wage Policy

The statement that a wage rate should measure the social opportunity cost of a particular category of labor hides a number of issues that could be of great relevance. Attention has been given to the possibility of the wage rate affecting the productivity of certain types of labor. There is also the possibility of a backward-bending-supply curve of labor. Wage payments may also affect attitudes toward family planning as well. The wage rate is also a factor in appraising labor's capacity and willingness to adapt to new social environments and new work routines.

If it is admitted that the competitive process does not automatically bring about the equating of wage rates and the social opportunity cost of the many categories of labor, then to achieve this important objective requires subsidies or taxes by the government as already argued. The point here is to emphasize that the varied roles (perhaps impact is better) of wage rates make it important to look at a number of things before concluding what the appropriate wage rate should be. Especially is it worth repeating that the existence of unemployment—open or disguised—does not thereby mean that the social opportunity cost of all labor is zero. It must also be understood that the payments transferred to the worker may be different from his social opportunity cost not only for ethical reasons, but also in order to accomplish some further objective associated with the development effort.

No wage policy pursued by the government can possibly perform all the demands that might be placed on it, and measurement difficulties open the way for important errors and even purposeful abuse. Again, however, these are not sufficient reasons for avoiding the whole issue.

C. Research Strategy

There is virtually an unlimited number of things we need to know about the development of underdeveloped economies. From the standpoint of research in the countries themselves, an area that seems to merit more attention than it has received, has to do with the impact of investment projects that have been established and are functioning. Systematic study of these projects, large and small, may be expected to lead to considerably more understanding of the implications of various uses to which investible resources are put than is now available. Private firms are not particularly eager to supply data to mere researchers, but new men beginning projects could perhaps be persuaded to do so. However, it is not only data from the investing firm or government corporation that is relevant, it is also the various side effects and interdependence effects that need attention. In some respects, the developing countries now undertaking formal plans supply excellent case studies of the impact of a great variety of projects on the performance of the economy. To trace the impact of these projects would not only reveal a great deal about allocation of investment problems, but also about how the economy responded to various types of inducements.

Especially needed are data on side effects and the extent to which the interdependence effects induces investment in other sectors. Also data that will supply information on conflicting policies may come from such studies. For example, in the discussion of the problem of the commitment of the labor force to new activities in Chapter 13, the conclusion was reached that this problem would be reduced, if new jobs imposed very little change in the social and family life of the worker. On the other hand, there are arguments that suggest that the upsetting of family and social life is an effective way to reduce the birthrate. Conceptually, one can introduce each effect into the *SMP* of the several projects and get the right answer. To do this one needs numbers, and to get numbers, one must examine projects that have been undertaken and put into operation.

Examination of the impact of projects could also reveal much about factor combinations, about managerial obstacles, about technical change, about the effect of training on labor productivity, and so on. These remarks really amount to saying that the empirical materials on which good development policy must rest can be accumulated only from observing the operation of the projects that are themselves part of development.

Evidently policies have to be made in the absence of adequate data, but it seems reasonable to believe that studying actual projects will provide information that will help relieve some of this inadequacy. International transplanting of empirical evidence is, of course, possible if done cautiously, but for reasons that have been explained cannot be done indiscriminately.

IX. Conclusion

No strategy or rule of thumb has emerged that contains a surefire cure to underdevelopment. An unusually gifted African student remarked upon completing a thorough and intensive course in development economics, "I know everything about economic development except how to tell my country to achieve it." Perhaps this is true with all who work in the field. The very nature of development economics does not lend itself to simple strategies the way (perhaps) static income theory does. But, insight and understanding can be increased, and it would appear that considerably more is known about development now than was the case a decade and a half ago. At least, it is known that it is much more complex than was thought then, and if any progress at all is to be made, more effort is required on everyone's part than was earlier suspected. It is, however, recognized as more complex because the process is now clearer, and perhaps seeing the process more clearly is a prelude to seeing the appropriate policies and strategies more clearly.

Bibliography

A good source of material on almost all the various strategies of growth commented on in the text is found in a collection of readings edited by Gerald M. Meier, *Leading Issues in Development Economics* (New York: Oxford University Press, 1964). Professor Meier also has an extensive bibliography for each of his leading issues. A few specific references may, however, be helpful.

The main statement of Rostow's stages is his *The Stages of Economic Growth* (Cambridge: Cambridge University Press, 1960). See also *The Economics of Take-Off into Sustained Growth* (New York: St. Martin's Press, Inc., 1963). Rostow edited this volume and contributed the introduction and one paper. The paper by Simon Kuznets (pp. 22–43) and the comments by Robert Solow (pp. 468–74) are particularly useful. Two very good reviews of Rostow's *Stages* are by Goran Ohlin in *Economic Development and Cultural Change,* IX (July, 1961) and H. J. Habakkuk, *Economic Journal,* LXXI (September, 1961). See also Appendix II of Everett E. Hagen, *On the Theory of Social Change* (Homewood, Ill., The Dorsey Press, Inc., 1962). See also Alexander Gerschenkron, *Economic Backwardness in Historical Perspective* (Cambridge: Harvard University Press, 1962). An excellent survey of the stage approach to the study of growth and history is Bert F. Hoselitz "Theories of Stages of Economic Growth" in *Theories of Economic Growth,* ed. by Hoselitz (New York: The Free Press of Glencoe, 1960).

The most careful empirical work on the terms of trade of relevance here is

Charles P. Kindleberger, *The Terms of Trade, A European Care Study* (New York: John Wiley & Sons, Inc. and The Technology Press, 1956). Professor Kindleberger has also attached importance to "transformation" in his *Economic Development* (New York: McGraw-Hill Book Company, 1958), Chap. 7. A profitable discussion of the various forms the terms of trade may take is W. W. Rostow, "The Terms of Trade in Theory and Practice," *Economic History Review*, No. 1 (1950). See also H. W. Singer, "The Distribution of Gains between Investing and Borrowing Countries," *American Economic Review*, XL (May, 1950); Raul Prebisch, "The Economic Development of Latin America and Its Principle Problems," *Economic Bulletin for Latin America*, VII (February, 1962); J. R. Hicks, "An Inaugural Lecture" *Oxford Economic Papers*, V (June, 1953); and Gerald M. Meier, *International Trade and Development* (New York: Harper & Row, Publishers, 1963). Werner Baer, "The Economics of Prebisch and ECLA," *Economic Development and Cultural Change*, X (January, 1962) reviews the terms of trade and other arguments associated with the argument that trade between rich countries and poor harm the latter. The most determined opponent of the declining terms of trade thesis is Gottfried Haberler; see, for example, his "Terms of Trade and Economic Development" in Howard S. Ellis (ed.) *Economic Development for Latin America* (New York: St. Martin's Press, Inc., 1961). On a more general level see Gunnar Myrdal, *Development and Underdevelopment* (Cairo: National Bank of Egypt, 1956), and the two papers by Hla Myint mentioned in the bibliographical material to Chapter 7.

On the short-run stability problem see the paper by Henry C. Wallich, "Stabilization of Proceeds from Raw Material Exports" in the Latin American volume just mentioned and two numbers of *Kyklos*, Fasc. 2 (1958) and Fasc. 3 (1959) both of which were devoted to a series of papers on this subject.

On agriculture the collection of papers edited by Carl Eicher and Lawrence Witt, *Agriculture in Economic Development* (New York: McGraw-Hill Book Company, 1964) is a useful beginning for further reading on this subject.

For the Big Push see Harvey Leibenstein *Economic Backwardness and Economic Growth* (New York: John Wiley & Sons, Inc., 1957), Chap. 8; Paul N. Rosenstein-Rodan, "Notes on the Theory of the Big Push" in the Latin America volume noted above; Ragnar Nurkse, *Problems of Capital Formation in Underdeveloped Countries* (Oxford: Basil Blackwell, 1958); H. W. Singer, "Balanced Growth in Economic Development: Theory and Practice," *International Development* (New York: McGraw-Hill Book Company, 1964); and John B. Sheahan, "International Specialization, and the Concept of Balanced Growth," *Quarterly Journal of Economics*, LXXII (May, 1958). On the Hirschman problem, his book is *The Strategy of Economic Development* (New Haven: Yale University Press, 1958), and Hla Myint, "The Demand Approach to Economic Development," *Review of Economic Studies*, XXVII (February, 1960) is an excellent review.

For the capital output ratio see *The Capital Development Needs of the Less Developed Countries* (New York: United Nations, Department of Economic and Social Affairs, 1962); the Meier volume mentioned in the first paragraph of this bibliography pp. 101–104; W. B. Reddaway, *The Development of the Indian Economy* (Homewood, Ill., Richard D. Irwin, Inc., 1962), Appendix C., and R. F. Harrod, "An Essay in Dynamic Theory," *Economic Journal*, XLIX (March, 1939).

A survey of planning in various countries is contained in Everett E. Hagen (ed.) *Planning Economic Development* (Homewood, Ill., Richard D. Irwin, Inc., 1963). See also, Hollis B. Chenery, "Development Policies and Programmes" *Economic Bulletin for Latin America*, III (March, 1958) for a formal approach to planning. Harry G. Johnson, *Money Trade and Economic Growth* (London:

George Allen & Unwin, Chap. 7 and Edward S. Mason, *Economic Planning in Underdeveloped Areas* (New York: Fordham University Press, 1958) discuss more general problems associated with planning.

On the relevancy of economics to development, see Everett E. Hagen, *On the Theory of Social Change* (Homewood, Ill., The Dorsey Press, Inc., 1962) and a review of this book by David C. McClelland in *Economic Development and Cultural Change,* XII (April, 1964). Other "noneconomic" approaches to economic development are David McClelland, *The Achieving Society,* (Princeton: D. Van Nostrand Co., Inc., 1961) and J. L. Sadie, "The Social Anthropology of Economic Underdevelopment," *Economic Journal,* LXX (June, 1960).

A review of the various aspects of the aid issue is Edward S. Mason, *Foreign Aid and Foreign Policy,* (New York: Harper & Row, Publishers, 1964) for Council on Foreign Relations. See also the articles in Chapter 9 of Lyle Shannon (ed.), *Underdeveloped Areas* (New York: Harper & Row, Publishers, 1957) and Howard Wriggins, "Foreign Assistance and Political Development" in Robert E. Asher (ed.) *Development of the Emerging Countries* (Washington, D.C.: The Brookings Institution, 1962).

INDEX